A Subaltern Studies Reader, 1986–1995

D1648688

A Subaltern Studies Reader, 1986–1995

Ranajit Guha, editor

 University of Minnesota Press

Minneapolis

London

Chapters 1 and 8 copyright 1992 by the Regents of the University of California. Reprinted from *Representations* 37 (winter 1992), pages 27–55 and 1–26, respectively. Chapter 7 first appeared in Partha Chatterjee, *The Nation and Its Fragments: Colonial and Postcolonial Histories*, copyright 1992 by Princeton University Press. Reprinted by permission of Princeton University Press. Poetry in chapter 1 reprinted by permission of Manazir Aashiq Harganvi.

Published by the University of Minnesota Press
111 Third Avenue South, Suite 290, Minneapolis, MN 55401-2520
Second printing 1999
http://www.upress.umn.edu

Printed in the United States of America on acid-free paper

Library of Congress Cataloging-in-Publication Data

A Subaltern studies reader, 1986–1995 / Ranajit Guha, editor.
   p.   cm.
   Includes index.
   ISBN 0-8166-2758-4 (hc : alk. paper). — ISBN 0-8166-2759-2 (pb : alk. paper)
   1. India—History—British occupation, 1765–1947. 2. India—History—
1947– I. Guha, Ranajit.
   DS463.S77   1997
   954.03—dc21   97-18632

10 09 08 07 06 05 04 03 02 01 00 99   10 9 8 7 6 5 4 3 2

Contents

Acknowledgments

The Editorial Collective of *Subaltern Studies* wishes to thank Shahid Amin, David Arnold, and Partha Chatterjee for their hard work in putting together the manuscript of this volume and Ranajit Guha for agreeing to write the introduction. It also wishes to thank the secretarial staff of the Centre for Studies in Social Sciences, Calcutta, for their assistance in the preparation of the manuscript.

The Editorial Collective is grateful to the following for their permission to reprint these articles in *A Subaltern Studies Reader*: The Regents of the University of California for Gyanendra Pandey's "In Defense of the Fragment," from *Representations* 37 (Winter 1992): 27–55; Princeton University Press for the extract from Partha Chatterjee, *The Nation and Its Fragments: Colonial and Postcolonial Histories* (1992), pp. 116–34; and Oxford University Press, Delhi, for Ranajit Guha, "Chandra's Death," from Ranajit Guha, ed., *Subaltern Studies V* (1987): 135–65; for Gautam Bhadra, "The Mentality of Subalternity," from Ranajit Guha, ed., *Subaltern Studies VI* (1989): 54–91; for the extract from David Hardiman, *The Coming of the Devi: Adivasi Assertion in Western India* (1987), pp. 1–11, 18–54; for David Arnold, "The Colonial Prison," from David Arnold and David Hardiman, eds., *Subaltern Studies VIII* (1994): 148–87; and for the extract from Shahid Amin, *Event, Metaphor, Memory: Chauri Chaura, 1922–1992* (1995), 115–90.

Introduction

Ranajit Guha

The editors of *Subaltern Studies* have done me an honor by asking me to introduce this collection of essays. It is representative not only of the intellectual range spanned by the project but also of certain distinctions the contributors maintain between themselves within an agreed orientation. This has indeed been a hallmark of *Subaltern Studies* from the very beginning—this insistence on a solidarity that would not reduce individual voices, styles, and approaches to a flat and undifferentiated uniformity. It is a strategy that is not without its risks, of course. It has opened us to attack from those party-liners, one-horse riders, and other monists who had looked for the straight and the steady and the singular in our work only to find us wanting. But we have taken that risk in order to generate and continually renew a space that is vital to a project like ours. For its very existence, in concept as well as practice, depends on its ability to negotiate the tensions of an irreducible noncoincidence within it—a stubborn remainder that is an essential condition of its creativity and the source of its energies.

It is perfectly consonant with such a strategy that the editorial collective should call on me to add a few introductory words to the volume. For my place in this project is one that stands for a certain difference within its history. It is a difference of generations, which sets me apart from each of the other contributors by at least twenty-five years. Much of what gave *Subaltern Studies* its distinctive character and individuality during the first decade of its career—that is, roughly the period covered by these essays—is owed to this hiatus, confirming some of Wilhelm Dilthey's insights into the phenomenon of generation.[1] In an article published over a century ago and left largely unnoticed, he argues that a simple chronology of individual lives studied in succession is not enough for the history of the social sciences. For such history to be situated in life itself it is necessary for its narrative to be informed by yet another concept of time, namely, that of generation. The latter, a descriptive term for the temporal span of lives lived together in a community, helps us to focus, he says, on "the relationship of contemporaneity amongst individuals"—that is, their sense of shared childhood and youth and of a maturity reached nearly at the same time taken as "the basis for a deeper bond between such people."[2]

A generation, conceptualized thus, acts not only as a force for continuity but also as one that promotes diversity and change, since what it inherits is always less than the whole of its ancestral culture. Humanity, says Dilthey, does not grow like the annual ring of a tree, and cultural transfer over time is necessarily incomplete. Important parts of the achievement of forebears are inevitably lost to the successors—a point he illustrates by showing how ancient Greek thought was assimilated by the Italian Renaissance in less than its full measure, and even that took centuries.[3] But tradition is eroded by time not only in the long run. It suffers some loss even by being handed down from one generation to the next, and the modification this brings about gains in depth and scope as the inheritors set to work on their legacy with all the revisionist energies that belong to their own time and their own world—in sum, to their own life as distinct from that of their predecessors. Thanks to this generational appropriation a culture opens up as a field of difference ready to be sown with doubt and turn into an encounter between the experience of one life span nearing its end and that of another about to make its debut.

The political and cultural history of India, prior to independence, has not been wanting in such encounters, as witness those, for instance, between Surendranath Banerjee's generation and that of Aurobindo Ghosh's within the Swadeshi movement, between Tilak's and Gandhi's within nationalist politics of the years immediately following World War I, between Rabindranath Tagore's and Buddhadeb Basu's in Bangla literature, between Girishchandra Ghosh's and Sisirkumar Bhaduri's in the theater, and so on, although much work needs yet to be done on their implications. However, the virulence of such encounters acquired a new intensity and meaning after the transfer of power, as became obvious when the generation that had reached its maturity during the last two decades of the Raj met that of the Midnight's Children in the turbulence of the 1970s.

That decade—or, to be more precise, the years between the Naxalbari uprising and the end of the Emergency—has often been described as a period of disillusionment and *Subaltern Studies* as one of its outcomes. There is nothing wrong with this observation except that it is stuck at a level of generality and helps little to explain how and precisely in what sense our project may be said to owe its formation to the disillusionment of those times. For even illusion does not work in quite the same way for the young and the old. It comes in two forms—the illusion of hope and the illusion of recollection, according to Kierkegaard. "Youth," he says, "has the illusion of hope; the adult has the illusion of recollection. . . . The youth has illusions, hopes for something extraordinary from life and from himself; the adult, in recompense, is often found to have illusions about his memories of his youth."[4]

Read in the light of this observation, the questions that gave voice to the disillusionment of the 1970s assume the significance of an ontological divide between generations. There were two kinds of such questions, which, bunched loosely together, were as follows:

1. What was there in our colonial past and our engagement with nationalism to land us in our current predicament—that is, the aggravating and seemingly insoluble difficulties of the nation-state?

2. How are the unbearable difficulties of our current condition compatible with and explained by what happened during colonial rule and our predecessors' engagement with the politics and culture of that period?

Each of these spoke, no doubt, of disillusionment caused by failed possibilities. However, there was something indefinite about that sense of failure. Phrased in interrogatives it carried the suggestion that things had not run their full course yet and a turn for the better could not be ruled out. In other words, the mood characteristic of this disillusionment was one of anxiety suspended between despair and expectation and projected, as such, into the future. Yet with all that was common between old and young in the future-directedness of this mood, it varied significantly between the two instances in its temporal articulation. For the disillusionment that surfaced in that anxiety contemporaneously for both generations within the same decade, that is, within a "now" each could call its own, had its source in two rather differently conceived pasts.

The past that the first set of questions had as its referent was clearly that of the generations whose adolescence and youth had coincided approximately with the last twenty years of colonial rule. It was a past pregnant with a possibility specific to their time and the expectations it held for them—that is, the possibility of an imminent end to the Raj and the birth of a sovereign nation-state. Yet when both independence and nationhood actualized, finally, in the transfer of power, the generation for whom these had been the sine qua non of a future beyond colonialism felt betrayed. This was a frustration that could hardly be avoided. For these hopes and ideas, which had ignited and spread so well in the heat of an embattled nationalism, died down as soon as power was grasped. What had glowed once as an immense possibility turned to ashes as mere opportunity, and barely a handful even of that. No dreams could survive in that climate of hardship and uncertainty. For Indians who had already reached adulthood by that fateful year, 1947, loss of illusion would come therefore as the remembrance of a gigantic promise that had bitten but managed somehow to get away.

The disillusionment of the Midnight's Children (a generation so named in a brilliant stroke of apt self-description by one of its most inventive children) was of a different order altogether. Recollection had little to do with it, if only because they had nothing to recollect as a past prior to independence. Born to citizenship in a sovereign republic, they had their nationhood with all its promise already constituted for them. It was a promise that relied on the nation-state for its fulfillment. Since that failed to materialize even two decades after Britain's retreat from South Asia, the despair that seized the younger generation in the 1970s could truly be ascribed to a disillusionment of hope.

To dismiss that historic despair simply as youth's impatience with those official agencies and institutions that had failed to deliver the future to it would be to take a narrowly statist view of that phenomenon. For there was more to it than the drama of Naxalite clashes with the organs of the state and the violence of counterinsurgency measures adopted by the latter. The critique addressed to the rulers of the day extended far beyond them to all incumbents of authority within the civil society. Insofar as these were identified largely with the older generations, the revolt of the 1970s amounted to youth calling age to account. The summons, served in a manner conspicuous for its excess rather than its wisdom—as in the beheading of a statue of the great nineteenth-century scholar and reformer, Iswarchandra Vidyasagar, in a Calcutta park—won the rebels no friends. Yet the very wildness of such gestures drove the point home, albeit scandalously, that tradition would not pass unchallenged. The tradition in question ranged all the way from intellectual culture, such as that associated with the so-called Bengal Renaissance, to the highly valorized ideals of Indian nationalism during its encounter with the colonial regime.

What came to be questioned was thus not only the record of the ruling party, which had been in power for over two decades by then, but also the entire generation that had put it in power. The young born, like Saleem Sinai, "handcuffed to history," were eager to break away from what that "history" meant for them as the legacy of a past made up of what they regarded as the utopian dreams, hollow promises, and unprincipled political behavior of their elders. Since the latter had defined their identity as Indians precisely in terms of such utopias, promises, and politics, and had imbibed the concomitant values for moral and spiritual sustenance during the long night of British rule, they found themselves, the morning after, on the wrong side of an ontological divide. The doubt voiced so raucously by the youth echoed in the ensuing debate as the self-doubt of those under interrogation. It made them question why they were let down so badly by a future that had looked so good as a possibility simply waiting to come true. And since "expecting a possibility, I come from this possibility toward that which I myself am,"[5] what, they wondered, did its failure make of their being what they were?

The turbulence of the 1970s and its pain owed a great deal to this clash of doubt and self-doubt, interrogation and response between generations. One of its many unsettling effects was to bring the impact of the twenty-year-old nation-state's crisis to bear on a settled and in many respects codified understanding of the colonial past. A body of knowledge and interpretation relating to that past, which had been taken for granted and authorized academically as well as politically (the extreme politicization of academic work in history under the aegis of the Government of India—officialization, for short—being one of the principal features of education during this period), was now subjected to doubt in such a way as to lose its certainties.

Subaltern Studies, a child of its times, was drawn from its very inception into the argument that broke out. What made that possible and indeed necessary was not only its place in the sequence of generations, which led, of course, to a continuous dialogue with the proximate age groups, but also its freedom from institutional constraints. An assortment of marginalized academics—graduate students yet to complete their dissertations, two or three very young scholars only recently admitted to the teaching profession, and an older man stuck at its lowest rung apparently for good—it had the advantage of owing no loyalty to any department, faculty, school, or party. With no curriculum, no dogma, no official line to guide it, no professor, prophet, or politburo to watch its every step, it was an outsider only too eager to listen to and participate in the controversies agitating the space beyond and around the temples of learning and the political headquarters. When the noise of the first exchanges was heard in the streets, it did not seek refuge behind intellectual or moral palisades, like some others among its contemporaries, but rushed out and joined.

Thanks to that sense of freedom (and, one might add, impetuosity), it was possible for us to inaugurate our project with the words: "The historiography of Indian nationalism has for a long time been dominated by elitism—colonialist elitism and bourgeois-nationalist elitism."[6] With the obligatory invocation of gods and manes left out of this exordium, indeed with the gods of Britain's neocolonialist scholarship and the manes of Indian bourgeois-nationalist scholarship confronted so polemically, a statement of this kind was irreverence approaching sheer impudence for many in authority. If they failed to kill the project simply by ignoring it or by broadsides ranging between the narrowest possible partisan attacks and some of the ugliest slanders ever heard in Indian academic discussion, it was only because our critique of elitism was rooted in an understanding of the configuration of power, which was as well supported by research as it was informed by theory. The domain of politics, we argued, was structurally split and not unified and homogeneous, as elite interpretation had made it out to be. To recall the words in which this thesis was formulated in the statement mentioned above:

> What is clearly left out of this un-historical [elitist] historiography is the *politics of the people*. For parallel to the domain of elite politics there existed throughout the colonial period another domain of Indian politics in which the principal actors were not the dominant groups of the indigenous society or the colonial authorities but the subaltern classes and

groups constituting the mass of the labouring population and inter-
mediate strata in town and country—that is, the people. This was an
autonomous domain, for it neither originated from elite politics nor did
its existence depend on the latter.[7]

The co-existence of these two domains or streams, which can be sensed
by intuition and proved by demonstration as well, was the index of an
important historical truth, that is, the *failure of the Indian bourgeoisie to
speak for the nation.* There were vast areas in the life and consciousness
of the people which were never integrated into their hegemony.[8]

This insight, which stands sharply in contrast to a characteristic blind-
ness of elite discourse, has had a great deal to do with whatever is distinctive about *Subaltern Studies.* All the essays presented in this reader,
as well as the nine volumes of the series and the thirteen monographs
published in as many years by the members of the collective since
1982,[9] when the project made its debut (not counting their numerous
contributions to periodicals and anthologies, or the writings of those
who have been working along with the project without being formally
associated with it), bear witness to that distinction. This can be grasped
in all its scope and detail only by a comprehensive study of what
amounts to an extensive body of writings, which cannot be undertaken
here. All that need be done for introductory purposes is briefly to highlight the importance of this thesis for the thematization of our work on
South Asian history and society.

To thematize requires a project to select its objects, deploy them
in a bounded field, and submit them to disciplined inquiry. Consequently, the procedures of selection and delimitation commit thematizing to one or more points of view, which must, in every instance, run
ahead of the project concerned and pilot it to the site of investigation.
What may or may not catch its eye is therefore prefigured in thematization. The failure of elite discourse, in both its imperialist and indigenous nationalist varieties, to identify, far less interpret, many of the
most significant aspects of our past follows from a thematization
framed rigidly by the presuppositions of its monistic view of colonial
power relations. *Subaltern Studies* has sought to undo the crimping
and concealing effects of that failure by means of an alternative mode
of thematization—that is, by thematizing the structural split of politics
as its central concern. What follows is a brief review of some of the
salient aspects of that alternative.

Displacing the Question of Power

With the structural split of politics recognized as fundamental to the history of colonialism in South Asia, the study of power could no longer be left standing where elite discourse had set it up as an exclusively elitist agenda. Displaced, it now acquired, in *Subaltern Studies*, the status of a question straddling the fault line of that split. A beacon, so to say, whose function would be to illuminate rather than hide the nonunitary character of that politics, it would draw attention to "the other domain" treated in dominant discourse as of no importance or even as altogether nonexistent.

It follows from the notion of a structural split that the domains defined by it are always and inevitably in touch with each other. This does not take away from their autonomy any more than the contiguity of two states sharing a common border takes away from the sovereignty of either. By the same token too, the politics of colonial India has never been anything other than an articulation of the mutuality of two interacting yet autonomous domains. To cite what was said about such mutuality in our preface to *Subaltern Studies I*:

> We recognize of course that subordination cannot be understood except as one of the constitutive terms in a binary relationship of which the other is dominance, for "subaltern groups are always subject to the activity of ruling groups, even when they rebel and rise up." The dominant groups will therefore receive in these volumes the consideration they deserve without, however, being endowed with that spurious primacy assigned to them by the long standing tradition of elitism in South Asian studies. Indeed, it will be very much a part of our endeavour to make sure that our emphasis on the subaltern functions both as a measure of objective assessment of the role of the elite and as a critique of elitist interpretations of that role.

Considered thus, the study of colonialism opens up in entirely new ways to bring into relief the manifold diversities that it has been beyond the oversimplified elitist interpretation to cope with. From now on it would have to reckon with two indigenous protagonists and not just one, that is, the elite, privileged by the dominant discourse to deal with the rulers on behalf of all the colonized. In other words, it would no longer suffice to regard politics merely as the sum of all transactions between the masters themselves. For every transaction of that sort would henceforth require a reference to "the other domain" for an understanding of its implications, and the presence of the subaltern would make itself felt even in a scenario where its name has been dropped from the list of actors by oversight or design. All of which adds yet another dimension to South Asian history, making it even more complex than ever before.

Most of these complexities derive from the urgency with which this approach insists on the recognition of such entities and forces of civil society as are usually left out in the cold by elitist studies of politics. The analysis and description of power in colonial India, it argues, must no longer rely on the fatuous concept of the "prepolitical." The invidious hierarchization of South Asian culture into "higher" and "lower" levels or into degrees of "backwardness," according to a blinkered statist view that did not acknowledge, because it could not see, the articulation of politics in areas and phenomena inaccessible to the apparatus of the Raj, would cease henceforth to exercise the undisputed authority invested in it by an academic tradition complicit to imperialism.

Defining the Colonial State as a Dominance without Hegemony

The monistic view of Indian politics has a certain advantage for elite discourse. It permits the latter to commit itself to the uncomplicated notion that the colonial state was generically the same as the metropolitan state that had sired it, even though it might have warped a little under "Asiatick" conditions. It carries little weight with this view that the symptoms of such "warping" made the Raj unlike anything within the metropolitan experience in some essential respects. For the difference, trivialized as mere administrative failure or blamed simply on "native character," is dismissed by it as unimportant. One is thus saved the trouble of confronting the question, What was it that could justify lumping Britain, the world's most advanced democracy, the Mother of Parliaments, generically with the autocracy it had set up in South Asia? How could a state constituted by its citizens be said not to be fundamentally different from a colonial state that was a state without citizenship?

What makes it possible for colonialist discourse to sideline or altogether avoid this question is the assumption that colonial rule in South Asia was based on the consent of the colonized just as much as the rule of the metropolitan bourgeoisie in a sovereign Western country is based on its citizens' consent. An unexamined liberal-imperialist postulate made grotesque, on occasions, by the claim that the Raj was a "rule of law," it continues to inform neocolonialist writing until today as one of its basic tenets. What it does, in effect, is to endow colonialism with a hegemony denied it by history.

An important aspect of *Subaltern Studies*, thematized in a number of polemical and expository ways, has been to subject this hegemonic presumption to a thoroughgoing critique. It has tried to show that there is nothing in the record of the Raj, considered on empirical grounds alone, to justify any pretension to a rule by consent. The facts of the case do not support the thesis, put forward by some Cambridge scholars, that Britain's rule in South Asia was based on the collaboration of its subjects. For no authority can claim voluntary collaboration (except as a Nazi euphemism) from its subordinates without allowing the latter a choice not to collaborate, and such a choice was, of course, incompatible with the autocracy that was the very essence of that rulership. Far from being blessed with the agreement and cooperation of those on whom it had imposed itself by conquest, the incubus known as the Raj was a *dominance without hegemony*, that is, a dominance in which the movement of persuasion outweighed that of coercion without, however, eliminating it altogether.

There is an Indian nationalist version of this spurious claim to hegemony, as well. People's consent to the rule of "their own" bourgeoisie was anticipated, according to it, in the anticolonial campaigns launched by the leading party of the elite—the Indian National Congress—and actualized subsequently, since independence, in its long tenure of governmental power. Here again *Subaltern Studies* has developed a wide-ranging critique to put this claim in a radically different perspective. Based on research into some of the most powerful agitations of the colonial period, especially those known as the Noncooperation, Civil Disobedience, and Quit India movements, it demonstrates how on one historic occasion after another and in region after region the initiative of such campaigns passed from elite leaderships to the mass of subaltern participants, who defied high command and headquarters to make these struggles their own by framing them in codes specific to traditions of popular resistance and phrasing them in idioms derived from the communitarian experience of working and living together. It is only a naive and somewhat deceitful historiography that has made such anti-imperialist mobilization into the ground for bourgeois claims to hegemony, whereas the evidence speaks of it as precisely the ground where such claims were contested by the mobilized themselves.

Since *Subaltern Studies* did not start by investing the bourgeoisie anticipatively with hegemony, it has been spared the embarrassment of those tendencies that had expressed enthusiasm about the ascendancy of the Congress to power in independent India as the fulfillment of a historic promise of rulership by consent and were proved wrong again and again by the developing course of events, especially those since the 1970s. The hollowness of such hegemonic pretensions is so painfully obvious in Indian politics today as to require no elaboration here. Suffice it to say that its thematization in our project so far has been informed by a vigilance about the impact that the scramble for power among elite groups has on their relations with the subaltern. The latter used as pawns in the vicious competition between the dominant elements end up, inevitably, as their victims. The story of that victimization, the strength and structure of the resistance it meets from its objects, and above all the implications of a dominance desperately striving for a hegemony that continues to elude it are by now part of an already substantial volume of *Subaltern Studies* writings.

Investigating the Relation between State and Civil Society and Its Tensions

A good part of the current difficulties besetting India on so many fronts is a direct legacy of the Raj. The latter was conspicuous for its failure to assimilate the society of the colonized to itself. The result was an uneasy imbrication of what stood for the state with what stood for civil society, making for a myriad of misfits and an apparently perpetual tension. Of the numerous and many-pronged attempts made by the colonial state to assimilate the indigenous society to itself there was none that was not fully or at least partially thwarted. If it was the aim of the Raj to paint India red, as that bold metaphor would have it, all it succeeded in doing was to produce a motley of haphazard daubs. Yet it was precisely the inconclusive nature of that engagement that made the resulting image historically so complex, interesting, and above all unique. It was unique in the sense that the relationship of state and civil society in every constituent part of the image was so specific to the South Asian experience, so utterly did it belong there in light and space, that for all the confusion of the indigenous and the alien in its texture, and indeed because of such confusion, it stands sui generis at the very limit of translatability by Western codes. To study colonial India is therefore to seek a path toward that specificity and to let its distinctiveness show up in interpretation.

Not the least important of reasons why this specificity has not been thematized thoroughly or thoughtfully enough is the notoriously statist disposition of academic work on South Asian history. It bends all too easily in favor of the point of view of the state, adopts its perspective without asking questions, and ends up by concentrating selectively on those parts of the colonial experience that are limited to this optics. And even these are considered only for their relevance to the administrative and institutional functions of the state, and not in terms of the tension that relates it to its other—the civil society.

The recognition of that tension is, by contrast, central to *Subaltern Studies*. Its critique of the universalist pretension of capital leads logically to a thematization informed not by any primacy attributed to the state but by an awareness of the unresolved problems of its negotiation with civil society. These problems, exemplified by the growth and intensification of communal, casteist, regionalist, and other particularist interests, find their place in this project not as they do in a conventional South Asian studies program, with modernity and tradition, development and underdevelopment, progressivism and conservatism, and West and East ranged on opposite sides, but as witness to the historic threshold that the so-called universalism of a Eurocentric reason and its engine of global expansion—capital—failed to cross in the age of colonialism.

However, the function of a threshold is not only to turn its back on some intrusive externality. It also faces in and inaugurates thereby the space a dwelling has as its own. This enables the latter to look out to what is beyond and to let that into its environment on its own terms. The result is to allow an incoming light to blend with one that is local, transforming both. The advent of Europe's reason in South Asia as part of a colonial cargo also had a transformative impact, no doubt. But thanks to the indigenous society's refusal to dignify an alien rulership with hegemony, the transformation shaped up essentially as a process of Indianizing the idioms of modernity imported by the Raj.

Some of these idioms were rejected as altogether incompatible, while others were admitted to South Asian culture in much the same way as the languages of the subcontinent made room for European words in their vocabularies. To say *gelash* for "glass," *tebil* for "table," *teram* for "tram," *istimar* for "steamer," and so forth, is, in each instance, to allow an English phrase to come into an Indian language, but to do so strictly on terms set by the host, which is Bangla here. The initiative of such assimilation rests entirely with the latter, as witness, among other things, the characteristic interposition here of a vowel splitting up, respectively, *g* and *l*, *b* and *l*, *t* and *r*, *s* and *t*. Modernity, too, has gone through a process in which the harshness of statist intervention acting on its behalf and the haughtiness of its civilizing claims were overcome by stratagems of adaptation so authentically Indian that only a Eurocentric scholarship, unfortunately not confined to Europe alone, could mistake it for Westernization.

Rescued thus from the shibboleths of Westernization, the question of modernism in India leads to other and more fundamental questions. These fall roughly into two groups. First, there are those that turn inward to ask how this process of modernization that is India's own links up with the still obscure process of nation formation as articulated in nationalism, nation-state, and generally nationhood, and whether the apparently unresolved tension between state and civil society is not indeed the epiphenomenon of a deeper and basic conflict between state and community mediated by a still far from fully formed civil society.

Second, there are those questions that face outward to confront the supposedly universal status of the European experience—the universalizing function of its capital, the universality of its reason, and the complicity of capital and reason in elevating the particular brand of European modernity to a universal model valid for all continents and all mankind—in short, questions that cast doubt on the presumption of what is European and modern as paradigmatically metropolitan and on the elevation of its history, a bundle of national and regional specificities like any other history, to Universal History.

We had set out on this survey with an array of questions in order to index the difference between two proximate generations—those of the Midnight's Children and their immediate predecessors—in their involvement with the project of *Subaltern Studies* as it emerged from the turbulence and anxieties of the 1970s. We conclude, again, with questions bearing on the difference between the South Asian and European experiences in the age of colonialism, nationalism, and modernism. No attempt has been made here fully to answer these questions. For the aim of this introduction is simply to try to let a beginning disclose itself, if in no more than the barest outline. A beginning, true to itself, has to begin with questions.

Notes

1. Wilhelm Dilthey, "Über das Studium der Geschichte der Wissenschaften vom Menschen, der Gesellschaft und dem Staat" (1875), pp. 31–73, in *Gesammelte Schriften*, vol. 5 (Stuttgart: Teubner Verlag, 1957). For our citations of and reference to Dilthey, see sec. 2 of that article, pp. 36–41.

2. Ibid., p. 37.

3. Ibid., pp. 38–39.

4. Søren Kierkegaard, *The Sickness unto Death* (Princeton, N.J.: Princeton University Press, 1983), p. 58.

5. Martin Heidegger, *The Basic Problems of Phenomenology*, trans. Albert Hofstadter, rev. ed. (Bloomington: Indiana University Press, 1988), p. 265.

6. Ranajit Guha, ed., *Subaltern Studies I* (Delhi: Oxford University Press, 1982), p. 1.

7. Ibid., p. 4.

8. Ibid., pp. 5–6.

9. Shahid Amin, *Sugarcane and Sugar in Gorakhpur: An Inquiry into Peasant Production for Capitalist Enterprise in Colonial India* (Delhi: Oxford University Press, 1984); Amin, *Event, Metaphor, Memory: Chauri Chaura, 1922–1992* (Delhi: Oxford University Press, 1995); David Arnold, *Police Power and Colonial Rule: Madras, 1859–1947* (Delhi: Oxford University Press, 1986); Arnold, *Famine: Social Crisis and Historical Change* (Oxford: Blackwell, 1988); Gautam Bhadra, *Iman o nishan: Unish shatake banglar krishak chaitanyer ek adhyay* (Calcutta: Subarnarekha, 1994); Dipesh Chakrabarty, *Rethinking Working-Class History: Bengal, 1890–1940* (Princeton, N.J.: Princeton University Press, 1989); Partha Chatterjee, *Bengal, 1920–1947: The Land Question* (Calcutta: K. P. Bagchi, 1984); Chatterjee, *Nationalist Thought and the Colonial World: A Derivative Discourse?* (London: Zed Books, 1986); Chatterjee, *The Nation and Its Fragments: Colonial and Postcolonial Histories* (Princeton, N.J.: Princeton University Press, 1993); Ranajit Guha, *Elementary Aspects of Peasant Insurgency in Colonial India* (Delhi: Oxford University Press, 1983); Guha, *An Indian Historiography of India: A Nineteenth-Century Agenda and Its Implications* (Calcutta: K. P. Bagchi, 1988); David Hardiman, *The Coming of the Devi: Adivasi Assertion in Western India* (Delhi: Oxford University Press, 1987); Gyanendra Pandey, *The Construction of Communalism in Colonial North India* (Delhi: Oxford University Press, 1990).

1 / In Defense of the Fragment: Writing about Hindu-Muslim Riots in India Today

Gyanendra Pandey

I

This is not a paper. It is a preliminary statement of some of the difficulties of writing one on the history of violence—more specifically in this instance the history of sectarian violence in colonial and postcolonial India. The history of violence has been treated in the historiography of modern India as *aberration* and as *absence*: aberration in the sense that violence is seen as something removed from the general run of Indian history: a distorted form, an exceptional moment, not the "real" history of India at all.[1] Violence also appears as an absence—and here the point applies more emphatically to a field wider than Indian history—because historical discourse has been able to capture and represent the moment of violence only with great difficulty. The "history" of violence is, therefore, almost always about context—about everything that happens around violence.[2] The violence itself is taken as "known." Its contours and character are simply assumed: its forms need no investigation.

The statement presented in the following pages is very general, a bare outline of a larger argument about the nature of evidence and the modes of analysis and representation employed in historical discourse. I proffer it in this form in the hope that it will focus some points for consideration in a way that a more detailed statement might not. But I do so with some hesitation. One reason for hesitation is that the formulations presented here are far from being adequately worked out at this stage; by the nature of things, they may never be adequately worked out.

Another reason for hesitation is that I have had to adopt in this piece a more personal tone than is perhaps, as yet, common in social science and history writing. My statement arises in large part out of the experience of the Bhagalpur "riots" of 1989, which figure in some detail in the later part of this essay. In writing about this experience I make considerable use of personal impressions and insights gathered as part of a ten-member team sent out under the aegis of the People's Union for Democratic Rights (PUDR), Delhi, to investigate the situation in Bhagalpur. The use of the "personal" in academic analysis is, however, something that many of us are still learning to negotiate, and I remain uncomfortable about what may appear as an excessive intrusion of the author's self in the pages that follow.

Finally, and perhaps most important, I hesitate because my criticism of some of the most significant writings on contemporary social and political conflict in India may appear ungenerous, especially in respect to scholars and activists who have come out boldly against the sources of oppression and exploitation in our state and our society. I can only say that the kind of criticism (and self-criticism) presented here would have been impossible but for the pioneering investigations and studies of individuals like Asghar Ali Engineer and organizations like the People's Union for Civil Liberties (PUCL) and the PUDR.[3] It is possible that my criticism of their writings on contemporary politics and strife will appear academic and of little immediate relevance. I should like to believe, however, that there is some dialogue between the "academic" and the "political," and that some of the arguments in these pages will contribute in a small way to the continuing debates on vital political issues of our times.

The present statement deals with the historiography of sectarian strife. This historiography functions, and has long functioned, in a political context where the rhetoric of nationalism is of central importance. In recent times, especially over the last two decades, this rhetoric has taken on a new tone and a different kind of stridency. The highly centralized state power that now goes by the name of the Indian nation-state has spoken more and more brazenly on behalf of a get-rich-quick, consumerist "middle class" and its rural ("rich peasant") allies. In furthering the ambition of this sectional interest, the state has shown a willingness to mark all opposition as "antinational"— whether this opposition has been located in the industrial working class, among the rural poor, or in other regional and local movements.

The "fragments" of Indian society—the smaller religious and caste communities, tribal sections, industrial workers, and activist women's groups, all of which might be said to represent "minority" cultures and practices—have been expected to fall in line with the "mainstream" (Brahmanical Hindu, consumerist) national culture. This "mainstream," which represents in fact a small section of the society, has indeed been flaunted as *the* national culture. "Unity in Diversity" is no longer the rallying cry of Indian nationalism. On the contrary, all that belongs to any minority other than the ruling class, all that is challenging, singular, or local—not to say, all difference—appears threatening, intrusive, even "foreign" to this nationalism.

Writings on Indian politics need to foreground this state-centered drive to homogenize and "normalize," and to foreground also the deeply contested nature of the territory of nationalism. Part of the importance of the "fragmentary" point of view lies in this, that it resists the drive for a shallow homogenization and struggles for other, potentially richer definitions of the "nation" and the future political community.

I do not suggest that resistance by the "minority" always, or even usually, functions consciously in this way. But the historian, social scientist, or political activist who stands back to analyze the conditions of Indian society will perhaps agree that this is an important part of what is happening. There is a historiographical issue involved here, too. For the narrow and diminishing view of nationalism described above is bolstered not only by a reference to current world trends in the economic and political practice of states, nor only by those who speak of ancient India as the cradle of civilization and the storehouse of all that is good and valuable in the contemporary world, but also by a "modern" and avowedly secular nationalist historiography that has reinforced notions of a natural Indian unity and an Indian national essence.

This historiography has elevated the nation-state—indeed, a contingent form of the nation-state as found in India today—to the status of the end of all history, so much so that "History," in schools, colleges, and universities in India, still ends for the most part in 1947. It has also created for us the neat binary categories with which we have all had to work: secular/communal, national/local (all too often read as "antinational"), progressive ("economic")/reactionary ("cultural")—categories that historians have only recently begun seriously to question.[4]

Even today, after decades of powerful and sophisticated history writing by left-wing as well as nationalist and other liberal scholars, the view from the "center" remains the recognized vantage point for a meaningful reconstruction of "Indian" history, and the "official" archive (government records or, for an earlier period, court records) the primary source for its construction. This historiographical practice fails, it seems to me, to lay sufficient stress on the provisional and changeable character of the objects of our analysis: "India" as well as "Pakistan," "Awadh," or "Andhra Pradesh," the Hindu or the Muslim "community," the "nation," "nationalism," and "communalism." By attributing a "natural" quality to a particular unity such as "India" and adopting its "official" archive as the primary source of historical knowledge pertaining to it, the historian adopts the view of the established state. This has surely happened in the historiography of modern India. The inordinate emphasis placed on the (given) unity of India and the unity of the struggle to realize "her" independence has meant that the history of India since the early nineteenth century has tended to become the biography of the emerging nation-state. It has also become a history in which the story of Partition, and the accompanying Hindu-Muslim and Muslim-Sikh riots of 1946–47, is given short shrift.

The history of sectarian strife in general, and of what is called "communalism" in India, has been written up as a secondary story. "Hindu" politics, "Muslim" politics, and Hindu-Muslim strife appear as minor elements in the main drama of India's struggle for independence from colonial rule, and they are associated usually with the machinations of the colonial ruling class. Histories of Partition, too, are generally written up as histories of "communalism."[5] These are, as one might expect, anything but histories of noble endeavor. They are not even, to any substantial degree, histories of confused struggle and violence, sacrifice and loss; of the tentative forging of new identities and loyalties; or of the rise among uprooted and embittered people of new resolutions and new ambitions. Instead they tend to be accounts of the "origins" or "causes" of Partition, investigations of the chances, the political mistakes, or the less amenable social and economic developments that allegedly brought about this tragic event. In this account, moreover, the tragedy appears as one that, for all its consequences, miraculously left the course of Indian history unaltered. In spite of the emergence of two, now three, independent nation-states as a result of Partition, "India," this historiography would seem to say, stayed firmly—and "naturally"—on its secular, democratic, nonviolent, and tolerant path.

Bipan Chandra's *Modern India*, perhaps the best textbook on the colonial period available to school-leavers and junior undergraduates, illustrates these points very well indeed:[6]

> On 15 August 1947, India celebrated with joy its first day of freedom. The sacrifices of generations of patriots and the blood of countless martyrs had borne fruit. . . . But the sense of joy . . . was mixed with pain and sadness. . . . [For] even at the very moment of freedom a communal orgy, accompanied by indescribable brutalities, was consuming thousands of lives in India and Pakistan. (Pp. 305–6)

There is "pain and sadness" at what can only be read as the hijacking of an enormously powerful and noble struggle. We read on:

> The symbol of this tragedy at the moment of national triumph was the forlorn figure of Gandhiji—the man who had given the message of *nonviolence, truth and love and courage and manliness* to the Indian people. . . . In the midst of national rejoicing, he was touring the hate-torn land of Bengal, trying to bring comfort to people who were even then paying through senseless communal slaughter the price of freedom. (P. 306; emphasis added)

Who hijacked the movement is not explicitly stated at this point, although other pages make it clear that Hindu and Muslim communalists, political reactionaries, and of course the British were to blame (pp. 296–97 and passim). This hijacking leads to senseless slaughter, hundreds of thousands of lives being lost as "the price of freedom." Something is elided here, however. Which people pay? For whose freedom? Rather than ask these questions, Bipan Chandra's textbook goes on to record how Gandhi died, assassinated in January 1948, "a martyr to the cause of unity," and how the people of India, "with confidence in their capacity and their will to succeed . . . now [after August 1947] set out to build the just and the good society" (pp. 306–7).

Here "Gandhi" and "the people" become symbols of the nationalist essence, the Indian spirit, and symbols that may easily be substituted for one another. "Gandhi" clearly stands in for the people in the nationalist account of India's anticolonial struggle. Similarly, with Gandhi gone, "the people" apparently take over Gandhi's work and march forward, unaffected by Partition, riots, refugees, and the like, to build "the just and the good society."

Sumit Sarkar's more critical textbook, meant for more advanced undergraduate and graduate students, puts forward a different argument but arrives at the same conclusion about the secular path of the Indian people.[7] Sarkar writes movingly of "the Mahatma's finest hour," from 1946 until his death in January 1948, when he labored almost single-handedly to try to restrain the passions that were leading to the slaughter of Hindus, Muslims, and Sikhs all over northern India. The futility of such "isolated personal effort" was, however, evident, the historian remarks.

"One might still argue," Sarkar says, "that the only real alternative lay along the path of united militant mass struggle against imperialism and its Indian allies" (p. 438). He goes on to describe in fairly optimistic terms the continuing potential for such struggle:

> Despite the obvious disruption caused by the riots, this possibility was by no means entirely blocked even in the winter of 1946–47. Five months after the August riots [the "great Calcutta killings" of 1946], the students of Calcutta were again on the streets on 21 January 1947 in "Hands Off Vietnam" demonstrations against the use of Dum Dum airport by French planes, and all communal divisions seemed forgotten in the absolutely united and ultimately victorious 85–day tram strike under Communist leadership which began the same day. (Pp. 438–39)

The author refers also to the "strike wave" of January–February 1947 in Calcutta, Kanpur, Karachi, Coimbatore, and elsewhere, only to add: "The strikes . . . were all on purely economic demands: what remained lacking was a sufficiently influential and determined political leadership" (p. 439).

I have quoted from two of the best general books on the history of colonial India and the Indian national movement, both from scholars writing within the Marxist tradition, to emphasize my point about the quite remarkable dominance of the nationalist paradigm in the writing on Partition and Independence. This history writing is part of a larger nationalist discourse, which finds powerful expression in films, journalism, and literature, as well. Partition was, for the majority of people living in what are now the divided territories of northern India, Pakistan, and Bangladesh, *the* event of the twentieth century—equivalent in terms of trauma and consequence to World War I (the "Great War") for Britain or World War II for France and Japan. The experience of World Wars I and II is commemorated in Western Europe and Japan through the erection of major national monuments. There is, not surprisingly, no equivalent for Partition in India. However, the erasure of memory goes further in this case.[8]

As in history writing, so in films and fiction, Indian intellectuals have tended to celebrate the story of the Independence struggle rather than dwell on the agonies of Partition. This statement requires considerable qualification. There has been a great deal of writing on Partition and the sectarian violence of 1946–47 in Punjabi, Urdu, and Hindi. But "Partition Literature" of the early period—of which Sa'adat Hasan Manto's devastating stories are the outstanding example—was largely confined to the strife-torn areas of Punjab and its environs in the decade or so after Partition.[9] Subsequent literary statements on this theme that have come out of northern India fall much more clearly within the secular nationalist problematic, for which Partition was a history gone wrong—a puzzling and in effect inexplicable failure. The classic of this genre is probably Rahi Masoom Raza's *Aadha gaon* (1966).

More remarkable still, sectarian violence and its consequences do not figure as a central motif in the Bengali literature of the post-Partition period. A recent study notes that while the famine of 1943 appears to have moved Bengali writers deeply, "the Partition of Bengal [dividing East Bengal, which became part of Pakistan in 1947, from West Bengal, which remained part of India] that . . . conclusively changed all erstwhile socio-economic configurations in and after 1947, never became a dominating theme of Bengali fiction even during the 1950s or shortly thereafter."[10]

In cinema, of course, the great Bengali director Ritwik Ghatak produced a series of unparalleled filmic statements about the pain, despair, and hopes of those dispossessed and displaced by Partition: *Komal Gandhar* (1959), *Subarnarekha* (1962), *Titash ekti nadir nam* (1973), and somewhat more indirectly, *Meghe dhaka tara* (1960). But Ghatak remains an exception—and not because of his brilliance alone. In Bengali cinema generally, as in the huge Hindi-Urdu film industry centered in Bombay, and in the large number of documentary films produced by the Films Division of India, filmmakers have paid relatively little attention to the history and consequences of Partition.

Among Hindu/Urdu films, the example that stands out against this trend is M. S. Sathyu's *Garam hawa*, a remarkable statement of the early 1970s that sensitively portrayed the collective insanity, the uprooting, the meaninglessness of existence, and the fear-laden searches for new meaning "elsewhere" that were the lot of so many people in the aftermath of Partition. The more recent television serial *Tamas*, based on Bhishma Sahni's novel of the same name published in 1972, has acquired a special importance because of the numbers it reached. However, the story marks a return to a less subtle nationalist statement in which *agents provocateurs* and mysterious evil folk pulling the strings from behind the scenes mislead an innocent and bewildered but brave people. Besides, partition is represented here in the likeness of a natural disaster in which human actions play little part, far removed from the run of daily life. As we have already noted, this is also the line that respectable, academic nationalist historiography has followed.

The reasons for this suppression of the history of Hindu-Muslim violence are not hard to find. Differences and strife between Hindus and Muslims persist in India today, and in relating the history of such strife there is the real danger of reopening old wounds. In addition, there is no consensus among us about the nature of Partition. We have no means of representing such tragic loss, nor of pinning down—or rather, owning—responsibility for it. Consequently, our nationalist historiography, journalism, and filmmaking have tended to generate something like a collective amnesia. Consciously or otherwise, they have represented Partition and all that went with it as an aberration. The day of the establishment of Pakistan, 14 August 1947, becomes an accident, a "mistake"—and one for which not we but "others" were responsible.

I should like to suggest, further, that our analyses of politics and strife in post-Independence India have run pretty much along the same lines. The following pages seek to demonstrate this through an examination of the historiography of "contemporary communalism." There is another incidental benefit that may flow from such an examination. Recent events and the writings upon them reveal, by their immediacy and uncertainty, many of the hazards of evidence and of representation from which historians of earlier periods sometimes believe themselves to be immune.

Although the immediate context for my observations is the experience of recent "riots," especially one in Bhagalpur in 1989, I wish to stress that the difficulties of evidence gathering and representation encountered here point to the folly of using accounts of, say, fifty or a hundred years ago as if they were somehow "transparent"—biased accounts to be sure, but accounts that may be balanced by setting them off one against another, by appropriate additions and subtractions, to give us a more or less adequate reconstruction of "history."

II

It has become commonplace in India now to describe one instance of strife after another as "perhaps the worst since 1947"; such has been the magnitude and brutality of sectarian violence in the 1980s.[11] In any event, Bhagalpur was one of the most devastating examples of Hindu-Muslim strife in the country since Partition. This round of violence began in the last week of October 1989; arson, looting, and murder spread from the city to the surrounding countryside and raged practically unchecked for several days. The situation was then brought under some sort of control by military and paramilitary forces, but an atmosphere of fear and terror remained for months afterward.[12]

Given the scale of the "riots" and the infamous role of the local administration in encouraging the attacks and suppressing evidence, it is impossible to establish the "facts" of this occurrence—what traditional historians like to call the "nuts and bolts" of the story. Possibly as many as a thousand people were killed in the course of the violence, most of them Muslims, but estimates of the casualties still vary enormously.[13] During the first days of the "riots," trains were stopped repeatedly at different places in Bhagalpur and its neighboring districts; from several of these, Muslim travelers were dragged out and lynched. No one can say for certain how many were killed in this way, even in particular incidents—not even disturbed travelers who were on these trains and saw people being pulled from their carriages. In the major attacks, in the rural areas as well as in the city, neither old people nor infants, neither women nor children, were spared. There is widespread feeling that women were abducted and raped on a large scale, but none of the surviving victims will talk about rape; the five specific cases recorded by the PUDR team that conducted investigations in Bhagalpur in January 1990 were incidents that Muslim women informants had themselves heard about.

What is beyond question is that the extent and ferocity of the attacks were unprecedented, even for a district that has seen much sectarian strife before, including "riots" in 1946. At the worst stage of the violence in October–November 1989, some forty thousand people were forced to leave their homes and live in makeshift relief camps. Destruction and looting of property occurred on a massive scale for several weeks. The fears generated among the heavily outnumbered Muslims were such that a great many were unwilling to return to their homes even three months after the initial outbreak of violence; an estimated ten thousand were still in "relief camps" toward the end of January 1990, apart from those who had moved in with relatives or friends in "safer" places in or outside Bhagalpur district. At this time many Muslims were pressing for the permanent retention of military or paramilitary forces in the vicinity of their villages or wards (*mohallas*) as the only trustworthy means for their protection, and some were demanding that they be given arms by the government for the same purpose. The air was still thick with rumors, and isolated attacks and looting continued to occur; one such incident was reported as late as March 1990.

How do we write the history of such an event? In Bhagalpur, the state's "archives," those official sources that generations of historians and social scientists have treated as core accounts, more "comprehensive" than any other source, are largely missing. Like historians generally, various teams of independent investigators visiting Bhagalpur have been eager to obtain the official account in order to establish "some overall picture" in the midst of an otherwise confusing investigation.[14] But the view from the center has largely been destroyed in this instance, at any rate for the first few absolutely critical days of the "riots." A *Sunday Mail* (Delhi) report of 11 February 1990, made after a fortnight-long investigation into the Bhagalpur carnage and its aftermath, sums up the situation in this manner:

> Crucial records of the period, especially those from the tables of [the] then district magistrate [DM] and superintendent of police [SP] are missing.
>
> Evidence strongly suggests that [the DM] in all probability destroyed the log book of the Central Control Room in which the many SOS received in the fateful week were recorded. The fresh log book that has been placed in the office strangely makes no mention of the incidents. . . .
>
> [The SP at the time], who has since gained notoriety, too has left his successor . . . without a clue to work [with?]. His records too show a single joint report on the Chanderi massacre [one of the worst incidents in the countryside], just because Patna High Court had issued a notice.

> Even the joint report of the DM and the SP on the first incident
> at Tatarpur Chowk [in Bhagalpur city] on October 24 that had lit
> the fuse is among the papers not traceable.
> The fact, incredible as it may sound, is that there is no statement
> of facts available in either the DM or the SP's office.

This kind of destruction or removal of records is of course not un-precedented: the British practiced it on a large scale in India after 1937, and no doubt there have been many other instances since Independence. What is less frequently observed, however, is the destruction entailed in the systematic construction of evidence on all sides, official and unofficial, when an event of this kind occurs. Violence produces the necessity of evidence gathering, of uncovering hidden processes and contradictions that we might normally prefer to ignore, but violence also wipes out "evidence" and even, to a large extent, the possibility of collecting it in a manner and form that is deemed acceptable by today's social sciences. Let me illustrate this with reference to the PUDR team's work in Bhagalpur.

In spite of the size of this team and the very long hours it put in during its eight-day visit to the district, our investigation was subject to severe constraints.[15] The majority of the people we spoke to in Bhagalpur were Muslims. They were the primary victims of the "riots"; they were in the relief camps; they were the people who were willing to, perhaps had need to, talk. Hindus in many of the badly affected areas met us with studied silence, if not hostility.[16] The Hindus we could speak with easily were from a narrow stratum: middle-class intellectuals, political activists, professionals, and officials with established opinions (or "theories") about what had occurred.

In addition, we were confronted with the problem when we met victims of the violence, or other eyewitnesses, of what questions to ask and how. The forms of our questions suggested particular answers, and there were particular answers that we were more ready to hear than others. This is a point to which I shall return. But we faced a further difficulty at the outset: How does one ask the victims of such barbarism—the father and son, or the mother and four little children, who survived because one was away and others managed somehow to hide in the fields from where they could see elders and young ones, kith and kin and neighbors, women and infants in arms, every one who was found in the Muslim quarter of their village being slaughtered—how does one ask such victims of terror for details of what they saw?

And yet one asks, because "investigators" are bound to ask. And sometimes the victims, survivors, and others standing by begin to talk without even being asked, because they have been asked so many times already, or because there is need for a public narrative of their suffering. However, this narrative too assumes a set form. It appears as a ritualized account, a collective memory or record that has been generated on behalf of the entire community—"Muslims" or "Yadavs" or "Hindus" or whatever. The standard practice in the affected *mohallas* and villages we visited was for us to be taken to a central spot where many people gathered, and the "elders" or the "educated" gave us what might be called the authorized account of local happenings.

The teams of three or four members that went to any one place tried to get around this screening by breaking up and talking to different groups individually. But in several places women and youth were restrained from holding independent conversations with us; in one village some of the local people (especially women) turned somewhat aggressively upon a woman colleague of ours and upon those village women who had continued to talk in spite of earlier signals asking them to stop. However, even when women, youths, or for that matter children spoke up separately and differences of emphasis and priority surfaced, their different accounts still emerged as part of a collective statement. The broad outlines of what occurred appeared to be known to everyone in the same way, and the concerns were common: the suffering of the collectivity, the need for protection and compensation, the identification of those who had proved to be friends in need (mainly religious organizations and, in places where the Left had a presence, left-wing activists and associations).

The PUDR team went to Bhagalpur three months after the outbreak of this violence, and it is possible to suggest that the ritualized nature of these collective accounts was much more firmly set by then. Yet I have no doubt that a collective memory, in a set form, will have come into being very soon after the occurrence of the events it describes. This has to do with the living conditions of the local communities, the history of past strife, and the difficult relations with the state. But it has to do with another factor as well: that the purpose of the public narrative is at least partly to impress a particular point of view on the state and its agents.

The situation produced by any large-scale outbreak of violence deepens the divisions that exist at any time between privileged people and common folk in India. Such situations also work to level communities and make entire groups that are under suspicion a part of the "common folk." At these times, the informants—distant villagers, illiterate artisans, faceless members of a makeshift relief camp, and even the elite of a community, such as medical practitioners or university professors—tend to become part of a collective subject that approaches the investigator as "a person of influence" and appeals to her or him for relief, justice, and mercy.

Consequently, much of our conversation with local people in Bhagalpur had to do with minute details of property losses, injuries, and deaths that we did not necessarily consider central to our investigation. We were asked repeatedly to come a little further, to this village or the next, to see for ourselves the destruction of this house, to make a note of these names, too. We were asked also to record "First Information Reports" and evidence where the police had allegedly failed or refused to record these, or at least to help in getting them recorded because, as a number of informants said, "We live under constant threat and may well be killed before anyone bothers to take down our evidence." We were met in other places with the bare response: "We don't know anything. We were not here."

Sometimes, as the denial of all knowledge of what occurred in a particular place indicates, the collective accounts we heard partook of the character of preemptive narratives. They were constructed, more or less consciously, in order to falsify particular "theories" or explanations of the course of events. "Hindus," who were accused of forming an armed procession and adopting extremely aggressive tactics during its course through the city of Bhagalpur, thus sparking off the violence of 24 October, declared that the procession was an ordinary religious one, like any other on important festive occasions, and that it was accompanied by large numbers of women and children singing devotional songs and playing on musical instruments as they went along. "Muslims," who were accused by the local administration and by others of making preparations for a "riot" from long before 24 October, declared all over the district and almost without exception that they had never had any quarrel with the Hindus and had no reason to fear a riot, that perfect amity had always existed between the Hindus and Muslims of the district and that "even in 1946–47," while the rest of northern India burned, there was no trouble in Bhagalpur.

Even where the defense of the immediate group or collectivity was not an issue, as when we spoke to urban professionals and intellectuals, the defense of something larger and more intangible was sometimes at stake: the "good name" of the city (or region), for example, or the very possibility of Hindus and Muslims living together in the future— as of course they must. It was this kind of thinking that led many people to stress the importance of letting bygones be bygones. Some similar reasoning perhaps lay behind the pronounced tendency to lay the blame for the strife on "outsiders": political leaders in Patna and Delhi, "criminal gangs," or a corrupt and spineless administration. The theory of "criminal" instigation and conduct of the riots has been especially popular. The argument is that "criminal castes" from across the Ganges (which flows west to east through the district just north of the city of Bhagalpur) came into the city and other strife-torn places in large numbers, that these castes (designated "criminal" by the erstwhile colonial regime) are the cause of much of the lawlessness in Bhagalpur even at other—"normal"—times, and that criminal gangs making free use of these "outside" elements were largely responsible for the violence of 1989.

The difficulties of evidence gathering are, however, only a part of the problem of reconstructing the history of such events. The question of how to write about such experiences, already hinted at, is equally hazardous. For there is the obvious danger of sensationalizing and thus rendering such strife and its consequences extraordinary, aberrational. Yet there is, on the other hand, at least an equal danger of surrendering to the demands of an academic discourse by sanitizing, "naturalizing," and thereby making bland and more palatable what is intensely ugly and disorienting. Academic discourse, too, tends to push the moment of violence into the realm of the exceptional and aberrant, as I shall try to show.

Discussions of sectarian strife in India find it necessary to try to balance an account of "Hindu" atrocities by some account of "Muslim" (or "Sikh") atrocities. So, a few weeks after our visit to Bhagalpur, the chief minister of Bihar spoke in a public announcement on the steps being taken to restore normalcy, of the numbers of Hindu temples and shrines destroyed in the district along with large numbers of Muslim holy places—against all the evidence, for no investigating team had reported a single Hindu temple or shrine damaged or destroyed on this occasion. So, too, a documentary film on the Bhagalpur violence made by an independent and enterprising filmmaker, Nalini

Singh, and shown on national television in March 1990 equated Jamalpur (the one Hindu village to be attacked in the course of the "riots") with Logain (the site of one of the worst massacres of Muslims), implying that the attacks and casualties were of the same order, although the most reliable estimates suggest that 7 people were killed and some 70 houses and huts were partially burned and looted in Jamalpur against 115 killed and the entire Muslim *basti* looted, burned, and destroyed in Logain.[17]

This allegedly "liberal" demand to document and present "both sides of the case" is frequently accompanied by the social scientist's search for those "outside forces" and "exceptional circumstances" that are in this view likely to be found behind such acts of extraordinary violence. In the case of Bhagalpur, journalists as well as other investigators have pointed the finger at "criminal" elements, at the local administration, and at the vicious propaganda of the Vishwa Hindu Parishad (VHP) and other militant Hindu organizations. As a newspaper report of 19 November 1989 has it:

> Is it possible that people who live together [have always lived together] and share each other's daily concerns—about food and drink, the marriage of daughters, and electoral politics—should become enemies overnight? . . . What have these people to do with the Babari Masjid and Ramjanmabhumi controversy? But the criminal elements of both communities saw their opportunity and very quickly indeed they filled the minds of the people with a poisonous insanity.

That this task of poisoning the minds of the people could be accomplished so quickly does not seem to raise any problems for the writer; its significance is never discussed. Instead we are told, "The Bhagalpur riots are not so much the product of sectarian ['communal'] feelings as a calamity brought about by the criminals."[18]

The moral of the story, which carries over from nationalist accounts of the pre-Independence period, is that "the people" are essentially secular. The same newspaper report goes on to say:

> The criminals are armed with rifles, guns, bombs, axes, choppers, spears, and the blessings of [powerful] political leaders. What can the people do? [*Bechari janta kare to kya kare?*] The members of both [Hindu and Muslim] communities wished to live together in peace and friendship but the criminals ultimately succeeded in spreading the poison among them.[19]

Explanations of violence in terms of "larger historical processes" are not so far removed from this kind of analysis as might appear to be the case at first sight. Instead of focusing on the activities of VHP propagandists and criminal elements or on dereliction of duty on the part of local officials, these explanations deal in the "criminalization" of politics; the "communalization" of Indian public life, not excluding the administration; and longer-term economic changes such as the rise of the "backward castes," emergence of new trading groups, unionization, labor troubles, and the like. The PUDR's careful and detailed report on the "Bhagalpur Riots," for instance, makes an elaborate—if somewhat confusing—statement regarding the complex of circumstances surrounding the outbreak of violence:

> A common simplification of the riots has consisted in placing the responsibility for them on criminals. We feel it may be more accurate to say that it was the sum of relations between criminals, the police administration, politicians, the dominant elite and the economy which are responsible and, at any given time, one or all of these— along with some local people—were significant factors and agents in the riots.[20]

Too often, however, the statement of complex long-term historical processes leaves little room for human agency and human responsibility and becomes a statement about the essential and unchanging ("secular") character of the majority of the people concerned. The "economic dimension" particularly tends to emerge as the master of all. Two examples from the work of Asghar Ali Engineer, perhaps the most prominent writer on the causes of recent sectarian strife, will serve to illustrate the point. On Jabalpur in 1961, he wrote:

> The *apparent cause* was the "elopement" of a Hindu girl with a Muslim boy. However, although it brought the powerful religio-cultural prejudices between the two communities into play . . . it was not the real reason. The *real reason* lay elsewhere. The Muslim boy was the son of a local *bidi* magnate who had gradually succeeded in establishing control over the local *bidi* industry. His Hindu competitors were very sore over this development. It was not insignificant that the *bidi* industry belonging to the Muslims in Jabalpur suffered heavily during the riots.

And on Bhiwandi in 1970, he wrote:

> [Bhiwandi] is a thriving centre of the powerloom industry, with quite a few Muslims owning powerlooms and a large number of

Muslim artisans working as weavers on these looms . . . . Also, being on the Bombay-Agra National Highway, Bhiwandi receives a large amount of revenue by way of octroi from the passing trucks. Its municipality thus has a handsome income. Local municipal politics, therefore, assumes [a] great deal of importance. Different parties and political groups vie with each other to wrest control of the Municipal Council. A section of Muslims with their increased prosperity due to the loom industry developed greater political aspirations, challenging the traditional leadership and this led to communal tension.[21]

In its more extreme versions, this economistic viewpoint tends to reduce all history to a fight for land and profit. Here is a journalist's account of the "economy of communalism" in Bhagalpur: "It would be simplistic to dismiss the recent Bhagalpur communal riot as a manifestation of the ugly face of our civilization. Attention must be focused on [the] ruined economy, dying industry and the decadent feudal agrarian structure of the area which provides food [fuel?] to such an event." Further: "Religion is no consideration among the buyers and sellers [of firearms]. Profit is the overwhelming motive. They have a vested interest in keeping the communal tension going. . . . Another factor that keeps it going is [the] profitability of relief camp operations [*sic*]."[22]

Obviously it is not my submission that economic interests and contradictions are unimportant. However, there is more than a narrowly conceived material interest to the history even of our times. Yet some of the most sophisticated writing in the social sciences continues to reduce the lives of men and women to the play of material interests, or at other times to large impersonal movements in economy and society over which human beings have no control. The thrust of this writing is to suggest that the "real" battle lies not where it might appear—say, in matters of history or notions of honor, or in the centrality of religion or people's attachment to particular cultural and religious symbols—but in the question of immediate material interests. In the quarrels at this level, furthermore, it is above all the elite groups that count. Let me quote the PUDR report once more: "The major material long term benefit the [rural] elite groups are likely to get from the present riots is land." Or again, regarding continuing tension between Hindus and Muslims in the villages: "One of the major factors contributing to this state of affairs is property, especially land, of those who left their homes. Threats continue to be made by those who have now set their eyes on either grabbing or buying land cheap."[23] But are these threats made by them alone?

Let me reiterate, at the risk of redundancy, that my point is not that land and property are of no importance in bringing about or perpetuating sectarian conflict. My point is that the emphasis placed upon these factors often leaves little room for the emotions of people, for feelings and perceptions—in short, little room for agency.

There is another aspect to this question of agency. The mass of "the people" appear to count for very little in our analyses of "riot" situations. It is economic interests, land struggles, the play of market forces, and frequently elite manipulation that make them occur. "The people" find their place, once again, outside history. By that means, perhaps, their pristine qualities (their "purity") is also preserved. For the message of much of the writing on sectarian violence in India in recent times is the same as that found in the nationalist histories of the pre-Independence period. It is to suggest that events like Bhagalpur 1989 do not represent the real flow of Indian history: they are exceptional, the result of unusual conjunctures. It is to pretend that their occurrence on the scale and with the frequency that we have seen in the 1980s still makes no fundamental difference to the essential "secularism" of the people and to our cherished national traditions: "secularism," "nonviolence," "peaceful coexistence."[24]

III

This is, to my mind, an unacceptable history. It is unacceptable not only because it tends to be reductionist and not only because it continues to ply a tired nationalist rhetoric. It is unacceptable also because, willy-nilly, it essentializes "communalism" and the "communal riot," making these out to be transparent and immutable entities around which only the context changes. In this section, I wish to dwell a little longer on the inadequacies of history writing in this vein.

A point that I have already made but would like to emphasize is that the grand narratives that we produce—and must continue to produce—as historians, political scientists, sociologists, or whatever—tend to be about "context" alone, or at least primarily: the "larger forces" of history that assemble to produce violent conflicts of the kind discussed above. One advantage, or if you prefer consequence, of such narrativizing is that we are able to escape the problem of representing pain. This is a sanitized history with which we are relatively comfortable. In it, violence, suffering, and many of the scars left by their history are suppressed.

It seems to me imperative, however, that historians and social scientists pay closer attention to the moment of violence and try in some way to represent it in their writings. There are at least two reasons for this. First, the moment of violence, and suffering, tells us a great deal about our condition today.[25] Second, the experience of violence is in crucial ways constitutive of our "traditions," our sense of community, our communities, and our history.

The scars of such experience are evident, for one thing, in the popular construction of the history that we live with—the construction of those brutish (or pious) characters that pass for "the Hindu," "the Muslim," or "the Sikh," all too often with quite terrifying consequences. I shall not try, in this brief statement, to analyze in any detail the changing self-image of the different religious communities and their constructions of the "other." A reference to some aspects of the image of "Hindus" and of "Muslims," as it appears in recent Hindu propaganda, may help, however, to illustrate the importance of the question.

Many observers have pointed to the new heights reached by Hindu militancy and propaganda over the last few years. This has been orchestrated most visibly by the VHP, and it plainly has had much to do with the increased frequency and scale of Hindu-Muslim strife in the 1980s. The point that is perhaps not sufficiently stressed, however, is that the violent slogans and demands of organizations like the VHP, and the "riots" they have sparked, do not poison the minds of "the people" only for a moment. On the contrary—given our history, the resources available to "secular" and "communal" forces in the country, the opportunism of most of our major political parties, and the continued and repeated outbreak of sectarian violence—the most outrageous suggestions about the "evil," "dangerous," and "threatening" character of the "other" community (or communities) come to be widely accepted and part of a popular dogma.[26]

Nothing but this acceptance can explain the kinds of atrocities perpetrated in recent instances of sectarian strife: the call to leave not a single Muslim man, woman, or child alive, which was acted upon in several places in Bhagalpur; the massacre of all eighteen Muslim passengers traveling in a tempo-taxi along with the Hindu taxi driver when they were stopped on a major country road two-and-a-half weeks after the cessation of general "rioting" and their burial in a field that was then planted over with garlic; the chopping off of the breasts of women; the spearing of infants and children, the spears with the victims impaled on them being then twirled around in the air to the accompaniment of laughter and shouts of triumph.[27]

What lies behind this insane and incredible brutality, I suggest, is the belief that the victims are real or potential monsters who have done all this and worse to "us" or will do so if given half a chance. In many cases, the alleged atrocities for which these actions are supposed to be just recompense are believed to have occurred "yesterday" or "the other day," in "the town" or a neighboring district or further away: in Bhagalpur the rumor that set off the major Hindu attacks in the countryside was that all the Hindu students living in Muslim-owned boardinghouses in a part of the city near the university (many of whom came, of course, from the villages of Bhagalpur) had been massacred on the first two days of the "riots."[28] In other instances, revenge appears to be sought for what "they" have done to "us," generally, in the past. The relevant point is that what appears to many of us as rabid and senseless Hindu propaganda is widely believed.

In one of its more "restrained" forms, this leads to the view that all Muslims in India are "Pakistanis": witness, we are told, their response in the course of any cricket match between India and Pakistan. Following from this is the argument that local Muslims are out to create another Pakistan, in one place after another—Bhagalpur, Moradabad, Meenakshipuram (Tamilnadu). By this juncture we are well into that realm where "Muslims" are represented as being inherently turbulent, fanatical, and violent.

Aggression, Conversion, Unbounded Sexuality: these are the themes that make up the history of the spread of Islam, as told by the Hindu historians and propagandists: "Wherever Muslim communities exist, there will inevitably be a 'dance of annihilation' in the name of Islam." It is the "religious duty of every Muslim" to "kidnap and force into their own religion non-Muslim women." Several pamphlets and leaflets distributed by militant Hindu organizations in places where strife has lately occurred show a "Hindu" husband and wife with two children ("Ham do, hamaare do" [Us two, our two]) by the side of a "Muslim" family—a man with four wives and numerous children accompanied by the self-explanatory slogan "Ham paanch, hamaare pacchis" (We five, our twenty-five).[29] Thus a whole new "common sense" develops, relating to the marital and sexual practices of "the Muslims" (here, as elsewhere, referring only to Muslim men), to their perverse character and their violent temperament.

It will perhaps suffice to illustrate the tenor of recent Hindu propaganda and beliefs about the Muslims if I reproduce here the substance of just one leaflet that was distributed in Bhagalpur sometime between the last quarter of 1989 and January 1990. Entitled "Hindu Brothers Consider and Be Warned," the leaflet asks:[30]

1. Is it not true that the Muslim population is increasing, while that of the Hindus is decreasing [*sic*]?
2. Is it not true that the Muslims are fully organized [prepared], while the Hindus are fully disorganized [scattered]?
3. Is it not true that the Muslims have an endless supply of weapons while the Hindus are completely unarmed? . . .
5. Is it not true that the Congress has been elected to power for the last forty years on a mere 30 percent of the vote: in other words, that the day the Muslims become 30 percent of the population they will gain power?
6. Is it not true that the Muslims will become 30 percent of the population in twelve to fifteen years' time: in other words, within twelve to fifteen years the Muslims will easily become the rulers of this country?
7. Is it not true that as soon as they gain power, they will destroy the Hindus root-and-branch, as they have done in Pakistan?
8. Is it not true that, when destroying the Hindus, they will not stop to think which Hindu belongs to the Lok Dal, who is a Socialist and who a Congressman [or woman], who belongs to the "Forward" castes, who to the "Backward," or who is a Harijan ["Untouchable"]? . . .
11. Is it not true that, after the conceding of Pakistan the land mass that remained was manifestly that of the Hindus? . . .
13. Is it not true that Hindus [*sic*] are prohibited from buying land or settling in Kashmir, whereas Kashmiri Muslims are free to buy land wherever they want in the country? . . .
16. Is it not true that Christians [*sic*] have their own "homeland"[31] or country, Muslims [*sic*] also have their own "homeland" or country, where they feel secure in every way, but Hindus have not been able to retain their country because under the banner of secularism it has been turned into a *dharmshala* [hospice]?
17. Is it not true that while Hindus are in power, Muslims can live safely, but as soon as the Muslims come to power, life will become difficult for the Hindus—that is, they will be destroyed? . . .

21. Is it not true that those Muslim women who have been divorced by their husbands are supported through the Waqf Committee by the government, with funds taken from the government treasury; which means that for the maintenance and joy- [or lust-] filled lives of the Muslims, the majority Hindu community has to bear an additional tax burden?

If these things are true, then Hindu brothers you must immediately awake—awake while there is still time. And vow to sacrifice your wealth, your body, your all for the protection of the Hindu people and nation and for the declaration of this country as a Hindu nation.

What follows from all this is of course a dread of "the Muslim" and the demand to disarm "him"—by disenfranchisement and deculturization: Muslims should adopt "our" names, "our" language, "our" dress. What follows is the demand that if the Muslims wish to stay in India, they must learn to live like "us." (Who? This is never very clear, but in the circumstances it does not seem to matter.) "Hindustan mein rahna hai, to hamse milkar rahna hoga" (If you wish to live in Hindustan, you will have to live like us); "Hindustan mein rahna hai, to Bande Mataram kahna hoga" (If you wish to live in Hindustan, you will have to raise the slogan "Bande Mataram" [Victory to the Mother]).

Alongside this argument is sometimes found the paradoxical one that "we" shall certainly provide justice to minorities like the Muslims for, since they are overwhelmingly local converts, it is "Hindu blood (that) flows in their veins."[32] But the central message remains: "Live like us" or, its blood-curdling corollary, face annihilation: "Babar ki santan—jao Pakistan ya kabristan" (Descendants of Babar—Pakistan or the grave, take your choice), a slogan that appears to have been taken literally by large sections of the police and the local Hindu population in Bhagalpur and some other places.

The obverse of this vilification of the "Muslim" is the promotion of a rather different image of the "Hindu" from that which has most commonly been advertised from colonial times to today. The emphasis in this militant Hindu propaganda is not so much on the nonviolent, peaceful, tolerant character of "the Hindus"—although astoundingly, even that proposition remains. It is rather more on how "the Hindus" have been tolerant for too long; they are "still too timid"; the need of the hour is "not tolerance but courage." "The Hindus" must now claim, are now finally claiming, what is rightfully theirs. If "Christians" have their own nation and "Muslims" have their own, why should "the Hindus" not have their own nation, their own country, their own state in the only territory they inhabit, where they form an absolute majority, and where they have lived for thousands of years? For too long "Hindus" have been asked to make concessions on the grounds of their "tolerance" and on the plea of "secularism"; they must be bullied no longer, they must make no further concessions. "Garva se kaho ham Hindu hain" (Announce with pride that you are Hindus) and "Hindu jaaga, desh jaagega" (The Hindus awaken, the nation shall awake), the walls of Delhi and other north Indian cities have proclaimed loudly over the last few years.

That there is nothing changeless or sacrosanct about all the traditions, values, images, and self-images associated with particular communities is strikingly demonstrated by the history of the *shuddhi* campaign conducted by the Arya Samaj and other Hindu organizations from the later nineteenth century onward. Lajpat Rai observed in his *History of the Arya Samaj*, published in 1944, that "the Arya Samaj, being a Vedic *church*, and as such a Hindu organisation, engages itself in reclaiming the *wandering sheep who have strayed from the Hindu fold*, and converts anyone prepared to accept its religious teachings."[33] The *shuddhi* movement was a direct response to Christian missionary attacks on Hinduism and their efforts at converting low- and, to a lesser extent, high-caste Hindus in the nineteenth century, and the Christian inspiration of Arya organization (into a "church") and of Lajpat Rai's language ("wandering sheep" to be brought back by their shepherd) is evident.

Lajpat Rai noted also that while *shuddhi* literally means "purification," militant Hindu practice of the late nineteenth and early twentieth centuries had transformed its meaning. It now applied to a range of practices: (1) *conversion* to Hinduism of people belonging to "foreign" religions; (2) *reconversion* of those who had at some stage in the near or distant past taken to a "foreign" religion; (3) *reclamation*, that is, raising the status of the *antyaj* (depressed) classes and making them fully Hindus.[34]

This redefinition of the Hindu community and of legitimate Hindu practice, and this adoption of "Christian" tactics like conversion, had something to do with the importance attached to numbers in the political and administrative calculations of the regime in late colonial India.[35] As the assertion of community identity gathered pace at many levels—Hindu, Muslim, Sikh, Ahir, Patidar, Nadar, Bihari, Oriya,

Telugu—and economic and political competition took on new dimensions, militant Hindu leaders and organizations called upon Hindus to give up "perverse" religious notions and practices; the "silly," "antinational" tradition of caste divisions; the restrictions on interdining and on travel overseas; and "fantastic" ideas of pollution and the consequent ban on reconversion that ensured that "millions of forcibly converted Hindus have remained Muslims even to this day."[36] In the 1920s, Arya Samajis and more orthodox Hindu leaders "rediscovered" the *Devalasmriti*, said to have been written a century or more after the Arab raids on Sindh, which prescribed lengthy rules for readmission into Hinduism of Hindus who had been forcibly converted, and in the 1930s "discovered" the *vratyastoma* rites (supposedly laid down in the *Atharvaveda* and the *Brahmanas*) for readmittance of those who were earlier judged to have fallen out of "Aryan" society.[37] Shastric authority had been marshaled for a new tradition.

What is true of "Hindu traditions," that they are neither static nor irreversible, is true of the traditions, images, and self-images of other communities. It may also be said to apply, *mutatis mutandis*, to what has for seventy years or more been designated simply as a "communal riot." The changing character and modes of sectarian strife even over this relatively short period need careful study, and it is necessary to emphasize that there is no essential "riot" around which only circumstances change.

Sectarian violence in the 1980s appears to have taken on new and increasingly horrifying forms. Recent strife between people belonging to different religious denominations has not been restricted to pitched battles on the streets or cloak-and-dagger attacks and murders in side lanes, which were the chief markers of earlier riots. The worst instances of recent violence—Bhagalpur in 1989, Meerut in 1987, the anti-Sikh "riots" in Delhi in 1984, the anti-Tamil "riots" in Colombo in 1983, the Hindu-Muslim "riots" in Moradabad in 1980, and others[38]—have amounted to pogroms, organized massacres in which large crowds of hundreds, thousands, and even, in places, tens of thousands have attacked the houses and property and lives of small, isolated, and previously identified members of the "other" community.

If just one or two deaths occur in an incident now, as a local leader of the Communist Party (Marxist) observed in Bhagalpur, it is not even considered a riot.[39] Attacks on young and old, the blind and the maimed, and women, children and infants; the aim of wiping out the "enemy" and hence physical destruction (of lives, property, tools for work, and standing crops) on a massive scale; the unashamed participation of the police; the lynching of "enemy" people found on trains or buses passing through the affected area—all these have become standard features of today's "communal riot."

When the lynching of railway passengers first occurred on a large scale in 1947, it was remarked that the country had just been divided: two new states were coming into being that needed time to consolidate their positions, and the armed forces and police had also been split; confusion, serious crime, and violence were almost inevitable. When such actions were repeated in 1984, it was said that a world leader and enormously popular prime minister had been assassinated, and that when a colossus falls some upheaval, some exceptional reaction, is only natural. Now it has become unnecessary to plead exceptional circumstances when people are lynched or burned alive in the course of sectarian strife; newspapers report these occurrences, sometimes on their inner pages, without special comment.[40]

Clearly, all this is not unrelated to other kinds of violence in the society, in other contexts—which also pass quickly from the domain of the "extraordinary" to that of the "everyday." Consider, for example, the cursory report on the deaths of five peasant volunteers from Bihar, among the tens of thousands who had streamed into Delhi in order to attend a rally organized by the Indian People's Front, who were run over and killed by a three-wheeler truck while they were sleeping on a pavement on the night of 7 October 1990,[41] or the reports on recent attempts at self-immolation by school and college students protesting against the institution of reservation in government jobs for people from "Backward Classes,"[42] which quickly retreated to pages 3 and 5 of the national newspapers after their first sensationalizing appearance in the press—which was, of course, no less problematical.

The discourse on violence brands events of this kind as "extraordinary" but treats them as completely ordinary, inconsequential, and unworthy of much attention. It is in this context that I turn, finally, to another "fragment" from Bhagalpur that provides a somewhat different perspective on violence, a different commentary on the meaning of "communal riots" today. I present this fragment here not as another piece, or even another kind, of "evidence." I propose it, instead, as the articulation of another subject position arising from a certain experience (and understanding) of sectarian strife, one that may say something about the parameters of our own subject positions and under-standings. In addition, this articulation provides a commentary on the limits of the form of the historiographical discourse and its search for omniscience.

The fragment in question takes the form of a collection of poems written by a college teacher in Bhagalpur, a resident of a mixed Hindu and Muslim, predominantly lower-middle-class locality that was not the scene of any of the "great" killings in 1989 but was nevertheless at-tacked repeatedly, traumatized, and scarred forever.[43] In Manazir Aashiq Harganvi's poems, written for the most part during the first five days of the violence, we get some sense of the terror and desolation that so many people in Bhagalpur experienced at this time. The poems speak of darkness, of long nights, and of those days and nights that seemed to run into each other without meaning and without end. They speak of the hysterical screaming that marked that time, screams for help that were, however, drowned out by the laughter and shouts of the attackers:

> Jaan leva hansi
> Bhayanak kahkahe
> Bachao ki awaazen
> Balwaiyon ke beech
>   phansi rah gayeen

[Blood-curdling laughter / Terrifying shouts / (Our) cries for help / Lost among the attackers.]

We have pictures of fields and corpses, and the impossibility of count-ing them:

> Ek . . . tin . . . sattar
> Sau . . . do sau . . . dhai sau
> Yeh ginti paar nahin lagegi
> Inhen ginne se pahle hi
> Tum aa jate ho
> Bam aur goli lekar
> Ginti ki tadad badhane
> Lamhe ki rupahli tasveer
> Koi dekhe aakar!

[One . . . three . . . seventy / One hundred . . . two hundred . . . two hun-dred and fifty / This counting will never end / For before it has ended / You come again / With bombs and bullets / To increase the numbers to be counted / If only someone could come and see / The beauty of this moment!]

We have a representation of the "wake," waiting for the darkness to end and some light to begin to appear, but also—and more dreadfully—waiting simply for the attackers to come again:

Dangai phir aayenge
Aisa hai intezar

[The rioters will come again: / We wait expectantly.]

Among these poems there are many that talk about rape: a metaphorical statement of the humiliations suffered by a community, or a literal description of events that occurred?

Mar gaye bete mere
Biwi mari
Aur yeh beti jise tum saath
        mere kankhiyon se dekhte ho
Beshumar hathon ne loota
        hai ise

[My sons have been killed / My wife is dead / And this daughter, whom you observe / out of the corner of your eyes / sitting by my side— / How many have looted her?]

Like the verse just quoted, there are many others that are addressed to neighbors and friends—or people who were once "neighbors" and "friends." Neighbors turned killers, people—known and unknown—running away from one another, and people ("all of us") afraid to look in the mirror for fear of what they/we will see. We have in them appeals and accusations. We have figures of emptiness:

Kuch bhi nahin rah gaya hai kahin

[Nothing is left anywhere.]

Aadmi bahut hi bauna ho chuka hai
Apni lambai ka jhootha ahsas bhi
        baki nahin bacha

[Man has become a midget / Unable any longer even to delude himself / about his height.]

Ham behad khokhle ho gaye hain

[We have been emptied (of meaning).]

        Aadhe-adhure log

[Half people, incomplete people.]

And the endless search for ourselves, our loved ones, our friends:

Khud apne aap ko dhoondte hue
Ab tum us kinare par khade ho
Jahan se koi nahin lauta
Koi nahin laut-ta dost
Ab to tum bhi nahin laut paoge
Yaad ki sirf ek shart rah jayegi
    ki jab bhi kahin
Fasad hoga
Tum bahut yaad aoge

[In search of yourself / You have now reached that shore / From where no one has returned / No one ever returns, my friend / Now you, too, are lost forever / There remains but one condition of memory that whenever, wherever / A riot occurs— / I shall remember you.]

It is a fragment that tells us a great deal about the Bhagalpur "riots" of 1989, and tells us also how much of this history we shall never be able to write.

Standard historiographical procedure since the nineteenth century appears to have required the taking of a prescribed center (of a state formation, a nation-state) as one's vantage point and the "official" archive as one's primary source for the construction of an adequate general "history." The power of this model can easily be seen in the writing of Indian history.

This is a procedure that is not easily discarded, both because states and nations are central organizing principles of human society as we know it, and because the historian must necessarily deal with periods, territories, social groups, and political formations constituted into unities or blocs. However, the fact of their constitution—by historical circumstance and by the historian—needs to be borne in mind. The provisionality and contested character of all such unities (the objects of historical analysis) must be underlined.

I should like to suggest, in opposition to the established procedure, that, with all their apparent solidity and comprehensiveness, what the official sources give us is also but a fragment of history.[44] More, that what the historians call a "fragment"—a weaver's diary, a collection of poems by an unknown poet (and to these we might add all those literatures of India that Macaulay condemned, creation myths and women's songs, family genealogies, and local traditions of history)—is of central importance in challenging the state's construction of history, in thinking other histories and marking those contested spaces through which particular unities are sought to be constituted and others broken up.[45]

If the provisionality of our units of analysis needs stressing, so does the provisionality of our interpretations and of our theoretical conceits. The arrogation of "total" and "objective" knowledge is no longer anywhere near as common as it used to be in historical writing. Nevertheless the temptations of totalizing discourses are great. The yearning for the "complete" statement, which leaves out nothing of importance, is still with us. That urge will remain an important and necessary part of the historiographical endeavor. At the same time, however, it would be well to acknowledge the provisionality of the statements we make, their own historicity and location in a specific political context, and consequently their privileging of particular forms of knowledge and particular relationships and forces to the exclusion of others. None of this is to deny the importance or efficacy of certain subject positions in a certain historical context. At the present juncture in India, however, the totalizing standpoint of a seamless nationalism that many of us appear to have accepted as social scientists and historians seems especially inappropriate.

The dominant nationalist historiography that insists on this standpoint needs to be challenged not only because of its interested use of the categories "national," "secular," and so on. It needs to be challenged also because of its privileging of the so-called "general" over the particular, the larger over the smaller, the "mainstream" over the "marginal"—because of its view of India, and all of South Asia, from Delhi alone.

The PUDR team of which I was a member happened to be in Bhagalpur on the eve of India's Republic Day, 26 January, in 1990. On the evening of the twenty-fifth, we heard extracts from the Indian constitution being read out on national television: "We, THE PEOPLE OF INDIA, having solemnly resolved to constitute India into a SOVEREIGN, SO-CIALIST, SECULAR DEMOCRATIC REPUBLIC and to secure to all its citizens: JUSTICE, social, economic and political; LIBERTY of thought, expression, belief, faith and worship . . ."[46] The remoteness of Delhi struck us on that occasion in a way that is hard to recapture in writing.

During the immediately preceding days, we had seen men, women, and children, with little bundles of their belongings, running away from their villages to "safer" places for fear of what might happen on 26 January. It was strongly rumored that on that day of national celebration, Muslims—"traitors" as always—would hoist black flags (or even the Pakistani flag) on their religious buildings and there would be another "riot." We had seen heated altercations among Muslim villagers and townsfolk, between those who said that running away only added to the alarmist rumors and the dangers and others who accused them of foolhardiness in the context of "all that has happened." We had been asked in a relief camp to take down "First Information Reports" and evidence because the police, who should have done this, were themselves the guilty party and, in many cases, were still ensconced in office. The words "justice" and "liberty" rather stuck in the throat at this time.

The remoteness of Delhi that I have mentioned is not a function of physical distance alone. I have no doubt that many have felt the same remoteness in Kota and Jaipur, in Meham and Maliana (Meerut), in Tilaknagar, across the river Jamuna from the capital of India, and indeed inside the old city of Delhi itself—where, too, talk of "justice" and "liberty" must often appear callous. We must continue to search for ways of representing that remoteness in the histories that we write.

Notes

1. See the many reviews of *Subaltern Studies* and of Ranajit Guha's *Elementary Aspects of Peasant Insurgency in Colonial India* (Delhi, 1983), which make the criticism that these works have concentrated too greatly on the moment of open revolt and violence. This criticism fits in with a more general trend in "peasant studies" and social history that has led to the recent emphasis on "everyday forms" of people's existence and resistance; see James C. Scott, *Weapons of the Weak: Everyday Forms of Peasant Resistance* (New Haven, Conn., 1985).

2. See Lata Mani, "The Female Subject, the Colonial Gaze: Eyewitness Accounts of *Sati*" (paper presented at a workshop on culture, consciousness, and the colonial state, Isle of Thorns, U.K., 24–27 July 1989), which makes a similar point about agency and the moment of suffering.

3. The same point needs to be made about the kind of historical and social science writing discussed in this chapter. I have taken my examples deliberately from some of the best Left and liberal scholars writing today. This is because it is among them, rather than among chauvinist "Hindu," "Muslim," or "Sikh" historians and social scientists, that there is serious debate about "secularism"/"communalism" and the meaning of sectarian violence. It seems to me also that a critique of their writings is not only harder to make but, in terms of building up an alternative to the dominant (chauvinist) political and ideological tendencies in India today, also the more necessary.

4. See, for example, Ashis Nandy, "An Anti-Secularist Manifesto," *Seminar* 314 (October 1985); T. N. Madan, "Secularism in Its Place," *Journal of Asian Studies* 46, no. 4 (1987); Partha Chatterjee, *Bengal, 1920–1947: The Land Question* (Calcutta, 1984); Dipesh Chakrabarty, "Invitation to a Dialogue," in Ranajit Guha, ed., *Subaltern Studies*

IV (Delhi, 1985); and Gyanendra Pandey, *The Construction of Communalism in Colonial North India* (Delhi, 1990).

5. For a discussion of the peculiar usage of this term in India, see Pandey, *Communalism*, 6ff.

6. Bipan Chandra, *Modern India* (New Delhi, 1971). Page numbers in parentheses refer to this edition.

7. Sumit Sarkar, *Modern India, 1885–1947* (New Delhi, 1983).

8. There is no equivalent, for example, to the debates in Germany about the meaning of the Holocaust and the whole experience of National Socialism. German historians and philosophers have battled with the question of whether this was a one-time aberration or something produced by a German "national character"; see Theodor Adorno, *Minima Moralia: Reflections from Damaged Life* (1951; reprint, London, 1974), and Karl Jaspers, *The Future of Germany* (Chicago, 1967).

9. See Muhammad Umar Menon, "Partition Literature: A Study of Intizar Husiain" (and the references he cites), *Modern Asian Studies* 14, no. 3 (1980); Aijaz Ahmad, "Urdu Literature in India," *Seminar* 359 (July 1989); Alok Rai, "The Trauma of Independence: Some Aspects of Progressive Hindi Literature, 1945–47"; and Surjit Singh Hans, "The Partition Novels of Nanak Singh," in Amit Kumar Gupta, ed., *Myth and Reality: The Struggle for Freedom in India, 1945–47* (Delhi, 1987).

10. Tapati Chakravarty, "The Freedom Struggle and Bengali Literature of the 1940s," in Gupta, ed., *Myth and Reality*, p. 329.

11. The incidents of strife in Delhi in 1984, in Meerut in 1987, and in Bhagalpur in 1989 have been reported in this way. For a still more recent example, see Tavleen Singh's report regarding comments on the Gonda riots in *Indian Express* (Delhi), 14 October 1990.

12. The details in the next two paragraphs are taken from the PUDR report *Bhagalpur Riots* (Delhi, 1990) and the notes upon which it is based.

13. While many local people put the death toll at not less than 2,000, the official figure for the number of people killed was 414 as of April 1990. The most careful unofficial calculations suggested that perhaps 1,000 people lost their lives, and that over 90 percent of them were Muslims; ibid., p. 1.

14. I refer here to our own efforts as a team of investigators. Satish Sabherwal and Mushirul Hasan also note the "wholly unjustified confidence" of the mass media in the official version of events in recent instances of strife; "Moradabad Riots, 1980: Causes and Meanings," in Asghar Ali Engineer, ed., *Communal Riots in Post-Independence India* (Delhi, 1984), p. 208.

15. As the PUDR report notes, the support given to its ten-member team by local activists of the Communist Party of India (Marxist) "effectively doubled our strength"; *Bhagalpur Riots*, p. 70.

16. It is worth noting that we were repeatedly pressed to go and see those places where Hindus had been the victims of attacks—notably, a village named Jamalpur and a few sections of Bhagalpur city. We had decided to visit these places in any case, even before our on-the-spot investigations began in Bhagalpur, precisely in order that we might see and hear "both sides."

17. *Bhagalpur Riots*, p. 17.

18. Ved Prakash Vijpayee, in *Navbharat Times* (Delhi), 19 November 1989 (translation mine).

19. Ibid. Here is an even cruder example of the same kind of argument: "In India the basic material is very good. I mean, the people. They are honest, intelligent and generous. They are only waiting to be drawn into the national mainstream. What is absent is

leadership of the right type"; A. S. Raman, "Leaders to Blame for Communalism," *Sunday Mail*, 14 October 1990.

20. *Bhagalpur Riots*, p. 6.

21. Engineer, "Causes of Communal Riots," in Engineer, ed., *Communal Riots*, pp. 36–37.

22. Sumitra Kumar Jain, "Economy of Communalism," *Times of India* (Delhi), reproduced in *India Pakistan Times*, May 1990.

23. *Bhagalpur Riots*, pp. 32, 37.

24. I should add that "secularism" and "communalism" are perhaps not the most useful terms to be applied in our investigations of the social and political consciousness of different sections of the Indian people. This is a point that is made by several scholars and also in my book, *The Construction of Communalism.*

25. A detailed newspaper report on the rape of two nuns teaching at a convent school in Gajraula, Uttar Pradesh, notes that the three rapists, wearing nothing but undergarments, addressed one another as "ustad" and "guru" (literally, "teacher" and "guide," here used roughly for "boss," "partner") while they held the nuns at gunpoint; *Hindustan Times*, 23 July 1990. This is the kind of brag commonly associated with young louts found teasing women and girls on Delhi buses and in Bombay films. It is worth pondering the question of how large the step is from this kind of molestation of women to the kind of violent assault involved in rape.

26. This applies, of course, not only to constructions of the different religious communities but also to stereotypes of different caste and tribal communities as "dirty," "mendacious," "turbulent," "ferocious," "criminal," and so on, stereotypes that have had wide influence since the nineteenth century, if not earlier.

27. All of these instances are taken from Bhagalpur (see *Bhagalpur Riots*, passim) but the examples could be multiplied from elsewhere.

28. The rumor was, in fact, malicious and baseless. Most students living in the boarding houses left as soon as the disturbances broke out, if they had not left a little earlier, and many were helped to get away safely by their Muslim landlords. The number of students killed or missing is now computed to be six: of these the bodies of only two students (one Hindu and one Muslim) have been found; *Bhagalpur Riots*, p. 12. However, in the disturbed and dangerous condition of the city and district in the first few days after the outbreak of violence, many students appear not to have been able to reach their homes directly. During this time, and indeed for long afterward, the story of the massacre of students was neither investigated nor countered by the district or the university authorities. On the contrary, it was publicized in the press, even aired on the radio (both local and BBC), and was readily and widely credited. It was still widely believed when we visited Bhagalpur at the end of January 1990.

29. See Asghar Ali Engineer, "On the Theory of Communal Riots," in Engineer and Moin Shakir, eds., *Communalism in India* (Delhi, 1985), p. 62; and leaflets and pamphlets collected by the PUDR team in Bhagalpur. The two preceding quotations in this paragraph are from a leaflet entitled *Bhagalpur ka sampradayik danga kyon?* issued in the name of the "People of Bhagalpur"; and Vinayak Damodar Savarkar, *Six Glorious Epochs of Indian History*, trans. S. T. Godbole (Bombay, 1971), p. 175.

30. Dr. Rajeshwar, Akhil Bharat Hindu Mahasabha, *Hindu bandhuon, socho aur sambhalo*, which is among the leaflets mentioned in note 29 (translation mine).

31. The English word is used in the Hindi text.

32. See A. Shankar, *Chetavni 2: Desh ko khatra* (n.p., n.d.). On some of the logical problems arising out of the declaration that Indian Muslims are converts (forcibly con-

verted) and the descendants of Babar at the same time, see Alok Rai, "Only Bigots Feel That Conversions Follow Invasion," *Times of India* (Lucknow), 13 August 1990.

33. Lajpat Rai, *A History of the Arya Samaj* (1915; reprints, New Delhi, 1967), p. 120 (emphasis added).

34. Ibid., p. 120 n.

35. On the impact of the Gait Circular, which suggested that separate tables be drawn up in the 1911 census for "debatable Hindus," for example, see ibid., pp. 124–25, and Kenneth W. Jones, "Religious Identity and the Indian Census," in N. G. Barrier, ed., *The Census in British India: New Perspectives* (Delhi, 1981), pp. 91–92.

36. See Vinayak Damodar Sarvarkar, *Hindu-Pad-Padshahi; or, A Review of the Hindu Empire of Maharashtra* (Madras, 1925), pp. 272–73. The words in quotation marks are from Savarkar, *Six Glorious Epochs*, pp. 154, 188, 192–93, and passim.

37. J. T. F. Jordens, *Dayanand Sarasvati: His Life and Ideas* (Delhi, 1978) pp. 170, 322 n.

38. For some reports on these, see Engineer, *Communal Riots*; Engineer and Shakir, *Communalism in India*; PUCL and PUDR, *Who Are the Guilty? Report of a Joint Inquiry into the Causes and Impact of the Riots in Delhi from 31 October to 10 November* (Delhi, 1984); Uma Chakravarti and Nandita Haksar, *The Delhi Riots: Three Days in the Life of a Nation* (Delhi, 1987); Stanley J. Tambiah, *Sri Lanka: Ethnic Fratricide and the Dismantling of Democracy* (London, 1986); and Veena Das, ed., *Mirrors of Violence: Communities, Riots, Survivors in South Asia* (Delhi, 1990).

39. Interview with Shri Arun, Bhagalpur, 20 January 1990.

40. Budaun and Bhagalpur provide instances in 1989.

41. "Five Rallyists Crushed to Death," *Hindustan Times* (Delhi), 9 October 1990.

42. The protests followed from a government announcement on 7 August 1990 reserving a percentage of government jobs for the "Other Backward Classes," in addition to those already reserved for the "Scheduled Castes and Tribes." For detailed reports on the agitation and protest immolations, see *Economic and Political Weekly, India Today*, and newspapers for September and October 1990.

43. Manazir Aashiq Harganvi, *Ankhon dekhi: Bhagalpur ke bhayanak fasad ko dekhne ke baad* (Bhagalpur, 1989) (translations mine).

44. Cf. Antonio Gramsci: "Is it possible to write (conceive of) a history of Europe in the nineteenth century without an organic treatment of the French Revolution and the Napoleonic Wars . . . ? One can say, therefore, that [Croce's] book on the *History of Europe* is nothing but a fragment of history"; *Selections from the Prison Notebooks of Antonio Gramsci* (London, 1971), pp. 118, 119. It will be clear, of course, that I cannot advocate the kind of "objective," "integral" history that Gramsci called for.

45. I might add that, given the very great difficulty, if not impossibility, of translating cultures and consciousness into alien languages, a new historiography also requires a more concerted effort to recover what we continue in India to call the "vernacular" and the dialect, in terms both of sources and of the medium of historical debate. Along with that, there is the need to recognize that the "vernacular" may also be the "national," in more ways than one.

46. Constitution of India, preamble.

2 / Chandra's Death

Ranajit Guha

I

This essay begins with a transgression—a title that is designed to violate the intentions for which the material reproduced herein has already served with two authorities—the authority of the law that recorded the event in its present form and that of the editor who separated it from other items in an archive and gave it a place in another order, a book of documents collected for their sociological interest. The movement between these two intentions—the law's and the scholar's—suggests the interposition of other wills and purposes. Whatever these were—anthropological, literary, administrative, or any other—they had, from time to time, given this material names and functions in some very differently constructed series and under different classifications. We know nothing of them except that they must have occurred. Yet the very fact that they occurred, in whatever unspecified ways, would justify yet another intervention—a return to the terminal points of the shift, the only visible sites of legal and editorial intentionality, in order to desecrate them by naming the material once again and textualizing it for a new purpose. That purpose is to reclaim the document for history. Here is to quote it in extenso.[1]

> [Mark of Invocation]
> . . . a dose at . . . and I made a paste of the drug again at dawn and administered it to Chandra. That did nothing to destroy the fetus. The next day when I went again to the same Kali Bagdi together with my mother and Chandra, he gave us an herbal medicine that

had to be taken thrice a day [*jori tin pan*] together with some *hori-tuki* (a wild fruit of medicinal value) and two tablets of *bakhor guli* (a preparation of herbs and rice used to induce abortion) diluted in lime water. On 12 Choitra[2] I prepared a paste of the medicine with my own hands and administered one dose of it to Chandra at a quarter past the second *prohor*[3] of the night. Then at about a quarter past the second *prohor* the fetus was destroyed and it fell to the ground. My mother picked up the bloody fetus with some straw and threw it away. Even after that the pain in Chandra's belly continued to increase and she died when it was still four to five *dondoes*[4] left of the night. Chandra's corpse was then buried near the [river's] bend by my brother Gayaram, his brother-in-law, and my mother's brother Horilal. I administered the medicine in the belief that it would terminate her pregnancy and did not realize that it would kill her.

When the other defendants were arrested on the basis of this deposition, Bhagaboti Chashin, mother of the deceased Chandra, also got a deposition written for her on the same lines as Brindra's, and alleged further:

Toward the end of last Phalgun,[5] Magaram Chasha came to my village and said, "I have been involved, for the last four or five months, in an illicit love affair [*ashnai*] with your daughter Chandra Chashani, as a result of which she has conceived. Bring her to your own house and arrange for some medicine to be administered to her. Or else I shall put her into *bhek*."[6] Two days after that I sent my daughter Brinda and my sister and my sister's daughter Rongo Chashani to Bhabanipur to fetch Chandra. The same day they returned to Majgram with Chandra Chashani at about a prohor after nightfall, and Rongu said that Chandra's mother-in-law Srimoti and her husband's sister's husband Magaram Chasha had given them a brass pot and a bell-metal bowl [in order to pay] for the arrangements to procure the drug required for an abortion.

And Kalicharan Bagdi, defendant, said in his deposition:

It was still some five or seven days to go before the end of the month of Phalgun in the current year when I was at my vegetable plot on the bank of the river one day. Rongu Chashani approached me there at approximately the second dondo of the day and said, "Please call at my house. When you do so, I shall tell you all I have to say." The following day I went to the house of Bongshi Bagdi of Majgram, but failing to meet Rongu Chashani there I was going back home when I happened to meet Bhagaboti Chashani who said, "My daughter Chandra Chashini is in the third month of her pregnancy. Please let us have a drug to terminate that pregnancy and we shall give you a pot and a bowl." I didn't agree [to her request]. The following day I was at my vegetable plot when at one and a half dondo of the day the said Bhagaboti Chashin came to me with an elderly peasant of the village Simla. He is Bhagaboti's son's father-in-law, but I don't know his name. Bhagaboti said, "Please give us a medicine to destroy the foetus. We shall pay for it in cash, if required." Since I didn't have the drug for abortion with me that day, I told Bhagaboti, "Please meet me here at this vegetable plot tomorrow and collect the medicine; your son's father-in-law need not take the trouble to call again." The next day I was at my vegetable plot. When the said Bhagaboti came to me at noon with her daughter Chandra Chashini and I asked for the price of the medicine on the understanding that Bhagaboti's son's father-in-law would pay it in cash, as promised the previous day, the deceased Chandra offered me one paisa (a copper coin valued at one sixty-fourth part of a rupee). I accepted that paisa, and after asking them to take their seat at the vegetable plot. . . .

II

How is one to reclaim this document for history? The ordinary apparatus of historiography has little help to offer us here. Designed for big events and institutions, it is most at ease when made to operate on those larger phenomena that visibly stick out of the debris of the past. As a result, historical scholarship has developed, through recursive practice, a tradition that tends to ignore the small drama and fine detail of social existence, especially at its lower depths. A critical historiography can make up for this lacuna by bending closer to the ground in order to pick up the traces of a subaltern life in its passage through time.

However, that is no easy task, as is made so painfully obvious by the material before us. The difficulty does not arise from its want of authenticity. On the contrary, both the prose and the presentation of the document speak of it as a genuine testimony to the event described. Written in rustic Bengali (some of which has inevitably lost its flavor in translation), it abounds in spelling errors. Characteristically, too, it has no punctuation and paragraphing (like those introduced by us in the English rendering). It begins with a mark of invocation that combines the customary sign *anji* (resembling the Bengali numeral seven, capped by a crescent) and the honorific word "Sree," duplicated for effect with the name of the deity, Hori. All this, taken together with an awkward mixture of country idiom and Persianized phrases borrowed from the language of the courts, speaks unmistakably of this writing as the work of a village scribe drafted in the service of the local law-enforcing agents. As such, it is witness to the force of the disciplinary thrust made by the colonial regime into Indian rural society by the middle of the nineteenth century.

But with all its authenticity, this document still fails to satisfy an important condition required by the normal practice of historiography. It is the condition of contextuality. For unless his material relates to a context, it is difficult for the historian to know what to do with it. This is particularly true of narrative material that makes sense only if it connects with what goes before and comes after it. That is why an urge for plenitude constitutes the driving force behind much of historical research—an unsatiated, indeed insatiable urge for more and more linkages to work into the torn fabric of the past and restore it to an ideal called the full story. It is therefore frustrating for that urge to come up against the phenomenon of fragmentation, that maverick which breaks into Clio's estate from time to time, stalls a plot in its drive to a denouement, and scatters its parts. Our specimen is one such untamed fragment, as the lost beginning of its first sentence and the missing end of the last so clearly testify. An anecdote with no known context, it has come down to us simply as the residuum of a dismembered past.

It would help if we could find a way of neutralizing the effects of decontextualization by situating this fragment in a series. For the principles according to which a series is constructed and the character of the constructing authority are all relevant to one's understanding of what is serialized. Historians know all too well how the contents of a series in an official archive or a company's record room derive much of their meaning from the intentions and interests of the government or the firm concerned. The material under study also belongs to a series, an editorially constructed series in a book of documents. But this has, alas, been designed with such scant regard for the contiguities of time and place, and its contents have been arranged under rubrics so excessively broad in scope, that serialization, in this particular case, is of no assistance at all in our search for a context.

That search is made all the more difficult by the mediation of the law. Each of the statements in this document is direct speech, but it is speech prompted by the requirements of an official investigation into what is presumed to be a murder. "Murder is the point at which history intersects with crime," says Foucault, and the site of that intersection is, according to him, the "narrative of crime" (*récit de crime*).[7] The discourse of the broadsheet, in which this genre is represented in its most popular and accessible form, has as its function "to change the scale, enlarge the proportions, make the minuscule grain of history visible, and open up for the quotidian its access to the narrative." It is indeed in this way that such narratives are able to "play a role in the exchange between the familiar and the remarkable, between the quotidian and the historic." The common murder, trivialized by the tolerance all cultures have of cruelty, uses precisely this discourse as its vehicle to cross the uncertain frontier that separates it from the "nameless butcheries" of a battle and make its way into history—"a history without masters, a history crowded with frantic and autonomous events, a history below the level of power and one that fell foul of the law."

If the discourse of the broadsheet helps to open a path for crime to enter history, it is the function of judicial discourse as a genre to cut off that path by trapping crime in its specificity, by reducing its range of signification to a set of narrowly defined legalities, and by assimilating it to the existing order as one of its negative determinations. The *ekrars* (a legal term for confessions or acknowledgments of guilt) that make up our text are witness precisely to such a process of detaching an experience from its living context and setting it up as an empty positivity outside history. It is a process intended to take out of these statements all that stands for empathy and pity and leave nothing to show for their content except the dry bones of a deixis—the "then" of a "crime."

How this process is put in operation by the discursive strategy of the law, how the latter gives the event a name and stamps it with a purpose, is shown by the order of the ekrars. In an all too obvious sense this corresponds to the punitive procedure of an initial deposition leading to arrests followed by other depositions. The authorial voice of the law interjects between the first two statements in our text to say so: "When the other defendants were arrested on the basis of this [Brinda's] deposition, Bhagaboti Chashin, mother of the deceased Chandra, also got a deposition written for her on the same lines as Brinda's and alleged further . . ." However, what is not so straightforward is the disparity between the actual sequence of events and its representation in the document. It emerges clearly from the information we have that the initiatives taken by Bhagaboti on hearing about her daughter's pregnancy and the transaction with Kali Bagdi *preceded* the administration of the drug by Brinda and her sister's death. Yet, in the order of the depositions Brinda had to speak first. Consequently, the "telling" began in medias res with an account of her part in the story and Chandra's death, and retraced its steps analeptically to fill in the background by two other accounts—Bhagaboti's and Kali's. In other words, the narrative in the document violates the actual sequence of what happened in order to conform to the logic of a legal intervention that made the death into a murder, a caring sister into a murderess, all the actants in this tragedy into defendants, and what they said in a state of grief into ekrars. Construed thus, a matrix of real historical experience was transformed into a matrix of abstract legality, so that the will of the state could be made to penetrate, reorganize part by part, and eventually control the will of a subject population in much the same way as Providence is brought to impose itself upon mere human destiny.

The outcome of this hypostasis is to assimilate the order of the depositions before us to another order, namely law and order, to select only one of all the possible relations that their content has to their expression and designate that relation—that particular connotation—as the truth of an event already classified as crime. It is that privileged connotation that kneads the plurality of these utterances recorded from concerned individuals—from a mother, a sister, and a neighbor— into a set of judicial evidence, and allows thereby the stentorian voice of the state to subsume the humble peasant voices that speak here in sobs and whispers. To try to register the latter is to defy the pretensions of an abstract univocality that insists on naming this many-sided and complex tissue of human predicament as a "case." For to take that word to mean, as it usually does, an "instance of thing's occurring" or a "statement of facts in cause *sub judice*"[8] is to confer on these statements the function of describing this death merely as a thing's occurring, as a fact shorn of all other determinations than being *sub judice*. It was as if there was no room in such description for a will or purpose and all that was said was meant to speak of an event without a subject. "The particular will of the criminal" is, according to Hegel, "the sole positive existence which the injury possesses."[9] To assume criminality and yet to exclude that "particular will" of the so-called criminal and substitute the empty factuality of a "mere state of affairs" for "the sole positive existence" of Chandra's "injury" in one's reading of these ekrars would be to keep their authors and their experience out of history. In contrast, to read these statements as an archive is to dignify them as the textual site for a struggle to reclaim for history an experience buried in a forgotten crevice of our past.

That struggle is nothing less than a contest between two kinds of politics. Each of these has as its aim to try to appropriate the event of Chandra's death as a discursive site—on behalf of the state in one case and on behalf of the community in the other. However, the fact is that the law, as the state's emissary, had already arrived at the site before the historian and claimed it as its own by designating the event as a "case," the death as a "crime," and the utterances that describe it as "ekrar." The consequence of this appropriation has been to clip those perspectives that situated this incident within the life of a community where a multitude of anxieties and interventions endowed it with its real historical content. Some of those perspectives could perhaps be restored if the stratagem of assimilating these statements to the processes of the law were opposed by a reading that acknowledged them as the record of a Bagdi family's effort to cope collectively, if unsuccessfully, with a crisis.

III

The Bagdis belonged to that nether end of the colonial society where extreme poverty and abject pollution converged to make them among the lowest in class and caste. One authoritative description in official literature placed them beyond the pale of the dominant caste Hindu society ("dwellers on the outskirts of Hinduism")[10] and another outside history itself ("lower Sudra people whose history in the majority of the cases is lost").[11] In Birbhum, a western district of Bengal where this particular family and their kin lived in a cluster of villages at the northernmost part of the area under Dubrajpur *thana*,[12] they were obviously agriculturists by occupation, as the male and female surnames Chasha and Chashani ("agriculturalist"; Chashini and Chashin are variants) indicate. They could thus be said to belong to the category of "cultivating caste" assigned to them by Risley in his ethnographic glossary.[13] But considered in the light of their actual function and standing in the local society, that designation must be understood as a euphemism for a rural proletariat. For even until fifteen years before the end of the Raj the Bagdis could be described, together with the other subaltern communities of that district, as "in the main . . . agricultural labourers" who "provide[d] the entire series of services for agriculture."[14] A survey made at that time of three thanas, including Dubraj-pur, showed what a "disproportionately small percentage of interests" they held "in the real landed property of the district."[15] While the Brahmans, who constituted only 6.48 percent of the population, owned 72.25 percent of all the land as proprietors, the Bagdis—9.13 percent of the population—owned no land at all. Again, while the Brahmans held 56.73 percent of the land as tenure-holders and 15.08 percent as ryots, the Bagdis' share was 0.24 and 2.37 percent, respectively. The proportions are reversed, significantly enough, in the case of land held as under-raiyats: 4.85 percent by Brahmans and 9.15 by Bagdis.[16] Nothing could speak more eloquently of the unequal distribution of resources between the purest and richest at one end of the social spectrum and the impurest and poorest at the other during the 1930s. In this respect the progress of British rule over a period of fifty years appears to have done little to change the condition of the Bagdis. For, as Risley observed on the basis of the 1881 census:

> Most of the Bagdis are also to some extent engaged in agriculture, usually as *kurfa* or under-raiyats, and comparatively few have attained the more respectable position of occupancy tenants. In Western Bengal we find large numbers of them working as landless day-labourers, paid in cash or kind, or as nomadic cultivators, tilling other men's lands on the *bhag-jot* system, under which they are remunerated by a definite share of the produce—sometimes one-half, sometimes less, as may be arranged with their immediate landlord. I can recall no instance of a Bagdi holding a zamindari, or even a superior tenure, such as *patni* or *mukarari* [types of landholding tenure], of any importance.[17]

Thus, as a labor force the Bagdis constituted a fertilizing sediment at the base of Bengal's agrarian economy, while being despised at the same time as a filthy deposit at the very bottom of its rural society. The comprehensive exploitation—economic and cultural—to which they were thus subjected robbed them of their prestige as well. As peasants they produced the wealth on the land by hard work, and as *lathials* (guards skilled in fighting with sticks) and nightwatchmen they guarded it for their landlord masters; yet they were stereotyped by the latter as incorrigibly prone to criminality. Again, it was the dominance of the upper-caste landed elite over this community that made Bagdi women a prey to male lust; yet they figured in patriarchal lore as creatures of easy virtue all too ready to make themselves available as objects of sexual gratification. For a measure of such hypocrisy, in which an indigenous feudal ideology blends with colonialist anthropology, one has simply to notice how the Brahmanical fantasy of the lascivious Bagdini who tempts the god Siva himself in Rameshwar Bhattacharya's *Sivayan* (especially in the *Bagdini Pala* of that ballad)[18] converges on the learned insinuations in Risley's *Tribes and Castes* about "the lax views of the Bagdis . . . on the subject of sexual morality"—as supposed to have been demonstrated by their willingness to "allow their women to live openly with men of other castes" and their tolerance of "sexual license before marriage" among their girls.[19]

The pressures exerted by such patriarchal morality could strain the resources of an entire community of Bagdis to the breaking point. That is what seems to have happened in the instance given in our text. The unfortunate family at the center of this crisis was headed at this time by Bhagaboti Chashani, a widow. (The document makes no mention of any male member of the family other than a son, and all the crucial decisions bearing, literally, on matters of life and death seem to have been left to Bhagaboti herself—a most unlikely thing to happen if a patriarch, in the person of a spouse, were around.) She had three children, including a daughter called Chandra. It was Chandra's pregnancy and the efforts to terminate it that involved the rest of the family and their kin in the developments that followed. Brinda, the other daughter, is the only female for whom no reference is made to any relatives by marriage. Since this omission occurs in the context of a total mobilization of the kin group, it can only mean that she was a single girl still living with her mother. There was nothing unusual about this, for in the nineteenth century the Bagdis of West Bengal were known to "practise both infant and adult marriage indifferently."[20] Brinda was obviously grown-up enough to walk all the way to her sister's village and back within a day and be entrusted to administer the drug to the latter and generally to look after her—a chore that would be customarily assigned, under similar circumstances, to any unmarried daughter in a traditional Bengali household.

Gayaram, the widow's son, helped in a different way. Being married, he mobilized the assistance of his wife's family. His brother-in-law Pitambar is mentioned in Brinda's *ekrar* as one of the three men—the others being Gayaram himself and his uncle, Bhagaboti's brother Horilal—who removed the corpse and buried it. Yet another member of Pitambar's family was his father, the elderly *chashi* of Simla whose presence was what apparently persuaded Kalicharan Bagdi to sell the drug for abortion. This is an important detail, which illuminates both the cohesion of a kinship network and the weight of male authority within it. The widow's word was not enough for Kalicharan; she had to be sponsored by a man whose standing, in terms of seniority, was the same as that of her late husband. In other words, the lacuna of male authority within the widow's own family had to be made up by that borrowed from another family allied to it by marriage.

Alliance by marriage brought help from other quarters as well. There was Rongu, the widow's sister's daughter, who, judging by her own statement and Kalicharan's, was a member of Bongshi Bagdi's household, a clear indication of her status as a married woman. However, there is no way to find out if Bongshi was her husband or father-in-law. Whatever the relationship, he has no role assigned to him in the document. By contrast, Rongu figures prominently as an escort for the pregnant woman on her way back to her parental home and as one of the party that negotiated the drug. Help also came from kinsfolk closest to Chandra by her marriage—from her mother-in-law, Srimoti, and her husband's sister's husband, Magaram. Together, they contributed a brass pot and a bell-metal bowl to pay for the abortion. But whether Magaram's contribution qualifies as help is another matter—a moot point of this affair, as we shall presently see.

The pot and the bowl, as the text tells us, were obviously not payment enough for the drug. The herbalist would not sell it except for cash. In rural Bengal under the Raj it was customary for such household utensils, usually regarded by a poor family as among its most valuable possessions, to be exchanged for goods and services or hypothecated for small loans.[21] Kalicharan's refusal to accept this mode of payment and his insistence on cash might have had something to do with the seasonal scarcity that generally hits the countryside toward the end of the Bengali calendar year. At this time, in Choitra (March–April), the village poor would have exhausted whatever savings in grain and cash they had made out of the winter rice harvest. Left with nothing after paying for some of their debts and those social obligations that occurred in this season, they would be busy soliciting loans again in money and grain in order to answer the landlords' and the superior tenants' call to clear all arrears of rent by *punyaha*—the ceremonial settlement of accounts due early the following month—as well as to stock up grain for sowing in monsoon and for consumption during the lean period until the next harvest. In Birbhum, as in all of the western Bengal tract known as Rarh, this is the season of heat and drought when, traditionally, starvation combines with creditors and rentiers to start the village poor again on their annual circuit of hypothecation of household goods against small loans of money and grain. Phullora, the heroine of the Kalketu episode of Mukundaram Chakrabarty's *Chandimangal*, spoke for all the indigent and lowborn people of that region in her lament:

> Anol shoman porey choiter khara
> chalusherey bandha dinu matia pathora.[22]
>
> [The drought of Choitra scorched like fire. / I pledged my earthernware bowl just for a seer of rice.]

That was in the sixteenth century. Two hundred and seventy years later, under colonial rule, the rigor of the season still drove the peasant to go begging for rice, but with a difference; what had to be pledged now was not earthenware but metalware. And yet, as bell-metal and brass objects piled up with the creditor, the amount of grain lent per unit of weight in metal would decrease. By contrast, the seasonal scarcity of cash increased preference for the latter in ordinary transactions. At such a time of the year, during the first fortnight of Choitra, Kalicharan Bagdi was astute enough to insist on payment in cash for his services, which were as highly specialized as they were urgently in demand. A poor peasant, forced by the drought to withdraw from paddy culture and left to fill in his day tending a patch of vegetables, he knew the price of his skill, as is evident from his ekrar:

> When the said Bhagaboti came to me at noon with her daughter Chandra Chashini and I asked for the price of the medicine on the understanding that Bhagaboti's son's father-in-law would pay for it in cash, as promised the previous day, the deceased Chandra offered me one paisa. I accepted that paisa.

One paisa! Not a great deal to ask for an expertise as valuable as his, or for a drug meant to deal with a matter of life and death. But by insisting on that particular mode of remuneration, Kalicharan, although a Bagdi by caste, put himself on a cash nexus clearly distinguished from the network of relations based on consanguinity and marriage. And this transaction—the intrusion of money into a tissue of anxieties shared by kinsfolk—helps considerably to undermine the abstract legalism of the text and heighten its drama by a play between the contrasting elements of venality and solidarity.

IV

The solidarity inspired by this crisis had its territorial base in a cluster of villages in the southwestern corner of Birbhum, within and around the Dubrajpur thana area. The document does not mention where Horilal came from. But we know for certain that his sister, Bhagaboti, and a niece, Rongu, were both married to Majgram men. Bhagaboti's own children, however, had to find their spouses elsewhere: the son, Gayaram, in Simla, and Chandra, the daughter, in Bhabanipur. The household to which the latter belonged was headed at this time by her mother-in-law, Srimoti, presumably a widow (there is no mention of her husband), whose daughter was married to Magaram of the same village. Bagdi marriage rules which insisted on partners being selected from two different sections within the same subcaste,[23] appear thus to have resulted, in this particular case, in a web of alliances covering three villages. At least two of these, Majgram and Bhabanipur, were situated, as the map shows, within about six miles of each other—indeed, an easy walking distance, for, said Bhagaboti in her ekrar, one day in the month of Phalgun she had sent Brinda and Rongu to Bhabanipur to get Chandra, and they returned to Majgram the same evening. Simla, the other village, was about two miles to the south of Majgram, not too far for an old peasant like Gayaram's father-in-law to walk on an occasion so urgent as this, but a little too much, perhaps, to cover on two consecutive days. Taken together, these villages formed a kinship region for six Bagdi families, all of whom felt seriously threatened by Chandra's pregnancy.[24]

They felt threatened because a child born of an illicit, that is, socially forbidden, liaison between persons related as kin could have dire consequences for an entire community. For, unlike Europe, where according to Foucault the "deployment of sexuality" had already emerged as an independent apparatus of social control since the eighteenth century and superimposed itself on the "deployment of alliance,"[25] in nineteenth-century India sexuality was still subsumed in alliance for all social transactions—for marriage, kinship, and "transactions of names and possessions"—and for all the theories that informed them. The control of sexuality therefore devolved on those authorities and instruments—*panchayats* (village councils), prescriptions, prohibitions, and so on—that governed the system of alliance. Speaking specifically of rural Bengal, one could say that the government of sexuality there lay within the jurisdiction of *samaj* (community, a term in which the institutional aspects of society and their moral and political attributes are happily collapsed). How a local samaj constituted either by a caste or subcaste or by a multicaste community based on one or more villages exercised its authority over the sexual conduct of its members can be seen from a number of other documents collected from the same region.[26] They, too, speak of conditions in the Rarh tract of western Bengal during the first half of the nineteenth century. Territorially as well as chronologically they belong to a tradition of rural politics that was dramatized, for one poignant moment, by the Majgram incident of 1849. As such, they may be used to illuminate some of the mechanics of discipline and punishment that are presupposed, although never explicitly mentioned, in the ekrars on Chandra's death.

However, unlike those ekrars this material does not relate to official justice. It belongs to that subcontinent of right and wrong that was never painted red. As such, it is witness to the historic, if largely unacknowledged, failure of the Raj to incorporate some of the most vital issues of indigenous social conflict within its hegemonic judicature. For each of these documents was addressed to a tribunal that functioned independently of and parallel to the network of colonial courts. Constituted at the village level of Brahman priests acting individually or collectively, or by the leadership of a caste or subcaste,[27] it operated by "a system of rules defining the permitted and the forbidden, the licit and the illicit,"[28] in a manner that had little to do with the codes and procedures of the *sarkar's ain* and *adalat* (government's law and courts). Those rules were an amalgam of local custom, caste convention, and a rough-and-ready reading—more often just recollection—of the shastras. The judgments constructed with their help came in the form of a prescription for ritualized penalty, technically known as *byabostha* (a vernacular adaptation of the Sanskrit word *vyavastha*). Nothing speaks more eloquently of the uneasy compromise of the shastric and the customary than the rustication of that word as *byabosta, bebosta,* or even *brobosta* at the hands of village scribes, or the verdicts appended by semiliterate Brahmans in bastardized Sanskrit to the inelegant Bengali prose of these petitions.

But the force of a byabostha was hardly undermined by hetero-doxy of idiom or disregard of grammar. That it was sought, without exception, by self-confessed offenders was itself evidence of that force. The latter derived directly from the authority of a samaj working insti-tutionally through panchayat and priesthood and ideologically through custom and shastra in order to prevent its "system of alliance" from being subverted by unauthorized sexuality. For the offense arose, in each instance, from a liaison outside the socially approved limits of sex-ual relationship, and the applicant for a prescriptive writ happened in-variably to be a relative of one of the partners in that liaison. To ask for a byabostha under such circumstances was therefore to incriminate one-self deliberately and to court the certainty of punishment by *prayash-chitta*, or penitential measures made up of fines, fasting, and feasting. But willing submission to such discipline was a preemptive tactic on the petitioner's part to ward off the ultimate social sanction of outcast-ing, the terror of which is conveyed accurately by the Bengali word for that practice—*jatmara*, literally, the destruction of caste. In short, it was fear rather than choice that induced people to seek byabostha and submit to prayashchitta.

The nature and extent of that fear can perhaps be best under-stood by considering a petitioner's relationship to the transgressor. In each of these documents a villager named the transgressor as a rela-tive, indeed as a consanguine in all instances but one (where it con-cerned a brother's wife).[29] In every instance, again, the relative was a woman and was referred to as "*my* daughter," "*my* sister," or "*my* sister-in-law." The paucity of male offenders in our sample is a telling index of patriarchal concern to exercise greater control over female than male sexuality. For the response of a samaj to sexual deviance was not the same for both genders. Since the prestige of a caste was higher or lower according to the degree of its purity—and the physi-cal constitution of women as well as their cultural construction as objects of male lust made them, in men's eyes, potentially the more polluting of the two sexes—a maiden's virginity, a widow's chastity, and a wife's sexual fidelity to her husband were all highly valorized by a samaj. Any violation of norms in this respect could pollute all of an offender's kin, especially her consanguines, and undermine the group's ability to sustain and reproduce itself by recruiting and ex-changing women through marriage. As a result, the first whispers of gossip (*janorob*)—most of the petitions testify to its power—alerted an entire kinship network, and a father, brother, or husband would presume a woman's guilt without any further evidence, apply for a byabostha, and make peace with priests and panchayats by submitting to whatever penalty was imposed by them. These impositions could be oppressive for some of the less affluent villagers: one of them asked for a writ and protested his poverty (*iha ati daridra*) at the same time in a desperate attempt to persuade the tribunal—in this case, his caste council—to limit the price of exculpation to a sum he could afford.[30] It was a measure of their fear of exclusion from caste that people put up with the tyranny of such prescriptions and their disciplinary jurisdictions.

That fear was the reciprocal of solidarity under these circumstances. The two must be taken together for any proper understanding of a community's reaction to the kind of crisis that erupted on the Bagdis of Majgram. For the object of solidarity was also the person who could, by her transgressions, bring shame upon those she would most expect to stand by her when found guilty and to share the rigor of all the penalties prescribed by her samaj. Consequently, the limits of solidarity within a kin group coincided with those of its members' dread of caste sanctions, and the terms used by ego to call for help would evoke a sympathetic but apprehensive response in reciprocal terms from the rest of the group. Thus, between siblings, a sister's cry in her distress would be addressed to her brother, and his answer would be inspired as much by his sense of obligation owed to a sister as by the fear of his own culpability accruing from any moral lapse on her part if such assistance were not offered. In other words, the reciprocals that made up a lexicon of kinship terminology corresponded to the reciprocities of solidarity and fear within that particular kinship group. A correspondence of this order can be discerned quite clearly in the mobilization of Chandra's relatives during the four critical days before her death. For, as shown in the accompanying chart, those who rallied to her support as her brother, brother's wife's brother, brother's wife's father, mother's brother, and, of course, mother, sister, mother's sister's daughter, and mother-in-law were also those who had the most to dread from caste sanctions because of the misdemeanor of one who related to them respectively as sister, sister's husband's sister, sister's daughter, daughter, sister, mother's sister's daughter or daughter-in-law.

Kinship Terms and Their Reciprocals Designating Relatives Who Helped Chandra (Ego)

Relative's Names	*Ego's Terms for Her Kin*	*Reciprocal Terms*
Gayaram	brother	sister
Pitambar	brother's wife's brother	sister's husband's sister
Pitambar's father	brother's wife's father	daughter's husband's sister
Horilal	mother's brother	sister's daughter
Bhagaboti	mother	daughter
Brinda	sister	sister
Rongu	mother's sister's daughter	mother's sister's daughter
Srimoti	mother-in-law	daughter-in-law

V

It is the interplay of solidarity and fear that situates this tragic episode firmly within the politics of patriarchy in rural Bengal. For it is the direct outcome of a patriarchal society's concern to protect itself from the consequences of female sexual transgression. That concern is clearly inscribed in the series of petitions for byabostha mentioned earlier. In each of them it is a man who comes forward to report a woman's "sin" (*paap*), it is some other men who validate his statement by formally witnessing it, and it is the authority of a male-dominated samaj, personified by a pandit or institutionalized by a panchayat, which issues the verdict of guilt and the writ for prayashchitta. By contrast, man's power over woman and over society as a whole is documented in the Majgram ekrars by a formal absence, the absence of Magaram Chashi. Although deeply implicated in all that leads to abortion and death, he stands outside the purely legal determinations of the incident. There is no ekrar taken down from him, for he is technically beyond the ken of the law: the law does not see him; it doesn't have to.

Yet, unlike Chandra, who is also absent and whose absence corresponds to her silence (the only glimpse we have of her alive is when a paisa changes hands from her to Kali, presumably in silence), he is given a voice in the text. He speaks through Bhagaboti Chashin, who quotes him as saying: "I have been involved, for the last four or five months, in an illicit love affair [*ashnai*] with your daughter Chandra

Chashani, as a result of which she has conceived. Bring her to your own house and arrange for some medicine to be administered to her. Or else, I shall put her into *bhek*." Three short sentences, and even these are not uttered by the speaker himself. But that does not stop them from taking hold of the document and charging it with the speaker's will. Indeed, the reported character of the speech helps, somewhat paradoxically, to emphasize its commanding aspect. It resonates like the voice of an unseen but pervasive authority. For it is Magaram's will that, thanks to this reporting, is allowed to set the scene, define its context, and determine all the action in it. The three sentences work together to that end, as is made clear by their modal differences. The unmarked and merely declarative first sentence stands in sharp contrast to the markedly imperative and intentional function of the other two. Taken together, they act as a fulcrum for all the initiatives that follow from that utterance—the alerting of a social network to the gravity of an unwanted pregnancy in its midst, the mission to bring Chandra back to her own village, the quick polling of resources for consultation and medication, the desperation of Brinda's attempt to destroy the embryo and save her sister, and the sad, furtive digging at dawn to dispose of the corpse. Magaram's voice thus dominates the text. It does so not merely by providing a cue for its drama but by elucidating its politics.

For what he had to say brought out into the open an element of power play that, although implicit in all the statements, was left to him alone to spell out. He could do so because he was not directly involved in the processes of the law himself: unlike the others, he was not a "defendant." Indeed, his was the only voice in the text to escape superimposition by the discourse of law and order, the only utterance that was not an ekrar. As such, it was possible for it to speak in terms of a power relation that was sited at a depth within the indigenous society, well beyond the reach of the disciplinary arm of the colonial state. There, in the unredeemed obscurity of a still active feudal culture, female sexuality was so relentlessly and comprehensively subject to surveillance that the only relief a woman could have from the combined rigor of a loveless marriage and domestic drudgery lay in subterfuge and secrecy. Subterfuge enabled her to dissolve some of the gall of interdicted desire in a socially approved discourse—that of the joke. Indeed, the joking relationship—a genre that, in the vocabulary of anthropology, marries the figure of a social contradiction to a figure of speech, that is, the tensions of unauthorized sexuality to those of irony—was not only allowed but positively encouraged, as witness the multitude of usages to that effect in the Bengali language. But sexuality that was not contained and subdued by jokes could be driven underground and flourish in the secrecy of an illicit and reprehensible passion.

The slide from subterfuge into secrecy was as common in Bengali society of that time as it was commonly suppressed, although nothing could be more difficult to document than the path such a slide actually took in any given instance and its critical moments. For a transgression of that order, born in secrecy, survived by stratagems of secrecy. Silence and evasion, fear and shame—all conspired to tolerate, or at least look away from, whatever exceeded the prescribed limits of sexual politics within a kinship group, so long as it was not forced out into the light of day by violence or by a rupture in the mute complicity of horizontal loyalties. We shall never know, therefore, how that eminently permissible joking relationship between a *salaj* (wife's brother's wife) and her *nondai* (husband's sister's husband)[31]—the reciprocal terms designating Chandra and Magaram as kin—turned into an *ashnai* (affair)—that is, whether it developed out of mutual affection or some force of circumstance subjecting a poor widow to the lust of a man of authority among her close relatives. Whatever the truth of the beginning of this affair, there is nothing in these depositions to illuminate any secrets of the heart. They only throw a lurid light on its end as the heartless rejection of a woman by the man who got her into trouble. That rejection shows where a liaison, with all that it might have meant as a relation of intimacy between two persons, stopped and social opprobrium against forbidden love took over.

In turning from his role of lover to that of a custodian of patriarchal ethics, Magaram speaks for all men in a semifeudal society and for male dominance itself. There is nothing remotely of a lover's sentiment in what he says, no acknowledgment at all of sharing any sexual pleasure with his partner. What comes through is the other male voice—not the one that croons so exquisitely about love in Bengali lyrics, but the disciplinary voice that identifies and indicts an offense against public morality to pronounce: "Abortion or bhek!" Or is it simply the same male voice speaking in one of its two distinct but complementary idioms, an idiom of feudal love rooted firmly in the inequality of gender relations and a penal idiom used for policing the second sex?

In any case, by pronouncing his ultimatum as he does, Magaram Chasha transcends his particularity and emerges as the universal male trying to make his sexual partner pay for a breach of morality of which he is at least equally guilty. For that is precisely what is involved in his threat to force a Boishnob's habit on Chandra as the only alternative to abortion.

To wear a Boishnob's habit, that is, to adopt the dress, ornaments, and body markings that make up the semiotic ensemble called bhek, is to move out of caste. As Akshaykumar Datta wrote in his authoritative work, *Bharatbarshiya upasak sampraday*, a near contemporary of the text under discussion, "Those who leave their castes and families and seek [spiritual] asylum with Lord Gouranga in their urge for world-abdication, must take the bhek."[32] But to this sense of a voluntary withdrawal from the institutions of Brahmanical Hinduism in favor of a way of life inspired by Chaitanya's teachings, another meaning accreted over time to make this word into a euphemism for loss of caste. The result was a semantic spread that reduced, indeed reversed, the force of choice that was there in the original idea, and bhek came to signify loss of caste by expulsion rather than by abdication. For a conversion to the Boishnob faith was often the last refuge of a person excommunicated by his or her samaj as punishment for violation of caste codes. It was a measure by which a local Hindu society sought to defend its hierarchical and sacral structure. But such surgical operation did not always have the desired effect. The wound it inflicted could fester and infect the community by those very freedoms that it was the object of the discipline to exclude in the first place. For an outcaste could return to his or her village in bhek and undermine the authority of the samaj by transgressions for which, as a Boishnob, he or she was no longer answerable to the guardians of Hindu morality.

An incident mentioned in a petition of 1853 tells us how two victims of caste oppression in Nabosta (within the Nanoor thana of Birbhum) turned the tables on their persecutors in precisely this way. There a widow called Saki and a man, Ramkumar Ghose, found guilty of a supposedly illicit liaison, were forced to leave the village when the engine customarily used for the destruction of caste (jatmara) was turned on and life was made impossible for them by denying the right of interdining with their kin and by cutting off the ritually indispensable services of priests and barbers (*amara napit puruhit get mela sakole atok koriachhi*). However, the couple got themselves initiated into the

Boishnob faith by someone called Jagomohon Foidar in Bahmon-khondo, a neighboring village, and returned to Nabosta after some time, causing much consternation among the authorities who had organized their expulsion. For, as the latter complained, the woman now began openly to live with her lover in the same household and to share his meals, defying thereby some of the basic rules governing sexuality and commensality in a Hindu widow's life. She was even "seen to wear bangles on her arms," an emblem of marital status strictly prohibited for a widow. Yet there was little that the village leaders could do about such outrages in their midst, for they recognized, to their great chagrin, that "Boishnobs were under no obligation [to abide by any caste discipline] [*boishnober pakshe daya nai*]."³³

Not all who were driven thus by casteism to embrace the Boishnob faith had the courage of this widow and her lover to stand up to the local despots who had muscled them out of home and village. On the contrary, most of those who were forced into bhek drifted into *akhras*. These were a type of communal settlement of Boishnobs that served not only as the principal site of their residence and ritual activity but also as a limbo for all the dead souls of Hindu society. Here the disenfranchised of all castes gathered into a secondary society, a large part of which was constituted by women excommunicated for their deviation from the approved norms of sexual conduct, a deviation encouraged, and often imposed, by male lust and brutality. It was, therefore, not uncommon to find a large congregation of derelict womanhood in an akhra—victims of rape and seduction, deserted wives, women hounded out of homes for rebelling against marriages to which they had been committed as infants, women persecuted by their husband's families for their parents' failure to pay up the dowries contracted for marriage, women with children born out of wedlock, or simply women left in the lurch by their lovers. But the largest group of female outcastes was made up, in most akhras, by Hindu widows ostracized for defying the controls exercised on their sexuality by the local patriarchies.

In an ironical twist, however, the asylum a woman found in an akhra could turn out to be a transfer from one variation of patriarchal dominance to another. This other dominance did not rely on the ideology of Brahmanical Hinduism or the caste system for its articulation. It knew how to bend the relatively liberal ideas of Vaishnavism and its loose institutional structure for its own ends, demonstrating thereby that for each element in a religion that responds to the sigh of the oppressed there is another to act as an opiate. It is the opiate of bhakti on which the engine of oppression turned in this particular case to make of the *sebadasi*—literally, "a woman devoted to [spiritual or divine] service"—an object of male exploitation for manual labor and sexual gratification. Indeed, exploitation of this order has been established long enough to constitute a tradition that has continued well into our own times. It is a continuity that feeds on the tragic institution of Hindu widowhood in rural Bengal, especially among its subaltern population. As a sympathetic and acute observer reflects on some of his findings from a recent visit to an akhra in a West Bengal village not far from where Chandra died:

> I couldn't help wondering where all these sebadasis came from? . . . An answer occurred immediately to my mind. In this wretched land there is no dearth of widows, hence no want of sebadasis either. Is there any scarcity of poor, dependent, childless widows in the countryside? How they go through the ritual of adopting a guru in order to escape from the aggressive lust of their husbands' elder or younger brothers, how they happen to congregate in akhras, who are the people who attract them, seduce them, and infect them with venereal diseases—who is to write the social history of all that?[34]

Some of the local male informants spoke to this observer with bitterness about the uses made of religion to corrupt women. This was a censure that had all the force and falsity of a half-truth insofar as it correctly identified a canker at the heart of rural society, but failed at the same time to discern its etiology by refusing to acknowledge the factor of male complicity in what religion did to women. Thus, said one,

> How many of these sebadasis you see here are genuine devotees? The great majority of them are flotsam. Nobody knows where they come from. They are recruited by procurers. It is the same story for all akhras. Corrupted themselves, it is they who would bring other people's wives and daughters here in the name of religion and corrupt them as well.

Another villager described these akhras as "abortion centers." According to him,

> parents in these rural parts, sometimes bring an unmarried daughter to such an akhra, if she happens to conceive, and leave her there for a month or so. The villagers are told that the girl has been sent to serve the family's guru. It is only after a successful abortion that the

girl returns home. Occasionally, a girl dies [in the process]. Well, there are men who will undertake to dig a pit in the sandbank of a river and hide the corpse there. The police would look away. The police station is far away. The guru sends his votive offering there at regular intervals. Everything is in order.[35]

It was as a variation on this theme that Magaram Chasha had pronounced his ultimatum: "Arrange for an abortion, or she must be dumped in an akhra!" This attempt to shirk parenthood by the destruction of an embryo or by consigning its carrier to living death in an akhra earns for Magaram a place in a historical relationship of power, a relationship of male dominance mediated by religion. It is a relationship that is overlaid and obscured, in our text, by the law's concern to assign criminality to one or more of the "defendants" in this "case." But the project to reclaim this material for history calls for a movement in the opposite direction, so that the pall of abstract legalism is penetrated in order to identify the murderer's hand as that of patriarchy in its dual role of the cynical lover and the authoritarian samaj.

VI

In the end, as this document shows in no uncertain terms, patriarchy won out. Magaram's ultimatum produced the desired effect. The pregnancy was terminated. Both the fetus and the body that had carried it for three months were put out of the way. But it was by no means an easy victory. The solidarity born out of fear contained within it *another solidarity* activated by a different, indeed contradictory, principle—namely *empathy*. If it was the power of patriarchy that brought about the first, it was the understanding of women that inspired the second.

The ekrar taken down from Brinda is instructive in this respect. Here she concentrates meticulously, for the most part, on the procurement, preparation, and administration of the drug that killed Chandra. This is precisely what the law wants her deposition to do. In its eye she stands nearest to the crime as its *immediate* agent and is, therefore, required to describe the process of its commission in all detail. So we are given an account of her part, spread over four days, in obtaining the ingredients for the drug, mixing them for medication by the right dosage twice a night, and caring for the pregnant woman for the next twenty-four hours until the latter ejects the fetus, bleeds to death in extreme pain, and is buried. It is only when, at this point, the sequence of medication, abortion, death, and burial grinds to a halt that she exclaims: "I administered the medicine in the belief that it would terminate her pregnancy and did not realize that it would kill her." With these words she comes out of the metonymic trance of her deposition and identifies herself no longer as a defendant speaking of a crime but as a person speaking of her sister and as a woman speaking of another woman. The recollections of that night of violence—of Chandra's body racked by fever and pain, of a plucked fetus, of hemorrhage and death, of a corpse surreptitiously buried in the darkness before dawn, and the recollection, above all, of the supreme violence of a man's rejection of a woman impregnated by him—combine to produce an utterance that defies the ruse of the law and confers on this text the dignity of a tragic discourse.

What we have here is indeed a classic instance of choice overruled inexorably by necessity—by fate, in short. For Chandra was killed by the very act that was meant to save her from living death in a ghetto of social rejects. Yet here, as in all tragedies, the triumph of fate helped to enhance rather than diminish human dignity, the dignity of the women's choice to terminate the pregnancy and their determination to act according to it. The contradictions through which they picked their way to arrive at that choice were a measure both of its gravity and its complexity. They could not defy the authority of the samaj to the extent of enabling a widow with a child born out of wedlock to live honorably in the local society. It would be a long time yet before such a thing could happen in rural Bengal. Historically, therefore, abortion was the only means available for them to defeat the truly cockeyed morality that made the mother alone culpable for an illicit childbirth, threw her out of society, and allowed the father to go scot-free. Under these circumstances their decision to go ahead with the termination of Chandra's pregnancy acquired a content very different from what Manaram had on his mind when he confronted her mother with that alternative. It was for him merely a ploy to save his own face. But for the women who had gathered around Chandra at this crisis the destruction of the fetus was a desperate but consciously adopted strategy to prevent the social destruction of another woman, to fight for her right to a life with honor within her own society. The decision to which Bhagaboti, Brinda, Rongu, and Chandra herself were party amounted thus to an act of resistance against a patriarchal tradition that was about to claim yet another woman as its victim, and their resistance took that characteristic form often adopted by the oppressed to subvert the designs of their oppressors in the guise of conforming to them.

Seen in this light the activity of women assumes a remarkable salience in this text. Indeed, such activity is one of the most visible aspects of an event that is otherwise so shrouded in secrecy and shame. It is women who generate most of the movement in it. Men have a part to play as helpers, but they do so clearly as auxiliaries: Kali Bagdi, who has to be coaxed to sell the drug; the elderly peasant from Simla mobilized simply to add a nodding consent to Bhagaboti's decision to go ahead with the abortion; and the three male relatives who figure as undertakers. By contrast, the initiative for all that follows Magaram's threat lies with the women. It is they who make up the party that travels to Bhabanipur and brings the young widow back to her village. It is they again who clinch the deal with their herbalist, get hold of the drug, administer it, and care for Chandra as she lies convulsed with pain. The exclusion of men from these interventions is hardly fortuitous. They are excluded because such interventions relate to a domain regarded as woman's own. It is the domain of the female body where, according to Simone de Beauvoir, "pregnancy is above all a drama that is acted out within the woman herself" in terms of the contradictory pulls of the immanence of her body and its transcendence: "The pregnant woman feels the immanence of her body at just the time when it is in transcendence."[36] The rhetoric and the development of this drama lie, on the one hand, in the immanence of that body as it "turns upon itself in nausea and discomfort," making the flesh feel like nothing but "a gross and present reality," and, on the other, in the body's transcendence as "the flesh becomes root-stock, source and blossom . . . a stirring towards the future," when by "carrying [the fetus within her] she feels herself vast as the world."

If, therefore, in many societies like the one under discussion natal care lies exclusively with women, this is so not simply because men would have it that way. On the contrary, this may well be a sign of patriarchy's retreat in the face of woman's determination to assert her control over her own body at a time when, in pregnancy, she knows that "her body is at last her own, since it exists for the child who belongs to her."[37] This knowledge constitutes a challenge that is genuinely dreaded by male authority. For it operates in an area of liminality not strictly governed by the will of husbands and fathers—an area that appears to the latter as fraught with uncertainty and danger, since women speak here in a language not fully comprehensible to men and conduct themselves by rituals that defy male reasoning.

Hence the elaborate structure of patriarchy's self-defense set up precisely to meet this challenge—the shastric injunctions that condemn woman's body as impure by definition at childbirth, the physical exclusion of that body from domestic space immediately after parturition, the quarantine imposed by prohibitions and purificatory rules to ensure the safety of the social body from parturitive pollution, and so on. That such prescriptions should so often be accompanied by an equally prescriptive male chorus in praise of motherhood is quite in order. For such idealization serves a twofold purpose—on the one hand, as a foil to those bans and exclusions that symptomize the fear by which male dominance seeks to defend itself, and, on the other, as a technique to defuse the threat that woman's consciousness poses to patriarchy at every childbirth in a traditional society.

That is why the Bagdi women of Majgram chose a far from instrumental role for themselves even as they pooled their resources and wit to arrange for an abortion demanded by a man speaking for all of the local patriarchy. As a role situated within the social domain of childbirth, it defined their independence negatively by excluding men from all those decisions and initiatives that were vital to the termination of Chandra's pregnancy. What is equally, if not more, important is that even in their apparent complicity the women acted in accordance with a project that was by no means identical with Magaram's. The latter had made out his ultimatum as a choice between abortion and bhek for Chandra. Either of these would have served his own purpose, which was to get himself off the hook and escape social sanction. Since all he wanted was to destroy the evidence of his guilt, it could have been achieved as well by the physical destruction of the incriminating embryo as by the social destruction of the person who carried it. However, for the women who had rallied in support of Chandra, the alternatives were by no means of equal value. In their judgment abortion, with all its risks, was preferable to bhek. This was a choice made by women entirely on their own in order to stop the engine of male authority from uprooting a woman from her place in the local society.

To explain this resistance merely in terms of the obligations of *kutum* (kin) is to ignore what is distinctive about it and what sets it apart from kinship solidarity. It is a fundamental condition of such solidarity that the relation between the genders within the group, whatever its structure, should remain cohesive and nonantagonistic. For without such cohesion there can be no reproduction of species, hence no kinship. But that relation turns antagonistic whenever a termination of pregnancy is enforced by patriarchy. On such occasions man's authority stands so clearly opposed to woman's interest that no subterfuge, theological or sociological, can hide the truth of their relationship as one of dominance and subordination. No experience, other than that of rape, elucidates sexual politics more forcefully for the woman. Betrayed and bleeding, she sees a core of coercion in what she believed was mutual consent and an abstract masculinity in the person she thought was her lover. Simone de Beauvoir writes of the bitterness of this disillusionment thus:

> When man, the better to succeed in fulfilling his destiny as man, asks woman to sacrifice her reproductive possibilities, he is exposing the hypocrisy of the masculine moral code. Men universally forbid abortion, but individually they accept it as a convenient solution of a problem; they are able to contradict themselves with careless cynicism. But woman feels these contradictions in her wounded flesh; she is as a rule too timid for open revolt against masculine bad faith; she regards herself as the victim of an injustice that makes her a criminal against her will, and at the same time she feels soiled and humiliated. She embodies in concrete and immediate form, in herself, man's fault; he commits the fault, but gets rid of it by putting it off on her. . . . It is at her first abortion that woman begins to "know." For many women the world will never be the same.[38]

It is this knowledge of man's bad faith that makes woman wiser about the limits of a solidarity that pretends to be neutral to gender. The rounded, unitary world of kinship can never be the same for her again. "Soiled and humiliated," she has recourse to an *alternative solidarity*—a solidarity of women. Not an "open revolt" armed with trumpet and banner, it is still a visible and loud enough protest in a society where initiative and voice are given to man alone. For when a victim, however timid, comes to regard herself as an object of injustice, she already steps into the role of a critic of the system that victimizes her. And any action that follows from that critique contains the elements of a practice of resistance. In rallying around Chandra at the hour of her rejection by Magaram and the samaj he spoke for, the women of Majgram transcended the limits of kinship relations. In choosing abortion as an alternative to bhek, they defied the sentence of living death that had already been pronounced upon Chandra. That she lost her life as a result of this effort made by the other women to save her is the truly tragic import of Brinda's despair as she said, "I administered the medicine in the belief that it would terminate her pregnancy and did not realize that it would kill her." That tragedy was a measure, for its time, of the strength of women's solidarity and its limitation.

Notes

I am grateful to my colleagues of the Subaltern Studies editorial team and to Ahmed Kamal, Rajyashree Pandey, and James Scott for their comments on a draft of this essay.

1. This document is published as item no. 380 in *PMCS*, my abbreviation for Panchanan Mandal, ed., *Chithipatre Samajchitra*, vol. 2 (Calcutta, 1953), pp. 277–78. It is taken from the archives of Viswabharati University. Its date is given as 1255 according to the Bengali year. Since the event of which it speaks occurred in the month of Choitra (see note 2), the corresponding date, according to the Christian calendar, should be A.D. 1849. Some of the proper names in the document appear in several variations: the surname Chashani as Chashini and Chashin, and the prenoms Brinda as Brindra, Rongo as Rongu, and Kali as Kalicharan. These variations have been retained in the translation.

2. Choitra is the twelfth month of the Bengali year and corresponds roughly to the second half of March and the first half of April.

3. *Pohor* and its variation, *prohor*, are a measure of time roughly equal to an eighth part of a twenty-four-hour day. "A quarter past the second pohor of the night" may therefore be taken to correspond approximately to three-quarters of an hour past midnight.

4. *Dondo* is a measure of time equivalent roughly to twenty-four minutes, so that the expression "four to five dondoes left of the night" may be taken to mean an hour and a half to two hours before dawn, and the expression "second dondo of the day," a little less than an hour after sunrise.

5. Phalgun is the eleventh month of the Bengali year and corresponds roughly to the second half of February and the first half of March.

6. The habit of a person belonging to the Boishnob sect.

7. This and the other extracts quoted in this paragraph are taken from Michel Foucault, *Moi, Pierre Rivière, ayant égorgé ma mère, ma soeur et mon frère* (Paris, 1973), pp. 269–71. My translation of these extracts is intended to be more faithful to the original than that of the English edition of this work published as *I, Pierre Riviere . . .* (Harmondsworth, 1978), pp. 204–6.

8. *The Concise Oxford Dictionary*, 6th ed. (Oxford, 1976), s.v. "case."

9. *Hegel's Philosophy of Right*, translated with notes by T. M. Knox (Oxford, 1967), para. 99, p. 69. Knox's comment on this passage is relevent to my argument: "Crime exists as a fact, an event, and it is 'positive' to that extent," he writes, "but as an event it is not differentiated by any criminal character from other events such as accidents. As a crime it exists only for those who understand it from the inside, i.e. as a *purposeful* action, and so considered, it lacks the positivity of a *mere* event: it is made something genuinely positive, a crime and not an accident, by the presence in it of the criminal's will, and in this sense it is 'positive' only because it carries out his conscious purpose"; ibid., p. 331.

10. H. H. Risley, *The Tribes and Castes of Bengal*, vol. 1 (reprint, Calcutta, 1981), p. 43.

11. Government of Bengal, *Final Report on the Survey and Settlement Operations in the District of Birbhum, 1924–1932* (Calcutta, 1937), p. 17. All further references to this work will be cited as *Final Report*.

12. See note 24 for further details of this identification.

13. Risley, *Tribes and Castes*, p. 37.

14. *Final Report*, p. 15.

15. Ibid.

16. This statistical information is derived from "Comparative Statement Showing the Interests in Land of Certain Castes in Thanas Suri, Khayrasol, and Dubrajpur in the District of Birbhum," in ibid., p. 71.

17. Risley, *Tribes and Castes*, p. 42.

18. Rameshwar Bhattacharya, *Siva-samkirtan va Sivayan*, ed. Jogilal Haldar (Calcutta: Calcutta University, 1957), pp. 225–77.

19. Risley, *Tribes and Castes*, pp. 39, 41.

20. Ibid., p. 39.

21. In Bibhutibhushan Bandyopadhyay's *Pather Panchali*, a bell-metal dish changes hands from a poor Brahman woman to the village barber's wife for half a rupee. The time of that story is the early decades of this century, but the practice has apparently continued well into the postcolonial period; see *Bibhuti racanabali*, vol. 1 (reprint, Calcutta, 1979), pp. 145–46, and N. K. Chandra, "Agricultural Workers in Burdwan," in R. Guha, ed., *Subaltern Studies II* (Delhi, 1983), pp. 243, 247.

22. Mukundaram Chakrabarty, *Kavikankan-candi*, p. 1, ed. Srikumar Bandyopadhyay and Biswapati Chowdhury (Calcutta: Calcutta University, 1958), p. 262.

23. "A Bagdi cannot marry outside the sub-caste, nor inside the section to which he belongs. Thus a Tentulia must marry a Tentulia, but a man of the Salrishi section, to whatever sub-caste he may belong, cannot marry a woman of that section"; Risley, *Tribes and Castes*, p. 38.

24. My identification of these villages is based on *Alphabetical List of Villages, West Bengal*, ed. P. C. Banerjee (unpublished typescript, Office of the Superintendent of Census Operations, Government of West Bengal, Calcutta, 1956), and *Final Report*, appendix 7, p. 2 (map), and index to appendix 7, p. 2 (village list). Majgram has been identified with the only village of that name (although spelled "Majhgram") in the *Alphabetical List*. Bhabanipur could be either of the two villages of that name, both nearly equidistant from Majgram at about six miles to the north within Rajnagar thana in one case and to the south within Dubrajpur thana in the other. I prefer the latter, as forming a better cluster, if taken with the third village, Simla, an abbreviation for Simlakuri, about two miles south of Majgram.

25. Michel Foucault, *The History of Sexuality*, vol. 1 (London, 1978), pp. 106–7.

26. *PMCS*, pp. 166–68, 175, 176, 179–80. The total number of these documents—all from Birbhum and Bankura—and their dates as shown in parentheses, are 225 (1840), 227 (1804), 229 (1819), 240 (1823), 241 (1824), and 247 (1834).

27. For specimens of an individual constituting such a prescriptive authority, see *PMCS*, documents 225 (pp. 166–67) and 247 (pp. 179–80). The collective authority of a group of six Brahmans is sought in another document—227 (pp. 167–68). In 229 (pp. 169–70) the petitioner addresses the leadership of his caste.

28. Foucault, *The History of Sexuality*, vol. 1, p. 106.

29. *PMCS*, 240, p. 175.

30. Ibid., 229, pp. 169–70.

31. I think Ronald B. Inden and Ralph W. Nicholas are a bit too restrictive in their description of the range of joking relationships in Bengali society. The *salaj-nondai* relation, together with a few others they do not mention, could be quite legitimately added to their list; Inden and Nicholas, *Kinship in Bengali Culture* (Chicago, 1977), pp. 31–32.

32. The ritual of bhek is described in this work thus: "[Sect leaders called] Goswamis usually rely on their [assistants called] Foujdars and Chhoridars for this ceremony. The latter would get an acolyte to go through the ritual of head-shaving and bathing, confer on him a stylized knot on a waist-band (*dor*), a loin-cloth (*koupin*), an outer garment (*bohirbas*), a characteristic mark of the sect on his forehead (*tilak*), a lesson in ritual gestures (*mudra*) as well as a water pot (*koronga; ghoti*), a necklace for telling beads (*japomala*) and a three-stringed necklace for wearing (*trikonthika galomala*). They would then instruct him in a *mantra*. They charge a minimum fee of one and a quarter rupee for all this. Moreover, offerings of food (*bhog*) have to be addressed to Lords Advaita, Nityananda and Chaitanya on this occasion and Boishnobs fed in a large banquet. It is popularly believed that the institution of bhek (*bhekasram*) was created by Lord Nityananda"; Akshaykumar Datta, *Bharatbarshiya upasak sampraday*, ed. Benoy Ghose (Calcutta, 1970), p. 105.

33. *PMCS*, 248, pp. 180–81.

34. Sudhir Chakrabarty, "Gabhir nirjan pather ulto banke," *Baromas* 6, no. 2 (April 1985): 4.

35. Ibid., pp. 4–5.

36. These and the other extracts quoted in this paragraph are taken from Simone de Beauvoir, *The Second Sex* (Harmondsworth, 1984), pp. 512–13.

37. Ibid., p. 513.

38. Ibid., pp. 509–10.

3 / The Mentality of Subalternity:
Kantanama or *Rajdharma*
Gautam Bhadra

I attempt in this chapter to focus on certain features of what may be called the subaltern mentality. It is well known that defiance is not the only characteristic of the behavior of subaltern classes. Submissiveness to authority in one context is as frequent as defiance in another. It is these two elements that together constitute the subaltern mentality. It is on account of this combination that the poor and the oppressed have, time and again, and in different histories, made voluntary sacrifices in favor of the rich and the dominant, at least as often as they have rebelled against the latter.

Certain assumptions made here need to be emphasized. First, the idioms of domination, subordination, and revolt, I believe, are often inextricably linked together; we separate them here only to facilitate analysis. If this is true, it follows that subordination or domination is seldom complete, if ever. The process is marked by struggle and resistance. The purpose of my analysis is precisely to highlight some of these tensions with reference to a particular text.

The Text

The text under discussion is a long poem called *Kantanama* or *Rajdharma*. It was written by one Dewan Manulla Mandal, who lived in a village called Fakanda, now situated in Balurghat subdivision, West Dinajpur, West Bengal. The text was discovered in 1913 (1320 B.S. [Bengali era]) by the noted Bengali scholar Nalinikanta Bhattasali while he was engaged in a search for old Bengali manuscripts. The exact transcription of the manuscript, with all its typical spellings and local usages, was later published by the Dacca Sahitya Parishat. Bhattasali wrote an introduction and added notes to the text, which I have found useful.[1] Let us introduce the poet in his own words:

> Fakanda is the name of my village,
> Gurai Mandal that of my father,
> And I thus, humble fellow,
> Am his son,
> Dinachpur is my Sirasthan [Sudder area].
> Jobsa is the name of my pargana [revenue district],
> While my *chakala* [subdivision] is in Bhongra.[2]

The village of Fakanda lay in the zamindari of the famous Kasim-bazar Raj. The area was named Kantanagar, after the founder of the house, Krishna Kanta Nandi. It was within five miles of Bairatnagar, a place of ancient legends and archaeological remains. Inquiries made by Bhattasali in Manulla Mandal's village revealed that Manulla had often worked as a copyist of texts such as *Mainamatir Punthi*. He also wrote a long narrative in verse about the old kingdom of Bairatnagar. Bhat-tasali was confident that the manuscript of the text of *Kantanama* that he had discovered was written in the author's own handwriting. The text runs to sixty pages and the date given on the last page is 1250 B.S. (1842–43), a couple of years before the zamindar Krishna Nath Nandi died. Krishna Nath figures very prominently in Mandal's book. It was during Krishna Nath's rule that Mandal felt the urge to write the book. Kantanama and Rajdharma were names given by the author himself; he referred to the text by these names, although more often by "Raj-dharma" than by "Kantanama."[3]

From the text is evident that the author was a member of the hereditary Mandal family; he refers to male ancestors of five genera-tions. He belonged to a joint family. At the time of composition of the book he was an old man and was seemingly under severe personal stress. He had experienced economic distress because of a fire that de-stroyed his house and property. By the time he came to write the book, Mandal had lost all his relatives, including seven sons. "My seven sons have been taken away from me, hurting me greatly. What happiness can be there if sons die before the father?"[4] And again, "Yet another calamity befell me. My house and possessions were destroyed in a fire. And then God gave me a dream."[5]

It is necessary to underline here the social significance of the terms *mandal* and *dewan* in the context of the rural society of Dinajpur during the late eighteenth and nineteenth centuries. *Mandal* was the term for the head man of the rural community and referred to the family of the original settlers of the village. In the nineteenth century *patwaris* and mandals were gradually incorporated into the revenue system of the zamindars and became their salaried agents. It has been suggested, however, that in Dinajpur, where the zamindars were relatively less powerful, mandals retained some of their old autonomy and customary position. A mandal was the representative of his "community"; he was "one of the persons of the village who bear in the estimation of the community the highest character of responsibility and trustworthiness." He was an arbitrator of disputes and a spokesman who represented peasants to the authorities. He was not generally on the payroll of the zamindar but certainly enjoyed certain privileges at the time of revenue assessment.[6] In fact, many mandals in the area under discussion belonged to the *khudkasht* (resident husbandman cultivating his own land) category of peasants—prosperous and enjoying *sir* lands (in which the owner has exclusive rights) at concessional rates. This land was the mandal's *jot* (land in which owner has occupancy rights), which sometimes extended over a fairly large area. Most mandals were Muslims and were hereditary resident cultivators.[7]

Manulla also held the title of dewan. *Dewan* generally meant the principal officer of a big zamindari establishment.[8] But in Dinajpur and Rangpur *dewan* had a specific meaning. People who pleaded the case of peasants in court or to the zamindar and were well versed in laws and regulations of settlement were called dewans. Various settlement officers have commented on the influence these dewans exercised in the affairs of the village and their capacity to regulate the connection of the rural community with the outside world.[9] It is therefore not surprising that Manulla Mandal's connection to his own village should take on a particular significance in the text. Bhattasali had also witnessed how Manulla's descendants, engaged in cultivation and living in the same village, had a familiarity with the local court. Long residence in a particular village was characteristic of a khudkasht peasant. Being a mandal and a dewan, therefore, it is very likely that Manulla, in his long poem, spoke not only as a prosperous peasant but also as a leader of the village community to which he belonged.

Manulla wrote his poem within the tradition of the medieval Bengali *panchali* (devotional poems) or *mangal kavyas* (ballads celebrating the glory of a deity). Like all other poets in this tradition, he avers that he was asked to write by his destiny or fate (*bidhi*) or God (*niranjan*), at a time of intense personal and familial crisis. His sufferings, he later realized, were but a trial intended to prove his suitability for the task that fate had kept in store for him. As he wrote, "A purposeless existence in this world—such indeed must have been my destiny. Two-thirds of my life passed in happiness, the last one-third was to be full of sorrow. I stayed back [in the world] for a useless existence. I lost my way and became unhappy. The world became barren for me." In the context of this depiction of a sorry and fruitless life, he recounts:

> On hearing this Niranjan spoke,
> Cry not, he said, my blue-eyed boy.
> You can write off your brothers or sons as illusions.
> Only I can take you across
> [the ocean of existence] in your final days,
> I have judged your mind and found you pure,
> You are indeed dear to me.
> Why do you think your life is wasted?
> You will live in heaven,
> And I shall never forsake you.
> . . . .
> Go and write the story of the King—
> Your name will reign supreme in this world.[10]

Manulla repeats this story several times: that he received a divine order to write down in poetic form the exploits and glory of the zamindar. He sees his material and familial crises as following from this divinely appointed task:

> And the lord began to wonder how the deeds
> of the king could be propagated in the world.
> The narrator of the exploits of the virtuous
> king must pass the test of having his relatives
> killed by me.
> . . . . . .
> Only he who does not forget me even in suffering
> will qualify to write this story
> That will bring salvation [literally benefit]
> to the king's ancestors. . . .
> . . . .
> Helpless, I have to write down the words of God.
> O my fate,
> Your heart is made of stone,
> You have dealt me a severe blow
> And [thus] made me record the exploits of the King.[11]

This is a familiar theme within the medieval panchali. From Mukundaram to Manik Datta—the well-known writers of the *Chandi Mangal* and the *Manasa Mangal*—to the lesser-known writer of the poem *Gosain-mangal,* written in Coochbehar, medieval authors almost invariably cite divine inspiration as explanation of their reason for writing. This was characteristic of the particular mentality in which an individual's writing was not seen as the product of his own talent but as ordained by God, fate, or destiny. Chandi or Dharma or Manasa or Vishnu or Allah or Niranjan was the real actor, while the mortal author was merely an instrument of divine will. Manulla was thus communicating his own thoughts within a well-established tradition, using the forms of *lachari* and *dopadi.* His losses and sufferings were personal and his own experience was the basis of his poem; yet the author transcended his own experience by placing it in a wider framework of religion and divinity. Everything in that framework was predestined and expressed the work of Niranjan or Allah. To write *Kantanama* was a task to be performed, and through this Manulla would achieve the ultimate mission of his life.

At the same time, *Kantanama* was not merely a piece of literary self-fulfillment. Manulla intended to read it at the court of the zamindar, hoping to be materially rewarded for his effort. He thus thought of his spiritual future as well as of immediate material gain: "I write *Rajdharma* at the bidding of God. When shall I be able to read it before the king? God willing, I should read it before the king one day. Otherwise there is no security for me."[12] His expectations of the king are equally clearly stated: "The king began to think of all the sufferings of the writer who was writing about his deeds. If I give him an elephant loaded with wealth, he thought, even that will not compensate his sufferings."[13]

A historian has suggested that a local village official called Brajanath Hazra encouraged Manulla to write this poem, but there is no evidence to this effect.[14] Nor is it clear that Manulla really got an opportunity to read his poem before the zamindar. However, he also had a general audience in mind. A refrain in *Kantanama* or *Rajdharma* runs:

The king, an incarnation of dharma,
Never mentions *babat* [cess].
Know this,
O you, the community of *praja* [subjects]
That God is merciful.[15]

Throughout his work Manulla Mandal never forgets this *prajar samaj*. His own experience, his social role, his own despair and hopes, are all expressed in a language and consciousness that is permeated with a religiosity meaningful to rural society. Its expression is perfectly in tune with the panchali tradition of medieval Bengali poetry. The following passage will ring familiar to any student of Bengali panchalis:

> With great care
> Shah Manulla has written this story
> As told to him in a dream.
> He who listens to it with devotion
> Will be saved from all misfortunes.
> He who plagiarizes this book
> Will have donkeys for parents,
> Will be born in poverty, and
> Will have his desires unfulfilled.
> Go to hell he will in the end
> And his family line will be terminated,
> While he who takes care of this book *Rajdharma*
> Will be rewarded with a place in the world of Baikuntha.[16]

The Cultural World of Manulla

Fakanda is now an obscure village in Dinajpur. But it has its own culture, and Manulla was aware of that. There was a strong tradition of *pirism* among the peasants in Dinajpur, mostly Rajbangshis and Muslims. Many Rajbangshis had been converted to the *pir* variant of Islam and were called the *nasyas* (lower-caste men who converted to Islam).[17] The strength of this tradition made it difficult for the Farazis to penetrate this region in the nineteenth century.[18] Even after their partial success in the early twentieth century, pirism thrived as before. It was noted by an acute observer in the early nineteenth century (1807) that there was hardly any village in this district that did not contain a *pirsthan* (place of worship).[19] Official statements of the 1930s confirm this impression. Along with this, Vaishnavism had spread among the Rajbangshis and survived the onslaught of a Kshatriya movement led by Rai Bahadur Panchanan Barman.[20] These two religious movements—Vaishnavism and pirism—have always overlapped, producing shifting and indeterminate boundaries. For both Satya Pir's song and Manasa's song the group of singers often remained the same; only the symbols and the dress changed.[21] In the two big locally held fairs, called

Nek Marad and Gopinather *mela*, people of various communities participated without hesitation or inhibition.[22]

G. A. Grierson noted this development in his study of Rangpur and Dinajpur. He found illiterate minstrels roaming the countryside reciting to peasants the ballads of Mainamati and Gopichandra.[23] He also discovered in this area a ballad, adapted from the Bhagavat, that described the birth of Srikrishna. His comments are worth quoting:

> The third specimen is a song describing the birth of Krishna. It is by far the most popular song among the Hindus of the district. It is not extant complete but I have been able to collect many pieces and to repatch them into something like the original song which no doubt originally existed. I have been able to produce a pretty fair text; as there is hardly a line of which I have not obtained two or three copies. Considering the great distances from each other at which the places were whence I obtained the fragments, it is wonderful how they agree; especially as it is not customary for the reciters to possess written copies, or even to be able to read them if they did.[24]

The unity and similarity of the textual content of the songs current over a vast region of north Bengal indicate the existence of a vigorous oral tradition. The illiterate singers of villages have continued within that tradition, making improvisations but retaining the overall structure of the *pala* (drama or narrative poem).

Alongside these palas and songs there was also a tradition of Kathakata. Putatively of ancient origin, this tradition was popular in rural Bengal as late as the last decades of the nineteenth century. The *kathaks* (*katha* means tale; a *kathak* is a storyteller) recited Vaishnava stories before rural gatherings. It was a performing art requiring considerable histrionic skills on the part of the performer. The speaker told stories from the Puranas, always explaining their moral import, adapting them to suit the taste of the local audience but successfully delivering the moral contained in these stories.[25] It has been stated in official documents that high-caste Brahmans from various areas visited Dinajpur annually at a particular time of the year, and their presence, daily norms, and discourses created great excitement among various categories of people in Dinajpur.[26] A typical description of this type of art performed by the Brahmans is given by a person from another part of Bengal—from the Rarh area—where this art form was quite popular. In this case the narrator's mother arranged for the performance in order to keep a pledge she had made to the gods.

A raised platform was erected at the Atchala and all the people of the village were invited to listen to a reading of the Ramayana. . . . In the evening the reader began to read the text. The village was small. About fifty to sixty men and thirty to forty women came and took their place in the audience. The *pathak* [reader] at first read out three or four verses from the Ramayana and then began to explain them. What a range of strategies he had for interpretation. Sometimes he would act, sometimes he would use a characteristically male language, on other occasions he would begin to lament in the soft voice of a woman, and so on and so forth. He thus performed for one and a half hours. The audience listened with rapt attention. Every day this type of performance was put on. It wasn't the same people who turned up every day to listen. . . . Few among the audience were educated, and even for those who were their education stopped at *pathsala* [village primary school] level. Yet they were able to grasp the sense of the highly Sanskritized language used by the kathak. . . . The audience came for two reasons. It was thought that listening to a recitation of the Ramayana conferred *punya* [merit] on people; they used to come to earn such punya. Second, if they did not come, my mother's vow would be broken and she would become a sinner. They could not do that to her. For this reason also, they attended the performance.[27]

Bankimchandra also once noted the role that "the dark and plump" *kathak thakur* (Brahman kathak) played in preaching certain moral values among rural people:

The ploughman, the cotton-carder, the spinner, or even the person without food—they all learned [from listening to the kathak]. They learned that *dharma* was eternal and divinely ordained, that to be self-seeking was demeaning, that there was a thing called *pap* [sin] and a thing called *punya* deserving punishment and reward, and that life was not meant for one's self [i.e., for one's own pleasures] but for others.[28]

Thus Kathakata performed certain distinct services. It popularized Brahmanical culture through highly effective fables and stories, upholding certain standards of morality and values derived essentially from the culture of the elite. However, within its framework there was always ample scope for accommodating elements that emerged out of the lives of ordinary people. Through twists and turns in the narrative, through varying emphases, through additional commentaries, the kathak always made references to local affairs and incidents. The text he used usually contained a variety of themes, ranging from Sanskritized moral tales to erotic descriptions of prostitutes or humorous descriptions of different types of sweets. His songs made up a mixed bag, containing Sanskrit verses as well as local Bengali songs. A successful kathak was always responsive to the moods of the different types of audience he encountered, for these could be, at times, highly sensitive and responsive to his performance.[29]

Throughout the eighteenth and nineteenth centuries many local chieftains in their own interest began to popularize various Vaishnava and Sanskrit texts in this region. The Raj families of Coochbehar and Dinajpur took the initiative in this matter.[30] The panel of sculptures at the famous temple at Kantanagar in Dinajpur, for example, contains a full depiction of the life of Krishna.[31] In this cultural world we can probably discern the interaction of two elements: the classical, or *marga,* with the popular, or *jana.* Through the Kathakata and extensive translation of the various texts of the Puranas and the Bhagavat there could have been a conscious attempt on the part of the local zamindari house to spread and uphold certain kinds of values and moral frameworks among the lower orders. But this was an active and two-way process. The popular and folk elements continuously changed and absorbed the classical in their own way. Grierson describes the perception of the Bhagavat by the singers themselves in the villages of north Bengal: "They have found them in songs, and it is not their business to alter things written in the Satya-yuga. Sometimes they are unable to explain whole passages, saying 'it is Satyayuger Katha, how are we to know it?' For other words they have a traditional meaning."[32] Incomprehension, ambiguity, and tradition made the popular reception of these classical tales quite distinct from the appreciation they received in the shastric world. Many local versions of various incidents of these epics and of the Puranas were composed, catering to an altogether different rustic audience. *Angad's Raibar* (the story of Angad abusing Ravana), for example, was universally popular among the peasants. It was later expunged from the standard edition of Krittibas's Ramayana by its famous editor Dinesh Sen, as it was supposed to be vulgar.[33] This type of acceptance, adaptation, and rejection is mutual at both levels and is an expression of power relations between the dominant and the dominated. Thus, while one can discern certain "classical" (marga) elements in "popular" (jana) culture, the blending is never entirely harmonious.

As opposed to this vertical interaction between the classical and the popular elements of culture, another type of connection was horizontal, taking place among the various trends within popular culture itself. Here, many contiguous local and regional cultural groups overlapped with each other. In north Bengal the cult of Sona Rai was an example of this. He was, at one place, known as the protector of the field, while at another place he was the god of tigers. Somewhere else he was a Vaishnava saint who had saved the Koran from desecration, while at yet another place he was a pir and had saved the Hindu religious texts from a similar fate.[34]

It was almost impossible to distinguish Madari (a Muslim sect) *pirs* and the Naths (a sect of worshipers of Gorakhnath) in Dinajpur.[35] Here the Niranjan of the Naths and the Allah of the Madaris were almost interchangeable. There were, and still are, a large number of small ruined buildings in this area, and these are used both by the Burhana pirs and the Nath *jogis* (ascetics) for purposes of worship.[36] One of the major features of these types of cultural interaction is to be seen at the linguistic level. Here, recourse is often had to the consonance of sounds or images to transform one god into another, a procedure that appeals more to popular conceptions of godheads, as well as to popular responses to alliteration, rhyming, and other rhetorical devices, rather than to any elaborate structure of reason and argument. The following is a typical example of such transformation:

> Dharma has assumed the form of a *Yavan*.
> Sporting a black cap and wielding a bow and arrows
>> He rides a powerful horse,
>> And is a terror to the world.
> The formless Niranjan has become a heavenly avatar,
> The word *dam* constantly on his lips.
> Brahma became Muhammad,
> Vishnu, Paigambar, [and]
> the holder of the trident [i.e., Shiva]
> transformed into Adam.
> Ganesh changed into Ghazi
> Kartik into Kazi
> And the *munis* [hermits] all became fakirs.[37]

This particular type of transformation and mutuality between two cultures, Hindu and Muslim, has generally been hailed by liberal scholars as proof of the tolerance or "syncretism" practiced by Hindus and Muslims at the popular level. This, however, is not an entirely satisfactory formulation. It is true that these transformations do show a certain tendency to transgress the boundaries of official or formal Islam and Hinduism. There was a flexibility in these types of movements that may have made it comparatively easy for the lower orders to bypass the rigid and formal structures of elite culture in a feudal society.[38] In our area, Grierson provides an example. Side by side with the recitation of the Bhagavat and Puranic palas there existed a tradition of bawdy and satirical rhymes in which everything turned into its opposite, every action led to an unintended and unconventional end. This was a way of pointing out the inconsistencies of this world. Such songs were quite popular in the rural areas of north Bengal.[39] So, in this culture, there was a mixture of many things that cannot be formalized in accordance with a hierarchical principle and that could not be easily appropriated by elite culture. At the same time, this mutuality of Hindu and Muslim gods does not imply their fusion. Brahma becoming Muhammad and Ganesh becoming Ghazi did not mean that they had lost their separate identities. As gods they usually retained their separate significations. Nor does a bland theory of "tolerance" help much in understanding the acute intolerance and sectarianism that popular sects sometimes displayed toward one another.

The imprint of both popular and elite culture, that is, of both *jana* and *marga*, can be traced in Manulla Mandal's text. The author begins his poem with an invocation to Vishnu or Hari:

Hari is the ultimate wealth [possession];
He is the essence of everything.
Without him there is no salvation.
Ill-fated are those who do not know [the power of] Hari,
For to hell they are eternally condemned.

But Hari is, at the same time, Niranjan, the symbol of the Naths and the Burhana *pirs*. Time and again Hari is replaced by Niranjan:

Of forms he has none.
Like the air, he is without color or shape.
By the power of his *nur* [light]
He created the world
And nurtures it as a father.[40]

Manulla Mandal was aware of Puranic and Sanskritic traditions, and often cites instances from these. He describes Baikuntha, the abode of Hari, and mentions the Kalki avatar. He writes thus about the court pundits of Krishna Nath: "They know the Tantras, the Puranas and the great Bhagavat. They know even the Chaitanya-Charitamrita."[41] He adds, "Whatever I have written in this book has support in the Bhagavat Puran."[42] At the same time he was aware of the local tradition. He made a copy of Sukur Muhammad's *Gopichandrer Geet*, and wrote a poem about Bairatnagar that contained the ballad "Ghazi Kalu and Champavati."[43] It is not unnatural, therefore, that this Hari could be easily interchanged with Niranjan or Allah. In his book, God can easily say, "I am Ram, I am Rahim, and I am Hari."[44] Once again, the alliterative mechanism works, and the glory of Hari can easily be expressed in the *nur* of Allah.

Thus, Manulla's book stands at a symmetrical intersection of traditions where Baikuntha finds its counterpart in Behesht, where Hari and Niranjan reflect each other's forms. Manulla moves freely in both traditions and borrows images and arguments from both; at the same time, he changes them in the process. This gives the text flexibility and plasticity, and also helps Manulla fashion his stories and messages more effectively.

Dinajpur: Its People and History

The history of the district of Dinajpur has been characterized by an official in very clear terms:

> With the breaking of the Dinajpur Raj (1800–1808), the history of the district ceases to be of interest to the outside public. The old saying that "happy is the country that has no history" may fairly be applied to Dinajpur, in which no important events of political nature have occurred to disturb the even tenor of administration and material development.[45]

This is typical of the colonial view: "no important events of political nature," hence "no history." But Manulla's *Kantanama* is full of "events," events important for his life and village. His overall concern was with the Kasimbazar zamindari and its development, but he also wrote as a ryot who was concerned about zamindari demands, especially the extra cess, or *abwab*.

It has been argued recently that in this area there were a few big zamindaris and families who came from outside the district and who maintained control within it through zamindari *amlahs* (functionaries) and extensive establishments.[46] On the other hand, as a consequence of the breakdown of older zamindari houses like the Dinajpur Raj family, zamindari officials and substantial peasant proprietors reaped the maximum possible benefit. Through the *kuthkanidars* (undertenants) they established contact with the zamindar to pay revenue and transferred the burden of rent onto the tenants. This class provided the big *jotedars* (proprietors with large landholdings) of the later period. In areas where land was abundant it was these big farmers who organized cultivation, controlled capital and foodstock, and fought zamindars if the terms were not favorable to them. Buchanan-Hamilton has eloquently described their power: "Whenever one of them is discontented, he gives up his farm, and retires with all his dependants to some other estate, where there are waste lands which his stock enables him to clear. The village which he left is then for some years unoccupied, unless the landlord can find a fugitive of the same kind." This type of mandal peasant could create a lot of trouble for the zamindar, the *izaradar* (leaseholder) and the state; from time to time their threat to withdraw from cultivation would even take the more serious form of defiance.

The small peasants and tenants were, in many ways, forced to depend on them, to bow to their will. In another well-known passage Buchanan-Hamilton has underlined the nature of this dependence: "It is true, that these large farmers exact enormous profits for whatever they advance to their necessitous dependants but still they are of infinite use to these people, who without their assistance would be instantly reduced to the state of common labourers and often to beggary."[47] This mutuality of dominance and dependence has also been stressed by later writers. It has been said that ordinary ryots were extremely wary of dealing directly with outsiders.[48] For Europeans and native officials the mandals were often the only contact with the village people. It seems that collectors like Grierson and Sherwill were always associated with fresh measurements or tax, and as such were unwelcome visitors to the village. State officials and the amlahs of landlords were also considered "outsiders," a source of potential threat.[49] In this context of tension and distrust between the zamindari establishment and the peasant, the conciliatory ideology of *rajdharma* preached by Manulla Mandal in his *Kantanama* acquires special significance.

One of the major issues in the tension between landlord and peasant was the question of *abwab*. In general, abwab is considered by historians to have been an illegal cess and an extra burden on the peasants who, because of their helplessness and the superior political power of the landlords, had to pay up and suffer.[50] In Bengal there were three categories of these extra payments: abwab, a regular cess to be paid at regular intervals; *mathot* (from *matha*, or head), payment taken for official needs and purposes; and *kharcha*, a payment for the expenses on revenue collection.[51] In practice the distinctions often got blurred. Although the colonial government banned these in the late eighteenth century, the peasants still had to pay these cesses to the zamindars. A colonial historian has explained this in terms of the "mysterious passive sentiment" of the Bengali peasant.[52] In actual practice payments of abwab had much to do with the nature of the relationship between ryots and zamindars.

In many cases in Dinajpur, the ryots agreed to pay the abwab only as a gesture of compromise. In many areas the khudkasht peasants concealed the actual amount of land under cultivation, opposing any attempt on the part of the zamindar to measure the land afresh and to reassess the rent. The ryots agreed to pay some cess as "compensation" to the zamindar, provided he did not insist on fresh measurement.[53] In most of these cases, the imposition of abwabs and *mangans* (cess) was a tacit compromise between ryots and zamindars, not an easy victory for the landlords. The amount collected varied from estate to estate. There are several instances of estates where the landlord succeeded in completing a fresh measurement with the result that the peasants of that estate refused to pay any extra cess. In other estates, where the new measurement was not made, the ryots, without apparent protest, paid various dues as abwab, mangan, and kharcha. There are also reports of cases where the peasants themselves took the initiative in paying extra amounts to salvage the prestige of zamindaris in crisis.[54] At the same time, many zamindars did not hesitate to levy the cess from their ryots by using the threat of force. However, they also kept up the appearance of making all these impositions look like voluntary gifts from the peasants. They actually described these dues, in their local languages, as *bhiksha* or mangan (kinds of beggary) by the landlord from his subjects.[55]

Various other cases show the involvement of headmen or prosperous ryots in the collection of abwabs. On the occasion of a visit of a new zamindar to his estate, it was often these "big" ryots who collected dues from the poorer ryots and offered *nazar* (tribute) to the new master. In lieu of their services they received *siropa* (gifts) and concessions. The collection of abwabs often became a source of income and of authority for the bigger ryots.[56] However, in all these attempts there was a notion of justice grown out of custom, experience, historical dispute, and the actual agrarian situation of the area. Excessive collection or continuous imposition of the new abwabs or mathots might well lead to an explosive situation like the *dhing* (revolt) against Deby Singh in Rangpur in 1783. This point was stressed in a petition from the zamindars of Rangpur that underscores the role of custom in agrarian disputes:

> The ryots of this country objected to engaging for any certain quantity of land and to the revenue being fixed, on account of its being contrary to the custom of country and the lands never having been measured according to *ruckha bandi* [a measure of land], they paying revenue only according to the quantity of land actually cultivated by them after deducting *moojraee* of a certain part remitted to them as an engagement. . . . If the settlement be not made with them according to the established custom of the country, they desert. . . . If the *bundabasts* [settlements] be not concluded agreeably to the customs of the country, the collections will be endangered.[57]

When there were agrarian disturbances in Baharband against the zamindar of Kantanagar, the peasants, the zamindar, and the government alike referred to *kanoon* (rules) and *raj-ul-mulk* (laws of the kingdom) as the basis for their action.[58] What constituted the particular kanoon in question was ultimately decided through a process of struggle. The willingness or reluctance to pay abwab or to allow the landlord to measure the area under cultivation depended on the economic logic as well as the power equation as it existed between the landlord, the big ryots, and the lesser peasants. Specific instances of deference and defiance in such matters were determined by the specific context. But there was no legally defined limit to how much the landlord could demand of the peasant: there was nothing written or definitive about it. It was kept vague and judged by the nebulous boundaries of "custom": landlords and cultivators had each their own interpretation of kanoon. In some cases the payment of mathot or abwab was a compromise between two contending groups; in other cases it was a forced exaction but taken in the name of some freshly invented tradition; in still other cases it was paid voluntarily, owing to a kind of attachment that the peasant felt toward the overlord—a notion of duty to a landlord rightly or wrongly perceived to be in need of such service.

Abwabs became a contentious issue with the zamindari family of Kasimbazar. The case of Krishna Kanta Nandi, the *bania* (agent) of

Warren Hastings, was typical. Through political connections, manipulations of *izara* (lease) contracts, and *benami* transactions (under false names), Krishna Kanta, starting in 1764, slowly built up his extensive landed property all over Bengal. He defeated Rani Bhawani in a series of legal and political games and consolidated his position in Dinajpur by buying the two most prosperous and contiguous parganas of Baharband and Bhitarband in Rangpur.[59] Thus came into being the zamindari of Kantanagar, with "an illegitimate origin in the obscure depths of eighteenth century politics and intrigues."[60] After the death of Krishna Kanta's son, Lokenath Nandi, the zamindari came under the management of the Court of Wards from 1804 to 1820, during the minority of Harinath Nandi. Harinath Nandi was involved in a prolonged lawsuit with his relatives and died shortly after becoming zamindar. Due to the minority of Krishna Nath Nandi, the Court of Wards took charge of the zamindari again in 1832 and administered it until 1840. The amlahs and managers who ran the administration on behalf of the Court of Wards also shared in the spoils, becoming izaradars themselves. The zamindari house was vertically split because of an unsavory tussle between Krishna Nath Nandi and his advisers, on one side, and Rani Susarmayi and Rani Hara Sundari, his mother and grandmother, on the other.[61] With two parallel administrations and "uncontrolled gatherings of the *Muffassil Umlahs*," the condition of the ryots became worse, and the income of the estate fell.[62] Even when Krishna Nath finally became zamindar in 1840, the situation did not much improve because of his intemperate behavior and reckless administration. Finally, in the face of a charge of willful murder, he committed suicide in 1844.

Thus there was no dearth of tension and conflict in this so-called peaceful district. The colonial government failed to recognize this reality because of its limited view; Manulla, however, did not fail to mention some of these events. *Kantanama* is intended to interpret rajdharma as well as to chronicle some of the events that marked the rule of the zamindars of the Kasimbazar house.

Rajdharma: The Face of Terror

One important source of rajdharma lies in terror and coercion. Manulla never forgot that he was a ryot, a subject, or that the Nandis were the zamindars. God had appeared in his dream and asked him to write the text, but as soon as he woke up he worried: "I am terribly afraid to write about the exploits of the King. Who knows, the King may dislike it. After all I am a subject and he is the King. He might be a sinner [i.e., one who ignores the words of God] and develop a dislike for me."[63] Manulla repeatedly reminds himself and his reader that he would not have written his book at his own initiative: "Helpless, I have to write down the words of God. . . ."

> The faith wavers,
> my mind is impure,
> I am narrating the deeds of the King,
> As I have seen them in a dream,
> . . . it is with great fear that I write,
> I am terribly afraid.[64]

"It is with great fear that I write" is a sentence that recurs often in the first half of the poem. Manulla was also aware of the distance between the ruler and ruled: "Will the King understand my suffering? He will recognize his own work, but will he understand my pain [grief]?"[65] Thus his praise and eulogy of the "king" or landlord, all his protestations of loyalty and devotion, are evoked at least in part by fear of the zamindar's power. In all the praise addressed to the overlord, terror is the mark by which the subordinate differentiates himself from the superordinate, the expression of a cosmic helplessness by the author offering testimony of his very material, earthly terror.

The terrorizing power of the landlord is of course the subject of many volumes by colonial observers. Even in the remote area of Dinajpur, an official wrote:

> Every village has, it is true, an Officer attached to it called a *Kotwal*. . . . Besides the Kotwals, landholders entertain the *paiks* [footmen], but these men never quite reach the threshold of the zamindar's *sudder cutchery* during the night, and their duties by day are confined to seizing the *ryots* and committing all sorts of violence under the orders of their masters in the prosecution of most objectionable extortions and most cruel oppression. . . . The proportion of *paiks* entertained by the zamindar averages about one per village. . . . If a zamindar has twenty villages, he has but one cutchery; at the break of day he sends forth his twenty *paiks* to levy his rents, who towards the close of the day, return with the sums they may have collected, bringing also with them, all such, as either may not have been able to meet the suddenness of the demand, or who may have had courage enough to dispute the justness of the claim. This is the sum of the *paik*'s "duty."[66]

Buchanan-Hamilton also gives a detailed description of the elaborate establishments by which the zamindar extorted rents and coerced defiant peasants. He comments in particular upon the power and authority of zamindari amlah necessary in Kantanagar.[67] On the same subject, Manulla says:

> Like the moon of the heaven sitting along with his stars, the zamindar sits with his amlahs.
> . . . He has a canopy over his head.
> . . . The Chief Diwan is Herkolots sahib.
> . . . The chief Nazir is Gangadhar Ghose, a name dear to god.
> . . . Durgacharan Babu is the head of the Cutchery, he is *sheristadar* [highest managerial officer] of the King.
> . . . Everybody is in his place, the king in his *darbar* [royal court] the whole Sabha is radiant.[68]

A peasant like Manulla, however prosperous, had to take cognizance of the power of this establishment, and deify it. This ritualized description, suggestive of a cosmology and a divine plan revealing itself in the physical arrangement of the royal court, was perhaps part of the strategy the peasant used to adjust himself to zamindari power. Subordination seems almost desirable by such a glorification of the source of oppression.

The capacity to punish has always been a signifier of royalty. It is through the exercise of such power (*danda*) that the king preserves the moral order of dharma. From the Manusamhita to the Mahabharata to the localized Puranas in medieval Bengal, the terrorizing power of rajdharma or danda is described in exalted terms.[69] In a typical passage of the Mahabharata, Arjuna, the legendary hero, says this of danda: "O King, Danda protects and rules the subjects. Even when everybody sleeps, Danda remains awake. The wise have described Danda as the principal dharma [*dandam dharmam bidurbhudha*]. Most sinners do not commit crimes for fear of *rajdanda*. It is the natural law of this world: Danda is the foundation of everything [*ebam samsidhiki loke sarvam danda pratisthitam*]."[70] As we can see from this, in the marga tradition, danda is fused with moral order. Disruption and withdrawal of danda mean the breakdown of social order, crisis in caste society, even a total reversal of the existing patterns of domination and subordination. Everybody is within the pale of danda; no subject is beyond it. The exercise of danda is natural and good; its suspension unnatural and bad. Danda and dharma thus became synonymous; "dandam dharmam bidurbhudha." This type of identity places rajdharma in the dual world of morality and terror, the one associated with the other in such a manner that it becomes impossible to draw a boundary between them.[71]

This picture is present in the *Kantanama* but with a difference. We do not have the speech of heroes like Arjuna or Bhisma; rather, the peasant, the subject of terror, is given speech. The exercise of terror by the king is explained and depicted in the *Kantanama* through the behavior of the peasant, the object of danda rather than one who wields it.

The story begins with the terrorized subject. Krishna Kanta establishes his zamindari and his rule: "Kantababu became the King in the year seventy-two; he was declared the zamindar in [B.S.] 1772. God has favored him. . . . The two annas of the area have been given in the name of Kantababu. The Maharaja circulated his *parwana* [warrant] throughout his *bhum* [area] and named the Pargana Kantanagar after his own name."[72]

In this way Manulla describes the establishment of a new zamindari, the exercise of a new power through the parwanas, through the measure of renaming an old place. The success of the landlord showed he had the support of God because of the good deeds of his previous lives. If success was a reward for the inherent goodness and merit in a man, Kantababu, who had been able to establish his order (*dohai*) in this area, naturally deserved to be respected: "The pargana belongs to Kantababu. It bears his name. All the subjects recognize that and salute him." Again, "Kantababu became the ruler of the *Dowani* pargana. He has found it easy to collect rents from this area."[73]

Kantababu, however, following the proper norms, did not go beyond the limit imposed by *insaf* (justice) "He never demands abwab. All the subjects [*praja*] live in great happiness."[74] But there are erring prajas, people incapable of understanding the goodness of Dharmaraj Kantababu. They are bad and defiant subjects, while Manulla himself, by implication, conforms to the ideal: "The Raja has got a kingdom [*mulk*]. Its name is Baharband. The story of this area is puzzling [*dhandha*]. The country is wicked, its people are wicked. There, no one pays rent, no one accepts authority."[75]

The area of Baharband, even according to the official documents, was well known for its recursive tradition of rebellion. Mir Kasim as well as Rani Bhawani of Natore had their times of trouble in this pargana. When Krishna Kanta Nandi purchased the estate *benami* (under a fictitious name) on account of his influence over Hastings, he wanted to make his holdings lucrative by introducing "scientific administration." At this the dominant and prosperous khudkasht ryots of the area were up in arms. In a petition to the East India Company they talked of their customary rights; referred to the earlier history of the pargana, in which "bad" zamindars were often taught a lesson; and spoke in favor of "their ancient settlements" and "raj-ul-mulk." The zamindar, Lokenath Nandi, son of Krishna Kanta, gave his own interpretation. He upheld "the universal law of empire," as well as the absolute authority of the landlord over his ryots. He also rejected the complaints as a conspiracy of the big ryots to disguise the actual area of land under their own cultivation to avoid proper measurement, and to shift the burden of the rent onto the poor ryots. Failure in effecting a compromise led to a revolt of these "artful ryots" under the command of Hargovind Bakshi, Mohan Bakshi, and Maniram Hazra.[76] Forces led by Goodlad, the collector of Rangpur, eventually crushed the rebellion on behalf of Kasimbazar Raj.[77]

It is to this incident that Manulla alludes in his poem. His aim was to represent rajdharma. Baharband was a place where lived the wicked subjects, as opposed to good and loyal subjects elsewhere. Their rebellion arose not out of their misery and poverty or a sense of acute oppression, but on account of their wicked nature, their innate desire to defy all authority. They were rich enough to possess elephants, yet they refused to pay because "it is a wicked [*khal*] kingdom, its subjects are also wicked" and "they do not accept the King and do not pay the revenue. In an organized way, they forbade everybody to pay revenue. They know nothing better than to cause trouble. They said to the Raja: 'We do not recognize you.'" Kanta Babu himself went to the pargana with his army, with the result that the ryots retreated and went into hiding:

> The King sent summons to the subjects.
> From a distant place, they sent back their reply:
> "We do not recognize you and we will not pay any revenue.
> Return to your own house for your own benefit [safety].
> If you apply much pressure, the consequence may be worse. Then you
>   will not be allowed to return to your house [country] alive."

In the eyes of Manulla, the king ought to be patient and kindhearted: "Even after hearing this, the king refused to be angry. He feels compassion toward his subjects." But his entreaties were repeatedly met with defiance. Ultimately, however, finding them to be "compulsive troublemongers" and having lived without provisions for twenty days, the king's patience ran out. He now gave a fitting reply to the strength of the organized peasantry, a reply known to everybody through the ages:

> Failing to get hold of any of the subjects,
> the king turned furious and set fire [to the villages].
> All the houses in the country were destroyed by fire.
> The prajas received what they deserved.
> One and all were punished in the right measure,
> The rent for three years being collected all at once.
> The king's authority was proclaimed all over the country.
> Pacified, the prajas returned to their houses.[78]

The burning of houses, the beating of people, the taking of all rents due in a single installment were the outcomes of the exercise of danda. In Manulla's opinion this was the only recourse open to Kanta Babu. If his subjects refused to obey, they transgressed the limits of prajadharma and violated the code of behavior sanctioned to subjects. In order to rectify this lapse the exercise of legal power was necessary, for without danda the bad praja cannot be restored to the right path. To establish authority is the beginning of rajdharma, and to punish the subject who deviates from his own dharma is its sacred duty. In the last resort, through the exercise of terror—danda—prajadharma was restored. Rajdharma's quality had thus been fully vindicated:

> Without objection, they accepted the King's judgment
> [and] paid rent, including cess on grazing land.
> The King, kindness personified, felt sorry for the subjects.
> In justice [*insaf*] he relinquished the cess for ever.
> It is thus that he collected the revenue,
> And named the pargana Kantanagar after himself.
> The pargana is Kantanagar,
>   And the King is called Kantababu.
> The Prajas all accept this
>   and salute the king.

He who did not understand the glory and significance of rajdharma is, according to Manulla, "a thoroughbred savage."[79]

Refusal to be terrorized by danda is equally a crime, for the danda of the king is not arbitrary or blind. Krishna Kanta gave his subjects the chance to correct themselves; he condoned their initial defiance. His exercise of power was tempered by kindness, limited by justice, or insaf. Hence, Manulla suggests that while the use of terror and coercion was legitimate and the ideal praja was expected to fear the king's power, the king, too, had the moral right to coerce only so long as the exercise of royal power was moored in the notion of insaf, or justice.

Limits to Rajdharma: The Nature of Insaf

The institution of abwab illustrates well the notion of insaf as it was actually practiced. In the day-to-day existence of zamindari, the regular payment of rent is a point around which the relation between a landlord and his peasants revolves. To collect rent is the right of the zamindar, and, in the opinion of Manulla, the peasants are duty bound to pay. But to measure the land, to collect revenue, and then to ask for abwab and mathot are, according to him, clear instances of oppression, be-insaf, zulm. We have seen how the issue of land measurement vis-à-vis the collection of abwabs became a bone of contention between landlords and the substantial peasantry in Dinajpur and Rangpur in the early nineteenth century. In the late eighteenth century, Lokenath Nandi rejected the demand of his khudkasht ryots, who opposed measurement and instead offered a cess as compensation. The powerful ryots of Baharband and Gayabari fought the zamindars successfully for the most part of the nineteenth century, until they were defeated by Rani Swarnamayi. However, in other areas the khudkasht ryots were not so powerful; they lost ground on the issue of land measurement. Hence, the collection of abwabs gradually became a contentious issue. It is interesting to observe that Manulla's discussion of abwabs is significantly different in tone and content from his discussion of danda. The collection of abwabs involved the practice of insaf, and here Manulla often sees the zamindar as the offender. After praising Nal, Harischandra, Karna, Bali, and Yudhisthir, all well-known mythological kings, Manulla introduces a king called Srishchandra, his own creation: "Srishchandra was a king and a great archer. . . . No one was able to match him. . . . He passed his days happily [until] he became the victim of a bad intention after a long period." What was this bad intention? He began to take mathot for the *annaprasan* ceremony of his son, for mortuary rites in connection with his father's death, and for the marriage ceremony of his son. As a consequence, "God became angry with him, the peasants suffered much for the payment of abwab. God with his own hands made the King a sinner."[80] Srishchandra's name cannot be found in any Purana, and he is clearly created as a counterimage of good kings like Bali, Nal, and Yudhisthir. To collect mathot on all these ceremonies was clearly an act of oppression. Using the structure of Puranic tales, Manulla depicts the imagined experience of an oppressive landlord. At the same time he places Krishna Kanta and his successors within that Puranic tradition.

Kanta Babu followed the rules of rajdharma because "he does not even utter the word 'abwab,' he is dharmaraj [himself]." Under the reign of his son Lokenath, the subjects were very happy because "he never oppressed anyone in the name of abwab."[81] Krishna Nath also belonged to the same category. Yudhisthir in the *Mahabharata*, too, belongs to that tradition: "Yudhisthir was famous in this world for his truthfulness. He never uttered the word 'abwab.'"[82] There was, obviously, no discussion of abwabs in the *Mahabharata*, but Manulla's Yudhisthir is made in the image of a just zamindar at Dinajpur, the sign of that insaf being that he does not collect illegal cess and abwabs from peasants.

Manulla is not unique in pursuing this theme. It is also present in the ballads of Mainamati and Gopichandra, so popular with illiterate Muslim peasants, weavers, and the Yugis, agricultural laborers and lime-makers of north Bengal. Through the work of Sukur Muhammad, Manulla was familiar with these stories. In the kingdom of Manikchandra, "the great righteous king," the tax was levied per plow and everybody was prosperous. The images of prosperity in these stories are identical with those used by Manulla to describe the Baharband ryots. It was the bad amlah, usually an outsider, who urged the raja to extract abwabs. The condition of the whole estate deteriorated, and the ryots appealed to God, who advised them to curse the king. "The King became greedy for wealth [*dhana-kangali*]. Dharma Niranjan would judge it." Ultimately, the half-naked peasants wished death on him and thus caused his death. Throughout this ballad of Manikchandra, the anger against the dhana-kangali (greedy) reverberates like an echo.[83] On this point Manulla is close to Gopichandra's *git* rather than to any shastric literature.

In Manulla's *Kantanama* this oppression has been perpetrated by the officials of the zamindar. Their presence was immediate and real to the peasantry; the landlords were far away—in Kasimbazar and Calcutta. In the *mahals* (estates) the amlahs were all in all. During the king's minority and management by the Court of Wards, their oppression increased.[84] Manulla gives a typical description of the situation during the period of the minor Raja Harinath. His description may be paraphrased thus: The amlahs collected money from the ryots but showed it as their own borrowings from the latter, and thus the estate became a defaulter in the eyes of the government. "They gave a bad name to the ryots," says Manulla, "and became *izaradars* [themselves]. Inflicting losses on the king [i.e., the treasury], they laid the blame at the door of the ryots. They pleased the king by promising *daul* [rent collections] and obtained their izara at the court. Returning to the country, they ruined the pargana." According to Manulla, they imposed cesses under various names, such as *bandobust, daul, milani,* and so on. The pargana was plunged deep into chaos.

Manulla's descriptions are amply confirmed by official documents. Izaradar oppression was, perhaps, even greater. During the time of the minority of Krishna Nath, the izaradar had hold of the pargana; as Manulla puts it: "Krishna Nath, being a minor, was innocent [of the affairs of the estate]. The Sahibs now became the *mukhtiars* [representatives] for the king, [and] Shyamkishore made arrangements in the collectorate [for the izara]."[85] According to official documents, Shyamkishore was an active patron of a faction of local amlahs and was "a man of business [who was] well acquainted with and engages in speculations."[86] He was a typical product of the permanent settlement, a relentless pursuer of profit from rent and speculation in land. Manulla gives an eloquent description of this man and his activities:

> He speaks only the language of violence. Nobody dares to speak in his presence. Summons came [from him] declaring all current rents as arrears. It was as if the pargana trembled [in fear]. The order from the collectorate was for the arrears to be paid within three *years.* But he [Shyamkishore] collected it all in three months. Varieties of abwabs he took from the ryots. He sold their jewelry, even their pots and pans. He respects nothing, not even *hurumat* [honor].

The izaradar did not respect custom and cared nothing for natural calamity, and the invocation of *izzat* or hurumat cut no ice with him. Eventually the peasants ran away:

> No water, no cultivation,
>   no prosperity in the household.
> The izaradar still exacts his dues under so many
>   pretexts.
> The people desert and flee from the pargana.[87]

This was a part of "normal" life for the peasantry. There was nothing unusual about their having to sell their essentials in order to meet the excess demands of rapacious farmers and the agents of zamindars. Desertion was quite common, too. In the songs of Gopichandra, the singer says, "The peasants sell their plows, their yoke, and all their agricultural implements to meet the demand of rent; they even sell their own infants."[88]

Their actual experience of amlahs and izaradars made the peasants despise immediate authority and created in them the expectation of justice from a higher, distant authority.[89] Manulla makes this distinction throughout his writing: amlahs and izaradars are not synonymous with the king but are his (bad) agents because they do not conform to the dictates of honor, or hurumat. What was the way out of this misery? "Prayer" is Manulla's considered answer: "Those of us who cannot escape, think of God. How long before the king ascends the throne? Let the king grow up and take charge of the kingdom: this is what we, the subjects, pray for."[90]

But why is the king necessarily more just, more responsible, and kinder than the izaradar and the amlah? To answer this question, Manulla postulated a general principle that was central to his notion of rajdharma. To take abwab or not, to be generous or not, to obey the preceptor (guru) or not—these were merely outward expressions of a general principle of dharma. They were the specific signs of a general principle, and there could be numerous variations on these signs in a specific situation. Manulla explains the point:

> Like a father the king looks after his kingdom with care
>   and attention.
> Others oppress with injustice for they know not any
>   kindness.
> Without the father the son becomes helpless like the
>   destitute [*kangal*] from Nadia,
> An orphan, he has no one to turn to.
> Likewise, the praja is the son
>   And the raja the father.
> [If] the father leaves his ward [*praja*]
> The praja becomes miserable.
> The father is both a preceptor and a friend.
> Know it for sure then
> [that] the father is the god Niranjan himself.
> . . . .
> The raja is for the praja as father is to son.
> Who else would value the praja as a son?[91]

The crucial feature of rajdharma is this relationship of father and son, through which the relationship between the king and his subject is viewed. It is a relationship, in colloquial language, of "ma-baap."[92] The father punishes and also looks after his son. This duality of chastisement and protection is the basis of rajdharma. The authority of the father and the submission of the son are matched by the helplessness of the son in the absence of the father. Manulla cites one example after another from the Puranas in support of his theory. Nal, Bali, Karna, and Yudhisthir were all rewarded in heaven precisely because they had conducted themselves in accordance with this ideal of rajdharma: "They looked after their subjects as sons [putra bhave palan kaila]."[93] Conversely, Srishchandra was rebuked by the messengers of Yama in hell for not behaving in a fatherly way toward his subjects.[94]

All the zamindars of the Kasimbazar Raj were made (by Manulla) in the model of these mythical heroes—their exact replicas. They treated their subjects as their own sons.[95] In this way, the Puranic kings and the zamindars of the Nandi family all became instances of dharmaraj, and a Puranic framework of time could be superimposed on a chronology that was local and specific. In the Mahabharata and the Puranas the same ideas and epithets are expressed to explain rajdharma as the relation between ruler and ruled.[96] In the Bhagavat, it has been said, the prajas, being sons, were even entitled to offer pindas (offerings to dead ancestors) after the death of the king. They remain before the king as "children before a father."[97]

In this notion, there was a fusion of the two opposing ideas of dominance and subordination. In the consciousness of the peasant, the king or the lord was duty bound to look after him. The authority of the father in a family is taken as "given" or "natural," so the lord's authority over his domain, by this analogy, becomes "natural" and "everlasting." This analogy from family to society and from society to the state comprehends various levels of authority and submission and makes these part of a whole order. Hence a particular landlord or king could be bad, but monarchy and landlordism were part of a "good and beneficial" arrangement. The king had certain duties toward the peasant, not as a part of the legal rights of the peasant but derived from a general moral and social order. The peasant had duties toward the king. Everybody in this hierarchical order accepts the chains of duty and moral obligation.

This was not just a figment of Manulla's imagination. We encounter the same theme in a petition that Rani Bhawani made to the East India Company against her izaradar in 1775:

> I am an old zamindar and not being able to see the griefs of my ryots, I agreed to take the country as farmer. . . . The high ground of Rarh yielded nothing for want of water and in Bhaturia, which is very low, the gentlemen [the officials of the company] took the pool-bandi [embankment] into their own hands and made the banks and

in August 1773, the banks broke and the ryots' ground and their crops failed by being overflowed with water. I am a zamindar, so was obliged to keep the ryots from ruin and gave what ease to them I could by giving them time to make up their payments and requested the gentlemen would in same manner give me time when I would pay up the revenues but not crediting me, they were pleased to employ Dulal Roy as *Sejawal*. . . . The two men [Dulal Roy and Paran Bose] . . . have depopulated and destroyed the country. I am an old zamindar. I hope I have committed no fault. My country is plundered and the ryots are full of complaints. . . . For this reason I am ready [to offer the same amount] and will take care that the *sircar* suffers no loss.[98]

It is irrelevant to ask here whether the rani's sentiments were genuine or not. The language of the petition and what she has to say of her duty as an old zamindar are what interest us. In the history of the Dinajpur Raj, too, an anecdote expressing a similar kind of mutual responsibility between the landlord and his subjects has been reported. When Raja Radhanath was faced with the prospect of bankruptcy, the headmen of all the villages sought a meeting with the "king" to work out an arrangement whereby they could assist the landlord in this time of crisis. The king agreed, pitched a tent, arranged a "solemn ceremony," and dressed himself accordingly. The ceremony was in the end cancelled, as certain amlahs did not favor the idea, but the anecdote reflects the notion of mutuality of duties between the ruler and the ruled.[99] As a famous passage in the *Mahabharata* puts it: "The first body of the subject is the king, the subject is also like the body of the king. Without the king, there is no country, without the country there is no king."[100]

Thus, by relating the day-to-day experiences of the peasant to the traditions of the *smritis*, the Puranas, and the sayings of wise men, Manulla transforms the mundane into the heavenly, the natural into the supernatural. The personal and historical experiences of Manulla thus become generalized beyond his immediate space and time.[101]

Transgression of Rajdharma: The Story of Harinath

Manulla also speaks of a rajdharma that might be interfered with by the ruler himself, and the consequences that would follow. Those who ruled according to rajdharma went to *baikuntha* (the abode of Hari, i.e., heaven) and those who violated his norms went to *narak* (hell): "If you do good, your place will be in baikuntha. If you do otherwise, you will be sent to narak." There is a clear distinction between the worlds of dharma and adharma, sin and merit: "The place in opposition to dharma is narak, the kingdom of Yama, riven with dissension, while Niranjan, the Lord, rules over baikuntha, the abode of dharma."[102] Srishchandra and Shyamkishore went to hell forever and were physically punished for their actions. From Yudhisthir to Lokenath, everybody who acted according to rajdharma was rewarded with a place in heaven.

The life of Harinath, the son of Lokenath Nandi and the father of Krishna Nath, was, however, not so simple. Harinath was a righteous king, but during the last days of life he deviated from the principles of rajdharma. This incident is crucial for the narrative of *Kantanama*, and Manulla describes the event at least twice. A peasant went to see Harinath and complained against the oppression of an izaradar. Harinath listened to the complaint but gave no decision. For thirteen days the peasant waited for a royal decision, but the king did not even attend his darbar. Reduced to poverty and despair, the peasant eventually managed to find the landlord sitting in his darbar. But, as Manulla says: "The doorkeeper did not allow him into the darbar. Being forbidden, he called out to the king. The king heard the cry but did not respond. . . . Being a king he refused to listen to the complaints of the subject. Nor would the sentry let him [the peasant] enter. The *praja* went away, wiping his tears." Thus Manulla brought two specific charges against Raja Harinath:

> Although a raja he does not attend the darbar everyday. Also unbecoming [of a king] is the fact that he does not listen to the complaints of the prajas. If the praja has to pay for food at the royal palace, or go without it altogether, this is yet another sin that attaches to the raja.

Harinath went to baikuntha all right, but he remained there in extreme discomfiture, for "Niranjan wrote *gunah* [sin] against the name of the righteous king."[103]

> No cool breeze soothes his person, which always burns [as though] from summer heat. Restless inside, with sweat running down all over his body, he finds [the situation] unbearable. "Oh, save me!" cries out his soul in desperation, and even though he is in Baikuntha itself, he still has to pray to God.

God eventually came in the disguise of a Brahman and explained the cause of his suffering. He also said that the suffering would last forever, for it was *bemiyadi*, without any time limit. The king pleaded for remission. Showing compassion for him, God said, "'Well, only a part may be remitted. Ten annas of your sin will remain for what you have done to your praja.' As soon as the Brahman uttered this, the king's suffering was lessened by six annas. The king now realized that this person [the Brahman] was none other than God himself."[104]

Pap and punya are the two most important themes of this discussion that goes on in baikuntha between the zamindar and God in the shape of a Brahman. Yet the peasant-poet's imagination shows all the signs of the political order in which the peasant lives. Just as the king was expected to respond kindly to petitions by the peasants and occasionally reduce their burden of rent, God, in response to Harinath's petition, did the same. The relation between landlord and peasant has been replicated in baikuntha as a relation between Hari and Harinath. Similarly, the punishments meted out in hell are reminiscent of the physical torture the peasants suffer at the zamindar's establishment.[105]

Manulla's heaven, by contrast, overflows with various items of food. For a peasantry used to hunger and physical deprivation, it was perhaps natural that "heaven" should represent all that was materially desirable:

> Rice was served with a variety of dishes. The plates were made of gold; so were the bowls and waterpots. . . . The king ate the meal with great relish—milk, curds, sweets, *khir*, and butter. The meal over, the king put some betel leaves in his mouth and was offered a golden hookah. He was now very pleased.[106]

Through this description of heaven and hell Manulla upholds the hierarchy of authority. To Niranjan every devotee is a ryot, a subject. "It is God, the master of all living beings," he writes, "who rules all men as his subjects and looks after them as a father."[107] The landlord in fact is shown to be afraid in the presence of God. Fearing punishment, "the king began to cry: alas I do not know what . . . calamity fate has decreed for me."[108]

But the lapses in this exercise of rajdharma are temporary. Stability and order are natural. And, in Manulla's narrative, the restoration of stability comes through sacrifices made by the subject. Harinath committed lapses because of his bad behavior with his praja; he suffered for that. His exculpation comes when God asks an ordinary praja, Manulla, to relate to others the story of the dynasty to which

Harinath belongs. But in order to qualify for this noble task that God has entrusted, Manulla had to pass the test of suffering and thus lost everything—his family and his houses:

> The king's thoughts turned to the writer and the sufferings he had borne in order to document royal deeds. . . . "In narrating to the world the exploits of my dynasty [the king said], my subject has sacrificed his father and sons. For my exploits the writer suffers." Thus the king laments over the misfortune of the subject. . . . "Our exploits have been propagated in this world. For that my subject has lost his sons and brothers."[109]

But Manulla is duty bound to do this; any subject is duty bound to help his lord in times of distress. As God says to Manulla: "Do the work in the interest of the king. You can be sure that your work will be everlasting."[110]

Thus the initiative of the subject is recognized, but in favor of the lord, not against him. Manulla is here a successor of Kalu Dom, a model in medieval Bengali literature of old, trustworthy servants. Kalu sacrificed his life and made Lau Sen, his overlord, victorious in a battle. Manulla's worldly sufferings are given a similar meaning: it is because he passes the test of suffering that he qualifies to write the history of the raj. This alone can reduce the king's sufferings in hell. Manulla's sacrifices show his loyalty to the king and to the divine order that kingship represents. It was also, one might say, a clever, if unconscious, ploy to ensure that his sufferings were after all not in vain, that they brought him adequate rewards from the royal court. We do not know if the strategy worked.

God, the King, and the Subject: The Question of Submission and Autonomy

In *Kantanama*, God—the king or the landlord—and the subject—Manulla—interact in a manner that deserves to be treated separately. Manulla wished to please the landlord, so he wrote about the deeds of his family. But the text is not simply supplicatory in tone. In the first place, Manulla wasn't even sure that the text would please Krishna Nath Nandi. What if it only aroused his anger? The fear of a negative reaction terrorized Manulla so much that to bolster his self-confidence he often invoked God's support. God's authority is superior to that of the landlord. It is interesting to note Manulla's strategy for self-protection. It speaks of the fear that even a subject who is praising the landlord feels. But in this imagined, hierarchical community, one's superiors also had their superiors, and one could always appeal to—or in the name of—the higher authority.

And this gives Manulla a voice of his own, a certain degree of autonomy even when he is submissive. It is interesting that he manages even to abuse the very landlord whom he was supposed to please. If the landlord dared to treat him badly because he did not like Manulla's poem, he would show himself up as a "mean" person (*pamar*). Only a king who was a "thoroughbred fool" (as God would say, Manulla hastens to add) would be unable to sympathize with the heartfelt sorrow of the subject.[111] Thus, by counterposing the authority of God to that of the landlord, Manulla not only saved himself from the ire of the master but also issued a veiled threat to him in case his expectations were not fulfilled. Manulla in fact even goes beyond this. He makes Harinath, the landlord, suffer in baikuntha because of his lapses from dharma. His redemption is only possible through Manulla's act of writing the text, and in the narrative, Harinath is forced by God to recognize this. But again, the ultimate actor, as Manulla says, is God himself. Harinath was forced to commit lapses because Manulla was destined to write the book: "Niranjan has confused the king because of the need to have his exploits written."[112] Thus, all the acts of Manulla, according to the order of God, are not meant for his own liberation but for that of his master.

Through his act of writing Manulla was, thus, an agent of God, and was outside the pale of the landlord's judgment. His own decision was also irrelevant here. Manulla is "entrapped in religiosity." He has, as Marx would have said, either not yet found himself or has already lost himself again. All his initiative belongs to the other world; his supplication and protest have their source in other worlds. Religion here becomes the opium of the people. But it is also, as Marx himself recognized, the sigh of the oppressed. Manulla is caught up in an endless cycle of transference: he creates a god whom he believes to be his own creator.

Manulla is not really representative of poor, indigent peasants. He was a Mandal, a headman whose social world was that of the well-to-do peasant. How then does *Kantanama* help us to understand the culture of the subordinate classes? Is it not the mentality of the substantial ryot that *Kantanama* documents? There may have, of course, been interesting and important differences between the thoughts of a poor peasant and those of a Mandal, and we cannot make *Kantanama* stand in as a substitute for evidence reflecting more directly the thought world, say, of a sharecropper or a landless laborer. However, it seems to me that we would be erring in the opposite direction to think that there could be no exchange or sharing of ideals or ideas between classes, or that classes, even when they were in conflict, did not learn from each other. There is, prima facie, no reason to assume that classes, like scholars, are deaf to each other, that ideas cannot travel across the boundaries of class. The cognitive map that Manulla had of the world may easily have been shared, although not necessarily wholly, by a poor peasant.

There is yet another reason why Manulla's text may be thought to have a general significance. If we were to think of subordination not as a static and fixed property of particular classes but as a process and a relationship, which people could enter into or reproduce in different contexts of hierarchy, the relevance of Manulla's text becomes apparent. In his statement, we begin to see the different elements in the cultural repertoire of rural Bengal that are marshaled and arranged in order to communicate to his masters his feelings of loyalty and submission. Hence, Manulla's text is of interest to us not simply because it allows us to see a particular form in which a peasant may try to present his view of rajdharma to his landlord in order to get material benefit as well as merit. What makes the text rich are its contradictions and ambiguities—the fact that a text ostensibly written to please the landlord should carry within it its own moments of irony, fear, resistance, and resentment.

From recent researches it can be shown that, time and again, the subordinate classes have risen in rebellion because of their faith in some moral order, out of an urge to restore justice. Rajdharma can be seen to have played a similar role. The praja recognizes his first identity as praja (subject) against the raja (as king) in terms of rajdharma. He thus becomes conscious of the marks of his distinction. This is the first step of self-recognition, without which rebellion is impossible. The peasant's submission is not to a particular king or to a lord but to a universal law such as rajdharma. Even at the moment of abject submission he, in his own way, internalizes the principle of rajdharma, on whose basis he might recognize or challenge any violation of it. From the same belief structure, he can rationalize both defiance as well as submission. During the Rangpur rebellion of 1783, peasants raised slogans against Devi Singh, saying "Dine zalim kutha asht" (the religion of the oppressor is short). The religious message that teaches submission also forms the basis of rebellion. Again, at the very moment of insurrection, peasants are quite capable of accepting a theory of kingship such as rajdharma, while rebelling against a particular king. Thus collaboration and resistance, the two elements in the mentality of subalternity, merge and coalesce to make up a complex and contradictory consciousness. How this consciousness overcomes and transcends its contradictions is another question.

Notes

For specific references and detailed quotations, see the Bengali version of this article in *Anustup*, autumn, 1987. However, essential notes and references have been cited. All the translations are mine. I am grateful to Dipesh Chakrabarty, who has thoroughly edited this essay and helped me formulate my ideas. I thank Ranajit Guha, Partha Chatterjee, and Gayatri Chakravorty Spivak for their comments.

1. Dewan Manulla Mandal, *Kantanama* or *Rajdharma*, ed. Nalinikanta Bhattasali (Dacca Sahitya Parishat Granthabali, no. 8, 1320 B.S., Calcutta, 1913; cited hereafter as *KN*).

2. *KN*, p. 80.

3. Introduction by Bhattasali, ibid., pp. 14–19.

4. *KN*, p. 5.

5. Ibid., pp. 8, 16.

6. *Papers Regarding the Village of Rural Indigenous Agency Employed in Taking the Bengal Census of 1872* (Calcutta, 1873, Bengal Govt. selections, no. 47), pp. 27–28.

7. F. O. Bell, *Final Report on the Survey and Settlement Operations in the District of Dinajpur, 1934–40* (Calcutta, 1942), pp. 9–11, para. 42; p. 88, para. 72.

8. Francis Buchanan-Hamilton, *A Geographical, Statistical and Historical Description of the District or Zilla of Dinajpur* (Calcutta, 1833), p. 250.

9. Bell, *Final Report, Dinajpur*, p.16, para. 16; F. W. Strong, *Eastern Bengal District Gazetteer: Dinajpur* (Allahabad, 1912), pp. 33–34; F. Hartley, *Final Report on the Survey and Settlement Operations in Rangpur, 1931–38* (Alipore, 1940), p. 45, para. 20.

10. *KN*, pp. 9–11.

11. Ibid., pp. 75–76.

12. Ibid., p. 82.

13. Ibid., p. 91.

14. S. C. Nandy, *History of the Cossimbazar Raj*, vol. 1 (Calcutta, 1986), p. 286.

15. *KN*, p. 105.

16. Ibid., pp. 106–7.

17. Strong, *Gazetteer: Dinajpur*, pp. 36–37. *Report on the Survey and Settlement of the Churaman Estate* (Calcutta, 1891), p. 9.

18. Bell, *Final Report, Dinajpur*, p. 11, para. 12.

19. Buchanan-Hamilton, *Description*, pp. 92–93, 111.

20. Bell, *Final Report, Dinajpur*, pp. 9–13; Atulchandra Chakraborty, "Pashim Dinajpurer tin laukik debata," *Pratilipi*, Ashvin 1388, 3rd issue; Golam Saklaen, *Purba*

Pakistaner sufi sadhak (Dacca, 1368 B.S.), pp. 63–68; Hartley, *Final Report, Rangpur*, pp. 84–87.

21. J. C. Sengupta, *West Bengal District Gazetteer, West Dinajpur* (1965), pp. 84–87.

22. Strong, p. 239; J. L. Sherwill, *Geographical and Statistical Report of the Dinajpur District* (Calcutta, 1863), p. 28.

23. G. A. Grierson, "The Song of Manik Chandra," *Journal of Asiatic Society of Bengal* 47 (1878): 35–238.

24. G. A. Grierson, "Notes on the Rangpur Dialect," *Journal of Asiatic Society of Bengal* 46 (1877): 201.

25. Dinesh Chandra Sen, *History of Bengali Language and Literature* (Calcutta, 1911), pp. 588–90; Sukumar Sen, "Kathakata," in *Bharatkosh*, vol. 2 (Calcutta, 1967), pp. 150–51. See also Bipinbihari Chakrabarti, *Khaturar itihas o Kushodvip kahini* (Calcutta, 1908).

26. W. K. Firminger, ed., *Bengal District Records: Dinajpur*, letter no. 194, dated 3 September 1787, vol. 2, 1786 (Calcutta, 1924).

27. Jogesh Chandra Roy Vidyanidhi, *Pauranik upakhyan* (Calcutta, 1361 B.S.), pp. 87–88. Cf. Dinendra Kumar Roy, *Sekaler smriti* (Calcutta, 1395 B.S.), pp. 42–43.

28. Bankimchandra Chattopadhyay, "Loksiksha," *Collected Works*, Samsad ed., vol. 2 (Calcutta, 1371 B.S.), p. 377.

29. Prankishor Goswami, *Kathakatar katha* (Calcutta, 1375 B.S.), pp. 19–20; Haripada Chakraborty, "Kathakatar punthi," in Ashutosh Bhattacharya and Asit Bandyopadhyay, eds., *Subarnalekha* (Calcutta, 1974), pp. 580–92.

30. Sashi Bhusan Dasgupta, *A Descriptive Catalogue of Bengali Manuscripts Preserved in the State Library of Cooch-Behar* (Calcutta, 1948); Sukumar Sen, *Bangla sahityer itihas*, pt. 1 (Calcutta, 1975), pp. 427, 447.

31. Gauri Shankar De, "Temple of Kantanagar," in *Proceedings of Indian History Congress* (Burdwan, 1983), pp. 592–603.

32. Grierson, "Rangpur Dialect," p. 226.

33. Sukumar Sen, *Bangla sahityer itihas*, pp. 424–25; Dinesh Sen, ed., *Krittibasi Ramayan* (Calcutta, 1955), introduction.

34. Sarat Chandra Mitra, "On the Cult of Sonaraya in Eastern Bengal," *Journal of the Department of Letters* (Calcutta University) 8 (1922): 141–72, 173–206.

35. Abdul Wali, "Notes on the Faqirs of Balia-dighi in Dinajpur," *Proceedings, Journal of Asiatic Society of Bengal* 72 (1903): 100; J. M. Ghosh, *Sannyasi and Fakir Raiders in Bengal* (Calcutta, 1920). For detailed descriptions on the Nath-Panthis, see Kalyani Mallik, *Nath-sampradayer itihas: darshan o sadhan pranali* (Calcutta, 1950), pp. 14–15, 102, 181.

36. Abdul Kalam Muhammad Jakaria, ed., *Sukur Muhammader Gopichander sanyas* (Dacca: Bangla Academy, 1974), pp. 92–94.

37. Bhakti Madhav Chattopadhyay, ed., *Ramai panditer sunya puran* (Calcutta, 1977), p. 160. Along with Professor Muhammad Shahidullah, the editor says that this part is a later edition and has been composed, probably, in the eighteenth century.

38. Cf. Mikhail Bakhtin, *Rabelais and His World* (Cambridge, Mass., 1968), chap. 1.

39. Grierson, "Rangpur Dialect," pp. 196–7.

40. *KN*, pp. 1–3.

41. Ibid., p. 87.

42. Ibid., p. 105.

43. Introduction to *Kantanama*, pp. 3–5.

44. *KN*, p. 71.

45. Strong, *Gazetteer: Dinajpur*, p. 27.

46. For the process, see Ratnalekha Ray, *Change in Bengal Agrarian Society, 1760–1860* (New Delhi, 1979), chap. 8; S. Taniguchi, "Structure of Agrarian Society in Northern Bengal" (unpublished thesis, Calcutta University, 1977).

47. Buchanan-Hamilton, *Description*, pp. 235–6.

48. Sherwill, *Dinajpur District*, p. 9; Grierson, "Rangpur Dialect," pp. 187–88.

49. *Survey and Settlement on Churaman Estate*, p. 36; *Survey and Settlement on Maldwar Wards Estate* (1891), para. 78.

50. Irfan Habib, *The Agrarian System of Mughal India* (Bombay, 1963), pp. 247–48; John R. Mclane, "Land Revenue Transactions in Eighteenth Century West Bengal," *Bengal Past and Present* 104 (1985): 1–23.

51. James Grant, *Historical and Comparative Analysis of Finances in Bengal*, in W. K. Firminger, ed., *Affairs of the East India Company (The Fifth Report)*, vol. 2, (reprint, New Delhi, 1984), pp. 205–31.

52. W. K. Firminger, *Historical Introduction to the Bengal Portion of the Fifth Report* (Calcutta, 1917; reprint, Calcutta, 1962), pp. 50–51.

53. Buchanan-Hamilton, *Description*, pp. 252–53.

54. T. Sisson, Judge and Magistrate of Rangpur, to Bayly, 2 April 1815, para. 35; Report of Mcleod on Crime, 30 September 1817, paras. 45–47, in E. G. Glazier, *Further Notes on Rungpore Records*, vol. 2 (Calcutta, 1876), appendix A, nos. 31–32.

55. T. Sisson to Bayly, 2 April 1915, para. 29.

56. Buchanan-Hamilton, *Description*, p. 236; J. H. Harrington's report to Charles Stewart on Pargana Swaruppore, 20 March 1790, Board of Revenue (BR), 22 March 1790, Proc. No.14/5, West Bengal State Archives (WBSA).

57. Petition of the Zamindars of Rungpur to Mr Purling, 1st of Aghoon, 1197, B.S., in Glazier, *Further Notes*, appendix G.

58. A petition from Zamindar of Baharband, Lokenath Nandi, BR, 16 June 1786, no. 30. Comm. of Revenue, 3 April 1786, Proc. no. 44 and 48, WBSA.

59. Somendra Chandra Nandy, *Life and Times of Cantoo Baboo*, vol. 1 (Calcutta, 1978), chaps. 2 and 4; vol. 2 (Calcutta, 1981).

60. Bell, *Final Report, Dinajpur*, p. 73, para. 55.

61. S. C. Nandy, *History of the Cassimbazar Raj in the Nineteenth Century*, vol. 1 (Calcutta, 1986), chap. 6.

62. J. W. Steer, 30 December 1835, Board of Revenue Wards (BRW), January 1836, no. 30, para. 30, WBSA.

63. *KN*, pp. 13–14.

64. Ibid., p. 17.

65. Ibid., p. 15.

66. T. Sisson, Magistrate Dinajpur to G. Dowdeswell, 11 July 1814, Judicial-Criminal, 19 August 1815, no. 1, paras. 2 to 4, WBSA.

67. Buchanan-Hamilton, *Description*, p. 252; Nandy, *Cassimbazar Raj*, vol. 1, pp. 44, 22.

68. *KN*, pp. 83–85.

69. Kaliprasanna Sinha, trans., *Mahabharat* (Bengali), Santi Parva (Basumati ed.), pp. 245, 253, 259; *The Mahabharatam* (Sanskrit, Arya Sastra ed.), p. 5999 (Sl. 138), p. 6022 (Sl. 16), p. 6037 (Sl. 104); Bhutnath Saptatirtha, ed. and trans, *Manusmritir Medhatithi Bhasya* (Calcutta, 1361 B.S.), pp. 633–38, Sl. 17–25; Panchanan Tarkaratna, ed. and trans., *Brihatdharma Puranam*, Uttar Khanda, 3, Sl. 13–19.

70. Kaliprasanna Sinha, *Mahabharat*, chap. 15, pp. 182–83, *Mahabharatam*, p. 5846, Sl. 6.

71. On rajdharma and danda, see Jan Gonda, *Ancient Indian Kingship from the Religious Point of View* (Leiden, 1966); Charles Drekmeir, *Kingship and Community in Early India* (Berkeley, 1962); and J. C. Heesterman, *The Inner Conflict of Tradition* (Delhi, 1985). I am most indebted to the classic work of P. V. Kane, *History of Dharmasastras*, vol. 3 (Poona, 1946), pp. 3–6.

72. *KN*, pp. 29–33.

73. Ibid.

74. *KN*, p. 28.

75. Ibid., p. 29.

76. All the descriptions and quotations are taken from translations of a representation from the ryots of Baharband; translation of the answer of Lokenath Nandy; and the humble petition of Lokenath Nandy, Zamindar of Baharband, Committee of Revenue, 3 April 1786, Proc. no. 49. See also "Particulars of the Reasons for Hutabood in 1189 B.S.," BR, 16 June 1786, Proc. no. 30, WBSA. For the early history of the pargana, see E. G. Glazier, *A Report on the District of Rungpore* (Calcutta, 1873), pp. 27–28, 84; Glazier, *Further Notes*, appendix C.

77. Nikhil Nath Roy, *Murshidabad Kahini* (1903; reprint, Calcutta, 1978), pp. 271–22.

78. *KN*, pp. 30–33.

79. Ibid.

80. Ibid., pp. 21–23.

81. Ibid., pp. 30–34.

82. Ibid., p. 20.

83. Ashutosh Bhattacharya, ed., *Gopichandrer Gan* (Calcutta University, 1965), pp. 1–6.

84. *KN*, p. 37. Cf. Anderson to J. P. Wards, Bankura, 13 May 1816, BRW, 31 May 1816, no. 30; Nandy, *Cossimbazar Raj*, vol. 1, pp. 45–46.

85. *KN*, p. 77.

86. Nandy, *Cossimbazar Raj*, pp. 173–74; BRW, May 1836, no. 48, WBSA.

87. *KN*, p. 78.

88. *Gopichandrer Gan*, p. 2.

89. The Arzee of the ryots of Purgunnah Lushkerpore, Proc. of the Provincial Council of Revenue, Murshidabad, 26 June 1775; the petition of the ryots, Pargana Silberry, ibid., 9 October 1779, WBSA.

90. *KN*, pp. 35–37, 77–78.

91. Ibid., p. 36.

92. Cf. Dipesh Chakrabarty, "On Deifying and Defying Authority: Managers and Workers in the Jute Mills of Bengal, 1890–1940," *Past and Present*, no. 100 (August 1983): 130–32. It must be noted, however, that in the colonial situation, this certainly had undergone some distortions where coercion was probably more pronounced than protection.

93. *KN*, pp. 19–20.

94. Ibid., p. 24.

95. Ibid., pp. 33, 38, 106.

96. Cf. *Mahabharat*, Santi Parva, chap. 87, p. 281. *Brahmavaivarta Puranam*, Mathuranath Tarkaratna, ed. and trans., chap. 90, Srikrishna Janmakanda, Sl. 6 (Calcutta, 1881–85); *Brihatdharma Puranam*, Uttar Khanda, chap. 3, Sl. 11.

97. Taranath Kavyatirtha, ed. and trans., *The Srimat Bhagavat* (Calcutta, 1373 B.S.), *skanda* 1, chap. 11, and *skanda* 4, chap. 21, pp. 282, 283.

98. Petition by Rani Bhavani, March 1775, quoted in A. B. M. Mahmood, *Revenue Administration of Northern Bengal* (Dacca, 1970), pp. 84–85.

99. E. V. Westmacott, "The Dinajpore Raj," *Calcutta Review*, 1872, p. 223.

100. *The Mahabharatam*, Santi Parva, chap. 68, Sl. 59.

101. Cf. R. Barthes, "Change the Object Itself," in *Image-Music-Text* (Glasgow, 1982), p. 165.

102. *KN*, pp. 18, 55, 59.

103. Ibid., pp. 55–59.

104. Ibid., pp. 63–67.

105. Ibid., pp. 23–24, for a description of *narak*, or hell. For similar descriptions of punishment for a revenue defaulter in the nawab's establishment, see "Madan Pala," quoted in Sukumar Sen, *Bangla sahityer itihas*, vol. 2, p. 487; for torture in the zamindar's establishment, see G. C. Dass, *Report on the Statistics of Rungpore for the Year 1872–73* (Calcutta, 1874).

106. *KN*, pp. 62–63.

107. Ibid., p. 4.

108. Ibid., p. 92.

109. Ibid., pp. 90–91.

110. Ibid., p. 12.

111. Ibid., p. 17.

112. Ibid., p. 56.

4 / Origins and Transformations of the Devi

David Hardiman

I

On 9 November 1922 about two thousand *adivasis*—the so-called original inhabitants or aboriginal peoples—who lived on the eastern borders of the Surat district of the Bombay presidency congregated in a field near a village called Khanpur. Coming from six different villages, they had gathered to listen to the teachings of a new goddess of great power known as Salabai. This *devi* was supposed to have come from the mountains to the east, and she expressed her demands through the mouths of spirit mediums. These mediums sat before the crowd under a *mandva*, a shade of leaves placed over a wooden frame. Holding red cloths in their hands they began to shake their heads and were soon in a state of trance. Then, as if reading from their cloths, they pronounced the commands of the Devi: to stop drinking liquor and toddy, to stop eating meat and fish, to live a clean and simple life, to bathe twice a day (men) or thrice a day (women), and to have nothing to do with Parsis. When they had finished, the adivasis filed one by one past a little girl who was dressed as the Devi, laying offerings of coins before her. They then sat down to a common dinner, known as *bhandara*, before dispersing.

This event was reported two days later to the assistant collector of Surat district by the officer in charge of Valod *taluka*.[1] It was the first eyewitness report of a Devi-inspired gathering to find its way into the records of the Bombay government. In the following days, as the cult spread into Surat district, fresh reports came thick and fast.[2] Everywhere adivasis were gathering together in large numbers to listen to the commands of the Devi. It was believed that those who failed to obey her would suffer misfortune at the least and perhaps become mad or die. By mid-November, the whole of Valod taluka was affected; by late November, the cult had spread to Bardoli and Mandvi talukas. No adivasi village in this area was left untouched. By 2 December, it had reached Jalalpur taluka and by 14 December Surat city and the coastal areas. In December, some new commands of the Devi began to be heard. Salabai was telling the adivasis to take vows in Gandhi's name, to wear khadi cloth, and to attend nationalist schools. Rumors were heard that spiders were writing Gandhi's name in cobwebs. It was said that Gandhi had fled from jail and could be seen sitting in a well side by side with Salabai, spinning his *charkha* (spinning wheel).[3]

Government officials expected it to be a passing affair. As one of them commented: "This is the tenth time within my knowledge that such rumours to stop drink are spread among Kaliparaj. Such rumours spread rapidly but the effect has always been temporary."[4] The officer's expectations were, however, to be proved wrong this time, for the Devi was to have a lasting effect on the area. In his annual report for 1922–23, the collector of Surat district, A. M. Macmillan, noted that the impact of the Devi continued, particularly in the area in which the adivasi *jati* (community) known as the Chodhris predominated. In that area, liquor and toddy drinking had to a large extent stopped, and there was a marked improvement in the material condition of the adivasis. In response to popular demand, Macmillan closed fifteen liquor shops in the region.[5] In the following year, Macmillan reported:

> The beneficial effects in the Chowdra areas of Mandvi where the effects of the movement persisted were obvious.
>
> The people did not require to borrow from sawkars to pay their land revenue instalments, as they had always previously done whether seasons were good or bad. They reduced their ceremonial expenses and so did not need to resort to sawkars for advances for this purpose. Their general appearance, and the appearance of their houses and villages is noticeably improved, and they are able to afford to use brass cooking vessels and to buy better clothes and ornaments for their wives.[6]

The Devi movement of South Gujarat had many features in common with adivasi movements in other parts of India during the late nineteenth and early twentieth centuries. In 1914–15, the Oraons of

Chhotanagpur were, for instance, enjoined by divine command to give up superstitious practices and animal sacrifices, to stop eating meat and drinking liquor, to cease plowing their fields, and to withdraw their field labor from non-adivasi landowners. Known as the Tana Bhagat movement, it "spread from village to village till it extended almost all over the Oraon country at one time."[7] As with the Devi, it took a nationalist turn, with invocations being made to the enemy of the British at that time, the German Baba.[8] Another such movement occurred in 1921 among the Bhumij of Chhotanagpur. In that year, a rumor spread that a new king had appeared on earth who was the incarnation of God himself. He told the Bhumij to give up taking liquor, fish, and meat. The movement spread very fast. People disposed of their chickens and goats in any way they could. In the following year, there was a bumper crop, which convinced the adivasis that their action had been correct. Three or four years later, the name of the king was revealed as being that of Gandhi Mahatma.[9] Many similar movements are reported in Stephen Fuch's *Rebellious Prophets* and K. S. Singh's *Tribal Movements in India*.[10] From this literature, it seems that almost all of the major adivasi communities of the middle Indian region, stretching from Bengal in the east to Gujarat in the west, have during the past century made such collective efforts to change their established way of life.[11]

Unfortunately, these accounts are for the most part sketchy, being confined either to short articles or to single chapters in more general studies of a particular "tribe."[12] There is not, to my knowledge, a full-length monograph that makes one such movement its subject. The available studies have been almost entirely by anthropologists rather than historians. In part, this is because there is a dearth of archival information on the subject. The government records and newspapers of the day provide a wealth of information about the contemporary nationalist campaigns of the Congress; about these relatively peaceful movements for collective reform they are virtually silent. In some cases, a government file may be found, as well as a few stray reports in the newspapers. Often we do not have even that. To a large extent, therefore, we have to rely on oral evidence taken from those who participated in these movements. Such evidence is not easily collected. The researcher has to go to the villages and share the life of the adivasis, often for prolonged periods. On the whole, it has been anthropologists rather than historians who have subjected themselves to such rigors. Relying often entirely on oral evidence, the historical accuracy of these anthropological accounts tends as a rule to be extremely low.[13]

There is another reason for the silence of historians about such movements, which is that they do not fit easily into the prevailing historiographies of modern India, these being, broadly speaking, either nationalistic or socialistic. Ranajit Guha has depicted the writing of nationalistic history as an attempt "to represent Indian nationalism as primarily an idealist venture in which the indigenous elite led the people from subjugation to freedom."[14] Such a historiography finds it hard to come to terms with the fact that these movements were started and carried on by the adivasis themselves. In some cases, there is a straight denial of adivasi initiative. Jugatram Dave has argued in his history of the Gandhian movement among the adivasis of South Gujarat that the Devi movement was inspired by the activities of Gandhi and his followers in the region in the preceding years. No account is taken of the fact that similar doctrines had been circulating among the adivasis of the area long before Gandhi arrived on the scene.[15] Another technique found in such writings is to relegate to insignificance the early stages of adivasi initiative while throwing a spotlight on the bourgeois social workers who commonly went to the adivasi villages at a late stage of the movement. A picture is thus drawn of dedicated nationalists going to virgin areas of adivasi backwardness to "uplift the tribals." A good example of this form of distortion is provided by Mahadev Desai's *Story of Bardoli.*

Desai's task is to explain the success of Gandhian social workers among the adivasis of the Bardoli-Valod region in the period after 1922. He begins his account by discussing Gandhian work in that area in 1921–22 and then follows it with the bald statement, "A strong wave of social reform had passed over the Kaliparaj community, a large number of whom had taken solemn pledges to abjure liquor, toddy, etc."[16] No mention is made of any Devi, the impression being given that the reforms resulted from the work of the nationalist cadres. He goes on:

> Ever since constructive work among these people has been making considerable headway, every year they have been having conferences and Khadi exhibitions, the models of their kind, and thanks to the efforts of Sjt. Chunilal Mehta and his wife, who have consecrated themselves to the services of this community, there are numerous people among them who live purer lives than their more fortunate brethren in the taluka. Many of their families spin and weave their own yarn, have abjured drink and exercise a great moral influence over the rest of their people. The school for the boys of the com-

munity under Sjts. Lakshmidas Purushottam and Jugatram Dave has turned out quite a number of workers who have gone into the villages to act as leaven to raise the lump.[17]

Whereas the high-caste Gandhian social workers are dignified with their individual names, the adivasis are depicted as a mere collective "lump" to be "leavened." There is no doubt as to who is the subject of this history.

Nationalist histories, written as these are to legitimize the position of the Indian bourgeoisie, are easily criticized at a factual level. All the evidence shows that the adivasis themselves initiated and carried on these movements. The fundamental task of socialist historians should be to expose such mythologies for what they are. Unfortunately, they have for the most part been more concerned with building their own mythologies. S. V. Parulekar begins his account of the movement among the Varlis of Umargam and Dahanu talukas of Thana district in 1945–46 thus:

> The basic cause of the mass upsurge of the Varlis lay in their abominable condition of wretchedness and their suppression by the tyrant landlords. They had rotted in these conditions for a century unnoticed and uncared for. . . . They lived in a mood of bitter despair. They were anxious to end their slavery. But they did not know how to do it. They needed somebody who would extend to them his helping hand, show them the road to their freedom, guide them, take their side against their oppressors and stand by them and lead them in their fight to be free men.
> This need was fulfilled by the Kisan Sabha.[18]

The history thus starts at the point at which the middle-class socialist leader arrives among a people whom Parulekar categorizes as "naive and innocent . . . aboriginal hill tribes."[19] They are raised quickly from their slough of ignorance to a state of advanced socialist consciousness:

> The experience of the bitter struggle through which the Varli had to wade had rapidly transformed him. His transformation had been so radical that he became a new being. He had been quite an innocent infant in understanding and consciousness. Straight from infancy he stepped into maturity. He has advanced with a breathless speed to overtake the peasants who had been far ahead of him by omitting many an intermediary step.
> He had developed a thirst for knowledge. He had become very keen to know all about Soviet Russia.[20]

The history ends on a note of triumph, claiming a great victory for the Varlis. In fact, the Varlis of the area continue to this day to be among the most exploited of all adivasi communities of western India. Such an account cannot even start to explain this paradox. The victory was not, in fact, of the Varlis, but of the Kisan Sabha leaders whose role as vanguard socialists appeared to have been vindicated. As history, accounts of this sort are in no way superior to the writings of the nationalists, for in both cases the adivasis are appropriated to an external cause. Their role in the making of their own history is correspondingly ignored.[21]

In such socialist histories, the religiosity of the adivasis is ignored, even though it must have had a profound bearing on their state of consciousness. As a rule, secular-minded socialist historians are either embarrassed by the existence of what they regard as mere superstitious belief and ignore it, or regard it as a form of primeval consciousness that is shed rapidly once the adivasis have been educated by socialist cadres. They confine their studies to highly militant struggles in which the economic cause of discontent appears to be of far greater consequence than any informing religious ideology. Less militant and more obviously "religious" movements, of the sort with which we are concerned here, appear to them to be suffused with a "backward-looking" or perhaps "petit bourgeois" religiosity, which they believe cripples the enterprise from the start. Such movements have, in consequence, been ignored.

There is little reason to believe that even if these historians did write such histories, the results would be at all satisfactory. This is because they subscribe to a dogmatic belief that religion is no more than a "hegemonic ideology" that is imposed on the peasantry by a dominant class so as to divide and rule.[22] Religion is seen as a political resource that is "used" by unscrupulous leaders to manipulate the peasantry for their own selfish ends. "Religion," it is argued, "is important for peasant consciousness not because peasant consciousness is inherently religious, but because religion is part of the ideological superstructure."[23] Only an impoverished historiography can be content with such formulations. All religions consist to a large extent of assimilated folk beliefs. It is this that gives them their mass appeal and great pertinacity over time. Religions are highly ambiguous, with seemingly identical sets of doctrines being made to serve quite contradictory causes. It is an elitist form of socialism that can view religion as merely an imposition from above.[24]

In this history of the Devi movement, I follow what I consider to be a more genuinely socialist course, which is to write a history of the adivasis in which they are the subject. The study is in this respect a part of the wider *Subaltern Studies* project, a prime aim of which is "to understand the consciousness that informed and still informs political actions taken by the subaltern classes on their own, independently of any elite initiative."[25] This consciousness was necessarily suffused with religion, for, as Partha Chatterjee says:

> the ideology which shaped and gave meaning to the various collective acts of the peasantry was fundamentally *religious*. The very nature of peasant consciousness, the apparently consistent unification of an entire set of beliefs about nature and about men in the collective and active mind of a peasantry, is religious. Religion to such a community provides an ontology, an epistemology as well as a practical code of ethics, including political ethics. When this community acts politically, the symbolic meaning of particular acts—their signification—must be found in religious terms.[26]

Religious belief and practice often reflected an aspiration for a better life, which was not merely located in the hereafter but also very much in the here and now. This aspiration grew from daily experience, representing an attempt to build a better future on an existing base.

II

To begin, we may ask where the Devi came from. Unfortunately, contemporary descriptions of the movement are very vague on this matter. Nobody seemed to know who had started it or why it had been started. There was considerable doubt about the place of origin and the direction in which it had traveled before it came to the attention of the authorities in November 1922. The propitiation cult thus appeared to have come out of the blue. This enhanced its mystery but at the same time made it all seem more bizarre and irrational. In carrying out my research, I felt that I needed to discover the origins of the Devi and her direction of travel, as I felt that this would help me to understand why the cult took the form it did and what it sought to achieve.

Statements about the origins of the Devi by officials and other contemporary observers were conflicting. B. D. Nasikwala, the Bardoli excise inspector, reported that the movement had started in Navapur taluka of West Khandesh and had spread west from there.[27] A. M. Macmillan, the collector of Surat, had a different view:

I have ascertained that the movement was started by Bhilbhagats in Kalwan and Peint [two talukas of Nasik district bordering Gujarat], who brought it to the Dangs. From there it was taken by groups of Dang Bhils to Nawapur (Khandesh) and Vyara (Baroda) to the states of Bansda and Dharampur, and to the eastern talukas of Surat.[28]

In a later report, Macmillan added that the movement had appeared originally in the previous year in northern Thana district.[29] This idea was backed up by a report from the police subinspector of Vyara taluka "that one Goddess Salebai is believed to have come in the form of apparitional wind from the Arabian Sea passing through Dang and Khandesh districts."[30] Others had different ideas. The nationalist leader of Bardoli taluka, Kunvarji Mehta, believed that the Devi had originated in West Khandesh but had come via Mulher and Salher in Baglan taluka of Nasik district.[31] The Baroda census report of 1931 said that it had been started in Baglan taluka by "religious zealots of the primitive revivalist type."[32] The police deputy superintendent of Baroda district of Navsari reported that "it is heard that certain butchers belonging to the Khandesh District have raised this trick in order to get the goats and sheep at low rate."[33] The suggestion that unscrupulous traders were behind the whole affair was put more forcibly by an American missionary working in the Dangs:

Some crafty "Ghantes," merchants from Nasik District, taking advantage of the ignorance and superstition of the simple Dangis, had brought in this cow goddess and instructed the people to sell their goats and chickens and grain for a mere pittance. These same merchants, who robbed the people of their few animals, sold coconuts for four times the proper price, saying the goddess must have offerings of coconuts, lest she bring sickness and death to their houses. From village to village, these avaricious merchants slyly followed the goddess and fleeced the people.[34]

Sumant Mehta, a Gandhian leader from Baroda who was active in the area at that time, wrote later in his memoirs that it was hard to discover the origins of the movement. According to one theory, it was started by adivasi teachers who believed that the habit of drinking liquor and toddy was ruining the adivasis. But this had never been proved. The Gandhian workers of South Gujarat had often made inquiries during the 1920s as to the source of the Devi, but they had failed to discover the truth of the matter.[35]

The only way in which I could get more information on this subject was to go myself to the Maharashtrian districts of West Khandesh (now Dhule) and Nasik and make inquiries among old adivasis. This I did in December 1981 and January 1982, traveling through the villages of Navapur, Sakri, Baglan, and Kalvan talukas. The general consensus of the adivasis whom I talked to in the Navapur and Pimpalner areas of West Khandesh was that the Devi had been brought by *gaulas*—spirit mediums—from the Kalvan area of Nasik district, via the Dangs. One old man said that the gaulas had a magic thread that had enabled them to walk on the waters of the Chankapur reservoir in Kalvan taluka.[36] Adivasis living in the valley that starts at Salher Mountain and runs east to the town of Mulher informed me that although the gaulas had come via the Dangs and were in many cases Dangis, they had brought Salabai from Kalvan taluka in the first instance. The towns of Abhona (near the Chankapur reservoir) and Vani were mentioned frequently.

I therefore traveled south to Abhona in the belief that I was at last reaching the source of the Devi. The first old man whom I met in the town, Morlidhar Jhadav, soon put me right: Salabai had come from the Gujarat side, via Surgana. Villagers in the area around Abhona with whom I talked during the next few days all, without exception, agreed with this. Salabai had come from Surgana via Chankapur to Abhona, and had then moved on in an easterly direction to the edge of the adivasi region. The goddess had been taken from one village to another by the villagers themselves; no gaulas had brought her. It seemed, therefore, that the gaulas who had taken the Devi from Kalvan to the Dangs and Khandesh must have started from Kalvan, in most cases being Dangi gaulas who had traveled south to "collect" the goddess. In a village between Abhona and Surgana called Delvat, I met an old adivasi, Ravji Pavji Powar, who was about sixteen years old at the time of Salabai. He had a fascinating story to tell:

At that time I decided to purchase some dried sea-fish [*bomla*, or "Bombay Duck"]. I set out on foot for the coast, going to Dharampur first of all. In Dharampur, I was told that Salabai had come and that I should buy a coconut for her before I proceeded. I heard the following rhyme being chanted:

"Ganji dongar chadla bai
Kachha sutane Salaibai."[37]

I then went to Dungri village, on the sea near Valsad, to buy the fish. The people told me that I could buy the fish, but that I could not eat it there because of the commands of Salabai. I could only eat it after I returned home. On my way back through Dharampur, I saw that Salabai was still moving about in that area. Mediums were holding red cloths and they were ordering the people to renounce liquor and meat and so on. I got back to Dalvat before Salabai arrived.

In June or July, after six months, people began saying that Salabai had come to Mankhed village in Surgana state. She took fifteen more days to reach Dalvat. . . . After that I had to throw away what remained of the dried fish I had bought in Dungri!

A couple of months before I started these inquiries in Maharashtra, I had already interviewed some adivasis of the Dharampur and Pardi areas. At the time, I had been baffled by the information, given to me by the majority of them, that the goddess (known there as the "Baya") had come from the Daman side, that is, from the coast. My initial hypothesis, based on this information, was that the goddess had come down the coast from the region around Surat city and had then gone inland. But now it seemed that the Devi had in fact originated in the coastal area around Daman and had traveled eastward to Kalvan, northwest to the Dangs, northeast to Khandesh, and then west toward Valod, Bardoli, and Surat.

The next step in my quest was, therefore, to tour the villages between Dungri and Daman. There I found that although everyone remembered the Baya, few had any idea where she came from. The little information I could get suggested that she came from the south, from the Umargam side. Traveling to Umargam, I met an old seaman called Babarbahi Machhi (of the fisherman caste) who told me quite categorically and with a wealth of convincing detail that the Baya or Mata had come from Palghar taluka in Thana district. My search had brought me back once more to Maharashtra, this time to the coastal region between Bombay city and the Gujarat border. My first trip to Palghar taluka brought disappointing results, and it was only after meeting Sudha Mokashi, a Bombay-based economist, that I was able to obtain better information. She had carried out her doctoral research among the fisherfolk of coastal Thana, and she agreed to accompany me to villages where she had good contacts.

From these interviews, it appeared that there was no Devi movement as such in the Palghar region. However, there was at the time an epidemic of smallpox, brought, so the people believed, by a goddess, or Baya. This goddess had to be propitiated. Female spirit mediums allowed themselves to be possessed by the Baya so that she could, through their mouths, make her wishes known. The mediums were known as *salabai*—woman (*bai*) who gives advice (*sala*).[38] While the ceremony continued, everyone had to stop eating fish and drinking liquor and toddy. To complete the rites, the villagers took a representation of the Baya in a basket to the border of their village. From there she was passed from village to village. It appears that she went only in a northerly direction, as I could not find any evidence of such a propitiation ceremony in the coastal villages of Vasai taluka, to the south of Palghar. My conclusion was, therefore, that the Devi movement originated as a smallpox propitiation ceremony that started in the fishing villages of Palghar taluka, probably in late 1921 or early 1922, and traveled northward and to the east before progressing northwesterly.

III

The maritime region of Thana, known as the Bandarpatti, consists of a narrow strip of land lying between the Arabian Sea and the Sahyadri Mountains. It is cut into by a succession of inlets, so that only the fishermen with their boats could travel at all freely from village to village along the coast. The chief fishing community of the Palghar area was that of the Mangela Kolis. They worked largely as fishermen, coastal traders and shippers, and laborers. Worshipping Hindu deities, they ate fish and meat, drank liquor and toddy, and sacrificed live animals to their gods and goddesses. They spoke a mixed Marathi-Gujarati dialect.[39] While carrying on their occupation, they traveled frequently to the ports of Gujarat, such as Surat and Broach.[40] The other major community of this area, the Vaittis, were mainly river fishers and peasant cultivators. These were the two communities chiefly involved in the propitiation cult of late 1921 or early 1922. The Son Kolis, the predominant fishing community to the south, do not appear to have been involved at all.[41]

Although my informants in Palghar taluka were sure that the phenomenon of that time was a smallpox propitiation ceremony, there was a seeming drawback to this explanation, namely that in 1921 and 1922 no epidemics of smallpox were reported in the area. On the contrary, the number of deaths from smallpox were the lowest for many years. In Thana district, smallpox mortality by year was as follows:[42]

1913: 269   1918: 264
1914: 314   1919: 268
1915: 94   1920: 51
1916: 129   1921: 54
1917: 250   1922: 48

In addition, there were no severe outbreaks of plague, cholera, or influenza in 1921 or 1922.

Smallpox statistics were, however, notoriously unreliable. Most villagers believed that the disease was caused by the smallpox goddess Sitaladevi, and that the government, in trying to stop her progress through such means as inoculation, would enrage her still further. As a result, they went to great pains to conceal outbreaks of smallpox from government officials.[43] It is not unreasonable to assume therefore that there was an outbreak of smallpox in coastal Palghar that was never reported to the government. The government presence in these coastal villages was very slight, as they were fishing villages that yielded very little land tax, and an outbreak could easily have escaped the notice of the authorities. In addition, to have a propitiation ceremony, it was not necessary that there be many actual cases of smallpox. Sitaladevi was considered to be present even if there was only one victim.

In fact, it was probably the very insignificance of the outbreak that allowed this particular smallpox propitiation ceremony to be transformed later into a ceremony with very different aims. If there had been a full-scale epidemic, it is probable that the rites would have remained embedded in their original context of smallpox. With this context soon lost, as the goddess traveled away from the original local outbreak, it became a freer force that was easily turned into a ceremony with its chief justification the renunciation of liquor and meat. The very *lack* of a major epidemic was thus a necessary precondition for the transformation of the cult.[44]

The ceremony that was held in village after village up the coast was remarkably similar to the smallpox propitiation rites described in the ethnographic literature. James Campbell and R. E. Enthoven have given detailed accounts of these rites in the Konkan (of which Thana district formed the northernmost portion).[45] The normal pattern was, first of all, for spirit mediums, known as *bhagats* in the Konkan, to allow themselves to be possessed by the goddess who had caused the outbreak, so that her wishes could be known. She could then be propitiated. This could involve worship at the shrine or temple of the smallpox goddess, Sitaladevi. In such cases, the ceremony often took a Brahmanical form. More often, however, the goddess was worshipped either at a public place, such as at a crossroads outside the village, or in the house of a person who was suffering from the disease. As it was considered that Sitaladevi had actually entered the body of the victim, he or she was worshipped as a personification of the goddess.[46] The deity could be worshipped in other forms. Most commonly, she was represented by a metal *lota* (drinking pot), on the neck of which was placed a coconut.[47] Often, a woman of the village was dressed to represent the goddess, and it was she who was worshipped.

The ceremony normally continued for about nine days, which corresponds to the duration of the disease in a person who survives, from the beginning of the symptoms to their subsiding. Lastly, the goddess had to be sent away from the village. In a few cases, she was made to enter an animal, such as a buffalo or goat, which was then driven far from the village and abandoned. But more common was the *paradi* ceremony, in which the goddess was enticed through offerings of food and sacrificial victims to quit the village. A large shallow basket was filled with cooked rice and other materials of worship, such as *kanku* (red powder). A goat was sacrificed and its head was placed on the rice.[48] The villagers then took the basket with its contents to the border of their village. In some cases, the basket was buried there and the ceremony was repeated with a fresh basket in the next village.[49] In other cases, the same basket was passed from village to village until it reached the sea, where it was immersed.

The propitiation ceremony of the Mangela Kolis and Vaittis conformed to this pattern. As their spirit mediums were normally female, women were possessed by the goddess and made her wishes known. One of these wishes was that they abstain from alcoholic drinks and meat and fish for the duration of the ceremony. The ceremonies were carried out in a number of different houses; these were normally the ones in which someone was suffering from smallpox. To close the ceremony, a basket was prepared full of objects that please the goddess, and it was taken to the border of the neighboring village. After the "departure" of the goddess, the people began once more to eat fish and drink liquor and toddy.[50]

The giving up of meat, fish, and alcohol for the duration of the ceremony was an important feature that does not appear in the accounts of Campbell and Enthoven. However, the people of the area insisted in interviews that this was a regular feature of such ceremonies. It is common in Hindu rites to avoid "polluting" substances during a ceremony, and the avoidance of flesh and liquor conforms to this practice. In addition, meat and liquor were considered to be "heating" foods, and as Sitaladevi—the "cool one"—was believed to be angered by heat, it may have been considered wise to placate her by abstaining from such substances while she was in the village.[51] There was also an absence of animal sacrifice in the propitiation rites of the Palghar area. Again, the local informants told me that this was the normal custom in their area.

From the coastal villages of Palghar, the goddess moved in a northerly direction. Why north? Probably because the people of this area had more cultural connections with the north than with the south. The gazetteer for Thana district of 1882 notes that in the coastal strip north of the Vaitarna River (which divides Palghar from Vasai taluka), the language of all classes, except for a few Maratha immigrants, was Gujarati rather than Marathi. Gujarati was the medium of instruction in government schools, and those who knew only Marathi could not easily make themselves understood in the region.[52] South of the Vaitarna in Vasai taluka, there was a high proportion of Marathi-speaking Christians—the product of the long Portuguese occupation of this area. If the goddess had been sent to the south, it is unlikely that these Christians would have passed her on. As it was vital that she be sent away as far as possible, it was wiser to send her northward where the people had the same beliefs.

In the Dahanu-Umargam area, the propitiation ceremony was taken up by the chief community of that region, the Gujarati-speaking Machhi community. Like the Mangela Kolis, the Machhis were for the most part fishermen, sailors, and laborers. Their religious and dietary habits were also similar. Enthoven mentions that they were strong believers in magic, the evil eye, evil spirits, and omens, and that they worshipped the goddess Sitaladevi during epidemics.[53] These Gujarati Machhis were found in coastal villages from Dahanu in Thana district to the area near Surat city.[54] Once they had taken up the propitiation ceremony, there was nothing to stop it from spreading up the coast as far as Surat.

In Umargam town, which has a large Machhi population, men and women were possessed by the goddess, which by then had become known generally as the Baya. They were not regular spirit mediums. In Umargam, there does not seem to have been a smallpox outbreak as such; the Machhis were merely propitiating a powerful goddess who could, in their eyes, cause them much harm. Those who were possessed sat before a *patla* (low stool) on which was placed a pot with a coconut and tree leaves sitting on the neck, kanku, and uncooked rice and other grains. The mediums shook their heads in the manner known in Gujarati as *dhunvu* (a verb meaning "to be possessed by a spirit or god"). They ordered everyone present to give up liquor, toddy, fish, and meat and to take a daily bath. The Machhis set free their goats so that they would not be tempted to eat them. After eight days, a married woman took the patla and pot on her head and immersed it in the sea. The goddess then passed on to the next Machhi village, where the ceremony was repeated. Like the Mangela Kolis and Vaithis, the Machhis went back to drinking liquor and toddy and eating fish and meat after the goddess had been sent on her way.

It was at this stage that the ceremony was taken up by the adivasis of South Gujarat, and in particular by the Dhodiyas. This was the chief adivasi community in the area stretching from Umargam taluka in the south to Mahuva taluka in the north. In 1921, the Dhodiya population was 130,307.[55] They straddled the border between Maharashtra and Gujarat, speaking a dialect that was basically Gujarati, but with some Marathi influence.[56] They were considered by government officials to be the most "civilized" of the "tribes" of South Gujarat, in that they lived a more settled life and were more efficient cultivators than the neighboring Varlis and Konkanas.[57] Despite this, they were hardly at all Hinduized in their religion, and they ate meat and were very fond of liquor.[58]

As the Dhodiyas and Machhis lived alongside each other, the Baya must have passed from the latter to the former in many villages. Atabhai Patel, a Dhodiya of Namdha, a village in Pardi taluka close to the border with Daman and Umargam, described in an interview what happened there. The Baya was brought by Machhis from Daman who came and told them of the visitation and the means they had used to propitiate the goddess. After the Machhis had completed their propitiation rites, the Dhodiyas of Namdha began to *dhun*. From house to house people became possessed. Atabhai's aunt was one of them. She had a patla with a red cloth on it, on which was a pot with a coconut. She told them not to eat fish, not to drink *daru* (country liquor), not to eat chicken, and to take a daily bath. After two days, she stopped "dhuning" and the goddess passed on to another house. Only while she was possessed did her family abstain from liquor and flesh.

At this stage, the propitiation wave was transformed into a movement for permanent social reform. It is difficult to find out exactly how this happened. The most likely explanation is that there was among certain Dhodiyas a climate of opinion in favor of social reform, and the propitiation ceremony, which involved renouncing liquor and flesh for a temporary period, provided a heaven-sent opportunity (in a literal sense!) to launch a movement for permanent reform. This was by no means the first time there had been an antiliquor movement among the Dhodiyas, and it was not unknown for such reforms to be furthered through spirit possession.[59]

Although the intentions of the Baya propitiation thus changed, the actual ceremony remained the same. The goddess proceeded from house to house, with Dhodiya men and women becoming possessed. The people of each neighborhood gathered and watched while the mediums sat before a pot and coconut, shaking their heads and pronouncing the commands of the Baya. These were to abstain from daru, toddy, meat, and fish and to take a daily bath. In some cases, tea was served as a substitute for liquor. The ceremony continued for a week to nine days (the latter figure recurred frequently in interviews), with the mediums being possessed at regular intervals each day. On the last day, the paraphernalia—patla, pot, coconut, and so on—was taken to the nearest stream and immersed. Although the Dhodiyas were expected to conform to the commands of the Baya permanently, the large majority did not in practice do so. A good number, however, maintained their reformed life for months, if not years. In addition, several of those who were possessed became "reformed bhagats"—spirit mediums who sought to heal their fellows by making them live the reformed life. As some of them were successful in this practice, they were believed to retain certain powers that the Baya had bestowed on them during her visitation.

The other important development at this stage was that the goddess ceased to move in a northerly direction up the coast and now started to move eastward toward the mountains. This was in accordance with Dhodiya custom. A. N. Solanki, the only sociologist to have carried out a full study of the Dhodiyas, mentions that when a goddess visits them and causes an epidemic, they carry out a propitiation ceremony that involves the preparation of a miniature wooden chariot, known as a *rath*. They "persuade" the goddess to enter this rath by carrying out sacrifices. They then take the rath to the border of the village and pass it on to the next village. The inhabitants of that village convey it to their boundary, and so it moves far away. Solanki notes, "These chariots are always moved from the west to the east so that all such chariots pass on with all their paraphernalia toward the hills and forests of the Western Ghats a few miles away."[60] Among the Dhodiyas, goddesses thus moved toward the mountains, and this is indeed what happened in 1922.

Before the mountains were reached, the Dhodiya community gave way to other adivasi groups. The chief of these were the Varlis and Konkanas. The Varlis, whose population in 1921 was 124,859, were found chiefly in Thana (in 1921, 86 percent of them lived in that district). There was, however, a sizable population of Varlis in southern Dharampur state. They were the most depressed of all the major adivasi jatis of western India, being exploited ruthlessly by landlords and moneylenders.[61] Among them, there was no sentiment for social reform and, although they were careful to propitiate the Baya when she reached their villages, they, like the coastal fisherfolk, relapsed into their old ways as soon as she had been passed on to the next village. The Konkanas, however, interpreted the message of the Baya in the same spirit as the Dhodiyas—as a call for permanent reform.

The Konkanas were the largest of all of the adivasi jatis of this region. It is hard to calculate their total population in 1921, as they were spread over several different administrative areas and in many parts called themselves Kunbis, so that in the census reports many of them were counted as Maratha Kunbis. Grierson estimated that there were 232,613 Konkani speakers.[62] This is probably an overestimate; 180,000 is, I believe, a more realistic figure for the early twentieth century.[63] The large majority of the Konkanas were settled in the fertile valleys of the Sahyadri ranges, in the region in which these mountains divided Gujarat from Maharashtra. By damming and channeling the numerous rivers running off these mountains, they were able to grow excellent crops. By tradition they had migrated to this region from the Konkan.[64] According to one account, they were soldiers who had served in Shivaji's armies and who, after campaigning in these areas, decided to settle there. In another account, the migration north was caused by the terrible Durgadev famine of 1390–1408, which devastated the Konkan.[65] Both traditions may have truth in them, for migration could have taken place in two waves. However, it is significant that the area that formed the heartland of the medieval kingdom of Baglan was inhabited predominantly by Konkanas. The capital of Baglan was Mulher, and even today the Konkanas of the valley running from Salher to Mulher maintain an elaborate irrigation system that is of great antiquity. In the sixteenth and seventeenth centuries, the kingdom of Balgan was renowned for its exports of high-quality rice, sugar, and fruit.[66] It is likely that these irrigation systems were constructed by the Konkanas after their migration north in the early fifteenth century, and that this jati formed the peasant base for this small but successful kingdom. Although the Konkanas of Nasik district and the Dangs were known as Kunbis, they were relatively un-Hinduized in their religion and were classified as adivasis. They ate meat and drank liquor.[67] Like the Dhodiyas, they had a reputation for being good agriculturists. According to the settlement officer for Nandurbar and Navapur talukas of West Khandesh: "In both industry and intelligence, they [the Konkanas] are immensely superior to Bhils and Mavchis. Their villages are substantial, their lands generally clean, well tilled and in constant occupation."[68]

In the area of Dharampur state in which the Dhodiyas and Konkanas lived side by side, the Baya propitiation ceremony of the Konkanas was identical to the one described above for the Dhodiyas. But once the goddess reached the eastern borders of Dharampur, where the Konkanas became the predominant jati, certain changes began to appear. The goddess ceased to be known as the Baya, becoming "Sellabai" or "Salaibai." There were local versions of the name "Salaibai" given to the women who had been possessed by the goddess in coastal Thana, but now the term was used for the goddess herself. Another name used for her was "Ghumribai." This came from *ghumri*, which is a noun meaning "the process of dhuning." In a few cases, the name of Gandhi was mentioned. For instance, a Konkana medium in the village of Behudna, which lay in Surgana close to the border with Dharampur, said when possessed: "Ghumribai, Ghumribai, Sellabai . . . Gandhi Maharaj, Gandhi Maharaj, Sellabai."[69] There was also the rhyme heard by Ravji Pavji Powar mentioned earlier:

> Ganji dongar chadla bai,
> Kachha sutane Salaibai.

"Ganji" was almost certainly a wrong pronunciation of "Gandhi," and the probable meaning was that Salabai, with the help of a weak thread (i.e., with considerable difficulty) had climbed Gandhi's hill. In Chankal village in the Dangs, an old Konkana told me: "In a song it is said that the woman Salabai was Devi. She came from the hill of Gandhi."[70] The ideal seems to have been that Salabai had been somehow generated by Gandhi, being based on an understanding that their programs of abstinence from meat and liquor were similar. However, the Konkanas had not heard of Gandhi at the time, and so the significance of the idea was lost on them and the rhyme became merely an empty incantation.[71]

The other innovation was a change in the closing ceremony in which the goddess was passed from one village to another. After each ceremony (lasting up to nine days), the paraphernalia of red cloth, pot, and coconut was either placed on a patla or put in a basket and carried to the border of the village by a young girl who had not reached puberty (she was normally between about eight and twelve years old). At the border, a hole was dug in the ground and the villagers filed past, throwing small coins into it. They also brought coconuts, which were broken; a portion was thrown in the pit and the rest eaten. The paraphernalia was then placed in the pit and buried. After that, the people of the next village began to dhun and the whole process was repeated.

The dressing up of women as a representative of the Devi was a common practice in propitiation rites.[72] Enthoven reported the following custom among the Bhils of Nasik district:

> When a severe epidemic attacks a village and will not yield to the ordinary remedies, a woman is selected from among the poorest classes and is well fed for several days; she is then dressed in fine clothes, placed on a cart, and escorted with great ceremony to the confines of the village by the whole of the residents. With her departure, the disease is supposed to depart too.[73]

The chief difference between this description and the Salabai propitiation ceremony of 1922 was that in the latter a prepubescent girl, rather than a woman, performed the role of goddess. This appears to have been novel; I have been unable to discover any reference to such a practice elsewhere. It was, perhaps, connected with the belief that this particular goddess—Salabai—demanded ritual purity, and a mature woman who was subject to the monthly cycle of "pollution" would not have been acceptable to her. In other respects, the use of such a representative of the Devi largely conformed to the practices recorded by Enthoven and Crooke.

The burying of the paraphernalia in a hole was likewise common in passing-on ceremonies for disease goddesses. James Campbell has described such a ceremony in a village near Bhiwandi in Thana district. An arch, or *toran*, was first erected at the boundary of the village:

> The villagers bathed, put on new clothes, and then a procession was formed. The *veskar* or village watchman walked in front, and next to him came the *patil* or the village headman, the *madhavi* or the village crier, and then the principal men of the village. On coming to the *toran* or triumphal arch the whole procession stopped. A hole was dug in the ground, and the village watchman put in it the head of a sheep, a coconut, betelnuts and leaves, and flowers. The *toran* or arch was then worshipped by each of the villagers.[74]

In the case of the propitiation of Salabai, the Devi-girl replaced the toran as the object of worship. Each villager filed past her, offering a coin to her by casting it into the pit. No sheep's head was buried, of course, as Salabai had ordered them not to take life. In other respects, the two ceremonies were similar.

On the whole, the Konkanas interpreted the message of the goddess to be a command to give up meat and liquor and to take a daily bath for the rest of their lives. In practice, many relapsed into their old ways after Salabai had gone, but a significant number appear to have kept to the commands for months and in some cases years. In contrast to the Dhodiya areas, however, hardly any Konkanas became reformed bhagats.[75]

In Kalvan taluka, where the movement now spread, much of the local trade and moneylending was carried on by members of the Shimpi and Teli castes. By tradition, the Shimpis were tailors and the Telis oil-pressers. They were found mostly in the small towns of the area, such as Abhona, Vani, and Kanasi. When Salabai reached these towns from the surrounding Konkana villages, the Shimpis and Telis also came under her influence. In Abhona, I was given a graphic description by an eyewitness of how one such Shimpi was possessed:

> He was just about to eat a dish of fish, but he suddenly kicked the plate away and began to dhun. He told us that he was under the effect of Salabai. We poured cold water on him to cool him down. He told us that we should not eat fish or meat, and that we should worship our gods by observing *arti* [waving lamps before a deity]. He also said that we should drink tea instead of liquor and should eat rice instead of flesh. He was possessed for three or four days.[76]

The propitiation ceremonies of the Shimpis and Telis were similar in almost every way to those of the Konkanas, with young girls of their community playing the role of Devi during the closing ceremony.

The Maratha Kunbi peasants of this area did not, on the other hand, take much interest in the affair. Some members of this community whom I interviewed denied ever being under the influence of Salabai. Konkanas said that Maratha Kunbis had watched their propitiation ceremonies in a passive manner and had refrained from eating meat and drinking liquor while Salabai was in the area. In the western part of Kalvan taluka, there were only a few Maratha Kunbis in a predominantly Konkana area, but eastward into the Deccan, the Konkana villages gradually gave way to Maratha Kunbi villages. As the Devi moved east, her power faded in direct proportion to the growing predominance of Maratha Kunbi villages. She disappeared in this direction not far to the east of Kalvan town. At this juncture, however, her progress and career took a dramatic new turn when she was taken up by Dangis. I was not able to discover how this actually happened, but it seems that some of them came to Kalvan taluka and carried her back with them to the Dangs.

The Dangs consisted of a maze of forested hills that formed a step between the Deccan plateau and the plains of South Gujarat. Stretching over nearly eighteen hundred square kilometres, the tract provided a formidable barrier between the two regions. Until the nineteenth century, the Bhil chiefs of the area remained unconquered by any outside power. After being subjugated by the British in 1830, the major chiefs were recognized as "Dangi rajas," each ruling over a separate tract.[77] The area was known for its fine teak, and the British took for themselves the monopoly of the timber.[78] The Dangs thus became an administrative peculiarity, for although in one respect it was a region of petty princely states, the effective rulers were British forest officers. The chief forest officer was also the political agent for the Dangi rajas, with magistrate powers.[79]

In 1921, the population of the Dangs was 24,576. Almost the entire population was adivasi. The largest single jati was that of the Konkanas, who were known there as Kunbis. No breakdown of the population is available for 1921, but a census of 1909–10 recorded 11,664 Konkanas and 11,064 Bhils.[80] The rest of the population was divided largely between Varlis and Gamits. The Bhils saw themselves as the aristocracy of the Dangs, and most of them claimed some relationship with a Bhil raja or one of the numerous subchiefs, a claim that could entitle them to a trifling share of the forest lease money. A missionary working in the Dangs in 1909 wrote of this class: "Every Bhil from the humblest to the most haughty expects the term [raja] applied to him when spoken of, and *every* one of them is proud of the fact that he is a Bhil or raja."[81] The Dangi Bhils were considered to be poor cultivators, preferring to hunt game in the forest with bows and arrows. They worked occasionally as field laborers for the more diligent Konkana peasants, receiving payment in grain. Despite this, they considered the Konkanas to be their subjects, a notion that justified periodic appropriations of their grain and livestock.[82]

It was to this forest region that Salabai was carried in August 1922.[83] She was brought by Konkanas, Bhils, and Varlis, who appear to have been so attracted by what they had heard of the Devi that they had gone to Kalvan taluka to find out more at first hand. There, several of them were possessed by her, after which they returned to the Dangs. In the Dangs they became known as gaulas. This would appear to be related to the world *gollo*, meaning "a staunch devotee of a mother goddess." They set about trying to reform Dangi society with the help of Salabai: "Their mission was to drive away *bhuts* [ghosts or demons] from the villages, and also to drive out the belief in bhuts."[84] Indubhai Patel, a Konkana of Chankal, a village in the heart of the Dangs, gave the following description of the movement there:

> For seven days those who were possessed [e.g., the gaulas] lived outside the village, as was the custom during this movement. They used to go to the village and clean some places, such as a cattle shed. If a man went to them without taking a bath, or if someone had eaten fish or crab, or if someone came who had drunk liquor, they used to know and they would beat the person. . . .
> On the seventh day of the dhuning, all of the men, women, boys, girls, and cattle took part. Food was prepared and a young girl or *kurli* was dressed to look like a Devi, with ornaments. We all went out of the village and dug a pit, and worshipped the goddess there. The girl's name was Salabai. Her sari was buried in the earth along with coconuts. Later on, some coconut plants came up there. After that we went to a place where a stream flows. There the gaulas told all of the women to give up witchcraft. A small stick was placed on the head of each woman and it was announced that she had given up

the evil crafts. Tea was then prepared. The women, both Bhils and Kunbis [e.g., Konkanas], had been asked to bring three or four *rotis*, or pieces of coconut. They then took a vow that they would not use evil crafts against others. The roti and coconuts were then given by the gaulas to the women.[85]

There are distinct parallels between this attack on superstitious beliefs in the Dangs in 1922 and the attack on bhuts by the Tana Bhagats of the Oraons in 1914–15. In April 1914, Jatra Oraon proclaimed to his fellows that Dharmes, the supreme god of the Oraons, had told him in a dream to give up ghost-finding and exorcism and belief in bhuts; to give up all animal sacrifice, eating meat, and drinking liquor; to give up plowing their fields, which entailed cruelty to cows and bullocks but failed to save them from poverty and famine; and to stop working as coolies and laborers for men of other jatis. Jatra Oraon then launched a movement to expel the old discredited spirits and adopt in their place new *babas*, or benign gods.[86] Similarly, in the Dangs the gaulas sought to rid the people of their superstitious fears of ghosts and evil spirits—which were considered to be particularly powerful there—replacing them with the worship of Salabai.[87] This worship entailed a thorough reformation of existing belief and practice.

In the Dangs, the list of Devi commands became more detailed and comprehensive. Not only were they to give up liquor, they were also to start drinking tea. In order that they would be firm in their renunciation of meat, they were ordered to sell off their goats and chickens, or release them in the forest. Cleanliness involved not only a daily bath but also careful cleaning of the house and cattle sheds, and using water rather than a leaf to clean the anus after defecation. Animal sacrifice was to stop, and coconuts were to be offered in their place. They were told that if they followed these commands they would become more prosperous.

The movement also became more of a community affair. Until then, possession had taken place in people's houses, with each village holding its own separate ceremony of the passing on of the goddess. Before this time, no attempt seems to have been made to force people to conform to Salabai's commands. In the Dangs, there was for the first time an element of compulsion. In Chankal, as we have seen, the gaulas beat those who failed to reform themselves, and it appears that in this they had popular support. In Chankal, I was also told that one of the oaths they took at this time was: "All are one. Bhil, Kunbi, and

Varli—all should behave as one!" Everyone, including the Bhil chiefs, took this oath and resolved to reform their lives together. The gaula's meetings were not just village affairs; people came from many villages to central places, where the atmosphere was like that of a *mela*, or fair. The gaulas sat under a mandva and carried on their dhuning before a large crowd. People in the audience became possessed and joined the gaulas under the mandva. Each night the gaulas slept under the mandva and began to dhun once more in the morning. It was because these meetings attracted such large crowds that the local authorities, for the first time in the history of the movement, were alarmed enough to report the matter to their superiors. A. C. Hiley, a forest official, told the collector of Surat that they were having great difficulty in finding labor for forest work.[88] He expressed a fear that the movement might lead to the obstruction of government work, even the damaging of government property.[89]

In the Dangs, the movement took a singular turn for which the gaulas do not appear to have been responsible. This has been described in a vivid manner by the American missionary Alice K. Ebey, who was living at the time in the headquarters town of the Dangs, Ahwa:

> "The goddess has come! The goddess has come to town!" With a shout and a rush, people—men, women and children—hurried to the government quarters, where stood a gentle old buffalo cow, with her forehead marked with a streak of red. This was the goddess, and the people bowed and worshipped and were about to bring offerings of coconuts and grain.[90]

Ahwa was not the only place where the Devi appeared in the form of a buffalo. Rustomji Sukhadia, an old Parsi whom I met in Vansda, had a similar story to tell:

> The adivasis of the area around Vansda thought that the Devi had taken the form of a buffalo. They followed the buffalo wherever it wandered. Eventually the buffalo wandered into Vansda town. I heard shouts of: "The Devi is coming! The Devi is coming! Make way for her!" I was curious and took a chair out onto my veranda to watch. The buffalo came surrounded by a large crowd of adivasis from outside villages. They were mostly Konkanas—though it was hard to tell as there were hundreds of them. They had garlanded the buffalo and were throwing flowers on the road before it. When I was seen watching I was told by some of them: "Get out! Only adivasis can see the Devi!"

The buffalo had come, so far as Rustomji Sukhadia could tell, from the direction of the Dangs.

Bavji Gavit, a Konkana of Shenvad, a village of West Khandesh which bordered the Dangs, told me a similar story, but from a more sympathetic point of view:

> Some time after the gaulas left, a buffalo came from the north side. We believed it to be the Devi. It visited every house. We considered it lucky if the buffalo defecated or urinated in someone's house. One man of Shenvad, Shivram Konkana, became richer after the buffalo defecated and urinated in his house. Many others also had good luck as a result. But after some time the buffalo disappeared, and nobody knew where it went.

The Devi could thus enter buffalo as well as men and women. In the eyes of the adivasis, anything, animate or inanimate, was liable to possession by spirits. It was also commonly believed that animals acted as the vehicles of disease goddesses. According to Enthoven:

> In some villages of Gujarat, when there is an outbreak of a serious epidemic, it is customary to drive a goat, a ram, or a buffalo beyond the village boundary, with the disease on its back. The back of the animal which is chosen for this purpose is marked with a trident in red lead, and covered with a piece of black cloth, on which are laid a few grains of black gram and an iron nail. Thus decorated, it is driven beyond the limits of the village. It is believed that an animal driven in this way carries the disease wherever it goes.[91]

Similarly, the Devi-buffalo, originally freed, no doubt, by an owner in conformity with the commands of the Devi, was allowed to wander where it wished carrying the Devi. The obvious drawback to this form of Devi-worship was that it could easily be made to look ridiculous by opponents of the movement. In Ahwa, some government officials grabbed the Devi-buffalo, held a public auction, and sold it for thirty rupees. According to Alice K. Ebey: "The goddess in a single hour became a domestic animal and the country was rid of a public nuisance." In Vansda, Rustomji Sukhadia, far from going away when told to by the adivasis, took up a stout stick and gave the Devi-buffalo a sharp whack. It careered away like any ordinary buffalo, much to the surprise of the adivasis. There is no evidence that this short-lived form of Devi-worship occurred at any other stage of the movement.

Another aspect of the Devi movement that received critical attention from the authorities at this stage was that of merchants who profited from the sudden demand for coconuts. Some suggestions were even made that merchants had engineered the movement with this end in mind.[92] Although this was not true, there was no doubt that some merchants did very well out of the affair. A shopkeeper in Ahwa brought in several sackloads of coconuts, which he sold at inflated prices. When the authorities heard about this, a policeman was posted at the shop to make him sell the coconuts at a reasonable price. Some merchants even followed the gaulas from village to village peddling coconuts at up to four times the normal price.[93] The gaulas appear to have reacted to this by ordering the adivasis to purchase their coconuts from particular shops. The two shops cited most frequently were ones owned by a Maratha trader called Shamji Patil in Abhona and Vani towns of Kalvan taluka. Shamji Patil was a middling trader who was not known particularly for his upright character or benevolence. Neither were his coconuts at all special. He appears to have been singled out purely because he sold his coconuts at a fair price.[94] Thus, far from being under the control of crafty merchants, the gaulas managed to keep this class firmly in its place by specifying shops in which coconuts could be obtained at a reasonable price.

From the Dangs, the gaulas took the movement into Sakri and Navapur talukas of West Khandesh and Songadh and Vyara talukas of South Gujarat. In both Sakri and Navapur talukas, there were sizable populations of Konkanas. The Mavchis were, however, the chief adivasi jati of Navapur. In Songadh and Vyara, there were only a few Konkanas, the chief adivasi jati being the Gamits. The Gamits and the Mavchis were in fact one and the same jati,[95] and they were concentrated chiefly in the three talukas of Songadh, Vyara, and Navapur. It is not possible to give the exact population of this jati in 1921, as the Mavchis were not counted separately from Bhils in West Khandesh. Grierson, however, estimated in 1907 that there were about 30,000 Mavchis.[96] In Gujarat in 1921, there were 64,573 Gamits. Their total population was thus about 95,000. The Gamits and Mavchis spoke a Gujarati-based language.[97] They were considered by officials to be, in contrast to the Bhils of Khandesh, an inoffensive and law-abiding peasantry.[98] In this, they were similar to the Konkanas.

Among the Gamits and Mavchis, the movement took the same form as among the Konkanas. The worship of the Devi often started in the houses of individual adivasis before the gaulas came. When the gaulas arrived, a mandva was erected and people came from miles around to attend the ceremony. A few local people usually joined the Dangi gaulas in the dhuning. The commands were like those in the Dangs. For the closing ceremony, a prepubescent girl was dressed as the Devi, a pit was dug, and she was worshiped there, with the adivasis filing past and throwing coconuts and other such objects of worship into the pit or coins onto a cloth. The pit was then filled in. In some cases, a communal feast was held in which all those present partici-pated. The gaulas then continued on their way, taking with them the money that had been thrown on the cloth.

This last feature gave rise to an accusation by government officials that the gaulas were spreading the Devi for avaricious ends. Many did indeed make a handsome profit from Salabai. Some also allowed their greed to get the better of them. In one village of Navapur taluka, a Konkana gaula was caught red-handed stealing money from the houses of the villagers. The people had left their houses unattended while they were at the Devi ceremony, which was held outside the village. As soon as the crime was known, the people beat the gaulas and chased them away.[99] This was the only such incident that I came across in inter-views. In no other cases was it suggested that the gaulas were at all greedy or hypocritical. The money that they took was regarded as a just reward for conducting the ceremonies of propitiation of the Devi. It was common to pay Dangi spirit mediums for such services. The Gamits and Mavchis who lived on the plains immediately adjoining the Dangs considered Dangi mediums to be particularly powerful. This was based on the belief that the deep forests and hills of the Dangs har-bored spirits of unusual power, so that the local mediums had out of necessity to be more skilled in their craft than those of the plains. When the plains adivasis were unable to placate spirits on their own, they often called in Dangi mediums. It was considered quite legitimate to pay them for such a service. The same held good with the propitia-tion of Salabai.

In West Khandesh, the gaulas did not go far beyond the Mavchi area. No doubt they felt that they were getting too far from home. Some, for instance, refused to go further than the railway line that ran east from Surat to Nandurbar, parallel with the Tapi River.[100] After the gaulas returned to the Dangs, the movement failed to develop any mo-mentum of its own. This was because it did not prove popular among the Bhils, who were the predominant adivasi group in Nandurbar taluka and the other parts of West Khandesh to the north and east of

Navapur taluka. In fact, excepting the Dangs, nowhere did the Bhils show any interest in the Devi movement. The goddess failed also to catch on among the Bhils of Vajpur taluka and, later, Rajpipla state. It is difficult to pinpoint the exact reason for this, but it may be significant that similar movements to change established lifestyles originating from the Bhils took a different form. Their movements were invariably focused around a single messianic figure. This was the case in the Gula Maharaj movement of 1938 among the Bhils of West Khandesh, the powerful Govindgiri movement among the Bhils of northeastern Gujarat in 1913, and Motilal Tejawat's movement among the Bhils of southern Rajasthan in 1922–23.[101] The Bhils seem to have preferred a centralized leadership. This was in keeping with their social structure, in which each Bhil was subject to the command of a Bhil chief.[102] The Devi movement, by contrast, had no overall leaders.

In South Gujarat, unlike the case in Khandesh, the movement did not lose momentum after the gaulas returned to the Dangs. On the contrary, it became stronger as it reached into the territory occupied by the Chodhris. The Chodhris were the smallest of the major adivasi jati of South Gujarat, with a population in 1921 of 76,118.[103] Although they inhabited the plains not so far from Surat city, they were not at all Hinduized in their religion, and in their customs they did not follow high-caste practices. They worshiped their own gods, drank daru and toddy freely, and ate all sorts of meat and fish—with the exception of cattle or horse flesh.[104] According to an assistant collector of Surat, writing in 1894: "Though they [the Chodhris] have a strong race feeling and a wrong-headed spirit of independence which makes them refuse to serve others or even Government, they are remarkably peaceful and law-abiding and proverbial for honesty and truthfulness."[105]

This so-called "wrong-headed spirit of independence" asserted itself most memorably in 1922–23 under the influence of the goddess Salabai. It was at this stage of the movement that we first came across Devi commands such as the demand for higher wages for labor, the refusal to work for anyone connected with the liquor trade, and the demand for a social boycott of the chief group that sold liquor, the Parsis.[106] The movement thus took a more assertive turn at this stage. The actual ceremony that the Chodhris took over from the Dangi gaulas remained basically unchanged, but there was a stronger emphasis on the final communal feast. This indicated that there was a greater stress on community solidarity among the Chodhris.

The only major innovation related to the passing on of the goddess, for which the Chodhris used a rath (a miniature chariot). The rath ceremony was a particularly important one among the Chodhris, and it has been described in detail by B. H. Mehta. The ceremony was held whenever the whole community was considered to be under threat. Men were first possessed by various spirits. The goddess responsible for the threat was then "persuaded" to enter a rath, which was taken to the border of the village, from where it was taken on by the people of that village. Afterward, the Chodhris gathered and held a communal feast. Mehta concluded: "The performance of the rite indicates the capacity of organisation and management of the people. Discipline, order, method, precision, attention paid to detail, are throughout evident."[107]

At the time of the Devi, a rough block of wood that symbolized the Devi was carried in the rath from village to village. The rath consisted of a wooden board, about twenty-five by thirty centimeters, with bamboo sticks at each corner, bent over to meet in the middle and with a cloth draped over the sticks. A small red flag was normally placed on top. The whole structure was about thirty centimeters high. There were no wheels. In some cases, a tablet bearing Gandhi's name was also kept in the rath.[108] After the close of each Devi ceremony, a rath that had been made by the villagers who had taken part in the ceremony was taken in a procession to the border of the village and passed on to the next village. The raths were passed from village to village in a westerly direction, toward the coast. They were eventually immersed in the sea by the people of the coastal villages. During this time, raths used to come through the villages near the coast once or twice a week for a period of nearly three months. Each time, the villagers diligently took the rath in procession, shouting "Devi ki jai!" or "Mata ki jai!" (Long live the goddess!) and passed it on to the next village.[109]

From the Chodhri villages, Salabai went westward toward the sea, along with the raths. In Bardoli taluka, members of the Dubla community organized propitiation ceremonies. The Dublas, also known as Halpati, were found throughout the plains of South Gujarat and northern Thana district. In 1921, their population was 159,238.[110] The large majority were agricultural laborers bound to a lesser or greater degree to high-caste landowners.[111] Although they lived in separate hamlets alongside the high-caste villages, they were in their religion and customs like adivasis.[112] They were kept firmly in their place by the high castes. Narhari Parikh has related how in Bardoli taluka in 1926, one high-caste landowner who ran a business decided to let a Dubla cultivate his land on a sharecrop basis. The other high-caste villagers were so upset that they forced him to go back on the agreement. "The Dublas are laborers: how can they be sharecroppers?" was the cry.[113]

In 1922, the high-caste landowners made no attempt to stop the Dublas from holding ceremonies to propitiate the Devi. To some extent, this was because many of the landowners themselves accepted the divinity of the Devi and her potential for mischief if not propitiated.[114] But, in addition, their control over the Dublas was so great that they had no fears that the Devi movement would encourage them in any way to become rebellious. Dublas of several villages came together at a mandva to worship the Devi in the normal manner. The sociologist I. P. Desai witnessed such a ceremony while still a boy in his own village of Parujan, which was dominated by Anavil Brahmans:

> The most loyal and obedient of the Dublas had the mandva by his house. The movement was not therefore seen as a challenge by the Anavil Brahmans. Some were standing and beating themselves with chains as they dhuned. They dhuned for several days. The Anavils then started to get upset as the Dublas were not coming for work. But they did not force the Dublas to work.

As anticipated, after the closing ceremony, the Dublas went back to work for their masters. Some gave up eating meat and drinking daru and toddy for a limited period; the majority went back to their old ways immediately.

In some cases, Patidars took part in the dhuning. Chhanabhai Luhar of Khoj, which was a Patidar-dominated village of western Bardoli taluka, gave the following eyewitness account of the propitiation ceremony:

> The Devi came from Akoti to Khoj. Three hundred Halpatis gathered. Ujaliats were also there, such as Luhars, Kumbhars, and Leva Patidars. When the Halpatis started to dhun, a Patidar woman called Kankuben Durlabhbhai Patel also began to dhun. She said as she dhuned: "Gandhi kuvama dekhay! Gandhi kuvama dekhay!" [Gandhi can be seen in the well!] The Halpatis who dhuned told them to leave daru and toddy and to take a daily bath. The dhuning continued for three days. They then took the rath to Ruva village.[115]

This appears to have been the general pattern in the Patidar-dominated villages. Whereas the Dublas repeated the normal injunctions of the Devi, the Patidar mediums, who were not in any case meat eaters or liquor drinkers, tended to stress the connection between the Devi and Gandhi. The Patidars of Bardoli had provided strong support to the nationalist movement over the previous two years. The district deputy collector, M. S. Jayakar, believed that they made up the idea of seeing Gandhi in a well so as to win adivasi support for the nationalist cause.[116] Although it seems that the idea originated in that area, it is unlikely that it was manufactured in such a calculating way. Shahid Amin has described how a spate of similar stories about Gandhi's supernatural powers spread among the peasantry of Gorakhpur district in 1921. He discounts the idea, popular among officials, that interested parties had planted such rumors and shows how they emerged from the whole structure of belief of the peasants.[117] Similar considerations would appear to have applied in Bardoli in 1922.

The idea of "Gandhi in the well" caught on rapidly. Throughout South Gujarat, people began peering into wells in the hope that they might receive Gandhi's *darshan* (vision of a deity or revered person). Normally, it was believed that Gandhi could be seen spinning his charkha. Sometimes Salabai was seen sitting next to him.[118] Large numbers claimed to have had such a vision.[119] One possible explanation, which was given to me by Madhubhai Patel of Navtad in Vansda taluka, was that what they in fact saw was a reflection of the wooden wheel fixed over the well to serve as a pulley for the rope. When he looked into a well at this time after hearing the story, this is what he himself saw. Through an act of faith, people must have fancied that they could see an image of Gandhi next to the actual reflection of the wheel. The idea would have been strengthened through the common folk belief in the magical power of wells.[120]

There were variations on this theme. Sometimes only the charkha was sighted in the well. At Abrama in Jalalpor taluka, people possessed by the Devi were saying: "See Gandhi in the roof, where the sun comes through the tiles. See Gandhi in the well."[121] Others claimed to have seen Gandhi spinning in the sun as it rose above the horizon early in the morning, or in the moon.[122] Some, while possessed by the Devi, said that they could see a vision of Gandhi on a white cloth that they held before them.[123] There was a common belief that spiders that had been possessed by the Devi were spinning the name of Gandhi into their cobwebs, and numerous sightings of such cobwebs were reported.[124] The people were also told by those who were possessed by the Devi that they should take vows in Gandhi's name.[125]

As the movement spread west from Bardoli taluka, the Gandhi content became stronger. In Devi meetings, the people were ordered, in addition to the normal commands, to spin on the charkha, to destroy foreign cloth and wear khadi, and to send their children to nationalist schools. Those who dhuned now "read" the commands from pieces of white khadi rather than from a red cloth, as had been normal at earlier stages of the movement. In Jalalpor taluka, the movement was even known as "Gandhi dekhay" (the seeing of Gandhi) rather than as the Devi movement. The local newspaper, the *Gujarat Mitra*, has given a description of the movement at this stage. The report concerns Nagdhara, a predominantly adivasi village on the eastern border of Jalalpor taluka:

> They are taking a bath two times a day and food once a day. Because of the commands of the Devi they have given up chicken, goats, the "sweet from the sea" [i.e., fish], and *daru-tadi*. When the Devi was there, there was an order that nobody could enter the *mandap* without *khadi*. Women also wore *khadi*. The fifteenth day after the Devi came was the last day. There was a dinner [*bhandara*] in the village and there was a *hartal* [work stoppage]. The whole village, including Ujaliats, observed the day off. The Ujaliats also enjoyed the festival. People were observing Gandhi in bottles of kerosene and in bottles of water at that time. Some Naikas and Dhodiyas took a vow to give up liquor and to control their marriage expenses. Mangela Vestu decided to give Rs. 125 to the *rashtriya shala* [nationalist school]. There was a procession, in which people shouted "Gandhiji ki jai!" and "Devi-Mata ki jai!" The Devi went to Satem village after that.[126]

In the coastal talukas of Jalalpor, Navsari, Chorasi, and Olpad and in Surat city, the communities that came most strongly under the influence of the Devi were the Kolis, Dublas, Ghanchis, artisan castes, and untouchables.[127] Among these groups, the Kolis associated the Devi with Gandhi most strongly. The Kolis were a peasant community with a population in Surat and Navsari districts in 1921 of 122,825. They were found mostly in villages near the coast, often farming rather poor land.[128] Few of them made a living from fishing, but they had a tradition of working as sailors on country craft, shipping goods up and down the coast. After this trade declined with the coming of the railways, many became expert construction laborers working in particular on steel railway bridges all over India.[129] From the late nineteenth century onward, many Kolis of Jalalpor taluka migrated to South Africa.[130] There, several took part in Gandhi's satyagrahas. Many of them returned to their villages after a few years, bought land, and built luxurious houses.[131]

During the noncooperation movement of 1920–22, the people of Jalalpor taluka had responded well to Gandhi's call, and nationalist schools were started in several villages.[132] The Kolis of Matvad, Karadi, and nearby coastal villages, such as Dandi (scene of the later salt satyagraha), were particularly enthusiastic supporters of the nationalist movement. It was not therefore altogether surprising when in late 1922 they took over a movement that by then already had a strong Gandhi content to it and converted it into a vehicle for furthering the nationalist cause. It proved a very effective vehicle. As Bhikhabhai Desai, secretary of the Jalalpor Taluka Congress Committee, said in February 1923:

> I have met many Devis in Jalalpor Taluka. Some people say there are 64, others 99 Devis in the taluka [presumably by "Devis" he meant Devi mediums]. They are spreading the message of Mahatma Gandhi. Government should spread social reform ideas among the people, but nowadays the Devis are doing this. Where volunteers have failed to popularize Mahatmaji's message, the Devis are now succeeding.[133]

This was the final of the many transformations of the goddess Salabai. Originating as a smallpox deity, she had become for the adivasis of the Pardi region a force for social reform and an inspiration for a new generation of "reformed" shamanistic healers. For the Konkanas of the Dangs, she had heralded an attack on prevailing beliefs in ghosts and demons and the practice of witchcraft, whereas for the Chodhris of the South Gujarat plains she had become the vehicle for a protest against their exploiters, the Parsis. The Patidars of Bardoli and the Kolis of Jalalpor, on the other hand, had seen her as an ally of Gandhi and a proponent of the nationalist cause. She had thus proved an open-ended force, emerging from a cosmos of belief and practice shared by peasant communities throughout this region but adaptable to a whole range of different aspirations and needs.

Notes

1. Report by Laxmishankar P., Mahalkari of Valod, 11 November 1922, Bombay Archives (hereafter BA), Home Department (hereafter HD) (Sp.) 637 of 1922. This description has been supplemented with information supplied to me on 28 October 1981 by Janabhai Chodhri of Ambach, one of the six villages that gathered that day.

2. These are in the Bombay Archives in a file entitled "The Kaliparaj Movement," BA, HD (Sp.) 637 of 1922 (hereafter KM).

3. B. P. Vaidya, *Rentima Vahan* (Ahmedabad, 1977), p. 177; Report by Collector of Surat, 14 December 1922, KM.

4. Report by Mamlatdar of Bardoli, 15 November 1922, KM.

5. *Land Revenue Administration Report of the Bombay Presidency, including Sind, for 1922–23* (Bombay, 1924), p. 43.

6. *Land Revenue Administration Report of the Bombay Presidency, including Sind, for 1923–24* (Bombay, 1925), pp. 39–40.

7. S. C. Roy, *Oraon Religion and Customs* (1928; reprint, Calcutta, 1972), p. 251.

8. Ibid., p. 250. Roy—a loyalist—denied that there was any anti-British content to this invocation. His denial is not convincing.

9. Surajit Sinha, "Bhumij-Kshatriya Social Movement in South Manbhum," *Bulletin of the Department of Anthropology* 8, no. 2 (July 1959): 16–19.

10. Stephen Fuchs, *Rebellious Prophets* (Bombay, 1965); K. S. Singh, ed., *Tribal Movements in India*, vol. 2 (New Delhi, 1983). In R. B. Lal's contribution to the latter collection, "Socio-Religious Movements among the Tribals of South Gujarat," a passing reference is made to the Devi movement on pp. 290–92.

11. In the pages of these books, there are reports of such movements among the Bhils of Gujarat, Maharashtra, and Rajasthan; the Gonds of Madhya Pradesh and UP; the Khonds of Orissa; the Bhatras, Halbas, Bison-Horn Marias, Dhurvas, and Dorlas of Bastar; and the Oraons, Santals, and Bhumij of Chhotanagpur.

12. Roy's examination of the Tana Bhagats, which occupies fifty-one pages of his monograph on the Oraons, is an example. It is perhaps the best description yet written of such a movement. More violent movements, which incorporated programs for collective reform, have received better attention; most notably, Birsa Munda's movement, which forms the subject of K. S. Singh, *The Dust-Storm and the Hanging Mist: A Study of Birsa Munda and His Movement in Chhotanagpur, 1874–1901* (Calcutta, 1966).

13. I say this after comparing some of the pieces in these collections with archival records that I have seen on certain Bhil movements in Gujarat and Maharashtra.

14. Ranajit Guha, "On Some Aspects of the Historiography of Colonial India," in R. Guha, ed., *Subaltern Studies I* (Delhi, 1982), p. 2.

15. Jugatram Dave, *Khadibhakta Chunibhai* (Ahmedabad, 1966), p. 15.

16. Mahadev Desai, *The Story of Bardoli* (Ahmedabad, 1929), p. 5.

17. Ibid., p. 6.

18. S. V. Parulekar, "The Liberation Movement among Varlis," in A. R. Desai, ed., *Peasant Struggles in India* (Delhi, 1979), p. 569.

19. Ibid., pp. 571, 578.

20. Ibid., p. 582.

21. This critique is based on Ranajit Guha, "The Prose of Counter-Insurgency," in R. Guha, ed., *Subaltern Studies II* (Delhi, 1983), p. 33.

22. "In a peasantry existing in a class-divided society, it is difficult to believe that

religious consciousness could be something internal to its own subjectivity and not hegemonic in nature"; Sangeeta Singh et al., "Subaltern Studies II: A Review Article," *Social Scientist* 12, no. 10 (October 1984): 11.

23. Ibid.

24. Nowadays, many Marxist historians have abandoned the vulgar base/ superstructure metaphor seen in use here. Historical determination is seen to be full of unevenness and lack of congruity and to involve altogether more complex processes; see Harvey J. Kaye, *The British Marxist Historians* (Cambridge, 1984), pp. 56–57, 98, 192–93, and Partha Chatterjee, *Bengal 1920–1947: The Land Question* (Calcutta, 1984), p. xxvi.

25. Dipesh Chakrabarty, "Invitation to a Dialogue," in R. Guha, ed., *Subaltern Studies IV* (Delhi, 1985), p. 374.

26. Partha Chatterjee, "Agrarian Relations and Communalism in Bengal, 1926–1935," in Guha, ed. *Subaltern Studies I*, p. 31.

27. Report of 25 November 1922, KM.

28. Macmillan, 14 December 1922, KM.

29. *Land Revenue Administration Report of the Bombay Presidency, 1922–23*, p. 43.

30. Report by police *naib suba*, Navsari, 15 November 1922, Baroda Records Office (hereafter BRO), Conf. file 327.

31. Vaidya, *Rentima Vahan*, p. 177.

32. *Census of India 1931*, vol. 19, *Baroda*, pt. 1, *Report* (Bombay, 1932), p. 386.

33. Report of 15 November 1922, BRO, Conf. file 327.

34. Alice K. Ebey, "Notes for October 1922," *Missionary Visitor*, January 1923, p. 24.

35. Sumant Mehta, *Samaj Darpan* (Ahmedabad, 1964), pp. 342–43.

36. Interview with Jhipru Lalji Konkni, Khandbara (Navapur), 10 January 1982.

37. The meaning of this rhyme, which is problematic, is discussed later in the chapter.

38. *Sala* means "advice" in the local dialect. The standard Marathi spelling is *salah*.

39. *Bombay Gazetteer* (hereafter *BG*), vol. 12, *Thana District*, pt. 1 (Bombay, 1882), p. 147; R. E. Enthoven, *Tribes and Castes of the Bombay Presidency*, 3 vols. (Bombay, 1920–22), vol. 3, pp. 1–3 (hereafter *TC*).

40. *BG*, vol. 13, *Thana District*, pt. 1, pp. 357–58.

41. Interviews with Son Kolis at Versova and Vasai, 6 May 1982.

42. *Annual Report of the Director of Public Health for the Government of Bombay, 1922* (Bombay, 1923), p. 22; *BG*, vol. 13B, *Thana District* (Bombay, 1926), p. 44.

43. For such beliefs about smallpox, see Digby Davies to W. H. Propert, 2 August 1884, in *Annual Reports on Western Bhil Agency, Khandesh, 1883–84 to 1905–6*, British Library I.S. BO 1/2; Ralph Nicholas, "The Goddess Sitala and Epidemic Smallpox in Bengal," *Journal of Asian Studies* 41, no. 1 (November 1981): 36. According to Gangaben Meher (interview, 20 December 1982), a Mangela Koli woman of Satpati (Palghar taluka), such fears used to be strong in their community, also.

44. This paragraph owes much to remarks made by Shahid Amin.

45. The best descriptions of disease propitiation in the Konkan and Thana districts are found in James Campbell, *Notes on the Spirit Basis of Belief and Custom* (Bombay, 1885), pp. 143–45; R. E. Enthoven, *Folk Lore Notes*, vol. 2, *Konkan* (Bombay, 1915), pp. 29–39; and R. E. Enthoven, *The Folklore of Bombay* (Oxford, 1924), pp. 266–67.

46. This practice was described by a missionary working in Thana district: "Instead of the people trying to keep from contracting the disease they flock to the house where there is smallpox and worship the person who has the disease"; Report by Mrs. Berkebile, *Missionary Visitor*, July 1909, p. 235.

47. It is a common belief in India that gods and goddesses reside in pots; W. Crooke, *Religion and Folklore of Northern India* (Oxford, 1926), pp. 88–89.

48. It was believed that spirits were fond of things like boiled rice, coconuts, and offerings of meat, and that these items were particularly efficacious in enticing them to leave a village; Enthoven, *Folk Lore Notes, Konkan*, p. 38.

49. Crooke notes that mother goddesses were associated with the earth, and offerings to them were accordingly buried; *Religion and Folklore of Northern India*, pp. 46–50, 106.

50. Information from interviews in Palghar taluka, particularly in Satpati village, 18–20 December 1982.

51. On the aspect of Sitala as "the cool one," see Susan Wadley, "Sitala: The Cool One," *Asian Folklore Studies*, 39, no. 1 (1980), p. 35.

52. *BG*, vol. 13, *Thana District*, pt. 1, p. 68.

53. Enthoven, *TC*, vol. 2, p. 399.

54. *BG*, vol. 13, *Thana District*, pt. 2, p. 673; S. T. Moses, "The Machis of Navsari," *Journal of the Gujarat Research Society* 3, no. 2 (April 1941): 62.

55. *Census of India 1921*, vol. 8, *Bombay Presidency*, pt. 1 (Bombay, 1922), p. 186; *Census of India 1921*, vol. 17, *Baroda State*, pt. 1 (Bombay, 1922), pp. 344–46.

56. G. A. Grierson, *Linguistic Survey of India*, vol. 9 (Calcutta, 1907), p. 124.

57. *Pardi Taluka Settlement Report, 1871* (Bombay, 1904), p. 44; *Administration Report of the Bansda State, 1888–89* (Ahmedabad, 1899), p. 11; *Chikhli Taluka Revision Settlement Report, 1897* (Bombay, 1899), pp. 9–10.

58. Enthoven, *TC*, vol. 1, p. 331.

59. "Some years ago, in the backward parts of the Surat district, some of the Kaliparaj young men who had got the benefit of education started a crusade against drink with the help of bhagats (religious preachers) and the sales of liquor fell very low"; testimony of Raojibhai Patel, April 1923, *Report of the Excise Committee Appointed by the Government of Bombay, 1922–23*, vol. 2 (Bombay, 1923), p. 371.

60. A. N. Solanki, *The Dhodias: A Tribe of South Gujarat Area* (Vienna, 1976), pp. 220–21.

61. Indra Munshi Saldhana, "Analysis of Class Structure and Class Relations in a Rural Unit of Maharashtra" (Ph.D. diss., University of Bombay 1983), pp. 116–24.

62. Grierson, *Linguistic Survey of India*, vol. 9, p. 130.

63. This is based on figures from a wide range of census reports and gazetteers.

64. According to Grierson, their language was a Marathi dialect with North Konkani elements. It had, however, been modified by the language of whichever region they were living in (Marathi, Gujarati, Khandeshi); *Linguistic Survey of India*, vol. 9, p. 130.

65. Enthoven, *TC*, vol. 2, p. 265.

66. *Songadh Taluka Settlement Report, 1902* (Baroda, 1902), pp. 3, 25; *Nandurbar Taluka Revision Settlement Report, 1895* (Bombay, 1896), pp. 3–4.

67. It may be noted that the Kunbis of Kolaba district—the area from which the Konkanas most probably migrated—were in the late nineteenth century meat eaters and liquor drinkers. They were, however, Hinduized in their religion; *BG*, vol. 11, *Kolaba District* (Bombay, 1883), pp. 54–62. Five centuries earlier, at the time of the possible migration, there is a likelihood that their religion was far less Hinduized.

68. *Nandurbar Taluka and Navapur Petha Settlement Report of 148 Villages, 1896* (Bombay, 1904), p. 2.

69. Interview with Chiman Powar, Behudna (Surgana state), 14 January 1982.

70. Interview with Indubhai Patel, Chankal (Dangs), 4 June 1981.

71. In interviews, all of the Konkanas who mentioned the Gandhi rhymes told me

that they only came to know who Gandhi was and what he was doing long after the Devi had gone.

72. Enthoven, *Folk Lore Notes, Konkan*, p. 30.

73. R. E. Enthoven, *Census of India 1901*, vol. 9, *Bombay Presidency*, pt. 1 (Bombay, 1902), p. 63. When the high castes of Nasik district held disease propitiation ceremonies, they selected an untouchable woman of the Mang caste to perform this role; Crooke, *Religion and Folklore of Northern India*, p. 127.

74. Campbell, *Notes on the Spirit Basis of Belief and Custom*, pp. 144–45.

75. In interviews in Konkana villages, I came across only one case of a man possessed by Salabai who started to heal people afterward by making them conform to her commands. The man—Bendu Gaula—relapsed into meat-eating and liquor-drinking after a few years, whence he "became less effective as a healer"; interview with Ravji Pavji Powar, Dalvat (Kalvan), 13 January 1982.

76. Interview with Anna Bala Savli (a Shimpi), Abhona (Kalvan), 12 January 1982.

77. D. C. Graham and J. Rose, "Historical Sketch of the Bheel Tribes Inhabiting the Province of Khandesh," in *Selections from the Records of the Bombay Government*, no. 26, new series (Bombay, 1856), pp. 231–35.

78. The British took what was called a "lease" from the rajas. The latter were paid a small annual sum, and the British exploited the timber. Needless to say, the Dangi rajas were never happy with this arrangement; D. B. Chitale, *Dang: Ek Samyaku Darshan* (Ahwa, 1978), pp. 20–22; Report by J. A. McIver, 12 July 1899, BA, Revenue Department (RD), 1901, vol. 151, comp. 949, pt. 1.

79. From 1902 onward, the chief political agent for the Dangs was the collector of Surat. The forest officer for Surat division (normally a white official) was the assistant political agent. As the Dangs represented by far the most important part of the Surat forest division, most of his duties were in the Dangs. He did not, however, live there all year round. The chief official residing permanently in the Dangs was an Indian who held the post of Dangs Dewan; G. E. Marjoribanks, *Working Plan for the Dang Forest* (Bombay, 1926), p. 4.

80. BA, RD 1911, vol. 120, comp. 636.

81. Report by J. M. Pittenger, *Missionary Visitor*, January 1909, p. 34 (emphasis in original).

82. M. S. Mansfield, "Narrative of British Relations with the Petty Native Estates within the Limits of the Khandesh Collectorate," in *Selections from the Records of the Bombay Government*, no. 26, new series (Bombay, 1856), pp. 166–67; *BG*, vol. 12, *Khandesh District* (Bombay, 1880), pp. 103, 600–601. F. G. H. Anderson and G. E. Marjoribanks, *Working Plan Report of the North Dangs Range Forests* (Bombay, 1912), pp. 3–4.

83. This date was given in a report by the collector of Surat, Macmillan, nearly a year later; *Land Revenue Administration Report of the Bombay Presidency for 1922–23*, p. 43.

84. Interview with two Konkanas, Manchhubhai Patel and Ikubhai Karbhari, in Kalibel (Dangs), 3 June 1981.

85. Interview with Indubhai Patel in Chankal (Dangs), 4 June 1981. The interview was written down in the Dangi language in my presence by a prominent social worker of the area, Chhotubhai Nayak. His brother, Ghelabhai Nayak, later translated it into English for me.

86. Roy, *Oraon Religion and Customs*, pp. 247–50.

87. See, for instance, the Bhil Agency Report for 1876–77, which noted that the witches of the Dangs had a fearsome reputation stretching even beyond the Dangs. The

Bhil Agency Report for 1881–82 notes that women labeled as witches were frequently put to death; *Annual Reports on Western Bhil Agency, Khandesh, 1873–74 to 1884–85,* India Office Library, V/10/1414.

88. A. M. Macmillan to Crerar, 1 December 1922, KM.

89. Report by Macmillan, 14 December 1922, KM. At the time, in August, Macmillan did not take much notice of this report and it was not passed on to Bombay. Only in December did Macmillan mention to Bombay what Hiley had told him in August.

90. Ebey, "Notes for October 1922," p. 24.

91. Enthoven, *Folklore of Bombay,* p. 257.

92. Ebey, "Notes for October 1922," p. 24.

93. Ibid. This was mentioned also by adivasis whom I interviewed.

94. Interview with Anna Savli, who knew Shamji Patil well, in Abhona, 12 January 1982. Shamji Patil himself never knew why he was so favored by the gaulas, but with adivasis from the north flocking to his shop to buy coconuts, he made a tidy profit at that time. Many of these adivasis walked great distances to make this purchase. There was nothing unusual in this. We have seen already how an adivasi of Kalvan taluka walked all the way to the coast to buy dried fish at a cheaper price. Likewise, adivasis often walked surprising distances over the hills to buy liquor.

95. In West Khandesh, members of this jati were also described sometimes as "Gavits."

96. Grierson, *Linguistic Survey of India,* vol. 9, p. 95.

97. Ibid., pp. 95, 119.

98. *BG,* vol. 12, *Khandesh District,* p. 101.

99. Interview with Sattarsingh Vasave, Chinchpada (Navapur), 9 January 1982. The adivasis of this area were almost all Mavchis and Bhils.

100. There was a rumor that if the gaulas tried to cross the railway track, it would shatter; Interview with Nura Vasave in Chinchpada (Navapur), 9 January 1982, and Jhipru Kokni in Khandbara (Navapur), 10 January 1982. In fact, some of the gaulas did go beyond the railway track in Navapur (and it did not break!).

101. For Gula Maharaj, see BA, HD (Sp.) 982 of 1938–42; for Govindgiri, see National Archives of India, Foreign Dept., Internal-A, 8–67, March 1914; for Motilal Tejawat, see National Archives of India, Foreign Dept., 428–P (secret), 1922–23.

102. John Malcolm, *A Memoir of Central India,* vol. 1 (London, 1824), pp. 551–53.

103. *Census of India, 1921,* vol. 8, *Bombay Presidency,* pt. 1, *General Report* (Bombay, 1922), p. 186; *Census of India, 1921,* vol. 17, *Baroda State,* pt. 1, *Report* (Bombay, 1922), p. 344.

104. *Mandvi Taluka Settlement Report, 1872* (Bombay, 1904), pp. 40–41; Enthoven, *TC,* vol. 1, pp. 292–93; B. H. Mehta, "Social and Economic Conditions of the Chodhras, an Aboriginal Tribe of Gujarat" (master's thesis, University of Bombay, 1933), pp. 189 and 392.

105. A. L. M. Wood, ACR 1893–94, BA, RD 1894, vol. 36, comp. 1305.

106. Report by Laxmishankar P., 11 November 1922, KM; Report by B. D. Nasikwala, 25 November 1922, KM; *Times of India,* 18 January 1923.

107. B. H. Mehta, "Social and Economic Conditions of the Chodhras," pp. 152–65. A description of a similar rath ceremony among Chodhras observed in 1964–65 is given in Augusta Glatter, *Contributions to the Ethnography of the Chodhris* (Vienna, 1969), pp. 151–52.

108. Macmillan to Crerar, 1 December 1922, KM. Relevant here is Shahid Amin's

observation that Gandhi, because of the fluidity of his supposed powers, could "stand in place of existing powerful beings and appropriate ritual actions connected with their worship, without upsetting the existing hierarchy of the divine and the deified"; "Gandhi as Mahatma: Gorakhpur District, Eastern UP, 1921–2," in Ranajit Guha, ed., *Subaltern Studies III* (Delhi, 1984), p. 46.

109. Interview with Ganeshbhai Patel, Karadi (Jalalpor), 1 January 1983; Maganbhai Nayak, Dhanori (Gandevi), 4 January 1983; Pragjibhai Nayak, Gandevi, 4 January 1983; and Premabhai Patel, Dihen (Olpad), 9 January 1983.

110. *Census of India, 1921*, vol. 8, *Bombay Presidency*, pt. 1, *General Report*, p. 186; *Census of India, 1921*, vol. 17, *Baroda State*, pt. 1, *Report*, p. 344.

111. See Jan Breman, *Patronage and Exploitation: Changing Agrarian Relations in South Gujarat* (California, 1974), for an explanation of the Hali system. The chief landowning castes of the area who exploited Dubla labor were Anavil Brahmans and Patidars. In 1921, there were 34,290 Anavils and 55,708 Patidars in Surat and Navsari districts.

112. Enthoven, *TC*, vol. 1, pp. 343–45.

113. Narhari Parikh, *Bardolina Khedut* (Bardoli, 1927), p. 30.

114. "Generally, the higher classes fear the magic of the lower classes. The fear is often the only means a Mhar or Mhang has of making the higher classes pay him his customary dues"; Campbell, *Notes on the Spirit Basis of Belief and Custom*, pp. 144–45. Enthoven noted that the Kanbis or Patidars of Gujarat "have much faith in sorcery, witchcraft and the influence of the evil eye. In sickness or in difficulty they consult a sorcerer. . . . They believe in omens and signs"; *TC*, vol. 2, p. 141.

115. Interview, 27 January 1982. "Ujaliat" means "white people," in contrast to "Kaliparaj," the "black people." In the context of South Gujarat, Ujaliat meant caste Hindus and others considered respectable in that area, such as Parsis, Jains, and Muslims.

116. Jayakar to Macmillan, 16 November 1922, KM.

117. Shahid Amin, "Gandhi as Mahatma." In my investigations of the nationalist movement in Kheda district, I did not find such beliefs to have been at all prevalent among Patidars there. In the early twentieth century, the Patidars of Kheda district were considered to be generally more sophisticated than those of South Gujarat, which may account for this; see Hardiman, *Peasant Nationalists of Gujarat: Kheda District, 1917–34* (New Delhi, 1981). In any case, I do not feel that such beliefs were central to the movement among the Bardoli Patidars.

118. *Times of India*, 18 January 1923.

119. In interviews, I recorded such claims in villages in Bardoli, Mandvi, Vyara, Mahuva, and Jalalpor talukas. In many cases, the people have remained convinced to this day that they had a genuine miraculous darshan of Gandhi.

120. R. E. Enthoven, *Folk Lore Notes*, vol. 1, *Gujarat* (Bombay, 1914), p. 86: "Some wells are noted as being the abode of spirits who have the power of effecting certain cures." People propitiated the spirits by throwing coins into the well. See also Crooke, *Religion and Folklore of Northern India*, pp. 64–67, where Crooke notes that wells were often considered to be oracles that could give "signs" to people.

121. Interview with Prabhubhai Patel, Karadi (Jalalpor), 1 January 1983.

122. Interview with Becharbhai Chodhri, Makanjher (Mandvi), 13 March 1982.

123. Interview with Fuljibhai Patel, Chasa (Chikhli), 10 November 1986.

124. Vaidya, *Rentima Vahan*, p. 177.

125. Ibid.

126. *Gujarat Mitra*, 21 January 1923; my translation.

127. For Surat city, see *Times of India*, 18 January 1923.

128. *Olpad Taluka Revision Settlement Report, 1928* (Bombay, 1930), pp. 9–10.

129. *Jalalpor Taluka Revision Settlement Report, 1899* (Bombay, 1900), pp. 84–5.

130. Assistant Collector's Report, 1898–99, BA, RD 1900, vol. 33, comp. 137.

131. Deputy Collector's Report, 1915–16, BA, RD 1917, comp. 511, pt. 4.

132. I have come across eight villages in Jalalpor taluka in which there were nationalist schools in 1921–22. The actual total was probably more.

133. Letter by Bhikhabhai Desai to *Gujarat Mitra*, 11 February 1923; my translation.

5 / The Colonial Prison: Power, Knowledge, and Penology in Nineteenth-Century India

David Arnold

I

Michel Foucault's *Discipline and Punish* begins with a horrific scene of public torture and execution in Paris in 1757. Boiling oil, molten lead, and sulfur are poured onto the body of the regicide Damiens as royal power wreaks its brutal revenge. Steel pincers pick at his flesh; horses pull apart his half-severed limbs. Slowly Damiens dies and his dismembered body is burned to ashes.[1] For Foucault, this grisly spectacle serves as prologue to that moment in the history of repression "when it became understood that it was more efficient and profitable in terms of the economy of power to place people under surveillance than to subject them to some exemplary penalty."[2] By the 1830s, eighty years after Damiens's execution, such spectacles of physical punishment had disappeared: "The tortured body was avoided; the theatrical representation of pain was excluded from punishment. The age of sobriety in punishment had begun."[3] In the new penology, the body ceased to be the main target of repression. In the closed and ordered world of the prison, the aim was not to torment the flesh but to reach beyond the body, "to correct, reclaim, [and] 'cure'" the "soul" of the prisoner. Punishment, Foucault quotes a contemporary as saying, "should strike the soul rather than the body." The violent expiation that once rained down upon the captive body was replaced by "a punishment that acts in depth on the heart, the thoughts, the will, the inclinations."[4]

The new penology found, according to Foucault, its definitive statement in Jeremy Bentham's "Panopticon" of 1791. In this theoreti-

cal scheme, warders, located in a central tower, command an unobstructed view of the entire prison. The cells are "like so many cages, so
many small theatres, in which each actor is alone, perfectly individual-
ized and constantly visible." So effectively does the Panopticon manipulate space and facilitate surveillance that brutal punishments are re-
dundant. The Panopticon, "this marvellous machine," as Foucault
described it, was to induce in each prisoner "a state of conscious and
permanent visibility that assures the automatic functioning of power."[5]

For Foucault, the prison was more than a penal institution, penology more than a discourse about prisoners and punishment. The
Panopticon was "at once a programme and a utopia,"[6] an exemplary
form of the diverse mechanisms and multiple discourses of power that
pervaded Western societies by the early decades of the nineteenth century. It was a form that had its analogues in the school, the hospital,
the mental asylum, the parade ground, and the factory. But the prison
was not seen by Foucault, as it has been by many Marxist writers, as
the stark expression of class coercion and repressive state power. "One
impoverishes the question of power," he told an interviewer, "if one
poses it solely in terms of legislation and constitution, in terms solely
of the state and the state apparatus." Power was "both different from
and more complicated, dense and pervasive than a set of laws or a state
apparatus."[7] For Foucault, there could be no "Foucauldian state"; nor
could power form the monopoly of a single class or cluster of individuals. Although the "techniques of power" might be invented to meet the
"demands of production" in a very general (and not merely economic)
sense, although power might, broadly speaking, be "consubstantial
with the development of forces of production," power itself was never
localized "in anybody's hands, appropriated as a commodity or piece
of wealth."[8] In thinking of the mechanisms of power, Foucault was
thinking rather of

> its capillary form of existence, the point where power reaches into
> the very grain of individuals, touches their bodies and inserts itself
> into their actions and attitudes, their discourses, learning processes
> and everyday lives. The eighteenth century invented, so to speak, a
> synaptic regime of power, a regime of its exercise *within* the social
> body, rather than *from above it.*[9]

It would not be difficult (or particularly original) to contrast Foucault's paradigmatic view of prison discipline and institutional surveil-

lance with a different perspective drawn from colonial India. There we are confronted, first of all, with episodes of resistance, of "revolts against the gaze," which suggest that prisoners were far from being the "docile bodies" Foucault described.[10] While there has been a tendency in the past to see prison protests as essentially a mark of the period of nationalist incarceration, particularly from 1920 onward, the more one explores the history of the nineteenth-century prison in India, the more frequent such episodes of resistance appear and the more significant they seem in the evolution of colonial penology.

Anand Yang has recently discussed one of these incidents in some detail—the opposition of prisoners in the jails of Bihar to the introduction of a common messing system in 1842 and 1845.[11] Until the 1840s, prisoners in the Bengal presidency had been allowed to purchase and prepare food for themselves: they were given a money dole to buy their own food and a place to cook in the prison yard. This enabled them to follow the requirements of their caste; it also relieved the tedium of prison life. But the consequences for prison administration could be chaotic. H. M. Cannon, inspector of prisons for Awadh, remarked in the 1860s, after this system had disappeared, that

> no-one who has not visited a large jail at meal times, under the old system (where every prisoner cooked for himself) can for a moment conceive the Babel of jabbering and confusion, the dirt and filth from spilt water, ashes, and newly constructed mud fire-places, the waste of flour and fuel, to say nothing of the peculation and total absence of all discipline, and the time afterwards expended in cleaning up and stowing away some hundreds of brass lotahs [water pots] and cooking vessels, with the accompanying hundreds of yards of string for drawing water.[12]

In a bid to strengthen jail discipline, curb this daily chaos, and make prison life more deterrent, the government decided that in the future prisoners would only receive food prepared for them by prison cooks and would eat it alongside other prisoners, regardless of their caste. This innovation sparked protests and hunger strikes, assaults, and eventually riots. But, argues Yang, echoing Foucault, the prisoners' opposition was not allowed to "turn back the development of a new system of discipline and punishment," and, by deploying its "overwhelming coercive power," the state ultimately succeeded in imposing the new messing system upon the prisoners.[13]

In fact, the outcome was more equivocal than Yang's account suggests. In the neighboring North-Western Provinces, resistance to messing was more protracted than in Bihar and effectively delayed the introduction of the new system for months, even, in some places, years. As late as 1854, it had still not been implemented in eight of the forty prisons in the province and in five others had been enforced only with respect to new or low-caste prisoners. Following a riot at Allahabad Jail in May 1846, the government decided that compulsory enforcement of messing should be avoided altogether if it was likely to provoke serious opposition and cause bloodshed.[14]

The conflict over messing was not an isolated episode. During the course of the century, there were a number of occasions when prisoners overpowered their guards, took over the jails, and temporarily dictated terms to the prison authorities. In April 1834, at Calcutta's Alipur Jail, the most important penal institution in British India at the time, the European magistrate was brained by a brass *lota*, and administrative control was only with difficulty restored.[15] Perhaps mindful of this incident, in April 1855, Bengal's inspector of jails ordered the confiscation of all unauthorized possessions from prisoners. He included lotas among the items to be seized, although they had not previously been prohibited. Fueled at this time of rampant rumor by reports that the seizure of lotas was an attempt to break caste and force conversion to Christianity, determined resistance broke out at several jails, notably Muzaffarpur and Arrah in Bihar. At the first of these, the district magistrate, faced with both the protests of the prisoners and a menacing crowd of opium-producing ryots outside the prison gates, agreed to return the confiscated lotas. Despite the evident loss of prestige this climb-down entailed, the provincial government approved the magistrate's decision and instead annulled the "injudicious, inconsiderate and improper order" of the inspector of jails.[16]

Such episodes of open defiance illustrate the authorities' difficulty in exercising effective disciplinary control over prisoners, especially during the first sixty years of the nineteenth century. They suggest, too, the ease with which disputes within the prisons could spill over into neighboring communities and attract outside sympathy. Far from being a captive domain in which discipline might reign supreme, the prison often became (as it did again during the nationalist era) a focus or symbol of wider defiance against the British. Thus, the connection between prison protest and popular revolt presaged by the jail disturbances of the 1840s and early 1850s in Bihar and the North-Western Provinces became a widespread reality with the wholesale liberation of prisoners and destruction of jails in Meerut, Kanpur, Allahabad, and elsewhere during the insurgent summer of 1857.[17]

In addition to acts of outright or covert resistance by prisoners, the prison system was honeycombed from within by laxity and ineptitude, by evasion and intrigue. When F. J. Mouat became Bengal's inspector of prisons in 1855, he found no effective prison system at all in the province, only an absolute want of "order, system, and method in the management of the prisons placed under my control."[18] J. Rohde, the Madras inspector, complained in the following year that

> the mode in which sentences are carried out . . . is very lax; we have
> no means of enforcing hard labour within the walls, and the work
> exacted outside is, to a labouring man at least, anything but *hard*
> labour; in most jails no fixed task is exacted, prisoners are too often
> employed with very little regard to the object of their being in prison;
> they have, outside the walls, access to their friends. There is too
> much community of feeling between the guards and the prisoners.[19]

Some twenty years later, in 1877, the president of the Indian Jail Conference observed that the "great practical fault of our jail system is that orders are not rigidly carried out." Another speaker took a similar view, claiming that the Indian prison was "entered without dread and inhabited without discomfort."[20] Where in all this, one might ask, was the Panopticon and the pervasiveness of penological power?

It was freely stated by some prison officers that the day-to-day running of prisons was largely out of their control and "almost entirely in the hands of the convicts themselves."[21] In the absence of trained supervisory staff and with senior prison officers weighed down with paperwork and administrative duties, the internal management of the prison was mainly left to ill-paid and corrupt subordinates—or to warders drawn from the convict population. The practice of using prisoners to run the jails began in Malaya early in the century and, because it was economical rather than because it was efficient, soon spread to Bengal and the rest of India. Convict officers served as overseers on work gangs or in jail workshops and as nightwatchmen in the prison wards or barracks. They were rewarded with special privileges (such as being allowed to smoke when possession of tobacco was forbidden to other inmates). Some even received small monthly payments. In the North-Western Provinces in the 1880s, they were provided with special uniforms, permitted to eat and sleep apart from the rest of the prisoners, and "to wear their hair and beards as in ordinary life."[22] The main objection to the use of convict warders was that they tainted the prison system with their own criminality and dangerously blurred the distinction between the watchers and the watched. One member of the 1877 Jail Conference called the employment of convict officers "an inversion of the order of things." Entrusting one group of convicts with authority over others, he said, broke down "the boundary . . . which should always strongly exist between convicts and their keepers. . . . It is more like burlesque than serious government to take a law-breaker and dress him up and pay him to act the part of upholder of the law."[23]

And yet (because it suited the authorities to turn a blind eye to their abuses), convict officers survived and flourished. A great deal of the actual, if illicit, power of the prison system flowed through their hands. They organized much of the smuggling that went on between the prison and the outside world and kept open lines of communication between prisoners and their friends and relatives outside. They were also held responsible for much of the extortion, violence, and sexual harassment that went on in prison. V. O. Chidambaram Pillai, a witness to the Indian Jails Committee of 1919–20 and himself a former prisoner, alleged that convict warders were the "medium of all the extortions, unnatural offences and tortures in jail." Convict warders, he said, organized the physical intimidation of new prisoners in order to extort money from them or simply to make them submit to their authority.[24] The prison created an institutional and social space that was colonized by other, unofficial, networks of power and knowledge than those represented by formal prison authority.

II

One of the ways in which the prison came to be colonized by middle-class nationalists from the 1890s onward was through the publication of prison diaries and memoirs recounting their experiences and struggles with the prison authorities.[25] It is more difficult, however, to gain access to the experiences of earlier generations of prisoners from other class backgrounds, especially the illiterate prisoners who formed the great majority of nineteenth-century convicts. But occasionally intercepted notes and messages provide some insights into their attitudes and concerns:

> Honoured Sir [ran a letter from a prisoner in Calcutta's Alipur Jail in May 1913], Our earnest prayer to Nirmal Babu is that we have received from that man, the sum of Rs.10, *ganja* [Indian hemp or marijuana]1 tola, opium 1 tola, and 2 soaps. The soaps are not required. I get soaps from the godown for washing clothes of Tulsi Singh. I am at present working at the *dal* godown as convict overseer. Everything there is at my disposal. Everything is done with my permission. The jemadar [warder] has full confidence in me.[26]

The writer, Sribande Ali, then went on to explain to "Nirmal Babu" that his friend Tulsi Singh "earnestly requested" him to send a petition to the prison governor on their behalf: "When the Governor will come to hold an enquiry into the matter, as to how provisions are stolen from the godown, we will point out how these things are managed. We know everything." After this thinly veiled threat to blow the gaff on Nirmal, Ali closed his letter with a polite request for further supplies: "Please send cash Rs.20, 4 soaps [so soap was useful after all!], *ganja* 2 tolas, 8 boxes of cigarettes, 10 stamps, and send a reply."

Not all prisoners who tried to send messages out of Alipur Jail concerned themselves with pilfered stores and smuggled ganja. One asked anxiously after the health of his father, although he too wanted a fresh supply of ganja, *biris* (cigars), cigarettes ("motor-car brand"), and sweets; another, sentenced for housebreaking, promised not to disobey his mother again—"if I come back this time."

Urgent messages also passed between prisoners within the jail. In July 1918, an undertrial prisoner named Laloo was sent the following note:

> Look here Laloo,
> Save us. Don't admit anything. If you confess then both you and we shall suffer. You should do what may save us all. Say you don't know anything. . . . This time we shall have to stand before the magistrate. Take care. Tell what I advise, or else I shall cut you when I get out. I shall take your life. My name is Bepin. You know me perfectly well.

Without female companionship, prisoners became enmeshed in homosexual relationships, not always of their own choosing. Some prisoners, echoing the idioms of Urdu poetry, wrote longingly to fellow inmates: "Know you Monmohan Rai that the moon has many stars but the stars have the moon only. So you have many but for me there is you only."

But often homosexuality formed part of the brutal commerce of the prison or figured in networks of power built around scarce resources and physical intimidation:

Dearest Latif [wrote Nilkanto in July 1917],
Received your letter yesterday and came to know everything. From this day you cannot expect anything from me. I have not been giving you Rs. 5 or 7 monthly for so long that you might become the *chokra* ["boy"] of Gaffur. However if you wish to be my chokra, come today anyhow . . . through Nos 10 and 11 wards. . . . Mind that this is my last letter.

A letter addressed to an adolescent prisoner named Khogenda (and which, like all these letters, must have lost much of its original flavor in translation) ran:

I told you on several occasions that if you consider me unsuitable to you, you may look elsewhere for others. But this you will not do. Because of you I was removed from the Remission system. You had better give up the idea of obtaining ganja from others, so long as I am here. If you attempt to do so, know this to be a settled fact, that I will kill you. I am ready for the gallows. The men to whom you gave two letters have brought them and they are in my possession. You also told them that he who will bear expense for your chokra, he will have unnatural intercourse with you. This is a fact, and I have proofs of it. I have further proof that [you] made a similar proposal to the night watchman of Ward No. 12 where you sleep. The man himself told me so. What do you think of me? I don't care for my life. It does not affect me a whit whether I am hanged or transported. . . . I am a match for the whole population of the jail. I am not one of those who take a kicking and buffeting in jail. . . . Be careful and think over the matter. This is good advice for you. Reply on receipt of this. Do not forget. If you do it will go hard with you. Wholly thine.

Shaik Yasin, a thirteen-year-old serving an eighteen-month sentence, wrote a briefer but no less pointed note in December 1917: "You Sala Musala, Had your father ever any chokra? You are a beggar. You, Sala fed Pancha and made friendship with him. Everyone should keep one man only. I go to cohabit with your mother. You don't speak to me, but I will tell everyone. I won't listen to you. Reply to this."

My purpose in citing these letters and offering an alternative view of the prison is not simply to suggest that life in India's jails had more the character of *Salaam Bombay* or *Our Lady of the Flowers* than of

Bentham's Panopticon or Foucault's *Discipline and Punish*, or to seek to dismiss Foucault by pointing out the great gulf between penological theory and prison reality (which would surely be true of prisons anywhere in the world). Nor do I want to suggest that the Indian prison was simply a poor imitation of an otherwise effective British model: rather, I am trying to identify what was different rather than what was "wrong," or, to put it another way, what was specifically colonial, about the prison system in India.[27] I will try to argue, first, contra Foucault, that one can find abundant evidence of resistance and evasion in the Indian prison system and a whole network of power and knowledge over which the prison authorities exercised scant control, but that this limited authority and control was partly the result of a pragmatic choice by the colonial regime, a recognition of its practical and political limitations, and partly a frank expression of its limited interest in the declared purposes of penal discipline and reform. But I also want to argue, rather more in accord with Foucault, that the prison was nonetheless a critical site for the acquisition of colonial knowledge and for the exercise—or negotiation—of colonial power. If one of Foucault's main ambitions was to show how a body of knowledge is created and structured, how a particular understanding of human society and the world comes into being, then, like Foucault, I see the prison not as an isolated institution, but as something representative of the ways in which colonial knowledge was constructed and deployed.

In making this connection with colonial power, I am well aware that the system of knowledge and power Foucault described was not defined by the operations of the state or by the aspirations of a single class. As pointed out earlier, for him power was something more pervasive, permeating society as a whole and not simply acting upon it as a form of state-managed social control. If one accepts this proposition (and certainly it is open to question), then the state in India played a disproportionate part in the ordering and disciplining of colonial society. Penology (like Western medicine, whose intimate connection with the prison will be examined later) was a more narrowly state-centered enterprise in nineteenth-century India than it was in contemporary Europe. Overall, then, I would argue that Foucault's broad conspectus remains highly relevant to any discussion of what might be termed "the colonization of the body."

Ashis Nandy claims to have identified a colonialism that "colonizes minds in addition to bodies" and produces "cultural and psychological pathologies" of such intensity that they have endured far beyond the formal termination of colonial rule.[28] However, this emphasis upon the psychological impact of colonialism inevitably gives prominence to middle-class rather than subaltern experience, and it tends to pass over unproblematized the question of the body, of its physical appropriation and ideological implication in the manifold processes of colonial rule and Western hegemony. By introducing the phrase "the colonization of the body" into a discussion of prisons, I want to highlight three main elements:

1. A process of physical incorporation by means of which the colonized were brought under various systems of discipline and control—in the prisons, as in the army and the police; in factories, plantations, and mines; in hospitals and in schools.

2. A process of ideological or discursive incorporation, effected through that vast agglomeration of texts, discourses, and institutional rules that concerned themselves with the physical being of the colonized and that, consciously or implicitly, used the body as a site for the construction of colonial authority and for the interrogation of indigenous society and culture.

3. An area of contestation between different understandings of the body, involving competing claims to speak for the body of the colonized and for its material, social, and cultural needs.[29]

III

The prison system that emerged in the late eighteenth and early nineteenth centuries in India grew out of the British preoccupation with the extraction of revenue and the maintenance of "law and order." In this sense, the prison was a strictly material adjunct to a colonial system of economic exploitation and political control. But just as in Europe the new penology helped to distance the age of the French Revolution and the Rights of Man from the "barbarities of another age,"[30] so in India the birth of the prison helped to draw a line of demarcation between colonial rule, which saw itself as uniquely rational and humane, and the "barbarism" of an earlier age or "native" society. By pointing to the extremes of cruelty and depravity exhibited in such practices as female infanticide, sati, and the self-immolation of pilgrims beneath the car of Jagannath, the West found a way to condemn India, a civilization that an earlier orientalist generation had held in such apparent esteem. The emphasis given to Indians' cruelty to their fellow men (and more especially women) articulated a growing contempt for India's religion, social practices, and governance and served, by contrast, to advance the claims of European humanity and reason and establish the West's credentials in speaking for the body of the colonized.[31]

The growing condemnation of brutal modes of punishment in the West thus found a singular resonance among the British in India. In the early years of its imperium in Bengal, the East India Company administered various forms of punishment inherited from previous regimes, including mutilation, branding, and whipping. But the late eighteenth century saw a reaction by Company men against what were increasingly regarded as inhumane—and, in the case of dacoity and murder, ineffective—forms of punishment. This shift in administrative thinking was exemplified by the abolition of mutilation in 1790, when Lord Cornwallis, the governor-general, substituted a sentence of seven years' hard labor for the amputation of one limb and fourteen years for the loss of two.[32] One of the consequences of the abolition of mutilation, as later of branding, was to encourage greater reliance upon imprisonment. "Imprisonment," commented T. B. Macaulay in December 1835, "is the punishment to which we must chiefly trust. It will probably be resorted to in ninety-nine cases out of every hundred." It was accordingly "of the greatest importance to establish such regulations as shall make imprisonment a terror to wrong-doers," while, at the same time, preventing it "from being attended by any circumstances shocking to humanity."[33]

In fact, imprisonment was far from being the universal form of punishment employed by the colonial state. Capital punishment (in contrast to the preexisting Islamic system of justice in Bengal) became a far more common penal sanction than previously, despite occasional complaints about its barbarity;[34] and one has only to think of the summary executions, whippings, and collective fines and the confiscations of land and other property used by the British virtually until their final days in India to realize that imprisonment was but one of the many modes of punishment deployed by the colonial power. Nor should it be imagined that reformers abolished "barbarism" overnight and instantly replaced it with modes of punishment less "shocking to humanity." Even when the political will was present, penal practice was slow to follow humanitarian theory. The public display of the bodies of executed criminals continued until 1836; a public gallows stood outside Madras Penitentiary as late as the 1880s. The practice of branding the foreheads of convicts (known as *godena*) only ceased in 1849, following the observation of a member of the Government of India that "it savours somewhat of barbarism and is opposed to the spirit of the age."[35] Despite repeated condemnation, bar fetters continued to be used to punish refractory convicts or prevent their escape, and in 1889 a government committee still looked forward to the day when "these barbarous appliances" would be "altogether abolished."[36] But, despite the retention of many of these "barbaric" vestiges of an earlier age, the ideological thrust of penal reform remained: however much the grim facts might seem to belie it, the British claimed to have introduced a more humane regime of punishment than India had ever previously known.

In December 1835, Macaulay called for the appointment of a committee to investigate prison discipline in India. This was partly prompted by alarm at the recent disturbances in Alipur Jail, uncomfortably close to the principal seat of British power in India. But Macaulay also saw it as a necessary adjunct to the work of the Law Commission with which he was currently engaged, arguing that "the best criminal code can be of very little use to a community, unless there be a good machinery for the infliction of punishment."[37] The prison in India was thus seen to be a necessary part of the evolving apparatus of the colonial state. Pressure for the creation of a more efficient and "humane" prison system came from within government circles and not, as in Britain, from individuals like John Howard and Elizabeth Fry on the margins of state power. Until the 1890s, or even later, Indian elites showed little desire to penetrate "the secrets of the prison house," while, apart from Mary Carpenter in the 1860s and 1870s, few British reformers showed much interest in Indian prisons.[38]

The Committee on Prison Discipline was appointed in January 1836, with Macaulay himself a member. Its report, published two years later, has been seen as evidence of the influence of Utilitarian thought on government in India at the time. Eric Stokes found in it "the authentic voice of the new Poor Law, of Chadwick and Southwood Smith." Its tone might be "sterner than that of Bentham," but there was "an obvious debt" to his *Principles of Penal Law* and to the Panopticon plan. Stokes cited as evidence the committee's recommendations that

> a penitentiary for all prisoners sentenced to more than one year's imprisonment shall be established in the centre of every 6 or 8 districts, and that a better system of classification of prisoners shall be adopted: that each prisoner shall have a separate sleeping place: that solitary confinement shall be much resorted to: that monotonous, uninteresting labour within doors shall be enforced upon all prisoners sentenced to labour: that prisoners shall be deprived of every indulgence not absolutely necessary to health, and that the management of each penitentiary shall be committed to an able trustworthy superintendent, either European or Native.[39]

Certainly, the language of the report and many of its recommendations echoed Bentham and the spirit of prison reform in North America and Europe. But no less striking is the frequency with which committee and its critics departed from Western precedent to stress the impracticality of simply importing the British model into India. Indeed, this was but the first of several occasions between 1830 and 1920 when proposals for reforms in line with current Western penological thought were rejected as impractical or inexpedient. In 1838, opposition to Benthamizing Bengal came most influentially from Lord Auckland, the governor-general. He was skeptical about the committee's proposals, particularly, but not exclusively, on grounds of cost: "Every reform of prison-discipline," he warned, "is almost of necessity attended at the outset with extraordinary expense." But he also argued that there were intrinsic differences between England and India that prevented any unqualified transference. An enclosed prison yard might be desirable and "not unwholesome" in England, but in India it would rapidly become a "sink of malaria." With respect to food, labor, and accommodation, there were in India "habits and an inveteracy of prejudice and of feeling" that created "opposing difficulties to the just management of prisons, such as are not elsewhere to be encountered." Where Auckland did concur with the committee was in seeing an insuperable problem of agency. How, he asked, was it possible to obtain among the natives of India "fitting instruments for control and management" when it was "principally upon a perfect tact and judgment, and an unwearying zeal, that the success of every scheme of discipline has been found to depend?"[40]

If in Europe or North America the new penology could present itself as not only humane and just but also as universal in its application, in India it constantly ran up against its orientalizing other. India, as Auckland's remarks about "inveteracy of prejudice and feeling" indicated, was seen as a land where local constraints—not just of caste and religion, but also of climate, health, funding, and agency—powerfully presented themselves. Orientalism, so often portrayed in recent scholarship as an empowering device, might here be better understood in negative and restraining terms, an obstacle colonialism threw up against the exercise of its own alien authority in the pursuit of a wider and more accommodating "economy of power." The necessity of establishing a system of prison administration according to the approved models of Philadelphia, Pentonville, or Paris was certainly a course that had its advocates in India, but it was a cause dogged by a persistent and pragmatic belief that the prohibitions of "prejudice" and climate had (almost always) to be respected.

It is not surprising, then, that little was done in the short term to reform India's penal system along Benthamite lines. Even the committee's recommendation that each province should have a senior officer solely responsible for jails was ignored until 1844, when the Government of the North-Western Provinces, more in the interest of economy than of reform, appointed W. H. Woodcock as its inspector of jails. This was followed by similar appointments in Punjab in 1852 and in Madras, Bombay, and Bengal in 1854. In the late 1840s, a start was made, too, on the construction of prisons along the lines, if not of Bentham's Panopticon, then of London's Pentonville Prison, which had opened in 1842.

Until the middle of the nineteenth century, India's prisons were uncertain places of incarceration, wanting both security and a clear institutional identity. Early colonial jails were generally buildings adapted from another purpose: the old Delhi jail was a converted *serai*. Fires were common, reputedly started by prisoners hoping to escape in the ensuing confusion. Some more substantial prisons built for the purpose had been erected from the 1790s onward, but by the 1850s many of these had also become dilapidated, overcrowded, and fever-prone. However, by mid-century, Benthamite ideas of prison management and construction had gained wide circulation among colonial officials. In 1855, J. Rohde, inspector of prisons in Madras, submitted a design for several new prisons, which he described as "a 'panopticon' on General [*sic*] Bentham's principle, of having every prisoner constantly under observation from a central point."[41]

Prompted partly by the events of 1857–58 and partly by reform of the Indian Penal Code, a number of central and district jails were built in the 1860s and 1870s on the Pentonville model, with a central watchtower, radiating cell blocks, and high-perimeter walls—among them were Salem, Lahore, and Allahabad jails. But their outward form could be deceptive. Agra Jail, built under Woodcock's direction in 1849 according to a "mixed" design, combined the economy of barracks, where a score or more of prisoners were locked up together at night, with individual cells where refractory prisoners could be punished with solitary confinement. It also had a building,

> similar to those at Pentonville, for carrying out the principle of solitary and silent exercise. This consists of a small central tower from which radiate to the circumference 25 subdivisions, separated from each other by a blank wall high enough to prevent communication from one to the other. On top of the tower stands the sentry who commands all the radii, and by an aperture in the centre of the tower, can look down upon the convict-cook below, who is, also in solitary silence, preparing food for his brother convicts.[42]

But C. G. Wiehe, inspector general of prisons in Bombay, who visited Agra in 1863, found that solitary confinement was rarely enforced and that the building intended for silent exercise and separation was already, after little more than a decade, no longer in use.[43] Multan Jail also had facilities for the complete separation of prisoners, but, as at Agra, they had not been used for years because, Wiehe reported, "it was found impossible to keep the men from communicating verbally with each other in these compartments."[44] At Salem Central Jail, there was "a most elaborate and expensive tower, placed in the centre of a circle of six different blocks of cells, originally intended for separate confinement," but here again, strict surveillance and separation were no longer practiced. The tower, already in ruins, was a danger to the jail's security, and, far from being run according to the "separate system," the prison housed 700 convicts instead of the 144 for whom it had originally been intended, with 4 or 5 prisoners crammed into a single cell.[45]

Nor did the situation change significantly in subsequent decades. In 1889, the Committee on Jail Administration in India reaffirmed the view that for "habitual" offenders, "silence and rigid discipline and segregation from other prisoners" were "the only means of rendering imprisonment distasteful," and yet it doubted the practicality of the single-cell system in India on both sanitary and financial grounds. In India, it further reported, sufficient numbers of reliable warders could not be found for the wages available, and hence a strict system of discipline and surveillance was simply unattainable.[46]

IV

Administrative attitudes and convict resistance were more likely causes of this failure to maintain Benthamite institutions than was the weight of prison numbers. Nineteenth-century India's prison population appears—at least at first sight—to have been relatively small. There was no "great confinement," perhaps because there was no great social or political upheaval, comparable to the Industrial Revolution in Britain, to occasion it. In 1838, the prison population of British India was stated to be 56,632 for a total population of 91.5 million people (equivalent to 0.06 percent).[47] Between 1863 and 1867, the average number of prisoners was put at 67,992 and in 1880 at 106,763, almost double the 1838 total but still a relatively small proportion of the population. The figure, however, varied from one province to another. In 1875, nearly 0.5 percent of the inhabitants of colonial Burma were in jail; in most other provinces, the figure was between 0.1 to 0.2 percent, and in Bengal and Madras it was less than 0.1 percent. In the late nineteenth century and the early years of the twentieth, numbers of prisoners appear to have been fairly stable at around 100,000 a year before rising steeply with the growth of political unrest at the end of World War I.[48]

But these figures are deceptive. They represent the daily average number of prisoners; during the course of a single year, a far larger number passed through jail, some sentenced to only short terms of imprisonment, others departing quickly for the gallows or the mortuary slab. In Awadh, for instance, the average daily jail population in 1862 was 4,342, but 15,428 individuals were admitted to prison, or remained there, in the course of the year.[49] In 1880 in Madras, 32,049 prisoners passed through provincial jails. Of these, 15,138 were released during the year, 4,445 were transferred to other jails, 312 were transported, 529 died in hospital, 26 escaped, and 55 were executed.[50]

Women formed only a small part of the prison population—8 percent in 1877, 5 percent in 1891. Of the 326,101 prisoners consigned to the jails of Lower Bengal between 1861 and 1865, 11,349 (3.5 percent) were women. Among the 4,458 prisoners in Awadh in 1862, there were 227 women (5.1 percent).[51] The reason for this striking disparity between the sexes is unclear. It suggests either that women did not commit the kinds of crimes—murder, dacoity, cattle theft, and housebreaking—that most frequently brought male offenders before the colonial courts, or that they were treated more leniently by magistrates and judges. Perhaps an awareness of the nature of prison conditions discouraged magistrates and judges from sending women, especially women from the "respectable" classes or in purdah, to prison in the first place.[52] But toward the end of the century, this policy, if such it was, seems to have changed as the state became increasingly involved in disputes over conjugal rights and an increasing number of women were sentenced to imprisonment for murdering their husbands or infant children. For most of the nineteenth century, however, because there were so few women in jail, little provision was made for their separate accommodation and supervision, and they were often relegated to the worst parts of the jail, a situation to which Mary Carpenter drew pointed attention in the 1860s.[53]

Apart from sentencing policy and the frequency of escapes and executions, two other factors governed the size of India's jail population during the nineteenth century. One was the prodigious mortality. In the first sixty years of the century, death rates not infrequently reached 25 percent; that is, a quarter of all prisoners perished in a single year. They died mainly from cholera, malaria, dysentery, and diarrhea. In Mangalore Jail in 1838, 151 out of 263 prisoners (57 percent) perished, nearly half of them from cholera. At Meerut in 1861, prisoners already weakened by famine were hit by cholera, and mortality soared to 62 percent. In the prisons of Lower Bengal, 40,550 deaths from disease were recorded between 1843 and 1867 alone.[54] Although sickness and mortality rates fell after the 1860s, because of the construction of healthier jails and as a result of improved sanitation and medical attention, imprisonment for even a minor offense was often tantamount to a sentence of death. Port Blair in the Andamans in particular remained a notorious deathtrap.

Mortality tended to be highest among newly arrived prisoners who entered jail in a debilitated and demoralized state, especially in times of famine, disease, and insurrection. Migrants and nomads, hillmen and tribals perished in large numbers—from unfamiliarity with a confined and sedentary life, from abrupt changes of climate and diet, from neglect at the hands of their jailers, or from the "nostalgia" and "peculiar despondency" that overcame them.[55] Accounts of rural insurrection in India conventionally close with military defeat and judicial sentence; too often the real end—for Santhals, Gonds, Mundas, Mappilas, and the rebels of 1857—came with a wretched death from cholera, tuberculosis, or dysentery, with the cremation or burial of the last bones of rebellion inside a prison yard.[56]

Another factor that caused the number of prisoners to fluctuate significantly from year to year was the effect of food shortages and famine. High grain prices, the loss of agrarian employment, and fear of imminent starvation provoked a sharp rise in rural crime levels, and these in turn swelled the prison population. G. S. Sutherland, a participant in the Indian Jail Conference of 1877, traced a close correlation between wheat prices and prison numbers in Awadh between 1869 and 1876. He estimated that high prices pushed the number of prisoners 15 to 30 percent above ordinary levels.[57] Reviewing the famines of the late 1870s, the Government of India's sanitary commissioner similarly observed that the

> jail population . . . rises and falls with the price of grain. As prices range high, it increases; as prices fall, the jails become comparatively empty. The strength of the prisoners in a province in other words is an index of distress, and the jail of every district fulfils to a large extent the functions of a poor-house as well as a jail.[58]

It was alleged by colonial officials that the poor deliberately courted imprisonment during periods of extreme hardship; for them, it was said, prison was "our father-in-law's house," a place where food and shelter might always be found. This claim was used as evidence that India's laborers were lazy (preferring to steal when times were hard rather than find work) and placed little value on their liberty when threatened by hunger. This was part of the case for making prisons as deterrent as possible so that they would not be "hotels for the starving poor." Stricter discipline and a more repugnant diet ("of the *coarsest, plainest and least agreeable* description compatible with health") were accordingly recommended.[59] Some laborers may indeed have sought refuge in prison as a way of escaping from famine. But the manner in which much famine crime was committed and the strength of popular antipathy to the prison cast considerable doubt upon this explanation.[60]

It was generally assumed that prison was a place of confinement for the laboring poor and the "criminal classes," and that the diet, labor, and punishment of prisoners should reflect such lowly origins. The colonialists' fear was that the prison was never quite deterrent enough. The view of the 1838 Prison Discipline Committee was that the convict was "really and apparently in a better situation as to lodging, clothing and food" than was the bulk of the population.[61] Rohde, the Madras inspector, was even blunter: "Imprisonment," he declared in 1856, "is a boon to the greater number, they are better clothed, and better cared for, than nine-tenths of them ever were in their lives."[62]

In actuality, though, prisoners were not exclusively drawn from the lowest classes,[63] and the prison did not treat all its inmates alike; rather, it distinguished between them on the basis of race, community, and, later, gender. In this sense among others, the prison stands as an archetypal colonial institution, not only reflecting and institutionalizing colonial ideas about essential social categories, but also constituting one of the key sites on which the ground rules of colonial engagement with Indian society were laid down.

One of the clearest areas of demarcation was race. European prisoners were invariably given privileged treatment. Control over working-class whites in India was maintained through a series of special institutions and practices—orphanages, workhouses, "lunatic" asylums, and repatriation.[64] These largely obviated the need for confinement in jail, except as a temporary measure or extreme sanction. But where imprisonment was deemed necessary, special provisions were made to ensure that it should not be excessively harsh or humiliating for members of the ruling race. "It would be cruel," remarked the Indian Law Commissioners in 1837, "to subject an European for a long period to a severe prison discipline, in a country in which existence is almost constant misery to an European who has not many indulgences at his command. If not cruel," they added, "it would be impolitic," when it was necessary for "our national character" to "stand high in the estimation of the inhabitants of India," to subject them to the "ignominious labour of a gaol."[65] Separate prison wards were reserved for Europeans, and at Ootacamund a jail was built exclusively to house European (and Eurasian) prisoners. When Wiehe visited it in 1862, he found "a small but substantial and two-storied building after the Pentonville model," accommodating only thirty-six Europeans.[66] They were fed a generous, European diet of mutton, beef, bread, and potatoes rather than the Indian ragi and dal. They were never placed under Indian jailers or subjected to forms of punishment and labor that might be considered demeaning. The European body maintained its privileged status even in confinement.[67]

The administration also found it politic to recognize the importance of caste among prisoners. Although it officially had no place in the colonial penal system—one of the judicial reforms of the early nineteenth century, for instance, was to remove Brahman immunity from capital punishment[68]—caste was nonetheless seen as too potent a factor to ignore in daily prison life. This privileging of caste was partly in response to the kind of overt opposition (led by Rajput, Brahmin, and Kayastha prisoners) encountered in Bengal and northern India during the 1840s and 1850s, but it was also based on a belief that Indians belonged naturally and essentially to castes and close-knit communities in a way that Europeans did not. Thus, a sentence of solitary confinement was thought to be much more of an ordeal for an Indian than for a European. Separation from caste and kin was reputedly the "only punishment that a Native dreads."[69] Except when exemplary punishments were deliberately sought, caste—or the colonial perception of caste—worked powerfully against the "individualizing" project on which the Benthamite Panopticon was premised.

There were prison administrators, like Woodcock in the North-Western Provinces, who held that the introduction of the new messing system in the 1840s was no real threat to caste. He regarded the issue as a mere pretext for opposing the introduction of a more orderly and effective prison regime.[70] But the administration as a whole took the view that caste was an essential part of a Hindu's religious and social identity and as such must be respected even in jail. Following a riot over messing at Allahabad Jail in May 1846, the secretary to the Government of the North-Western Provinces revealed the extent of official caution on this point when he wrote: "The ramifications of caste among the natives of this country are so numerous & European officers are so imperfectly acquainted with them, that it is hardly safe to entrust them with the execution of a measure so closely connected with that difficult subject." The attempt, he continued, to enforce common messing against the will of prisoners had occasioned such resistance and made the prison system so "exceedingly unpopular with the country at large" that the utmost caution was necessary in proceeding any further with it.[71] In April 1847, the government confirmed that it was still in favor of common messing and believed that "much benefit would result from such a system," but only "if it can be introduced without doing violence to the prejudices or the feelings of the people whom it affects."[72] The Court of Directors in London took a similarly pragmatic view, observing that any advantages to be gained by the messing system were unlikely to be "commensurate with the difficulties and risks attending its introduction." While the directors appreciated "the danger and inexpediency of giving way to insubordination," they felt sure that governments in India would not persist in "any measures calculated to excite alarm and discontent as interfering with the religious opinions and feelings of the natives."[73]

It was practical evidence of the willingness to accommodate such "opinions and feelings" that when Mouat visited Bihar Jail in 1856, he found 53 cooks preparing food for 504 prisoners. "It is true that the prejudices of caste in Bihar are very strong," he declared, "yet it seems preposterous that men of the same caste cannot take food from the hands of each other, and that every petty subdivision of the same fraternity should have rules and practices of its own."[74] In Awadh a few years later, the inspector of prisons was petitioned to allow Brahmans their own cooking spaces (*chowka* or *chula*) in prison. He was clearly reluctant to allow any return to the old messing system, which had only recently and with difficulty been supplanted elsewhere in northern and eastern India. Nonetheless, at Lucknow Central Jail, he "indulged" their "prejudices" to the extent of allowing every Brahman to bathe before eating and to mark out "his own 'Chowka' where he squats and receives his rations within the boundary of which no one is permitted to pass during meal time."[75] Among Europeans outside the prison administration, there was bewilderment, even rage, at the extent to which caste had been "basely and indecently succumbed to in our Indian Jails." From the viewpoint of an Evangelical like Alexander Duff, it was bad enough for the government to acknowledge caste rights and distinctions among its ordinary subjects. To respect them among convicts was "the very climax of sinful weakness."[76]

The importance attached to caste was further exemplified by the discussion of prison labor. As early as 1796, it was said that to compel high-caste convicts to work on the roads alongside "common criminals" would be for both them and their families "much more severe than a sentence of death."[77] Forty years further on, the Prison Discipline Committee opined that

> to force a man of a higher caste to work at any trade would disgrace him for ever, and be in fact inflicting a dreadful punishment not only on himself but on every member of his family. It would be looked upon as a barbarous cruelty, and excite nothing but indignation against the laws, in the strength of which the most dreadful crime would be forgotten.[78]

The committee suggested a way out of this dilemma by proposing that prisoners be put to work on a treadmill, since this form of labor would "shew no more favour to the foot of the rich Rajpoot than to the foot of a poor Chumar."[79] While accommodating certain aspects of high-caste status, convicts at the lower end of the caste hierarchy, belonging, for instance, to barber, washerman, and sweeper castes, were expected to perform their customary occupations in jail for the benefit of other prisoners and in the interests of prison economy. In this way, the prison tended to replicate, and extend formal colonial recognition to, the social hierarchy outside.[80]

In an attempt to define the essentials of caste and religion as they affected prison management, jail manuals became elaborate lexicons of bodily signs and ritual practices. According to the Bengal Jail Manual of 1867, any convict sentenced to rigorous imprisonment was to have his head shaved every fifteen days, but, it added,

> the Hindu will retain the *chooteeah* [*chutia*] or *sikha* [tuft]. The beard and moustaches of all prisoners shall be close trimmed or clipped, the beard of Mahomedans being left an inch in length. All prisoners to whom it should be justly offensive or degrading shall, at the discretion of the officer in charge of the jail, be exempt from this proceeding. Sikhs and Mughs must at all times be held exempt.[81]

Similarly, on admission to the prisons of the Bombay presidency,

> the Hindu [is] to retain the shendi; beard and mustachios of both Musalman and Hindu prisoners to be clipped, not shaved; European and Eurasian prisoners to be exempted from having their head shaved, the hair to be cut short only. Sikh prisoners to be exempted altogether from having their hair cut, except on purely medical ground[s].[82]

Despite the requirement that all Indian prisoners wear the prescribed uniforms, special consideration was shown in Bombay's jails to the dress appropriate to high-status communities. In addition to his prison clothes, a Parsi was allowed to wear an undergarment called a *sadra* and a Brahman was permitted to put on a *sowla* cloth while eating; both were allowed to wear the garments known as *janwa* and *kasti* if provided at their own expense.[83] Not all religious emblems and signs were afforded equal treatment, however. Sikhs might keep their uncut hair and even wear a turban in place of a prison cap. They could have a comb, wear breeches and a steel bracelet, but not keep a *kirpan* (dagger), an "undesirable object to entrust to prisoners in jail."[84] Despite these attempts to define the essential requirements of caste and religion, the recognition or denial of certain kinds of religious emblems in prison increasingly became a source of friction between the prison authorities and political or religious leaders who claimed to speak on the prisoners' behalf.

Underlying this policy was a belief that needlessly to violate the requirements of caste and religion in prison would be to inflict an additional punishment beyond that decreed by the courts, one that might be more onerous than the sentence itself. But, by the same token, there were certain situations in which religious conventions and social sensibilities could, it was felt, be justifiably transgressed, whether in the cause of prison discipline and economy or to heighten the punitive effect. As we have seen, the introduction of the messing system in northern India in the 1840s was partly motivated by a determination to make prison a more disciplined and deterrent place by deliberately ignoring caste sensibilities about the preparation and consumption of food. In a similar way, transportation of convicts from India to Southeast Asia, begun in the 1780s, was commended by the Prison Discipline Committee in 1838 as "a weapon of tremendous power" in view of Hindu antipathy to crossing "the black water." In India, it noted, a sentence of transportation was regarded with "indescribable horror." The impact of such a sentence on the convict was "little short of the effect of a sentence of death, whilst the effect of such a sentence on the bystanders is greater than the effect of a sentence of death."[85] Thus, transportation was deliberately maintained at a time when it was losing favor in Britain. Another measure of this sort, perhaps only rarely practiced, was to punish "violent and unruly" women by cutting off their hair, thus rendering their imprisonment a kind of institutional widowhood.[86]

In contrast to the reforming intentions ascribed by Foucault to

Europe's prisons (however imperfectly such goals may have been realized), in India until late in the nineteenth century there was little emphasis upon reform as opposed to confinement. The body of the "Oriental" might be disciplined, but his "soul" remained out of reach. The Prison Discipline Committee of 1838 certainly spoke of "attempts to reform the character" of prisoners as one of the cardinal objectives of the prison system, but it gave less weight to reform than to deterrence.[87] In Madras in 1856, Rohde considered the question of education to be one that "presents difficulties unknown in almost any other country." The provincial government rather confirmed the point when it strongly rejected his suggestion that Christian missionaries be brought in as a suitable agency for prisoners' education and moral reform.[88] The Indian Jail Conference of 1877 went a step further, observing that the idea of reforming prisoners, whatever its validity in the West, "has but little significance in India, where the great majority of criminals . . . need but little reformation." Anyway, it added, there were "practically no means of reforming those who do." The majority of Indian prisoners were "not materially below the moral level of the outside population," and no one would be "so visionary as to wish to apply any other standard to them." Moreover, it asked,

> does any one suppose that we, of an alien race, who, more often than not, live in entire ignorance of the character of those immediately about us, whose moral conceptions are rooted in Western soil, can do much by moral instruction to raise the moral level of the convicts in our jails?[89]

Like earlier commentators, the conference pointed out the difficulty of recruiting suitable warders in India for prisoners' moral reform. "The agencies by which the English reformer works," it said, "are in our hands but broken reeds."[90]

V

But if India's prison system despaired of reforming its inmates and reaching their "souls," it could still serve as an agency for a more practical form of colonial control over productive labor. The extensive use of convict labor on public works in late-eighteenth- and early-nineteenth-century India was not simply a way of keeping as many convicts as possible out of overcrowded jails, although that had its administrative attractions. It was a way of mobilizing scarce labor power, especially for road construction and repair. In the 1830s, thirteen thousand prisoners were employed in road gangs in Bengal alone.[91] They were also assigned to such tasks as clearing river beds, digging irrigation canals, and building their own prisons. In Singapore, Indian prisoners constructed two lighthouses, a cathedral, and the Government House.[92] One of the advantages from the colonial viewpoint of transporting convicts to Penang and Singapore was that they provided a cheap and fairly disciplined workforce in places where this was hard to obtain locally. Even the development of a penal settlement on the Andamans was a form of enforced colonization for which local labor could not be found.

But by the late 1830s, extramural labor was beginning to be viewed with official disfavor: discipline tended to be laxer than inside the jails; it was more difficult to prevent prisoners on road gangs from communicating with the public or escaping; and larger and more efficient sources of nonconvict labor were being tapped to meet the expanding needs of road, canal, and later railway construction.[93] Around the 1850s, a switch was made to industrial production within the prisons, but here too, reform often took second place to remuneration. Mouat, in his day the leading proponent of prison workshops in India, sought to justify them as part of prisoners' discipline and reform; reading Bentham and Beccaria had taught him that "idleness is the chief cause of by far the greater part of the constant war waged by the habitually criminal classes."[94] But the main attraction for the state was that by turning jails into "schools of industry," prisoners contributed substantially toward the cost of their own incarceration and produced, often for the state itself, high-quality goods and services. At first, prison wares were too poorly made to command much market value, but by the 1860s some prisons were achieving significant commercial success. Mouat took particular pride in Alipur and Hugli jails, "unparalleled," he claimed, "in prison management in the world." The former alone had an income of nearly Rs. 210,000 in 1861 from high-quality printing work and brought in a further Rs. 60,000 by manufacturing gunny bags—a total profit of almost Rs. 270,000.[95] Twenty years later, in 1881, as the trend continued, the jails of the Madras presidency produced goods worth Rs. 331,832, most of which were supplied to other government departments—for example, uniforms, boots, sandals and blankets for the police.[96]

Turning prisons into factories was not a policy without its critics, who claimed that discipline was being sacrificed to profit and that the line of demarcation between convict and warder was being dangerously eroded. "The law intends imprisonment to be a punishment," wrote one skeptic, "and therefore the first thing to be looked at in labour is not that it should be remunerative, but that it should render a residence in jail a matter of dread, apprehension and avoidance."[97] Wiehe agreed, commenting on the jail workshops in Calcutta that it was "scarcely possible to conceive a system more indulgent, less tentative in respect of moral reformation, and better calculated to promote the comfort of the convicts."[98] The policy came in for strong criticism again in the early 1880s, when the Military Department unilaterally reversed the Government of India's decision to favor jail manufactures over private contractors. Lord Ripon, the Liberal viceroy, took the view that jail manufactures "should be regarded not as a source of revenue, but as a branch of prison discipline." But for what he called "the admitted exigencies of sound prison management," he would have been "opposed to jail manufactures in India altogether."[99]

But, despite the critics, jail manufacturing continued to expand and flourish. If, elsewhere in the industrial age, the factory often resembled the prison, in India the prison largely anticipated the factory. With a combination of disciplined labor and a principle of profit, several major Indian industries sprang up behind prison walls—gunny bags in Calcutta, woolen goods at Agra, blankets at Bhagalpur, carpets at Hazaribagh—and convict workshops also specialized in the production of carpets and dhurries, papermaking and lithography. By the early years of the twentieth century, some jails had become so commercially successful that European industrialists complained of unfair competition from state-subsidized jail labor.[100] Certainly, the growth of jail industries was a remarkable development for a regime that was formally committed to laissez-faire and that otherwise denied aid to industry, but they were one indication of the higher priority colonialism gave to prison as a "school of industry" than as a "house of correction."

VI

If the colonial prison provided an orientalist model of a society constructed around an essentialism of caste and religion, it also, increasingly as the century progressed, became a model for the ordering of society according to the dictates of medical science and sanitation. One of the few areas where the colonial state had relatively unobstructed access to the body of its subjects, the prison occupied a critical place in the development of Western medical knowledge and practice in India.[101] Apart from the alarm generated by outbreaks of prison violence and indiscipline, it was the high level of sickness and mortality in jails that impelled official inquiry and reform. Although no physicians were included in the 1838 Prison Discipline Committee, by the 1860s the prison was being actively incorporated into the expanding realm of state medicine. In the absence of a professional prison service, civil surgeons were being appointed to run district and central jails. From the 1860s, prison inspectors general were usually drawn from the Indian Medical Service, and medical officers sat on several committees of inquiry set up to investigate disciplinary as well as health issues. By the end of the century, medical administration had come to be seen as "the most important of all matters affecting jail management."[102]

In accepting a responsibility for health inside the jails, the colonial state helped establish them as privileged sites of medical observation and experimentation. The importance of the colonial connection between medicine and penology was reflected in the voluminous medical literature that used prisoners as a source of statistical data and clinical observations or as a standard by which to calculate and evaluate the health of the population as a whole.[103] Although individual medical officers might be highly critical of prison conditions, collectively they endorsed prison practice and bestowed upon it an aura of scientific legitimacy.

The prison exemplified the role of colonial medicine as an agency of disciplinary control. It was, for instance, the responsibility of medical officers to decide whether prisoners were genuinely ill, merely "shirking" to avoid punishment, or suffering from self-inflicted ailments. They were required to advise whether a prisoner's mental and physical health was "likely to be injuriously affected by the discipline or treatment observed in the jail." Medical officers might thus exercise a moderating influence over harsh punishments, but sometimes they clearly allowed abuses to occur or sanctioned punishments without due regard to the physical and psychological consequences.[104] By entrusting responsibility for prison administration to the medical service, the state also drew a permissive veil over other forms of neglect and suffering. In concentrating on issues of diet, health, and sanitation, it distanced itself, for instance, from any active responsibility to educate prisoners. Health alone was the mark of a sound prison system.[105]

The importance of the prison as a site of medical observation and intervention stood in inverse proportion to colonial access to the rest of Indian society. At a time when most of India lay beyond any kind of medical and statistical purview, prisoners could readily be classified and counted. As early as the 1830s and 1840s, statistical tables were compiled to show the number of admissions to prison hospitals and the extent and causes of sickness and death among prisoners. Only among soldiers were comparable statistical exercises possible in the first half of the century.[106] Prisons were one of the main sources of information about cholera, epidemics of which periodically devastated the jails. At a time when medical science identified many diseases with poisonous miasmas and stinking effluvia, prisons presented a seemingly incontestible case for the relationship between fetid bodies, human exhalations, and epidemic disease. Prison officers responded by evacuating prisoners to temporary camps or sought to mitigate the ravages of disease by ordering improvements in ventilation and drainage.[107] Despite the appointment in the 1860s of provincial sanitary commissioners responsible for army and civilian as well as prison health, the crudeness of the general mortality data (and the virtual absence of morbidity figures) meant that prison data retained a "definiteness and value" that was "quite unique."[108] Jail-based medical investigations were not confined to cholera but also included typhoid, tuberculosis, kala azar, and meningitis, as well as malaria and ankylostomiasis (hookworm infestation)—these last two assuming a particular economic significance because of their prevalence among plantation laborers as well as prisoners. This statistical, sanitary, and medical reconnaissance of society, via the prison, of "biological traits" relevant to wider "economic management" reminds us of Foucault's account of a similar, if more generalized, process at work in eighteenth- and nineteenth-century Europe.[109]

Without wishing to make Indian jails sound like Nazi concentration camps, which clearly they were not, it is noteworthy how, in prisons, medical measures could be enforced, and observations and experiments carried out, that were deemed impractical or inexpedient elsewhere. For instance, given the extreme difficulty medical researchers had in obtaining corpses for dissection because of the intensity of Indian opposition to postmortems, the jail was one of the few permitted sources of cadavers. By the 1860s, it was standard practice to conduct a postmortem on every prisoner who died (the Bengal Jail Manual rather bizarrely suggested that one reason for this was to discourage prisoners from trying to escape by pretending to be dead!), and these postmortems facilitated the acquisition of medical knowledge about diseases like typhoid, where diagnosis on the basis of external signs and symptoms was unreliable.[110]

"In no cases are preventive and prophylactic measures so efficacious as among bodies of men so completely under control, as are prisoners in jails," remarked Mouat in 1856.[111] Indeed, medical opinion inclined to the view that in prison it was possible—even desirable—to ignore the cultural and social "prejudices" that obstructed Western medicine elsewhere and that indeed had previously been afforded recognition within the prison itself. As Rohde in Madras put it, "Outside a jail, prejudices are supposed to be insuperable, but within a jail there can be no excuse for neglecting any proper [medical or sanitary] precaution, or not compelling any observance which shall tend to remove the risk."[112] These were not hollow words. At a time when it still encountered strong popular resistance and evasion, vaccination against smallpox was compulsory for prisoners who could not demonstrate prior protection. Even a man in Punjab, sent to prison in 1911 for refusing to have his daughter vaccinated, found himself vaccinated.[113] Early trials in the use of immunization against plague, cholera and typhoid were conducted on selected (and reputedly "voluntary") prison populations in the 1890s and early 1900s. At Gaya Jail in Bihar in 1894, the Russian bacteriologist Waldemar Haffkine inoculated 215 of the 433 prisoners against cholera, although the Government of India, when it heard about this, was fearful that reports of compulsory inoculation in jail would stir up hostile agitation. Despite this, three years later, in January 1897, half of the inmates of Bombay's House of Correction were inoculated with Haffkine's experimental antiplague serum. In both cases, the tests conducted among prisoners (along with plantation workers and soldiers) were advanced as scientific evidence for the safety and efficacy of prophylactic measures and their suitability for public use.[114]

Quinine was also widely experimented with in jails, partly because of the exceptional facilities they offered for administering strictly regulated doses and for carefully observing their prophylactic effect. At a time when quinine encountered strong public resistance—because of its bitter taste, its unpleasant side effects, and a preference for indigenous febrifuges—the prison provided a unique opportunity to demonstrate its effectiveness. The drug was first systematically used in 1907 when Punjab's inspector general of prisons, G. F. W. Braide, instructed jail superintendents to give prisoners regular weekly doses of sulphate of quinine during months when malaria was prevalent. Ramadan happened to fall that year during the malarial season, but, in a way that indicates how the expanding claims of medical science were encroaching upon the old orientalist sensibilities, instructions were given that Muslim prisoners were not to be exempted from this treatment but were to receive their dose after sundown; "in no case" was the distribution of quinine to be "suspended or vigilance over it be relaxed during the period of the fast." Braide attached great importance to adequate and consistent dosage, and urged prison officers to use their influence and authority to ensure that every prisoner "actually receive the exact quantity of the drug fixed by the rules in force at the appointed times." The year 1908 proved to be one of the worst on record for malaria. In the four months from August to November, an estimated 90 percent of the population of Punjab suffered from malaria; 50 percent fell seriously ill. Over 400,000 deaths were reported, and the loss of productive labor was immense. But Braide's quinine policy appeared to be vindicated, because among prisoners, sickness and mortality rates were much lower than among the general population. It was admitted that prisoners were an atypical group, with few women, children, and old people among their number. Nonetheless, the fact that 90 percent of the public but only 10 percent of prisoners fell ill was used as evidence for the value of quinine, and the public was urged to follow the prisoners' example.[115]

Pioneering work on Indian diets was also carried out in prisons. Observations made on prisoners were used to inform comparisons with the diet and health of the laboring population in general and to work out differences between the nutritional and calorific value of Indian and European diets. In 1846, Dr. A. H. Leith conducted an inquiry into the causes of ill health among prisoners at Bombay's House of Correction. His attention focused on the prisoners' diet, which consisted of rice, dal, a little salt, and ghee. When Leith introduced an improved diet incorporating an antiscorbutic pickle and wheat flour instead of rice, scurvy disappeared, sickness rates fell, and there was an improvement in the body weight and health of prisoners.[116] Criticisms made by Mouat on the deficiencies of jail diets in Bengal ten years later stimulated fresh interest in the subject, and in 1861 (after his report had attracted attention in London) the Government of India asked each province to report on jail diets and to compare them with the food of the laboring classes outside. The resulting surveys provide interesting insights into rural diets at the time.[117] However, the nature and quantity of food provided for prisoners remained a continuing source of controversy, and several further investigations were carried out before World War I. An attempt was made to reconcile the requirements of health and economy with a penological desire to exclude anything—such as ghee—that might constitute an item of unaccustomed "luxury" for the laboring poor.[118] These investigations were also important in providing a measure for the amount of food or money to be given to seekers of state relief during famines, providing evidence of how much (more often, how little) food was needed to sustain life and support labor.[119] Once again, colonial knowledge, born of the prison, supplied a standard of wider utility.

Dietary data based on prison populations was also used to make "scientific" pronouncements about physiological differences between Indians and Europeans and even between different Indian "races." In 1912, Professor D. McCay of Calcutta Medical College compared jail diets in Bengal with those in the United Provinces and used the results to draw a contrast between the physical frailty of rice-eating Bengalis and the robust constitutions and martial bearing of the Rajputs and Sikhs of northern India, with their diet of dairy products, wheat, and meat. The prison evidence was taken as proof that the agrarian classes of the United Provinces were on a "distinctly higher plane of physical development" than those of Bengal:

> The general muscularity of the body is decidedly better and their capabilities of labour are greater. They are smarter on their feet, more brisk and more alive to the incidents of every-day life, and they do not present such slackness and tonelessness as one is accustomed to observe in the people of Lower Bengal.[120]

Despite the narrow nature of his evidence, McCay was confident that this showed how dietary "faults" could be corrected to the advantage not just of prisoners but also of agrarian society and the state. Jail diets were taken as a valid indication of the importance of food rather than heredity "in the formation and development of those attributes and qualities of mind and body that are alike the pride of the soldier and the envy of inferior races."[121] It seemed no more inappropriate to McCay than to many earlier colonial physicians to read civilian health from convict physiology.

VII

There are many histories of the colonial prison yet to be written. Concealed within its walls are many examples of unexplored subalternity, still obscured from us by the sheer density of the colonial record and overlaid by the more familiar narratives of prison life that emerged from the middle-class discovery of the prison from the 1890s onward. But looking back beyond that watershed, one can already see the nineteenth-century prison as a site of sporadic defiance and "everyday resistance," and of some success, in what might at first sight appear a most unpromising locale, in contesting and occasionally or temporarily negating the power and authority of the colonial state over the body of its subjects. Like Foucault, one might write a history of the technologies of corporal power as they manifested themselves in prison discourse and practice, although, it has been argued here, such a history would need to give much more consideration to the role of resistance in shaping the very nature of the prison system and to focus more centrally upon the prison as a site of state power and knowledge.

Out of the carceral gloom emerges a central discourse around the body of the Indian prisoner and its relevance to the wider colonization of Indian society. The prison was not cut off from all contact with and reference to the rest of civil society. On the contrary, it often served an exemplary role, showing how discipline and order could, or (not infrequently) could not, be imposed on indigenous society by an alien ruling class, how a desire to overturn cultural and social "prejudices" needed to be tempered by political pragmatism, how medicine might reign without its customary hindrances. Despite the iron fetters and the high walls, despite the exercises in internal exile and overseas transportation, the prisoner remained ineluctably, even defiantly, part of his or her own society. The colonial prison was, in many respects, a remarkably permeable institution, connected to the outside world through venal warders and communal identities, as it was later to be through political affiliations. What happened in the prison echoed in the streets and reverberated in the villages. In the mid-nineteenth cen-

tury, the colonial authorities felt obliged to recognize a continuum between the prison and the wider community and so abandoned any pretense at individualizing or reforming prisoners. It was politically expedient to do so, but it also reflected certain basic assumptions about
the essential nature of Indian—as opposed to Western—society.

And yet, paradoxically, the prison, especially in the later decades of
the nineteenth century and the early part of the twentieth, was also a
site where colonialism was able (indeed was obliged) to observe and interact with its subjects to a degree exceptional elsewhere. Where else did
it feed, clothe, house, and nurse its subjects? The body of the prisoner
was disciplined, but this was less in the service of moral reform than in
the cause of remunerative labor. While the need to respect the essential
attributes of caste and religon was acknowledged and enshrined in
prison manuals, the body of the prisoner might yet serve as a site of intensive medical investigation and experimentation. This, quite apart
from the role that confinement might have in the actual disciplining of
labor, made the prison integral to the wider dynamics of labor management under colonial rule. For all its superficial isolation and its obvious
physical and sociological peculiarities, the prison was repeatedly scrutinized as some kind of representative institution—in relation to caste, to
disease, to labor, and to diet. The body of the prisoner and the cultural
practices that surrounded it were constantly related to wider perceptions and imperatives alike among the colonized and the colonizers.

Notes

1. Michel Foucault, *Discipline and Punish: The Birth of the Prison* (Harmondsworth, 1979), pp. 3–5.
2. Michel Foucault, *Power/Knowledge: Selected Interviews and Other Writings,
1972–1977* (Brighton, 1980), p. 38.
3. Foucault, *Discipline and Punish*, p. 14.
4. Ibid., pp. 10, 16.
5. Ibid., pp. 200–202.
6. Foucault, *Power/Knowledge*, p. 159.
7. Ibid., p. 158.
8. Ibid., pp. 98, 159, 161.
9. Ibid., p. 39.
10. Ibid., p. 162. Resistance is given a more significant place elsewhere in Foucault's work. The statement "Where there is power, there is resistance" (*The History of
Sexuality: An Introduction* [Harmondsworth, 1984], p. 95) is closer to the spirit of the
present essay.
11. Anand A. Yang, "Disciplining 'Natives': Prisons and Prisoners in Early Nineteenth Century India," *South Asia* 10, no. 2 (1987): 29–45.

12. *Report of the Inspector of Prisons in Oudh for the Year 1862* (Lucknow, 1864), p. 33.

13. Yang, "Disciplining 'Natives,'" p. 42. See also *Report of the Prison Discipline Committee* (Calcutta, 1838), pp. 30–34. An earlier attempt (in the 1790s) to prohibit self-catering among prisoners in Bengal also ran into formidable opposition and had to be abandoned.

14. J. P. Woodcock, Magistrate, Allahabad, to Sessions Judge, Allahabad, 18 May 1846, North-Western Provinces (NWP) Criminal Judicial Proceedings, 5, 1 July 1846, India Office Library (hereafter IOL); C. B. Thornhill, Inspector-General of Prisons to Secretary, NWP, 27 January 1854, NWP Criminal Judicial Proceedings, 296, 14 February 1854, IOL.

15. *Prison Discipline Committee*, p. 63.

16. A. E. Russell, Magistrate, Tirhut, to Sessions Judge, 10 May 1853, Bengal Judicial Proceedings, 3, 7 June 1855, IOL; minute by Lieutenant Governor F. J. Halliday, 18 May 1855, ibid., no. 7.

17. John Kaye, *History of the Indian Mutiny of 1857–8* (London, 1870), vol. 2, pp. 42, 44–45, 192–93, 232; William Edwards, *Personal Adventures during the Indian Rebellion in Rohilcund, Futtehghur, and Oude* (London, 1858), pp. 3, 9–11. A further factor here was that the prisoners included Brahmans, Rajputs, and others, sentenced for affrays and similar crimes: many of them must have had relatives among the rebellious sepoys of the Bengal Army.

18. F. J. Mouat, *Report on the Statistics of the Prisons of the Lower Provinces of the Bengal Presidency for 1861, 1862, 1863, 1864, and 1865* (Calcutta, 1868), p. 2.

19. J. Rohde to Chief Secretary, Madras, 30 April 1856, *Report of the Inspector of Prisons, Fort St. George, 1856* (Madras, 1856), report, para. 6.

20. *Report of the Indian Jail Conference Assembled in Calcutta in January–March 1877* (Calcutta, 1877), pp. 47, 121.

21. *Report of the Indian Jails Committee, 1919–20*, vol. 1, *Report and Appendices* (Simla, 1920), p. 56; vol. 2, *Minutes of Evidence Taken in England, the Madras Presidency and the Andamans*, p. 34.

22. William Walker, *Rules for the Management and Discipline of Prisoners in the North-Western Provinces and Oudh* (Allahabad, 1882), pp. 42, 115–16.

23. *Indian Jail Conference, 1877*, pp. 70–72; *Report of the Committee Appointed to Enquire into Certain Matters Connected with Jail Administration in India* (Calcutta, 1889), pp. 49–51; *Indian Jails Committee, 1919–20*, vol. 1, pp. 68–71.

24. *Indian Jails Committee, 1919–20*, vol. 2, p. 268–69.

25. For the middle-class discovery of the prison in the 1890s and 1900s, see *Hitavadi*, January 1898, Bengal *Native Newspaper Reports*, for the editor's jail experiences; *Dnyan Prakash* (Bombay), 12 September 1898, Bombay *Native Newspaper Reports*, for Tilak's experiences in prison; V. D. Savarkar, *The Story of My Transportation for Life* (Bombay, 1950); and, for Gandhi in South Africa, *The Collected Works of Mahatma Gandhi*, vol. 9 (Delhi, 1966). For later examples of this genre, see C. Rajagopalachari, *Chats behind Bars* (Madras, n.d.), and *Rajaji's 1920 Jail Life* (Madras, 1941).

26. These letters are taken from *Indian Jails Committee, 1919–20*, vol. 2, pp. 406–10.

27. Foucault himself later conceded that the prison system he described in *Discipline and Punish* failed to operate with the precision its originators ascribed to it and that indeed it served to "manufacture" criminals; *Power/Knowledge*, p. 40. For the evolution of the prison system in Britain, see Michael Ignatieff, *A Just Measure of Pain: The Penitentiary in the Industrial Revolution, 1750–1850* (London, 1989), and William

174 / *David Arnold*

James Forsythe, *The Reform of Prisoners, 1830–1900* (London, 1987), and for a recent discussion of the difficulty of applying Foucault to a colonial situation, see Megan Vaughan, *Curing Their Ills: Colonial Power and African Illness* (Cambridge, 1991), esp. pp. 8–12.

28. Ashis Nandy, *The Intimate Enemy: Loss and Recovery of Self under Colonialism* (Delhi, 1983), pp. xi, 1–2, 30–31.

29. These themes are more fully explored in David Arnold, *Colonizing the Body: Epidemic Disease and State Medicine in Nineteenth-Century India* (Berkeley, Calif., 1993).

30. Foucault, *Discipline and Punish*, p. 39.

31. This contempt was perhaps most clearly and influentially expressed by James Mill, *The History of British India*, 5th ed. (London, 1858), vol. 1, pp. 176–83, 284–90, 309–11.

32. Tapas Kumar Banerjee, *Background to Indian Criminal Law* (Bombay, 1963), pp. 68–71, 129, 291–94. For a critical account of changes instituted by the early colonial regime in Bengal, see Jorg Fisch, *Cheap Lives and Dear Limbs: The British Transformation of the Bengal Criminal Law, 1769–1817* (Wiesbaden, 1983).

33. Cited in Banerjee, *Background*, p. 360. The phrase "shocking to humanity" echoes Sir William Jones's comment of 1788 on the "cruel mutilations practised by the native powers" of India; Mill, *History*, vol. 1, p. 176.

34. Between 1816 and 1827, roughly 9 percent of the 9,002 individuals sentenced by the Nizamat Adalat, the chief criminal court for Lower Bengal, were sentenced to death, 30 percent to transportation, and 19 percent to terms of between seven and fourteen years; Fisch, *Cheap Lives*, pp. 44, 100. In the North-Western Provinces between 1836 and 1842, from 5 to 16 percent of those sentenced each year by the Nizamat Adalat were sentenced to death; *Report of the Nizamut Adawlut North-Western Provinces on the Administration of Criminal Justice for the Year 1843* (Agra, 1844), p. 97.

35. Banerjee, *Background*, p. 119.

36. *Jail Administration in India* (1889), p. 53. For a critical account of India's penal system in the 1860s, see Mary Carpenter, *Six Months in India* (London, 1868), vol. 1, pp. 48–52, 103–5, 200–202, 297.

37. Cited in A. P. Howell, *Note on Jails and Jail Discipline in India, 1867–68* (Calcutta, 1868), p. 1.

38. Mary Carpenter, "On Reformatory and Industrial Schools for India," *Journal of the National Indian Association* 47 (November 1874): 278. I am indebted to Indira Chowdhury Sengupta for this reference.

39. Eric Stokes, *The English Utilitarians and India* (Oxford, 1959), p. 218.

40. *Report of the Committee on Prison Discipline*, p. 3.

41. Rohde, *Report*, "Construction," para. 27.

42. C. G. Wiehe, *Journal of a Tour of Inspection of the Principal Jails in India Made by the Inspector General of Prisons, Bombay Presidency* (Bombay, 1865), p. 38.

43. Ibid., p. 39.

44. Ibid., p. 53.

45. Ibid., p. 7.

46. *Jail Administration in India* (1889), pp. 13, 49; cf. Howell, *Note on Jails*, pp. 18–19.

47. *Report of the Committee on Prison Discipline*, p. 9.

48. *Annual Report of the Sanitary Commissioner with the Government of India, 1880* (Calcutta, 1882), p. 67; *Indian Jail Conference, 1877*, pp. 22, 125; *Indian Jails Committee, 1919–20*, vol. 1, p. 37.

49. *Report of the Inspector of Prisons, Oudh, 1862*, p. 16.

50. *Annual Report of the Sanitary Commissioner, Madras, 1880* (Madras, 1881), p. 40.

51. *Indian Jail Conference, 1877*, p. 104; Mouat, *Report on Statistics*, p. 4.

52. Fisch, *Cheap Lives*, p. 105, cites a major dacoity case in Bengal in 1821; among the 163 put on trial were 31 women, all of whom were discharged.

53. On women prisoners, see Carpenter, *Six Months in India*, vol. 1, pp. 51, 115, 202; Mary Frances Billington, *Woman in India* (1895; reprint, New Delhi, 1973), pp. 240–49; Fred. J. Mouat, *Report on Jails Visited and Inspected in Bengal, Behar, and Arracan* (Calcutta, 1856), p. 63; Wiehe, *Journal of a Tour*, p. 7.

54. Wiehe, *Journal of a Tour*, p. 45; Howell, *Note on Jails*, p. 124.

55. *Report on the Medical Topography and Statistics of the Ceded Districts* (Madras, 1844), p. 28; Mouat, *Report on Jails*, pp. 54–55; Home (Judicial), 98–124, May 1908, National Archives of India (hereafter NAI).

56. As in the case of Vasudeo Balvant Phadke of tuberculosis in Aden in 1883; V. S. Joshi, *Vasudeo Balvant Phadke: First Indian Rebel against British Rule* (Bombay, 1959), pp. 172–73. (I am grateful to David Hardiman for this reference.)

57. *Indian Jail Conference, 1877*, pp. 20–21.

58. *Annual Report of the Sanitary Commissioner, 1880*, p. 83. For a similar correlation between dearth and prison populations in Madras, see A. G. Cardew, Inspector General of Prisons, to Chief Secretary, Madras, 19 June 1896, Government Order 1026, Madras Judicial Proceedings, IOL.

59. W. H. Woodcock, to Secretary, NWP, 29 January 1846, NWP Criminal Judicial Proceedings, 19, 4 March 1846, IOL (emphasis in the original); *Prison Discipline Committee*, p. 104; *Indian Jail Conference, 1877*, pp. 20–21.

60. David Arnold, "Dacoity and Rural Crime in Madras, 1860–1940," *Journal of Peasant Studies* 6, no. 2 (1979): 145–49, and "Famine in Peasant Consciousness and Peasant Action: Madras, 1876–8," in Ranajit Guha, ed., *Subaltern Studies III* (Delhi, 1984), pp. 75–93.

61. *Prison Discipline Committee*, p. 104.

62. Rohde, *Report*, "Accommodation," para. 5.

63. Among the 4,458 prisoners in Awadh in 1862, 746 came from service communities, 905 from laboring and 2,157 from cultivating groups, 80 from zamindari families, 296 from trade and 68 from shopkeeping; 89 were beggars, 21 were weavers, and 16 were goldsmiths. In caste terms, there were 675 Brahmans, 612 Rajputs and Khatris, 219 "Buneas" (Bhuinyas), 51 Kayasthas, 910 Pasis, and 204 Ahirs; among Muslims there were 417 Sheiks, 230 Pathans, 195 Sayyids, and 183 Moghuls. There were 217 prisoners able to read and write; *Report of the Inspector of Prisons, Oudh, 1862*, pp. 54–55, 72–77.

64. David Arnold, "European Orphans and Vagrants in India in the Nineteenth Century," *Journal of Imperial and Commonwealth History* 7, no. 2 (1979): 104–27.

65. *The Indian Penal Code as Originally Framed in 1837* (Madras, 1888), appendix, pp. 95–96, note A.

66. Wiehe, *Journal of a Tour*, pp. 3–5. In 1877 (*Indian Jail Conference*, pp. 176–77), there were 1,232 European men and 16 women in Indian jails.

67. For later protests against this preferential treatment, see *Report of the United Provinces Jails Inquiry Committee, 1919* (Allahabad, 1929), pp. 241–47.

68. Fisch, *Cheap Lives*, pp. 81, 101.

69. Lord Mayo, minute, 3 March 1869, Home (Judicial), 3, 19 June 1869, NAI.

70. W. H. Woodcock, to Secretary, NWP, 30 May 1846, NWP Criminal Judicial Proceedings, 4, 1 July 1846, IOL.

71. J. Thornton, Secretary, NWP, to Secretary, Bengal, 1 July 1846, NWP Criminal Judicial Proceedings, 6, 1 July 1846, IOL.

72. Thornton to "the several judges," NWP, 30 April 1847, NWP Criminal Judicial Proceedings, 103, 30 April 1847, IOL. Cf. the Government of Bengal's response to the lota riots in 1855: "It is only when they imagine their caste about to be encroached on, that the prisoners are prone to rebel, or that their countrymen without the jail shew them any sympathy"; minute by Lieutenant Governor F. J. Halliday, 18 May 1855, Bengal Judicial Proceedings, 7, 7 June 1855, IOL.

73. Judicial letter to Bengal, 12 August 1846, cited in Banerjee, *Background*, p. 339.

74. Mouat, *Report on Jails*, pp. 76–77.

75. *Report of the Inspector of Prisons, Oudh, 1862*, p. 33.

76. Alexander Duff, *The Indian Rebellion: Its Causes and Results* (London, 1858), pp. 354–55.

77. Cited in Banerjee, *Background*, p. 343.

78. *Prison Discipline Committee*, p. 106.

79. Ibid., p. 110.

80. An attempt by the inspector general in Madras to make reconvicted prisoners perform certain manual tasks was overturned by the Government of India; Inspector General of Jails, to Chief Secretary, Madras, 12 April 1871, Madras Judicial Proceedings, 75, 19 April 1871, IOL; Secretary, Judicial, India, to Chief Secretary, Madras, 8 July 1871, Madras Judicial Proceedings, 98, 24 October 1871. It was thereafter directed that in assigning labor to convicts, "reasonable allowance should be made for caste prejudice, e.g., no Brahman or caste Hindu shall be employed in chucklers' work"; *The Madras Jail Manual* (Madras, 1899), p. 121. There was a similar dispute in Bombay jails in 1886 over attempts to make women convicts perform scavenging work; Bombay *Native Newspaper Reports*, January–February 1882.

81. George Alexander Hodge, *Bengal Jail Manual* (Calcutta, 1867), p. 69. See also Walker, *Rules for the Management and Discipline of Prisoners*, p. 54.

82. Cruikshank, *A Manual of Jail Rules for the Superintendence and Management of Jails in the Bombay Presidency* (Bombay, 1876), p. 26.

83. Ibid., pp. 58–59.

84. *Indian Jails Committee, 1919–20*, vol. 1, p. 156.

85. *Prison Discipline Committee*, pp. 86, 97.

86. *Indian Jail Conference, 1877*, p. 104; *Jail Administration in India* (1889), p. 68.

87. *Prison Discipline Committee*, pp. 38, 102.

88. Rohde, *Report*, "Education," paras. 1–3; government review, 7 February 1857, ibid. For a short-lived attempt to use literate prisoners to educate others at Agra jail, see Secretary, NWP, to Inspector-General of Prisons, 2 March 1854, NWP Criminal Judicial Proceedings, 112, 9 May 1854, IOL.

89. *Indian Jail Conference, 1877*, p. 34.

90. Ibid., p. 34.

91. *Prison Discipline Committee*, p. 17.

92. J. F. A. McNair and W. D. Bayliss, *Prisoners Their Own Warders* (London, 1899).

93. For a review of government policy toward extramural labor, see notes to Home (Judicial), 121–52, October 1882, NAI.

94. Mouat, *Report on Statistics*, p. 16.

95. Wiehe, *Journal of a Tour*, p. 17.

96. Notes to Home (Judicial), 121–52, October 1882, NAI.

97. Cruikshank, *Manual of Jail Rules*, p. 35.

98. Wiehe, *Journal of a Tour*, p. 23.

99. Ripon, memo, 16 August 1882, in notes to Home (Judicial), 121–52, October 1882, NAI. The debate continued in Home (Judicial), 328–51, June 1883, NAI.

100. *Indian Jails Conference, 1919–20*, vol. 1, pp. 124–25.

101. Colonial India was not, of course, alone in this respect: prisons were also a significant source of sanitary statistics and medical information in late-eighteenth- and nineteenth-century Britain; cf. Edwin Chadwick, *Report on the Sanitary Conditions of the Labouring Population of Great Britain* (ed. M. W. Flinn) (Edinburgh, 1965), pp. 49, 279–83. But I would argue that medical research and administration in Indian prisons had an exceptional role not only in medical research but also in creating a colonial discourse about Indian society and the Indian body.

102. *Rules for the Superintendence and Management of Jails in the Province of Assam* (Calcutta, 1899), vol. 1, p. 224.

103. E.g., James Hutchinson, *Observations on the General and Medical Management of Indian Jails and on Some of the Principal Diseases Which Infest Them* (2nd ed., Calcutta, 1845); A. E. Roberts, "Public Health and Vital Statistics," *Imperial Gazetteer of India: The Indian Empire* (Oxford, 1907), vol. 1, pp. 531–34.

104. Cruikshank, *Manual of Jail Rules*, p. 12; Savarkar, *Story of My Transportation*, pp. 112–13, 117–18; McNair and Bayliss, *Prisoners*, pp. 152–53.

105. *Indian Jails Conference, 1919–20*, vol. 1, p. 30.

106. E.g., *Report on the Medical Topography and Statistics of the Ceded Districts* (Madras, 1844), pp. 22–28, 52–57.

107. Mouat, *Report on Jails*, pp. 35–37, 43, 61; John Murray, *Report on the Treatment of Epidemic Cholera* (Calcutta, 1869).

108. Lankester, *A Report on Tuberculosis in India* (Simla, 1915), p. 35. For jail-based investigations of ankylostomiasis, see K. S. Mhaskar, "Report of the Ankylostomiasis Inquiry in Madras," *Indian Medical Research Memoirs*, no. 1 (Calcutta, 1924), pp. 10–11.

109. Foucault, *Power/Knowledge*, p. 172.

110. Hodge, *Bengal Jail Manual*, appendix, p. 400.

111. Mouat, *Report on Jails*, p. 43.

112. Rohde, *Report*, "Diseases of Prisoners," para. 14.

113. Home (Jails), 21–22, November 1912, NAI.

114. R. Macrae, "Cholera and Preventive Inoculation in Gaya Jail," *Indian Medical Gazette*, September 1894, pp. 334–38; Home (Medical), 37–47, April 1895, NAI; R. Harvey, "Note on Anti-Plague Inoculations," Home (Sanitary), 76, May 1898, NAI.

115. G. F. W. Braide to all Jail Superintendents, Punjab, 4 July 1908, and "Malaria in the Punjab and the Protection of Prisoners by the Use of Quinine in the Jails of the Province," Home (Jails), 11, January 1910, NAI. But even in prison, such prophylactic measures could meet evasion—by prisoners who spat out the quinine "poison" when the doctor was not looking; *Krishnakumar Mitrer Atmacarit* (The autobiography of Krishna Kumar Mitra [in Bengali]) (Calcutta, 1939), p. 323. I am indebted to Indira Chowdhury Sengupta for this reference.

116. A. H. Leith, "A Contribution to Dietetics," *Transactions of the Medical and Physical Society of Bombay*, n.s., 1, 1851–52, pp. 114–27.

117. *Report by Civil Medical Officers on the Nature, Growth, and Mode of Preparation of the Various Alimentary Articles Consumed by the Industrial and Laboring Population in the Several Districts of Bengal, North-Western Provinces, Punjab, Oude,*

and British Burmah (Calcutta, 1863); W. R. Cornish, *Reports on the Nature of the Food of the Inhabitants of the Madras Presidency* (Madras, 1863); *Report on the Diet of Prisoners and of the Industrial and Labouring Classes in the Bombay Presidency* (Bombay, 1865).

118. For controversy following the introduction of new jail diets in 1877, see "Corporal Punishment and Mortality in Indian Jails," *Parliamentary Papers*, C3316, 1882, pp. 3–25.

119. For the use of jail-based standards of diet and labor and the dispute that arose between W. R. Cornish, sanitary commissioner, Madras, and Sir William Temple on behalf of the Government of India, see J. C. Geddes, *Administrative Experience Recorded in Former Famines* (Calcutta, 1874), pp. 143–44; Cornish to Chief Secretary, Madras, 13 March 1877, Madras Sanitary Commissioners Proceedings, March 1877, IOL. The use of prisoners' health and diet as a basis for comparison with other social groups, such as factory workers, continued into the 1920s and 1930s; e.g., Ahmad Muktar, *Factory Labour in India* (Madras, 1930), pp. 234–39.

120. D. McCay, *Investigations into the Jail Dietaries of the United Provinces, with Some Observations on the Influence of Dietary on the Physical Development and Well-Being of the People of the United Provinces* (Calcutta, 1912), p. 188.

121. Ibid., pp. 135, 190.

6 / Remembering Chauri Chaura: Notes from Historical Fieldwork

Shahid Amin

SITA: *Surāj ke bāre mein pahila "case" Chauri Chaura-e-hauwwe.*
NAUJADI: *Chauri Chaura te hauwwe-hi—aur Dumri se sab kār bhail. . . . Sabke Raj ho gail, hamni-ke Raj nāhīn kailas—hamman utpāt kaileen, au(r) hamman-ke kuch nāhīn milal.*

On 4 February 1922, a crowd of peasants burned a police station at Chauri Chaura, a small town in northern India, killing twenty-three policemen. Gandhi's prompt condemnation of this "crime" led to a relocation of this day in the life of the nation.[1] To be a Gandhian in the spring of 1922 (and for some time to come) was to share in an authoritative recollection of this antinationalist "riot."

The "unforgettable event" was largely forgotten in nationalist lore; it came to be remembered only as the episode that forced Gandhi to call off his all-India movement of noncooperation with the British. Intrinsically meaningless, the significance of Chauri Chaura lay outside the time and place of its occurrence. An event without prehistory, it was quarantined inside the borders of a consequentialist past; that is, nationalist verse, political prose, and the memoirs of distinguished Indians all invoked the event *to explain* the termination of *one phase* of the Freedom Struggle. Chauri Chaura became "Chauri Chaura": the place and the people were erased over the construction of a momentous Event. The event was written out as it was recounted.

"Stoppage of the Non-Co-operation Movement of 1921"—this was the rubric under which a long demotic poem, published in 1931 to mobilize the nation, retailed the happenings of 4 February 1922.

179

"Gandhi's War; or, A History of Satyagraha," to give this broadsheet its full title, had no place for an "incensed 'public' [that] burnt the police station" in nationalist history proper; Chauri Chaura was the place where that history was made to stop. So strong was this desire to immunize Indian nationalism from the violence of Chauri Chaura that, oblivious of chronology, the poem ends the noncooperation movement with the calendar year 1921, a month before the infamous event that was to bring about its actual suspension.[2]

Contemporary nationalist prose on Chauri Chaura could get equally ungainly. In a "Brief Sketch of the Non-Co-operation Movement," written in August 1922, the "serious riots" of "the month of February" are phrased out by Gandhi's intentions and reactions. Babu Rajendra Prasad's awkward sentence, quoted here, is illustrative of the manner in which "Chauri Chaura" was to be recollected in nationalist historiography:

> In the month of February, serious riots took place at a place called Chauri Chaura, in the district of Gorakhpur and Mahatma Gandhi who had proceeded to Bardoli to lead a campaign of mass Civil Disobedience and had gone so far as to issue his message to the Viceroy and Government intimating his intention of mass Civil Disobedience had to suspend the campaign as a consequence.[3]

In his reminiscences, Sampurnanand, a leading nationalist of the United Provinces (UP), was even more parenthetic. "The last few months in jail had been dull and uninteresting," he recalled in his memoir of 1921–22. "There were no new faces to be seen. The movement had been suspended by Mahatmaji after the unfortunate incident at Chauri Chaura, in Gorakhpur, in which some policemen had been violently done to death by an angry mob."[4] The fact that the east-UP patriot deliberated on the "suspension" of the movement at some length is not the issue here. The "riot," or "riots," the term Rajendra Prasad used, still stands displaced in the memory of the distinguished nationalist.

There is, of course, an extensive judicial archive on the Chauri Chaura trials;[5] however, I am here more concerned with memory, less with the accounts of reluctant witnesses. I have not tried, in this essay, to rehearse the ways in which "facts" were prised out and judgment recorded. In a trial such as Chauri Chaura, the crux of the matter is to identify the "criminals" and mete out punishment, but this has simultaneously to be put across as the accomplishment of justice. My primary concern is with remembrance, not with the affidavits and testimonies that preoccupied the police and the magistrates for a full nine months after the "riot."

A Narrative of the Event

In late 1920, Gandhi was able to push through a radical program of noncooperation with British rule. *A-sahyog* involved a boycott of the commodities and institutions through which England was able to rule India with the aid of Indians. Gandhi, the author of this noncooperation movement, toured the country, campaigning for the boycott of foreign goods (especially machine-made cloth); a boycott of the legal, educational, and new "representative" institutions; and a symbolic refusal to participate in the colonial system of rewards and honors. Two dramatic affirmations—*swadeshi* and *ahimsa*—were to accompany this quintet of Great Denials and to presage in tandem the transition from British Raj to *swaraj*.

The movement toward swaraj was to be made possible by the creation of the new nationalist activist—the *satyagrahi*-volunteer. It has been suggested that Gandhi's ideas about the satyagrahi underwent a marked change after the violence that accompanied the anti-Rowlatt Act satyagraha campaign. (The campaign was the first all-India mass movement launched by Gandhi to protest against a set of laws that, under the guise of curbing terrorist activities, drastically curtailed civil liberties of the ordinary Indian; at several places the movement went beyond the limits set on it by Gandhi.) There was "little concern" until 1919 "about the distinction between leader and satyagrahi and the masses . . . or about the organizational or normative safeguards against the inherent unpredictability of a negative consciousness playing itself out in the political battleground."[6]

"The Congress is a demonstration for the mob. . . . Though organised by thoughtful men and women, . . . our popular demonstrations are unquestionably mob-demonstrations," Gandhi wrote, summing up the experiences of his triumphant train tours of 1920.[7] This nationalist manifestation of the people as the mob was in need of an urgent disciplinary solution.[8] In September 1920, Gandhi put forward a twenty-point program for controlling the "mobocracy" of the *darshan*-seeking crowds. To overcome "this mobocratic stage," it was obligatory for "every one to obey [the] volunteers' instructions without question."[9]

"Before we can make real headway," Gandhi concluded, "we must train these masses of men who have a heart of gold, who feel for the country, who want to be taught and led." He added, "But a few intelligent, sincere, local workers are needed, and the whole nation can be organised to act intelligently, and democracy can be evolved out of mobocracy."[10] *Mobocracy*—"an ugly word greased with loathing, a sign of craving for control and its frustration"[11]—required Gandhian volunteers to purge it of its originary, subaltern impurities. "Volunteers," almost by definition, had to stand apart from "demonstrators": they were to discipline nationalist exuberance by acting as the "people's policemen."[12]

By the winter of 1921, not "a few" but many thousand volunteers had overrun the nationalist arena. In fact, the numerical strength of these volunteers in a district (or its jail) came to be regarded as a manifestation of the "nationalist spirit" in a particular locality. The signing of the pledge form (after the various volunteer organizations had been outlawed in November 1921) was documentary proof of mass civil disobedience. The pledge forms were formidable three-part affidavits. They were constructed to function as a nationalist record and had, therefore, to be filled out in triplicate: one copy to be retained in the village, the other two to be lodged at the district and provincial headquarters. People became volunteers by pledging "in the name of God" to wear khaddar, practice nonviolence, obey the "orders of officers," "oppose as a Hindu the evil of untouchability," uphold the principle of religious amity and unity in a multireligious society, suffer all manner of hardships (including imprisonment), and refrain, if arrested, from asking for financial support for one's kith and kin.[13]

In mid-January 1921, a village unit (*mandal*) of such volunteers was set up in Chotki Dumri, a village one mile west of the Chauri Chaura police station.[14] A functionary of the Gorakhpur District Congress and Khilafat Committees had been invited to Dumri by Lal Mohammad Sain of Chaura.[15] Hakeem Arif, the man from Gorakhpur, gave a lecture on nationalism and Gandhian political economy, appointed some "officers," and took the evening train back to the district headquarters. The peasant "officers" of the Dumri mandal went about their business. Pledge forms were filled out, subscriptions (more on this problematic word later) were collected, and, in a characteristic self-construed extension of the Gandhian message, meat, fish, and liquor rather than retail outlets of foreign cloth became the target of picketing.

The clash with the police had its roots in the local volunteers' attempt, a few days before the Chauri Chaura "riot," both to stop trade in these articles and to enforce a "just price" for meat and fish in the nearby Mundera Bazaar. A police officer had beaten back the volunteers and had also administered a salutary thrashing to one Bhagwan Ahir, a demobilized soldier from the Mesopotamia campaign (and therefore a government pensioner) who had no business to be so demonstratively disloyal to the Raj. The leaders of the Dumri mandal then sent letters to others in neighboring villages, informing them of this oppression on the part of the local police.

All volunteers were urged to congregate at Dumri on Saturday, 4 February, a bazaar day at Mundera. Arrangements were made for this gathering (*bator*) at the village threshing floor, *khalihān*, also known as "kāli māi ka thān": raw sugar was collected for refreshments, gunny cloth was spread on the threshing floor, and garlands were prepared for welcoming the chiefs of the volunteers. The meeting was eventful. A debate on the best course of action took place, "influential persons" sent by the *thānedār* to dissuade the crowd were disregarded, and their sincerity was questioned. The "real" leaders were garlanded. Nazar Ali, one such leader from Chotki Dumri, bound the crowd together by oath, and the volunteers marched in serried ranks to the *thāna*, to demand an explanation from the thānedār and then mass picket the nearby Mundera Bazaar. It was this procession of volunteers that clashed with the police on the afternoon of 4 February 1922. Gupteshar Singh, the thānedār, was expecting the crowd; additional policemen had been sent from Gorakhpur. Eight armed guards arrived by the morning train, and these, along with the local constables and *goraits* and *chaukidārs* (rural policemen) from neighboring villages, had been assembled in an intimidatory fashion to dissuade the crowd from marching on the bazaar. The symbolic display of force failed, however; "influential leaders" had once again to be pressed into action to parley with the "*māliks*" of the crowd.[16]

Allowed to pass unhindered in the direction of the bazaar, the crowd celebrated the ineffectiveness of the police by derisive clapping and by shouting a common north Indian abuse: the thanedar, and by extension the *sarkār*, it said, were "shit scared!"[17] The police officers sought to recover lost ground by firing in the air. This signal was disregarded. It was as if the amber light, a cautionary sign of "danger ahead, retreat" was read as a precursor of green, "go ahead."

"Bullets have turned into water by the grace of Gandhiji" was the construction put by the crowd on the ineffectiveness of the symbolic firing. The crowd responded by rushing and brick-batting the police. This time the firing was for real; three of the crowd were killed and several injured, but the hail of stones from the adjacent railway track was overwhelming. The policemen retreated into the thāna. The crowd locked them in and set fire to the building by sprinkling it with kerosene oil seized from the bazaar. Twenty-three policemen, including the station officer, were battered and burned to death.

The death of the policemen was not the end of the "riot." Police property was systematically destroyed, rifles were smashed, and the bits of brass with which police *lāthīs* (bamboo staves) were capped to make them into deadly weapons were taken off. Over three dozen chaukidārs managed to escape by throwing away their conspicuous red turbans (*pagrīs*) and milling into the crowd. Their pagrīs were subsequently torn to shreds by the volunteers.

The crowd dispersed by nightfall. Many did not return to their homes but ran to relatives in distant locations. In a violent inversion of the role assigned to volunteers, the "abolition of thāna" was proclaimed as the sign of the advent of "Gandhi raj." By the time reinforcements reached the smoldering thāna, the villages were deserted. In police parlance, "the rioters had absconded."

Repression was immediate. Chotki Dumri was raided early next morning, but the "leaders" were not at home, and the identity of others had to await the naming of names and the discovery of incriminating documents. The fact of having signed the pledge form was documentary proof of being a volunteer and, by extension, of participation in the riot. Lists of volunteers were compiled from police and nationalist records, and where a name tallied with an identification in a confessional or "eyewitness" account, the peasant found himself in the dock as a Chauri Chaura accused.[18]

Historian's Dilemma

In the court, the accused chose not to speak about their "criminal" past. Faced with the tangible proof of deliberate disobedience—the pledge form—the peasant volunteers tried to distance themselves from their thumb impressions. "I am not a volunteer," asserted accused Aklu before the magistrate. Confronted with Exhibit 37, his pledge form,

Aklu responded, "I did get my volunteer form filled but I don't remember if I thumbmarked it."[19] "I am not a volunteer. The whole world paid 4 annas (as subscription). I also paid 4 annas, and I also signed a paper but I don't know if it was a volunteer form." "I am not a volunteer. Babu Sant Baksh Singh [the landlord] may have got my name registered in the Congress office." "I am a volunteer but I did not work as a volunteer." The ambiguity of these denials rests on a fine distinction between intentionality and fact: "I do not know if I became a volunteer"; "I am not a volunteer, but people called me a volunteer."[20]

It was this opacity of rebel speech that made me turn to the enforced utterances of *mukhbir* (approver) Shikari.[21] The judicial discourse on "Chauri Chaura"—"This Tale of Murder"—had left its impress on the event and the accused before the historian could enter the record room. Those arraigned were unwilling to talk about their political motivations and political expectations in the court because any true recollection there would have stuck them even more deeply within the mire of criminality prepared by the prosecution. In the court records, the silences and denials of the 225 jointly accused are superimposed and given meaning by the testimony of the approver (king's evidence and witness for the prosecution, as this figure is called in British and American jurisprudence, respectively). The paradox of the displacement of the rebel from the judicial record, the center-stage presence forced on the rebel/renegade (one who "sings for his life"), the problematic nature of the approver's testimony—all these were occasioned by the trial and the requirements for the production of penal truth.

The fabricated testimony of the approver, I suggested, was the condition for a historiographical possibility. In the Mir Shikari of the records, the historian has access to the actual words of a leading actor from Chotki Dumri. The presence of the grammatical first-person singular is, in this case, inadequate guarantee of the speaker's nearness to his own speech.[22] The I/we of Shikari's narrative echoes the events of 4 February in an instrumental voice that helped bring everybody named by it (apart from Mir Shikari) nearer judicial penalty. My essay on Shikari's testimony has been criticized for its ironic effects: subaltern history-writing, it is said, has written the subaltern out of existence. Texts and testimonies have displaced the people whose experiences these words signify.[23]

Recovering the event from judicial and nationalist record then becomes a task of some methodological complexity. Local informants and I together forged new narratives of the event, but we could not be oblivious to the judgment and the nation. In February 1989, I rushed from Delhi to garner reactions to an official celebration of Chauri Chaura, choreographed by a local politician who had been elevated to a ministership in Rajiv Gandhi's cabinet; during my visit in August 1988, I was not looking for just any informant, but for very special people, the "relatives of the rioters." For me, it was not simply a question of counterposing an immediate, local memory to an authoritative nationalist remembrance. The process by which historians gain access to memory is itself problematic; so is the relationship between recall and record.

Both in my quest and my knowledge of the "criminal pasts" of the deceased relatives, I felt like a colonial policeman! I was, of course, different; I was welcomed in Chauri Chaura as a local intellectual, the sort who travel halfway around the globe to come and talk to peasants in the neighboring district. Among the Dumri intelligentsia, I was "the visiting historian"; to my precious octogenarian "informants," I was the man from Delhi who was interested in their pasts. We inevitably talked about political pensions, but my concern with Bikram Ahir and Rameshar Pasi did not, I think, raise any major expectations in Chotki Dumri. Their relatives had seen enough promises turn false, I suspect, for them to pin their hopes on someone who did not have the usual markers of official standing—a chauffeur-driven Jeep and at least one sidekick to act as linguistic and cultural translator.

Which differences, I asked myself, were erased through affinity, and which remained, and which got created as we talked about the event, about Gandhi and about much else besides? How do these affect the possibility of generating a different narrative of Chauri Chaura and of Indian nationalism? Product of an encounter so moving as to have left me at times mouthing inanities, this essay eschews the temptation of an excessive concern with the writer's own "positionality." The irony of an old, low-caste woman using the same term, "sarkār," as a noun for the colonial government and as an attention-seeking honorific in our dialogue was not lost on me; nor was the use of "bābu," a term of endearment for children, which also designates members of a junior landed lineage and, more generally, any male superior to the speaker. My familarity with the local Bhojpuri dialect may have paradoxically accentuated the use of status markers in our coversation; my desire to research a history of Chauri Chaura in Chauri Chaura may in turn have helped forge a community of purpose. Historical fieldwork and the emerging narratives were seen by many to feed into a history. "Kitāb nikri! Kitāb!"—"a book will come out of all this"—was the cue used in Dumri to align memories into stories.

This chapter is based on fieldwork done in and around Chauri Chaura in August 1988 and February 1989. My major concern has been to try to give the event a prehistory. I attempt to do so by underlining the local contexts—nationalist or otherwise—within which most retellings begin and assume form. This, I hope, will help take out the element both of spontaneity and of stereotypicality from this police-peasant encounter. While interrogating several local narratives of the "riot," I have chosen to concentrate on familial accounts from Chotki Dumri. The recollections of Naujadi, the wife of a "rioter," and Sita, the son of a chaukidār, are deployed to construct the world of the peasant nationalists. These *otiyars*, to use Naujadi's remarkable Bhojpuri creolization of the familiar *volunteer*, were *Gandhi's men*, all right; everything connected with popular nationalism of the time was possessed of a generic "Gandhian" quality, but Naujadi's otiyars were Gandhian in curiously unrecognizable ways.

I seek to chart the distance that separates the volunteers of Gandhi's *Collected Works* from the otiyars of Naujadi's recollection. I also try to explore the possibility, with the help of Sita and Naujadi, of generating an independent narrative—a story that does not have crime for its title. The attempt is not quite successful. This narrative failure is not because the basic facts of the riot are incontrovertible: the same characters can, after all, be made to play several different parts. The failure of the independent narrative is illustrative, rather, of the power of judicial (and nationalist) discourse. The subalterns make their own memories, but not as they please. The gallows and the prison ensured that decades later judicial pronouncements would live to be heard in the familial recall of the event.

Dumri Records

The typical document available in Chauri Chaura is a certified copy of the punishment meted out to the convicted rioter for his "participation in the non-co-operation movement of 1922 (Chauri Chaura outrage)."[24] The equation of the "*kānd*" (outrage) of 1922 with the "freedom movement" of that year, the use of the verb "participate," and the third-person honorific (*bhāg liye the*) are grammatical signs of the relocation of the riot in the narrative of nationalism.[25] By 1972, that is, in the twenty-fifth year of Indian independence, the "rioters" were understood to have "participated" in "nationalist crimes." This late admission was not based on a radical rendering of the event: Gandhi's condemnation of the "crime of Gorakhpur" had ruled that possibility out. Instead, the power of the nation-state to reorder its prehistory was used simply to transform the record of death and imprisonment into one of reward and recognition: punishments were to be translated into pensions. When Naujadi, the wife of Rameshar Pasi, repeatedly refers to things "written on my paper" (*hamār kagda par likhal ba*), her paper is the same recent copy certifying that Rameshar had undergone eight years' rigorous imprisonment. Family records, favored by an entire generation of historians, turn out in Chauri Chaura to be fragments of a judicial sentence.

Could it be that very few records were generated in Chauri Chaura in the winter of 1921–22? Oral transmission was no doubt important,[26] but so were missives, written in the unsteady hand of a schoolboy or a semiliterate peasant. We have on (judicial) record three letters written in January 1922 by a volunteer leader of Chauri Chaura. In these successive letters, Lal Mohammad "Sain" offers his services to the Gorakhpur Khilafat Committee, reports on the success of his recruitment drive, and lodges a complaint against the local thānedār.[27] The crowd of 4 February, it will be recalled, had assembled in response to an express written communication.

Writing and recording were integral to the constitution of the volunteer movement. Completing the pledge form, securing thumb impressions, maintaining registers, and corresponding with district headquarters were important tasks of the mandal functionaries.[28] One of them, Lal Mohammad, was his own writer; Nazar Ali and Shikari, for their part, went around with a literate boy in tow. "I and Nakchched and Nazar Ali recruited 9 men. Nakchched wrote the forms," Shikari stated in the court of Judge H. E. Holmes.[29]

The district headquarters was full of nationalist paper. When the city police raided the Khilafat and Congress offices on 5 February, they carried away scores of registers, receipt books, maps, files, budget proposals, pledge forms, and abstracts of correspondence, including Lal Mohammad's letters. Most of these were put on record.[30] A similar raid on the mandal office of Burha Dih, a few miles north of Dumri, again yielded a rich haul.[31] Burha Dih had a developed sense of non-cooperation. In December 1921, the nationalist village *panchāyat* (council) was mediating in property disputes, and the mandal secretary had furnished the thana with a complete list of the illegal volunteer corps for "necessary action."[32]

Why is there nothing on record from Chotki Dumri, especially as the village was raided the day after the riot? The "Dumri papers" may not have been as wide-ranging as the Burha Dih collection, but nationalist paper there must have been at Dumri. It appears that the same police force that went about impounding each and every scrap of paper, including "waste" and "blank" paper,[33] deliberately destroyed the Dumri records in the early hours of 5 February 1922. Sita Ahir, the young son of Surajbali chaukidār, who was mourning the death of his father, recalled:

> When the thana was burnt, then everyone ran away. Not a soul, not even a little bird was left; only I remained [*Ek chirai ke put nāhīn hamār gauwān mein rahal*]. Nobody was willing to take charge of Chauri Chaura thana [*Kehu Daroga bīra na khat rahe Chauri Chaura ke*]. Then Lachman Singh, captain of Deoria thana—a very tough man he was—he came down at midnight to take charge of the Chauri Chaura thana. It was the month of *māgh*. . . . Then at the crack of dawn—I, of course, was crying by the feeding trough, and my mother, she was crying as well—Lachman Singh emerged from the Chamar quarters, walking up the railway track. . . . Then two of his *sipāhis* [constables] gave me a few mighty blows with their rifle butts. I forgot all about my [dead] father; I now thought only about myself. Oh yes! My body became stiff as wood [laughs].

Sita, now recognized as the village chaukidār's son, was ordered to lead the way to the houses of the Dumri leaders. "Najar Ali-Sikari ka ghar batāo," he quotes Lachman Singh in imitation Hindustani. "And so I took them along—*te liya ke chalalīn*," he recounts in local Bhojpuri. In Sita's recall, 5 February 1922 is punctuated by a series of forceful exhortations. All that happened in the village that morning echoes Lachman Singh's command, "Najar Ali-Sikari ka ghar batāo!"[34]

The raiding party wreaked its vengeance on just about everything. Doors of houses were broken, earthen ghee pots were smashed, and ghee was gobbled up by the mouthful. Onward to Shikari's house the police party went: "Khapra ke ghar rahe—paith gailān sab. Jaune dehri mein māren kul, taune mein se bhak-dena dhanwe nikre. Te kaha tāna kul, "dhān bāndho!" Kahlīn, nāhīn hajoor, hammen dhān-aun nāhīn laukat-ta, hamme apne dāda ke chāhat-tāni, ta inhān se lautalān kul." At Shikari's house—a substantial tiled structure—several large jars of rice were smashed, and the son of the dead chaukidār was asked to take the loot home. There is a noteworthy parallel here between the destruction and the extravagant eating that Ranajit Guha finds in peasant insurgencies and the symbolic and material damage done to peasant property by Lachman Singh and party.[35] To translate Sita's recall of the scene at Nazar Ali's house:

> And so [Lachman Singh] said, "Show us the house of Nazar Ali." And so I brought him there. . . . Nazar Ali's house was a thatched [hut]. One could see the *kolhu* [sugarcane press], etc. Then this "bugger" Lachman Singh [Lachman Singhwa!]—one box full of volunteer-paper was in the house—Lachman Singh brought it outside. . . . He brought the box out and started tearing and throwing away the papers. And he said, "'Sister-fucker!' lives in a thatched hut and goes out and commits such a big 'case'!" [*Eh sāla-bahanchod! etna bara "khēs" kar diya aur phoos hai nahīn ghar par!*]

At the thana, the volunteers had torn the police turbans to tatters; in August 1942, when police and railway stations were targeted by student and peasant nationalists to force the British to "Quit India," public burning of the red pagrīs was punished by collective fines of Rs. 20 per headdress burned;[36] in Dumri in the early hours of 5 February 1922, a police officer, fresh from the smoldering Chaura thāna, had wreaked his vengeance on the pledge forms. No wonder only one *pratigya patra* from the village could be produced in the court.[37] In Chotki Dumri, the police had destroyed the record.

What then are the narratives that can be tapped around Chauri Chaura? I could discover four: the stories of the youth, accounts from the Mundera Bazaar, the narratives of distant localities, and remembrances of surviving family members.

The Youthful Account

The narratives of the Dumri youth are thin on sequence, but they supplement the actions of a grandfather or a granduncle with physical prowess and cunning insight. The "otiyars" here appear as *pahelwāns*, trained in the literal and political *akhāra* (wrestling pit) of Nazar Ali, the leading wrestler of the village. For the grandson of Bikram Ahir (hanged in 1923), it is *bal* and *chhal* rather than *tyāg* and *tap* that constitute the "plot" of his story:

> Gandhiji had come, but he did not stop over; he just met people with folded hands and went away. The thāna was attacked twice. The first time it "failed." The second time, bullets turned into water by the blessings of Gandhiji.
>
> Nazar Ali, Bikram Yadav, and Neur used to wrestle at the akhāra. It was Nazar Ali's akhāra: he had two or three *bighās* of land. They did not farm every day—nobody does—they would set off with their lāthis and roam around [the jungle].
>
> One day, Bikram Yadav was grazing buffalo [in the jungle]; he came across a rifle. He deposited the rifle at the thana, thinking that this way he would earn goodwill [*khair-khāi*]. Bikram Yadav [consequently] became a chaukidar. This way [they] were able to infiltrate [*ghus-paith*] the thāna. The first thing they burned were the [thāna] records.

The account of Shardanand Yadav [Ahir] is peopled by cunning peasant-wrestlers and daredevil herdsmen, not by upright Gandhians. The power of the Dumri nationalists resides in tough masculine bodies; it does not emanate from an androgynous Gandhian sense of sacrifice.[38] Quite the contrary; the focus on *bal* (force)—Neur Ahir's body, according to his cousin Sita, was the abode of the goddess Durga— creates the space for the fictive presence of a dreaded Ahir *dacoit* of the 1920s.

Komal-Dacoit

In conversation, Shardanand briefly mentioned the name of Komal Yadav, the common caste marker obscuring the fact that Komal was no ordinary Yadav but the notorious "Komal and his gang" of the police records. Shardanand was unable to knit Komal into his sketchy account, but he reminded Sita, the eyewitness, not to leave the tough guy out of his story. Sita did not ascribe any leadership role to the dacoit (member of an armed robber band), but he admitted that it was Komal who had the "guts" (*karēja*, literally, "liver") to torch the police station: "'Leader' te nāhīn rahlān, Komal. 'Leader' te Najar Ali aur Abdulla rahlān, baki phuk-le Komal-e-ke karēja rahal." The interjection, "Komal always carried a spear," completed the picture. The irony of Komal's fictive presence emerges when counterposed with the police version of the story. "Expenditure of energy" in apprehending and prosecuting the Chauri Chaura rioters had "prevented the police from devoting their full energy to organised crime."[39] "Surveillance was poor" in 1922 and 1923 "and, to a large extent, over the wrong men." The district, noted the commissioner, "was harassed by bands of dacoits," notably "Komal and his gang." With the "capture and conviction of Komal . . . things improved" in 1924.[40]

> SITA: Komal was really a very tough Ahir. He cut his chains bit by bit. It took a full month. When just a little bit of the shackle remained, then [they] threw a rope from the outside. There was real strength in his strides, and his eyes, they were this big! He had the small bit of the *beri* [shackles] by the hand. His strides, they were powerful—like a Punjabi. He was from Sahuakot, and had been to jail many times. He got involved in this thāna affair as well. He was a pahelwān.
>
> NAUJADI: I have yet to see a stronger fellow than he. I saw him at the Gorakhpur Jail.
>
> SITA: He was tough and cruel [*jābir*], like a Punjabi.

Komal was no ordinary pahelwān. About this Naujadi and Sita leave you in little doubt. The real significance of the character Komal lies in the fact that "he got involved in the thāna affair as well." Police files offer an altogether different trajectory to the dacoit's career; from the Chauri Chaura court records, Komal is simply absent. Nevertheless, in local memory, Komal remains a powerful presence, one that evokes the magnitude of the violence at Chauri Chaura. It is the physical prowess of the Sahuakot Ahir that places him alongside Nazar Ali and his associates on that extraordinary day—a reminder of the idea of the tough otiyars in the minds of the Dumri folks, young and old alike.[41]

The Bābu-Saheb of Mundera

The tough otiyars of Dumri appear in the bazaar account as "rustics, ruffians, and rogues," in that order.[42] In Mundera, the riot is remembered as an episode from the history of the bazaar itself. Its hero is the legendary ruthless zamindar, Sant Baksh Singh, ably supported by his clever functionary, *kārinda* Awadhu Tiwari.[43]

After the riot, the rival Chaura Bazaar lay in ruins; Mundera, the *phulwaria* (literally, garden) of the Bābu-saheb (Sant Baksh Singh), rode the storm. Chandi Tiwari, the kārinda's grandson, draws on his memory of the event as follows:

> Satyagraha had started at the behest of Gandhiji. . . . [Volunteers]
> were insisting that the sale of meat, fish, and liquor be stopped.
> Grandfather requested the thānedār to beat the fellows down; it
> would be the end of the bazaar, he said, if these fuckers were allowed
> to carry on with their riotous ways [*dhīnga-karna*]. So Gupteshar
> Singh came. He had his sipāhīs bring these fellows in, and they were
> slapped and threatened [*do-chār thappar māra gaya, darwāya gaya*].

The Hindustani phrase implies that the thrashing of the volunteers
was as much the work of the kārinda as of the thānedār. In fact, the
construction—*māra gaya, darwāya gaya*—can be taken to include the
narrator as well as his grandfather. Chandi Tiwari's tone suggests that
Awadhu considered the volunteers to be mere peasants. These fellows,
or rather "fuckers"—for the high-caste cannot help abusing the subaltern even while reporting a conversation—no doubt meant mischief,
but police kicks and curses were considered adequate to rid them of
their pretensions. The Dumri otiyars took the beating more seriously
than expected, a surprise that is echoed in Chandi's recollection:

> After the volunteers had been beaten back [on Wednesday], these
> fellows sent out letters saying that we should all go to the bazaar
> [on Saturday]. And return they did in strength. And a whole lot of
> *goondās*, *badmāsh*, and *dākus* [i.e., rogues and ruffians] were there
> with the set purpose of looting Mundera Bazaar. And that's what
> [nearly?] happened.

But Awadhu Tiwari, the kārinda, stood up for the bazaar. He picked
out Ramrup Barai, a volunteer from Mundera (hanged in 1923), and
taunted the *panwāri*: "Ka ho Ramrup! Hamariye kapāre pe ee chūra
chali?" "This crowd is beyond my powers to control," replied Ramrup. Awadhu ordered him to "divert the crowd toward the thana." In
this, Ramrup was apparently successful: the bazaar was spared; the
thāna was burned.

It is hard to miss an element of filial exaggeration in Chandi's recall.
Awadhu Tiwari, by his own account, "remained the whole night on guard
in the bazaar,"[44] but the volunteers knew their geography; the procession did not require an astute diversion to find itself outside the thāna.

In the bazaar narrative, it is not so much the riot as the Bābu-saheb's
ability to stand up to its consequences that is the object of an exagger-
ated remembrance. Chandi recalls the "*loot-mār*" that accompanied
police investigations: "A 'force,' hundreds strong, including '*sowārs*'
[riders], raided the villages. . . . Whole hamlets were deserted; only the

old and the infirm remained" to face the wrath of the state.[45] "After 1922, Chauri Chaura Bazaar . . . was ruined because of the raids; Bābu-saheb on the other hand kept the police out of Mundera." This was a fantastic feat, and it is remembered as such:

> In 1922, when the thāna was burned, . . . the collector came. Sant Baksh Singh [Chandi recalls] went out to meet him at the station. They talked. The collector said, "Bābu-saheb! You got your bazaar saved and had my thāna burnt!" Sant Baksh Singh gave a [stunning] reply. He said, "Why shouldn't your thāna be burned, you who make a fetish of your laws [*Kyon na āp ka thāna jala diya jāe, jab āp kanoon se bor-ke roti khāne wāle hain*]. You people are hamstrung by rules and procedures: 'First fire blanks, then fire in the air, then below the knees.' Me! I would have fired to kill." The collector shook his head, and asked for help: provisions [*rasad*], some laborers, and cloth for the shrouds of the dead policemen. Bābu-saheb had all this supplied from Mundera without difficulty, but he did not let a single policeman enter the bazaar.

The dialogue between the Bābu-saheb and the collector was a powerful and imaginary one. Sant Baksh Singh was certainly in attendance at the railway station on 5 February—a clutch of public men had also arrived by then from Gorakhpur—but it was Chandi's grandfather who was "ordered" by the collector "to help with coolies and supply two *thāns* (bolts) of cloth and eight bullock carts." Mundera Bazaar *baniās* were made to supply food gratis to the troops at the thāna.[46] Awadhu Tiwari was, of course, acting on behalf of his *mālik*, and it is his master who figures as a hero, both in the Mundera Bazaar and in Tiwari's own family. A ruthless zamindar and a toady of the British, Sant Baksh Singh is remembered even today with a mixture of awe and adulation. Local memory credits him with protecting his subjects from the ravages of the law.

Mewa Lal Jaiswal, trader-intellectual, who frequents Ram Awadh's bookshop in the commercial wing of the local Arya Samaj *temple*, offers a view from the bazaar of the activities of the Babu-saheb:

> [After the thāna was burned] people pulled down their shutters and just scooted. Then Sant Baksh Singh rode into the bazaar on elephant-back. [He lived five miles away in Gaunar.] *Purāna rupaya* [old, regionally minted coins, collected as bazaar dues], ghee and *bhandāri* [i.e., provisions], he offered as gifts [*dāli*] to the English collector. It was then that the *Angrez* calmed down somewhat. Sant Baksh Singh said, "My phulwāri Mundera Bazaar will be ruined."

Stanley Mayers, the Gorakhpur police chief, was raiding the surrounding villages nonstop (he fell ill in the process).[47] It was this massive police hunt that made Sant Baksh Singh plead for "his people"; otherwise, Bābu-saheb had a reputation for keeping the police at bay.[48] "Even the postman had to enter the bazaar wearing 'civilian dress'!" For Mewa Lal, who made this observation, the divesting of the state's authority was enforced after the "riot," as well. The police, "when they came into the bazaar," did so "in 'plain dress.'" Sita and Naujadi describe a sea of red turbans (*lalri-e-lalri*) lashing out against the neighboring villages. The local chaukidār, however, "never saw any darogha or constable coming [in]to Mundera"[49] during the entire course of police investigations.

The inspector in charge of investigations was "won over." "My men will go with you, and my peons will get the culprits you want," the inspector was told:[50] "Hamāre qasbe mein koi sipāhi nahīn āyega (Bakri-shakri sab thāne mein 'supply' kar di). Jo 'list' chāhiye de-dijiye, ham pakrawa denge."[51] Mewa Lal Jaiswal maintained that this enabled Sant Baksh Singh to "shield the real ones": "Bābu-saheb got all the rogues and ruffians [*lafange, chor-chikār*] arrested." In this way, "these [low-caste] people [who were actually hanged and imprisoned] became [political] 'sufferers'": "Asli log 'back'-mein chale gaye [the real people went into the background]."[52] In Mewa Lal's account, the success of Sant Baksh Singh has paradoxically enabled the descendants of rogues and ruffians to draw political pensions for what can only be termed "wrongful confinement." There is nothing but convoluted high-caste pique to Mewa Lal's words. The Dumri crowd, we know, was composed of low- and middle-caste men—"a mob of enraged untouchable volunteers" is how they appeared to the Brahman magistrate—and the social composition of those convicted was no different.[53]

The Madanpur Narrative

The "real agents" (*asli log*) are again some other people in the narrative from Madanpur, a Pathan-trader-dominated village, thirty miles southeast of Chauri Chaura.[54] The Madanpur account places the riot in the context of a stylized understanding of the "nationalist movement," and it ascribes agency to the trader-cartmen who happened to be around on the afternoon of 4 February. "*Namak āndolan chal raha tha*—it was the time of the salt satyagraha," begins Mohram Sheikh of

Madanpur, pushing the event eight years into the nationalist future. "The volunteers were trying to encircle the thāna, but were being beaten back by the police." The peasants told the cartmen their plight; the *gāriwāns* replied: "Let us tether our bullocks, and then we shall see what can be done."

It is the Madanpur cartmen who suggested that stones lying by the railway track be used as missiles; it is they who supplied the kerosene for setting the thāna afire. Having caused the riot, the traders drove their carts, laden with rice and *gur*, back to Madanpur, threatening another thāna en route.[55] A massive police raid—a cannon is mentioned—on Madanpur (in late February) finds a village united and ready to defend its "criminals." Village elders parley with police officers. The English superintendent cries "real tears," saying, "*Hamāri 'insult' ho gayi hai*—we have lost face; our thana has been burned down." Guns looted from the police station are hidden in the village well; these lie undetected, but the police manage to arrest forty suspects. Appeals are made in the name of the nation: "Pahchānon mat! Āzadi ka sawāl hai! Yeh sab ke liye kiya gaya hai." To give evidence against these men would be to betray the country.[56]

The Madanpur narrative is an account of nationalist success. Transporter-traders from a distant village make their contribution (*yogdān*) while going about their business; exhortation on behalf of an ongoing struggle and the powers of a Muslim worthy enable the village to rescue its admittedly violent heroes from the clutches of judicial penalty.

Village solidarity is important to the successful denouement of this narrative. In Dumri, the story was altogether different. The village was deserted ("ek chirai ke put nāhīn rahal"), and Shikari had turned approver. There was no question of police officers parleying with village elders; Dumri felt the full impact of police raids. From the court records, we know the following sequence. Shikari makes a confession on 16 March; Chotki Dumri is raided early the next morning; eighteen persons are arrested and packed off to the district jail.[57] Sita Ahir recalls the raid (*chāpa*) of 17 March as follows: "A month after the riot, when people had started coming back to the village, there was a big raid. They surrounded the village from all sides. Whoever ventured out of the house—in the middle of the night, or at dawn, even for a crap—he was nabbed by the police."

Malaviya Saves Chotki Dumri

According to Sita, cannons had been brought over to blow Chotki Dumri up, but a legal luminary made an ingenious argument and saved the village from utter destruction:

> They had brought cannons with them. Madan Mohan Malaviya saheb then argued [*bahas karlān*]: "Sir," he said, "four-legged animals have not burned the thāna, cows and buffalo have not burned the thāna, birds have not burned the thāna. It is the two-legged creatures, men [*du-gora: manhi*] who have burned the thāna. Catch *them*! . . . If you fire the *top* [cannon], then all life—*chirai-chirau, goru-bachru*—will be destroyed." At this, the English agreed; cannons were not fired.

How are we to read this amazing account of Dumri's success in surviving the wrath of the avenging colonial force? There was no way in which Malviyaji, the veteran nationalist, could have pleaded with the police on behalf of Chotki Dumri: "*bahas*" (argument) is reserved for the courtroom, and the Allahabad pleader did not set foot in Gorakhpur until July 1922. But Malaviya had been in touch from almost immediately after 4 February. C. K. Malaviya, his son, toured Chauri Chaura as a member of a fact-finding team, and K. N. Malaviya was the counsel for the defense in the sessions court. Madan Mohan Malaviya pleaded the case at the Allahabad High Court.[58] Leading a team of five counsels, he had the number of death sentences reduced from 172 to 19. Malbiya-saheb was able successfully to negotiate the "rule of law" and restrict punishment to select individuals. The village as a whole, represented in Sita's voice by its living organism, young and old—"chirai-chirau, goru-bachru"—was saved by a clever lawyer. Or was it the younger Malaviya who interceded on Dumri's behalf and helped avert ruin in the spring of 1922?

The Great Betrayal

If this is how the shadow lines of punishment and justice are etched in Sita's memory, there is no ambiguity about the fact that the "case" had to await the discovery of an approver. "Mukadma chale ke jōg nāhīn rahe": there was very little chance of the case getting off the ground. However, Shikari's was not an individual betrayal; he was made to renege by that historic renegade, the Sikh zamindar of the Dumri estate whom the English had "rewarded" for his services during 1857 by the grant of a confiscated zamindari.

Sita picks up the thread of his narrative of how the village was saved, and the story takes on a different turn:

> And then, Sardar saheb, he is a toady of the English [*Angrez ke khair-khāh hauwwen. Inheen ke pakral gail*]. It was he the English got hold of. Then he [the Sardar] went out in search of his own men, his own tenants, and turned them into approvers [*uhe mukhbir bayān dihlān*]. It was these approvers who testified in court; it was then that the trial could commence, don't you see!

The grateful Sikh owners of the Dumri estate remain true to their renegade self; they betray the peasants in 1922, as they had the landed rebel, Bandhu Singh, in 1857. The contrast between the Sardar saheb (of Dumri) who offered his tenants as approvers and the Babu-saheb (of Mundera) who, as usual, held the police at bay, is a characteristic trope in most local retellings of Chauri Chaura. It is not the destruction of the state apparatus—the police station—that evokes the tumult of 1857. It is necessary help toward the reestablishment of colonial authority that marks the Sardars out as the object of scorn.[59]

A Powerful *"Mukhbir"*

"Shikari was also in the *kānd*, but became a *mukhbir*. Sardar Harcharan Singh made him *mukhbir* (approver)."[60] Sita's brief account of the making of the approver has an interesting tie-up with the Dumri-Sardars. Harcharan Singh, an old-time official of the estate, had brought Shikari's father (so said Sita) from Punjab. Mir Qurban was given "a pension" by the estate. Shikari was a man of substance who did not have to slave over his plot of land: "Shikari ke majgar ghar rahe . . . Shikari ke kheti bahut rahal, 12 bigha—akele rahēn, kheti karēn . . . Chamra-o bēchēn, obha-chobhi, jaise ki kauno bajār jāwēn, kauno na jāwēn . . . Kheti ke tāo aa ja te kheti-e karēn." When translated, this reads: "Shikari was a man of substance. With a large holding and additional income from leather trading, he lived alone; he had no need to slave on his four acres of land. He would sell skins and hides every now and then, or turn to agriculture, if it took his fancy."[61] This biographical information, which casts Shikari as a carefree, well-to-do individual, was not offered to explain Shikari's act of reneging. There is nothing in Sita's account that suggests a valid "reason" for

Shikari, of all people, turning approver. Sita, and especially Naujadi, remember Mir Qurban's son with a certain resignation, quite free of pique. In their recollections, Shikari appears as a powerful person, a leader of men, whose power was not lessened by his stellar performance in court. In fact, people in the village were still in awe of Shikari after his return from the trial. Nobody, affirms Sita, castigated him for his part in the proceedings: "Hai ke kahe? Dar ke māre, ee kehu kahe!—darāe sab." And why were they afraid rather than just plain angry? "Because he could [very well] implicate them in some other 'case.'"

Shikari's was then a successful return. Approvership had imbued the leader of Dumri men with an altogether different sort of power. That Shikari's son was elected the village headman (*grām pradhān)* in the late 1980s indicates that no stigma now attaches to the approver and his family. Ironically, the recounting of the event for the visiting historian took place at Shikari's old house. There really has been no getting away from Mir Shikari!

This is especially true with the eighty-year-old Naujadi, wife of Rameshar Pasi, incarcerated for eight years for his part in the riot. Naujadi, a low-caste woman, is the "Godmother" of Shikari's grandson. The little boy was "sold" for his weight in grain to the old Pasin, as his siblings had all died in infancy.[62] Naujadi, who regards herself as a "member of the [Shikari] household, then [1922] as now [1988]," remembers the powerful approver with hardly a trace of regret. For her, Shikari was first and foremost a leader of men: "Ek mutthi mein kihle rahlān. Unke mutle chirāg barat rahal." It was Shikari who kept everyone united. His was real power: "One could light a lamp with his piss," says Naujadi, wonderfully adapting a local epigram to her own ends.[63] After the riot, Naujadi's husband tried saving his skin by running away to his sister's village; all this was in vain, for Shikari had spoken. "Pahichān"—identification by the approver got one the gallows or the jail, but there was no vindictiveness in what he said.

For Naujadi, there was a certain inevitability about punishment; having challenged the might of the state in a frontal assault on the thāna, only temporary reprieve could be hoped for. There is no room in her recall for the "ones who got away." The immediate kin persuaded the "absconders" to come out of hiding: "Jab paulīn hāl ki [Rameshar] chutihēn te nāhīn, aa pa jaihēn [pulis] te mār ke bekām kar deihēn—te ānkhi se sab dekhat rahlīn. Te kahlīn, kahlīn, ki chutihēn te nāhīn, te kāhe ke deh radd karāwal ja—le āwa, unke bharti kar jāwal jā, te . . . bula ke le-ailīn." Naujadi knew well the treatment that awaited Rameshar; she had little hope of her husband successfully evading the police for long. *Bharti*—surrender (literally, to deposit)— was better than "having one's bones broken" by the police. Sita's uncle, Bikram (hanged in 1924) was forced out of hiding by the prospect of the raiding party arresting his wife in his stead.[64] The effect of police raids and Shikari's testimony was overpowering:

> Te māre gārad se, māre ghora se, "kham-kham-kham-kham," ailēn san, eh Bābu! Kehu dehri mein dharāil, kehu rahta [rasta] mein dharāil. Aa, eh Bābu! hum jhūt nāhīn kahīn, hamre Sikari-Bābu ke dehe ke biyān, nāhīn bhail na? Jahār [jānch] karlān, kahlān-sunlān, kehu ke bekār nāhīn karlān, haan! Bekār nāhīn karlān. Humman-o-lōgan ke pahichān karlān; bekār nāhīn karlān.[65]

Using evocative imagery, Naujadi is here saying that, although people tried to run away from the horses' hooves, when the mounted police came looking for culprits (*māre gārad se, māre ghora se*), it was in vain. With Shikari-bābu implicating his former comrades almost to a fault—"he also showed us up, but not without reason"—it really was the end of the road for Rameshar and Nageshar, and for Lal Mohammad and Nazar Ali.

But do I really wish to suggest that Shikari was never regarded as a betrayer in the village? Could not the resignation that I discovered in Dumri in 1989 have been an effect of the passage of time? Even as the approver performed for the prosection, his "accomplices" gasped with disquiet at the impersonal and transactional nature of Shikari's testimony. The connection between torture and speech was not hidden from the accused. Scores had been made to "confess"; at least two others had been short-listed as potential approvers, only to fall short and be hanged for their crimes. Faced with the Dumri leader's damning testimony, Abdullah of Rajdhani responded: "Shikari knows me from before. He has turned an approver and if he did not name a number of persons, how could he get off?"[66]

Abdullah (hanged on 2 July 1923), of course, never came back to confront Shikari outside the court, but Rameshar, Naujadi's husband, did return after eight years in prison. What did he think of Shikari-approver? We don't have access to Rameshar Pasi's memory; all we know is that Naujadi still remembers "Shikari-bābu" with respect untainted by rancor.

The One-Seven-Two of Chauri Chaura

If Shikari's role is etched out as a matter of fact, judgment, however, makes a shadowy but deadly appearance in Naujadi's recall. Every time the old woman refers to an assembly connected with the event, she uses the figure *ek-sau-bahattar*—172, to give it its proper Arabic numerical form. "Ek-sau-bahattar" people gathered on the morning of 4 February; "there are 172 persons mentioned on my paper."[67]

Now 172 was the number of "rioters" sentenced to death by the sessions judge in Gorakhpur; the High Court reduced the death sentences to 19 and acquitted 40 persons altogether. One-seven-two has remained, however, the "real number" for Naujadi. The reasons for this lie in the system of colonial justice. Under the Indian Penal Code, death was the "ordinarily right and appropriate" sentence to pass on each and every member of an assembly proven to have committed an offense under section 302/149. Section 302 was a murder charge; under section 149, each and every member of a crowd that committed a grave offense "was liable to punishment for that offence as if he had committed it himself." Judge Holmes had then quite rightly considered the crowd as one legal person, and, given "the adequacy of the evidence in each case, the conviction of these hundred and seventy-two men on the charge of murder was right, and indeed inevitable."[68] The Gorakhpur judge could have been a bit lenient, but he would then have had to explain why he was not doing his duty by awarding the maximum punishment. The natural inclination of district judges was to recommend the hangman's noose, secure in the knowledge that "no capital sentence can be carried out until it has been confirmed by the High Court."[69]

The contrast with eighteenth-century England is instructive. Douglas Hay has noted that although a very large number of persons were awarded the death penalty for relatively minor offenses, these were mostly commuted to lesser sentences on the recommendation of the local gentry. Discretion of the justices of the peace, magistrates, and the gentry, one might say, was the better part of eighteenth-century English justice.[70] In colonial India, the situation was quite the reverse. In cases such as Chauri Chaura, punishment was to be handed down in the districts, and it was then up to the duly convicted to appeal against the "ordinarily right and appropriate . . . death sentence."[71] Until justice could be won at Allahabad, all of Naujadi's "ek-sau-bahattar" were as good as dead. The dissonance between local punishment and provincial justice can be heard in the familial recall of the event. For Naujadi, who made the weekly trip to Gorakhpur Jail, a portion of which functioned in this case as a court, the initial 172 represented the crowd as well as the convicted.

The idiosyncratic in Naujadi's recall becomes intelligible in terms of the working of the judicial process.[72] Sita's comment, "Yes, Abdullah was in it—the first to be hanged," is equally revealing.[73] Abdullah topped the list of those sentenced to death by the High Court; it was in this alphabetical sense that "his was the first hanging." It would be a naive historiography that would expect to find subaltern recollections untouched by the prose and the procedures of punishment: judgment was, quite literally, a matter of life and death for Abdullah and 171 others. It is remembered as such.[74]

Those Who Willed It

This is not to suggest that all accounts of Chauri Chaura were identical with a judicial master narrative. The concerns of a Naujadi or a Sita were obviously different from the judge's understanding of "the case." There are variations in tone and emphasis even within the prose of the judiciary.[75] What unites the various orders of judicial discourse, however, is the connection they all seek between the burning of the thāna and the world of "politics" beyond Dumri. After a précis of the riot,[76] Holmes, the sessions judge, settled down to the business of connecting the occurrence with local nationalist politics: "This horrible tragedy is further shown by overwhelming and undisputed evidence to have been a direct outcome of an agitation styled the "non-co-operation movement" in the sense that if it had not been for that movement it could not have possibly occurred."[77] In their obiter dicta, the High Court judges went a step further. They apportioned the blame on accredited district Congress functionaries who were the "real agents" behind the whole gory affair:

> We cannot take leave of this case [they wrote] without an uneasy
> feeling that there are individuals at large at this movement, men who
> have not even been put on their trial in connection with this affair,
> whose moral responsibility for what took place at Chauri Chaura
> police station on the afternoon of 4 February 1922, is at least equal
> to that which rests upon such men as Nazar Ali and Lal Mohammad,
> who acted as leaders openly in the light of the day, and at least
> placed their own lives on the hazard along with the rest.[78]

The Allahabad judges "strongly suspect[ed]" that the Dumri leaders had in fact acted upon instructions sent out from the district headquarters.[79] Lal Mohammad Sain, who had initially arranged Hakeem Arif's visit to Dumri in January, sent a letter to Gorakhpur after the beating of the volunteers in Mundera Bazaar. In his "report," the Sain from Chaura made the usual gesture of political deference: "We therefore report this matter to you, Sirs, so that you could come over and ascertain for yourself. And it is because of you, Sirs, that we have not taken any offensive action, for we would act only after seeking the advice of [you] our *'afsars'* [officers]."[80] Much was made of this letter in the court. The judges suggested that since the confiscated Congress records contained no evidence of a written reply, "an oral answer was returned [to Chaura] . . . of such a character that those responsible for it could not commit it to writing."[81] Gorakhpur, in other words, was instrumental in causing the "riot" at Chauri Chaura.

The Presence of Gandhi

By contrast, there is hardly any place for the District Congress in the local recall of the event. It is Nazar Ali's letter—"*tār*" [wire], in Sita's words—summoning an urgent meeting at Dumri[82] that is the object of remembrance in Chauri Chaura; no one seems to recall Lal Mohammad's "report," which is lodged as Exhibit 95 in the court records. Hakeem Arif, the Gorakhpur nationalist, who for the judge "definitely formed . . . the local . . . Dumri circle . . . of the non-co-operation movement . . . in January 1922,"[83] is similarly displaced by the activities of the local volunteers. For Naujadi, it is an existing band of "otiyars," called into being by Gandhi, who confabulate and organize, unaided by people from Gorakhpur (*apne mein log "kumēti" kail*). The district headquarters is referred to by Naujadi once as the site of the jail, never as the seat of the noncooperation movement.

In Dumri, the district does not count. The being and becoming of the volunteers derives directly from Gandhi's personal appearance at the Chauri Chaura railway station on 8 February 1921,[84] eleven months before Nazar Ali, Shikari, and others turned full-time volunteers.[85] In Naujadi's recollection, that extraordinary visit is heralded by celestial apparitions—a snakelike figure and two everyday objects, a *barhani* and a *hēnga*, appeared over the Chauri Chaura skies.[86] "*Hamse tani-ye karēr rahlān, Gandhiji*—Gandhiji was only slightly

better built than I," recalled the eighty-year-old Sita, virtually establishing a physical connection between the people of Dumri and the author of noncooperation. Naujadi, for her part, makes an analogous
connection between Gandhi and his "otiyars." Her account begins,
"*Chauri Chaura mein pahile sab otiyar rahlān; Gandhi-Mahatma ke
jab raj ail—otiyar rahlān*—To begin with, all were otiyars in Chauri
Chaura; when Gandhi Maharaj's raj came, there were otiyars." The
phrase about the Mahatma is significant, for it suggests that the
"otiyars" inhabited the time of Gandhi-raj. This is a novel perspective
on the Rule of Gandhi. "Gandhi's raj" is then not an impending event
that had to be divined by a reading of its signs, nor is it an object at-
tainable by militant means.[87] For Rameshar-volunteer's wife, the time
of the "otiyars" *was* the time of "Gandhi-raj." The space created by
Gandhi at the Chauri Chaura station on 8 February 1921, "wearing a
dhoti as I do" (Sita), paradoxically left no room for the District Congress Committee.[88]

Was it just in familial memory that the Mahatma displaced every
other nationalist actor, apart from the local volunteers? Strands of the
connections with the district headquarters lie scattered throughout the
records. The Dumri unit was formally established by a district functionary; Nazar Ali had gone to Gorakhpur with a request for a drill in-
structor; Lal Mohammad sent up a written complaint about the beating of volunteers in Mundera Bazaar. Important as these events are for
a historical reconstruction, they seem to have slipped out of local recall. An erasure caused by time perhaps? Or could it be that those who
recounted "Chauri Chaura" for me were not privy to all that tran-
spired between Dumri and the district? It is significant that in our long
conversations, not a single district nationalist's name ever cropped up;
it was Gandhi and the volunteers who straddled the narrative space.
What we have here are mnemonic traces, perhaps, of a desire to construct a world larger than the local—a world of the otiyars from which
the Gorakhpur superiors are necessarily absent.[89]

Sita's Narrative

"In 1922, I was eighteen years old." Sita, the son of the village chaukidar, opens his account with the "*olantiyars*" and the picketing of Mundera Bazaar three days before the clash with the police. The volunteers
were picketing the sale of liquor, fish, and meat (*dāru, kariya-machri*)

in Mundera Bazaar; the *daroga* beat a few volunteers; that very night, Nazar Ali sent out urgent messages calling for a meeting on the next bazaar day. The meeting decided to "picket Mundera Bazaar after paying respects(!) to the daroga"—"daroga ke salām kar-ke rokal jai bajār-e-mein":

Olantiyar log Buddh-ke Murera Bajār mein je dāru piye, aa, kariya-machri kharīde, tē-ka rokal lāgal. Te Daroga du-teen olantiyar ke mār dihlān. Bas! Biepphe ke—Buddh-e-ke-rāt-ke chāron des chitthi bhēj dihlān. Nakched Kahar aur Najar Ali, duno-admi, duniya-mein chor dehlān—unke inhān chitthi chal gail: rāti-mān tār chal gail ki sanichar-ke Dumri mein michor hai. "Miting" mein ee bhail ke chal-ke Daroga-ke—sanichar ka roj rahal . . . bas! Inhān ee miting bhail ke Daroga-ke salām ka(r) ke rokal jāi bajār-e-mein.

It was a massive "meeting" (*michor*) that took place at the village threshing floor, also known as *kāli-māi-ke-thān*, the site of the local Kali shrine. "It was like a *mēla*, not one nook of the *kharihān* was without people. On that Saturday, by this time of the day, hundreds of people had gathered," recalled Sita on 17 August 1988. The daroga knew about the Dumri gathering. "The picketing of the bazaar had started." Awadhu Tiwari, the *kārinda* of Sant Baksh Singh, was at the thāna. He said:

"Mundera is jam-packed with volunteers, and there are still a lot of them in Dumri. . . . These people are uncontrollable [*bheriādhasān hauwwen*]. Fire blanks! [*Chuchiya awāj karīn!*]" The daroga had got eight *gārad* [armed guards] from Gorakhpur, but he did not have the collector's order to fire at the crowd; he could only fire in the air.[90]

Picketing, in Sita's account, the starting point of the narrative, appears as a matter of fact; it requires no context, no explanation.[91] Awadhu Tiwari, the "vigorous old" kārinda[92] of Mundera Bazaar, plays an important role. He appears as the local adviser to the thānedār; it is Awadhu who suggests the only possible line of action—firing in the air—that was available to the police officer who had armed guards but not the "*adar*" (order) to fire into the crowd.[93] Sita is very precise about the "eight" armed guards the collector had sent to the thāna after Awadhu had requested the dispatch of additional force for the protection of the bazaar.[94] So significant is the number "*āth-go-gārad*" that it plays an analogous role in Sita's memory to Naujadi's one hundred seventy-two.[95] Thus, the daroga had asked for eight guards, Lachman

Singh raided Dumri on 5 February with "eight sipāhis," and when the English bestowed recognition and a large zamindari on an Azmatgarh business house, including lands around Chauri Chaura, the *lāt-saheb* placed "*āth-go-gārad*" (eight guards) at their *kothi* (mansion). Numerical exactitude becomes intelligible in terms of the referents that uphold it.

The Policemen Dead

When Sita asserts that "nineteen died at the thana; nineteen were hanged," he creates a slightly flawed equation but one that establishes a symmetry between the extent of the crime and the degree of punishment. The High Court no doubt sentenced nineteen to death, but the toll of policemen was twenty-three. The transposition of the number of "rioters" hanged onto the number of policemen killed suggests a displacement far deeper than a simple error of four; it points to the silencing of the police in most local retellings of the "riot."

In Dumri, the policemen who died do not count. The trigger to the "riot," no doubt, is the ineffective firing in the air; the gathering in the village that morning is, similarly, in response to the police inspector's beating of volunteers. It is Nazar Ali and *his men*, however, who activate the stories. In Sita's account, there is a greater awareness of the tie-up between the thāna and the district (armed guards had been dispatched from Gorakhpur; "orders" had not been received from the collector to open fire) than there is knowledge about the local police force. Sita's considerable knowledge about the regular and auxiliary police is not deployed by him in the narrative of the "riot."

The force that confronted the Dumri marchers, we know from court records, consisted of armed guards, regular constables, and a motley collection of "rural policemen"—*chaukidārs* and *goraits* resident in their villages, and normally indistinguishable from peasants in appearance and attire. Of the two, the goraits (from *gor*, foot) were of inferior status, usually of the untouchable Chamar and Dusadh castes. Required to subsist on a small rent-free allotment, the gorait was very much a "servant of the zamindar," "employed to fetch, carry, and perform menial services," including plowing the master's fields free of charge. Attached to lowly untouchables, the term gorait had "become one of reproach" and was "by itself . . . a great obstacle to men of good caste taking up the post."[96]

Chaukidārs (from *chauki*, outpost, a "station"), by comparison, were paid servants of the state, had a dignified ancestry, and came from middling social groups. Mostly Ahirs or middle-ranking Muslims, a few, like Chedi and Tribeni Pande of Sant Baksh Singh's estate, even belonged to the upper crust of Brahmans.[97] Sita Ahir's grandfather, when he elected to leave the paternal home in the overpopulated southern tract by the River Rapti and follow his wife to her natal village Dumri, recently won over from the forest, also made the transition from being an errand-runner (*harkāra*) to a chaukidār. The chaukidāri of Satrohanpur village, just across the road from Dumri, falling in the newly carved jungle estate of the powerful merchant-banker family of Raja Moti Chand of Azmatgarh, then devolved in Sita's family. From the grandfather, it went to an elder uncle, then to father Surajbali, who was killed in the "riot." Sita's mother received Rs. 100 for her husband's death in the line of duty; her thumb impression survives on a receipt marked no. 447(13) in the court records. Harpal Chamar of Dumri, an erstwhile gorait whose lowly office had been merged with chaukidār by a special dispensation of 1919, survived "Chauri Chaura."[98]

After his father's death, Sita recalls being offered a post in the provincial constabulary. He passed the "physical"; his eyesight was normal: "Inspittar āil rahal; ānkhi rumāl-umāl bāndh ke ehi tarah ginaulas, te laukat rahe, sab gin gailīn." But Sita wanted to stay back, and desired the chaukidāri of a neighboring village. He had a widowed mother and three sisters to look after. The request was turned down at the highest level: "Kul Lāt-Governor, jarnail-pharnail jawāb deh dehlēn." Uma Chamar—"Umva," as Sita, inflecting a low-caste name with the requisite disdain, called him—had a prior claim. The chaukidāri of neighboring Bharatpur-Satrohanpur villages ended in Sita's family with the death of his father on 4 February 1922.

Chaukidārs like Sita's father were auxiliaries to the regular police stationed at the thāna. Chauri Chaura was a "third-class" police station, which meant that it had no more than eight constables and just one subinspector of police, or daroga. But the thāna covered over a hundred villages, and had about that many chaukidārs under it. Although not under direct everyday control, the chaukidārs had the thāna as their reporting station. These "rural policemen" were expected to report serious infractions of the law and to register the incidence of births and deaths in the village to the thāna every week.[99] They also had to walk up to the police station to receive their monthly pay. Saturday, 4 February, was payday. A large number of chaukidārs were present at the thāna, dressed in their officious red turban, or pagrī. On such occasions, they would be ordered around, pressed to labor gratis for the daroga or his establishment—perhaps to repair the tiles on the thāna roof, weed the garden patch of the thānedār, or run an errand to the nearby bazaar.

Subordinate to the force resident at the thāna, the chaukidārs were also made to appear a bit different. Not for them the starched khaki of the regular police, roughly textured to allow it to "breath" during the hot and humid months. Formalized in the 1870s, the dress of chaukidārs consisted of a *mirzai* (a padded jacket) of "blue drill," a four-yard-long red pagrī, and "the usual dhoti." From the waist down, it was the dhoti that was to keep the rustic chaukidār from rising above the ordinary peasant. The billowing oversize khaki shorts—popularly called "half-pant"—and the khaki "leggings" were not for chaukidārs.

Headdress apart, it was the *sarkāri* (official) blue coat that distinguished the chaukidār from a peasant. It was this official blue that got Dukhi Kewat (two years' rigorous imprisonment) into trouble with unfamiliar comrades on the evening of 4 February 1922. Dukhi attempted to make away with a dead policeman's rifle, which had survived an earlier attempt by some "rioters" to break it in half. He was set upon and beaten by a section of the crowd. Dukhi's black mirzai (subsequently displayed in court) was mistaken for a chaukidār's blue! "They considered that as he had on a black mirzai, he was a chaukidār," explained the "watchman" of Dukhi's village to the sessions court.

The lowly chaukidārs had only one thing in common with policemen proper—the red police pagrī. Everything about their attire, from neck to toe, was different—blue, not khaki; dhoti, not "half-pant"; leggings and boots, not unshod feet. It was the turban and its distinctive red color that proclaimed the two as a composite coercive corps of the state.

Great weight is in fact attached to the pagrī as headgear in most parts of rural India. With some communities, it is the headman alone who may wear the headdress; in Gujarat, it is a privilege violently guarded by the dominant caste of Patidars in Gujarat.[100] It was a significant gesture, then, to have conferred the pagrī on the lowly untouchable chaukidār along with the policeman proper. It was the pagrī that the chaukidārs flaunted the most; it was this four-yard strip of cloth that the peasants attacked even after its owner was dead. "The red turban was particularly offensive to the non-co-operation lamb," wrote the committing magistrate, gritting his teeth in anger. "Minute strips of these turbans, two or three inches long and quarter inch broad, were lying all over" the thāna on the morning of 5 February 1922.[101]

When Ram Lal Chamar, chaukidār of Lachmanpur, came for his pay on 4 February, he came sporting the headgear: "I had not had my uniform renewed for a long time and it had got torn. I had not brought my belt or lāthi. I had only come for my pay with my turban on."[102] Confronted with the crowd yelling "death to the red-turbaned bastards," Ram Lal threw down his pagrī at the thāna door and ran into a wheat field. Others, more fully attired, had to divest themselves of all their accoutrements. Manohar thrust his "uniform, *sāfa* (turban), belt, and *mirzai*, etc.," into a corner of the burning thāna "and, with an *angocha* of coarse cloth tied round [his] loins," ran out by the east door and joined the crowd. "They could not identify me; they were so many." Siddiq, the sole surviving constable (many more chaukidārs managed to escape), who was standing near a mango tree away from the thāna, saw the crowd bolt the door on the policemen seeking refuge in the station:

> I then knew that my uniform would kill me. I put off my uniform and ran off in my shirt. Running, . . . I heard a woman saying, "Here is a policeman going this way," pointing toward me. No one followed me. When I had gone a mile or half a mile, I seized a kerchief [*gamcha/angocha*] from a lad's head and ran on and then tied it round my loins.

Siddiq ran for another six miles to the next police station and filed "the first information report" on the riot. Badri, of Jungle Chauri village, also ran out half-clad, picking up a handful of stones (*kankar*) so that he would look like an average rioter. Jeodhan "threw off" his uniform and turban "and went out with kankar in both hands pretending to be one of the rioters and calling out 'Beat, beat.' Bhagelu of Sonabarsa, a late arrival, was spotted at some distance because of his brass-capped lāthi and a suspicious-looking bundle. He was accosted by five men carrying an injured comrade back to their village. "They put down the injured man and two men seized" Bhagelu. "One man wanted to open my bundle and said they would kill me if a turban should be found in it."[103]

There is no room in the Dumri stories for Bhagelu and his comrades. When Sita mentions the escape of a policeman (Siddiq), it is to identify the person who lodged the first report at the next police station. The violence of Chauri Chaura, gruesome as it was, is recalled in Dumri as a matter of fact. It is narrated from the point of view of those hanged in 1923, and not of the policemen killed at the thāna. The death of twenty-three policemen—the central figure in all nationalist narrations—fails to register as a fact independent of the burning down of that precinct. A son of a chaukidār, the wife of a "rioter," the grandson of a bazaar functionary—all relate the event as *the setting afire of the thāna.* "The day the thāna was burned" is how the event is phrased to impede the flow of quotidian and historic time. This is true as much of Sita's recollections in 1989 as it is of the more immediate recall of several witnesses in the court in 1922.

"Running away from the hail of stones, they locked themselves inside the thāna. The building was set on fire; whoever came out was thrown back into the flames" (Sita). All local accounts of the police-peasant encounter build up to the destruction by fire, paying particular attention to where the kerosene oil came from. "They got the oil from a storage tank next to the railway gate"; "from the Madanpur traders who had carts loaded with kerosene"; "from Mundera Bazaar"; "a canister of oil was there [at the thana], and there were matches, as well."

The last of these statements, by Naujadi, wife of Rameshar Pasi, allows for the incendiary agent to appear on its own! In Naujadi's "eyewitness account"—"we are only laborers, Sir, I am retelling what I have seen with my own eyes"—the blaze is all-consuming; it accounts for at least two young lives that, we know, were not lost that day:

> Singing and shouting, they [the volunteers] left for Chauri Chaura. . . . The roof of the thāna was tiled—this I shall never forget. . . . Then daroga saheb fired. They were hit.
>
> Then Bābu! they turned around. Turn back they did, and started throwing clods and stones. [*Hammani ke bar-majdoori karat tāni, sarkār! dekhli-ānkhi-ke kahat tāni. Bābu-ho!*] They turned back and started pelting [the police] with stones.
>
> A canister full of oil was kept there, and so were matches. . . . They started setting fire to the thāna. The *darogāin* was standing there. . . . They set fire to [the daroga's] house, burned him alive, his children, too! There the kids were—the two of them, back from school, standing with their satchels—they also threw them into the fire.

The daroga's two daughters, who, along with the mother, narrowly escaped death that day, here get thrown into the inferno. Naujadi does not relate how the trapped policemen were attacked and killed, their bodies charred by fire. That day, the thāna (and everybody and everything connected with it) was set ablaze.

The crowd outside the thāna was not looking for individual policemen; their actions were not animated by recollections of past enmities, to which the riot, as it were, was an answer. Harpal, the village chaukidār, kept popping in and out of the Dumri meeting, reporting on its progress to the thāna, one mile down the road. Unmindful of the local "watchman," the volunteers deliberated the course of their collective action.[104] The gathering then marched out to the thāna to demand an explanation for the forceful prevention of two previous attempts to picket Mundera Bazaar. The daroga would be given a chance to explain his conduct, perhaps made to apologize. Guns and muskets meant to terrorize them would be braved. The bazaar *would be* picketed. The *paulic* (public) would see that the police were powerless.

The "reasons" for the clash in local memory seem to lie outside an immediate history of police-peasant tension. The event follows the willful acts of the Dumri activists: "This is what they [had] decided. That they will 'pay their respects' to the daroga and then picket Mundera Bazaar. [*Ihe sab sarmat [sahmati] kailan ki thānedār ke salām kar-ke chalal jāi rokal jāi . . .* That's all" (Sita). Three thousand peasants—the activists distinctly attired—marching in unison to bow their heads before the thānedār in mock subjection before picketing Mundera *as volunteers*. That was the scenario, imagined, according to local recall, in Dumri that day seventy years ago.

Tension there certainly must have been between the village and the thāna. Two weeks before the clash, the thānedār had listed all the activists, village by village, paying special attention to the "leaders" and how they could be "shown" to have broken the bounds of the law.[105] Police constables had been attacked in the district; popular animosity lived in the proverb that "god punishes darogas by not usually blessing them with sons!"[106] In local memory, the event—"this burning of the thāna"—does not *result* from a *cause*; it is part of a story, a narrative activated by the local volunteers.

It is worth reminding ourselves that Sita Ahir, a major eyewitness narrator (died 27 August 1991) was the son of the village chaukidār killed in the riot. His father's death obviously figures prominently in

Sita's recall. The police officer, searching furiously for Dumri leaders the morning after the riot, saves a disconsolate Sita from the hard-hitting rifle butts of his sepoys and escorts him to the *thāna* where "nineteen(!) corpses were laid out side by side." The son is asked to identify the dead father and is unsuccessful. Surajbali chaukidar's body was unrecognizable: it was "charred like charcoal" (*jhaunsal . . . kāth ho gail [rahe] dehiye*).

Despite these details, Sita's account is really about the deeds of the Dumri activists. The police appear after the event, as the avenging "force" punishing Dumri rather than as kinsmen killed during the riot. Sita, the dead chaukidar's son, speaks *for* the village. Until his death in August 1991, old Sita was regarded as the most authoritative reteller of the *kānd* (event or outrage). Would Sita have always retold his story in this way? Perhaps not. The discourse of pensions may be at work here, aided by the fact that Sita's uncle, himself a former chaukidār, was hanged as a "rioter." Young Sita had visited Bikram, his uncle, several times in Gorakhpur Jail and had also made the long journey to Meerut Prison to be present at his hanging.[107]

Bikram Ahir, Sita's uncle, had a checkered career. A chaukidar for over fifteen years, Bikram had joined the regular police in the late 1910s:[108] "Chaukidāri hamre dādā ke de-ke apne 'line' mein bhailān. Par kawāid nāhīn pār lāge—bara kawāid tab hōkhe. Gor-or toot gail—pār nāhīn lāge. Itāpha ['istīfa'] de-ke ghar baith gailān." To paraphrase Sita in English, the "parade and drill" (*kawāid*) at the po-lice lines was very tough in those days; Bikram Ahir just couldn't take it. He resigned and came back to Dumri. On his return from the "Line," the shenanigans of his wrestler son got him a six-month jail sentence. Neur Ahir—a tough young lad of the local *akhāra*, who was to be subsequently employed as an informer by the police to get the Dumri leaders arrested, then arraigned in court, and finally released—had in 1920/21 stolen some timber from the nearby Tarkulha jun-gle.[109] The "*sirpat*" (sleepers) having been traced to Bikram's house, the father offered himself to the police in place of the son. A stint in jail meant that Bikram could not come back to his chaukidāri post. In any case, Sita's father had already succeeded to that position.

In late 1921, Bikram of Dumri was a recognized volunteer. A fat, officious-looking "Register of Volunteers of Gorakhpur," which had a rubber-stamp image of Mahatma Gandhi for effect, names Bikram as a volunteer.[110] In court, the "village policeman" presented this composite picture of chaukidār/volunteer Bikram Ahir: "This accused is Bikram of my village Dumri. . . . I saw him in a previous *sabha* [meeting] in Dumri in which he was wearing a Gandhi cap and as chaukidars move people on at fairs, etc., he was in that sabha making people sit down and acting as leader. He is a vounteer."[111] Bikram produced an alibi in court: he was, he claimed, fifty miles away on the day of the riot, buying a pair of bullocks. A receipt testifying to the purchase was produced in court; so were accounts of his major participation in the riot. Eyewitnesses apart, "a prima facie strong point against him [was] that he did not accompany his brother's widow when she went to the police station to get compensation for her husband's death."[112]

Sita's uncle and Neur's father was awarded the death sentence. Young Sita had visited his uncle several times in Gorakhpur Jail, and had also made the long trip with Neur to Meerut Jail where Bikram was to be hanged:

> In Meerut, the hanging kept getting postponed. It was to be on one day, but then it would get fixed for another. In this way, we stayed on in Meerut for one full month. I would see *chācha* every Sunday. After a month, *chācha* said, "You fellows go home and look after your work. Don't stick around here. Go back home." We came back to Dumri. Then the "wire" arrives that the hanging had been fixed for tomorrow!

It is not just a "rioter" uncle who displaces a policeman father. In Sita's and several other local retellings, the widow of the station officer assumes a role that is as significant as it is ubiquitous.

The Darogāin

Sita has an intriguing reference to the "darogāin," the widow of the daroga killed at the thana:

> When night fell, the darogāin was unhurt. Two or three men saved the darogāin—they surrounded her saying, "Don't kill her." The *olantiyars* wanted to throw her into the fire as well, but these men— Meghu Tiwari of Menhian—took her to his house. She was pregnant. They did not listen to her entreaties, and dishonored her [*beijjat karlān*]; he [Meghu] did not listen to her. With tears she wrote down her plight on her person. . . . And when the trial began . . . Meghu Tiwari got the gallows for his "*bahaduri.*"

The wife of the daroga figures in other local accounts as well. "She was pregnant. Meghu Tiwari took her" (*Darogaji ki istri garbhwati thīn. Meghu Tiwari usko lekar ghar chale gaye*) is how the episode was described in chaste Hindi by the Vaidji (naturopath) of Mundera.[113] For the Chauri Chaura judges, the "dishonoring" of the darogāin consisted in a *pardanashīn* woman (keeping purdah and so remaining inside her house) being confined in another man's house.[114] Mussammāt Rajmani Kaur described her escape as follows:

> The house was burning and my two girls were carried out and my servant was turned out and I followed. . . . As I got out of the house, there were 2,000 or 3,000 men round it, who were shouting. . . . Out of the mob, *one or two men said that we should not be beaten as I was pregnant* and we were women. The mob fell in with the view and I walked aimlessly with my daughters.
>
> I was met by two or three men who commanded me to follow them. I obeyed, as they said they would kill us. We followed them into a courtyard [*usāra* or *osāra*], where we were seated. We remained there all night and we were neither offered any refreshments, nor were we shown any hospitality, nor were we given any bedding. No womenfolk came near us.[115]

It was this passage that was paraphrased in the judgment. Even the committal "order," otherwise so full of abuse and anger, did not hint at any "*beijjati*": "She was given no food nor was she treated well," was all that Mahesh Bal Dixit, the committing magistrate, had to say.[116]

In Sita's and Naujadi's account, and in local memory more generally, the confinement of the darogāin by Meghu Tiwari amounted to a sexual assault on her person. So strong is this idea that the daroga's wife is the subject of obscene, sexist jokes at the Chauri Chaura petrol station, a meeting place for all the hoodlums of the area.

The figure of the "darogāin" is etched out in greater detail by Naujadi. Naujadi could not recollect Meghu Tiwari's name, but for her the Bābhan (Brahman) of Menhian appears surely as the culprit who, instead of protecting a pregnant (*sānpat*) woman, went out of his way to dishonor her:

> Hānn! Ohi Babu! Ahir hauwwe ki Bābhan? . . . [Bābhan], Ohi ke gharwa le gailān ki ijjat-pāni bachi rahi . . . sānpat na rahi! Okre ghar le gailān. [Uu] lehu lena [dhan] aur beijjat-o-karlān; Bedharam-o-karlān aur dhan-o le lihlān.

[It was to that Brahman's house they took her so that her honor and shame would be safe: she was pregnant, you know. But that fellow not only looted her but dishonored her, as well. This is how Meghu Tiwari disgraced the wife of thānedār Gupteshar Singh.]

But the darogāin, who remained in her house until "stones and kankar were thrown" [at the thāna],[117] is made to play a crucial role both before and after the riot. Let us go back to Naujadi's account of the police-peasant encounter. It is late afternoon of 4 February, and the Dumri *batōr* has just left for Chauri Chaura:

Singing and shouting [*gāwat-bajāwat*], they went at four in the evening; they went to Chauri Chaura through the thāna. The thāna was a tiled structure, this I cannot forget. *And the darogāin was standing.* And these people [Nazar Ali, Shikari, et al.] were on their march, singing and shouting. *And the daroga was seated. When they passed the thāna the daroga fired.* . . . *And the darogāin was pregnant*, she was standing and reasoning with the daroga to let the crowd go, but he did not pay heed, and fired.

Darogāin sānpat rahal, minha karat tāri: "chale jāe do, kāhe ko goli chalāega, chale jae do." Te ee na manlān, na manlān, chala delān.

In Naujadi's account, the darogāin is the voice of moderation and of justice. The riot occurs because the daroga pays no heed to her advice. The darogāin is no doubt looted and dishonored by some of the crowd, but still proffers the correct version of events. The sequence is confusing: for Naujadi, the darogāin is both confined for the night in Chauri Chaura, and she arrives (from Gorakhpur) the next morning to speak up for the *paulic*. But there is no doubting the importance of her "testimony": "Uhe darogāin! jab unhān-se inhān ailas—char-ke motor-pe gail—'tekasi' [taxi]-pe—uhe darogāin asal-asal bolali. 'Sarkar! Koi-ka dos[h] nahīn hai,' 'paulic' kuch nahīn dos[h] hai; hamāra goli chalāega, hamāra mārega." To translate this passage adequately is to prune it of its ambiguity.[118] Naujadi's attempt to mimic the speech of the high-caste *darogāin* results in grammatical slides, such that the possessive pronoun *hamāra* (mine), in the absence of a qualifier (husband), becomes the subject that causes the riot! "It was no fault of the public," she is saying to her interlocutors when apprehended. In Naujadi's version, the darogāin, witness to a tragic truth, lessens the enormity of a public occurrence by blaming her husband, albeit obliquely.[119] Further, it is the darogāin's crucial presence—and intervention—that saves Dumri from ruin: "Te darogāin je na rahe te kund par jae Dumri-Mundera!" (But for the darogāin, Dumri would have been totally destroyed). "Without her, there would have been apocalypse [sarvnāsh]" is how one person translated this emphatic statement.

We are back here to the theme of the crucial intervention that saves entire localities from utter ruin after the riot. Survival in the aftermath of "Chauri Chaura" is an important motif in all local remembrances of the event, with varying degrees of extraordinariness attached to it. In the Madanpur narrative, it might be recalled, it is village solidarity *and* a Muslim "worthy" (*buzurg*);[120] in Mundera, it is a legendary tough zamindar; in Sita's account, it is "Madan Mohan Malaviya sahab"; with Naujadi, it is the widowed darogāin herself who helps avert *sarvnāsh*!

Naujadi's Otiyars

An "otiyar" (volunteer) was one who begged for his food and who wore *gerua* (safflower-colored) clothes.

That is how Naujadi began her account on 18 August 1988. It was raining, the *nakchatra* was *Maggha*, and all of us—a small, inquisitive set—were sitting in the *osāra* of Shikari's old house. Sharfuddin, Shikari's son and the elected village chief of the village, had asked Sita and Naujadi, the two surviving witnesses to Chauri Chaura, to come over to his house. Besides Sharfuddin and myself, there were Shikari's four-year-old grandson, Shikari's daughter Jaibul, Sita Ahir, Naujadi Pasin, and a couple of young men from the village. The "interview" with Sita had concluded for the day; it was Naujadi's turn to speak into the portable tape recorder. She said: "In the beginning there were otiyars in Chauri Chaura. When Gandhi Mahatma's raj came there were otiyars. They asked for alms. Shikari Babu, this gentleman's father," Naujadi points to Sharfuddin, "was there; Nazar Ali was there, Salamat-father-in-law [bhasur] was there; Nageshar, my *dēvar* [husband's younger brother] was there; Rameshar was there." Naujadi, taken in by this roll call, uncharacteristically identifies her husband by his first name and not by the locution *hamār parani* (literally, "my life"). "And Awadhi was there. I am telling you the story of *that* time." With this temporal emphasis, Naujadi comes around to identifying the otiyars by their attributes. First they got organized; they got together and discussed things (literally, "did some committeeing") among themselves (*apne mein log kumeti kail*). And, like beggars asking for alms (*bhīk*), they asked for a pinch of grain (*chukti*). "They had flags, pink, no gerua, long shirts (*kurta*), caps, flags." She then turns to the otiyar's uniform.

> Chauri Chaura mein pahile sab otiyar rahlān. Gandhi-Mahatma ke jab raj ail—otiyar rahlān. Bhīk māngat rahlān. Babu-ke dāda rahlān [points toward Sharfuddin].[121] Ohmen Shikari-babu rahlān, Najar Ali rahlān, Salamat-bhasur rahlān. . . . Sahadat rahlān, Nagesar, hamre dēvar rahlān, Ramesar rahlān, Awadhi rahlān. . . . Sun tani! Oh-samay ke bāt ba!
>
> Okre bād mein inhān-se Sarkar jab apne-mein log "kumeti" [committee] kail, aa chutki māngat rahal, te ohi-mein khāt-o rahlān aa dharāt-o rahal. . . . Mane khāt-o apne-mein rahlān, aur dhara-jāt rahal jo bēsi ho.
>
> Khariyāni nāhīn let rahlān.[122] Jaise bhikmanga chutki mānge le na? Mānge-lān bhīk!—Ohi-tarah log bhīk māngat rahlān.
>
> Jhanda rahal, gulābi-kurta rahal—gerua-rang; dhoti rahal, topi rahal, aa jhanda rahal.

In Naujadi's mind, *chutki*, *bhīk,* and *gerua* clothes were what distinguished the otiyars of Chauri Chaura.

Chutki

"They would come begging and ask for a pinch of grain," says Naujadi, wife of Rameshar Pasi of Chotki Dumri. Demanding chutki was regarded as evidence of a volunteer past in the sessions court, as well. However, chutki was here so closely associated with *chanda* as to have become a synonym for "subscription." "We were all told to collect subscriptions (*chanda* and *chutki*)" is how Shikari's implicit distinction between these two was blurred in the official record of the trial.[123] In the judicial probe, *chutki was one fact among many* by which the accused were identified as volunteers: donning a Gandhi cap, patrolling the village at night, "behaving as a policeman" at a fair or a gathering, signing the pledge form—all these formed a set of incriminating evidence.[124]

With Naujadi, it was chutki that mattered most. It was what distinguished a "real" otiyar from a nominal one; her *dēvar* from her husband, for example: "Otiyar khāli uhe, chotka [Nageshar-dēvar] rahal. [As for Rameshar, her husband?] Are likhaule rahlān, mane māngat nāhīn rahlān. Uu [Nagesar] māngat rahal—gerua . . . sab pahir le-lena, lugga-kapra. [Ramesar] khāli likhaule-bhar rahlān." It was chutki-begging and not the signing of the pledge form (*likhāna*) that made a volunteer. And the volunteers asked for chutki, *like beggars*, Naujadi stressed, her voice rising in exasperation at my inability immediately to grasp the meaning of the term. "*Bhejyo māi, chutki!*—Send out a pinch of flour, mother!" was in fact a mendicant's cry in north India.[125] The housewife, before cooking the day's food, would set aside some lentils, rice, or flour as the share for the volunteers. It was not so much the "reason" but the reasonableness of the demand—"they did not come for it everyday, did they?" ("*roj nāhīn-na kahēn? . . . dusre-tisre din diyāt rahal*")—that Naujadi remembers today.[126] Out of the chutki so collected every third day or so, the volunteers would cook their own food; the surplus "chutki" they would stock up.

This is a short paraphrase of Naujadi's long statement on chutki.[127] What we have here is a housewife's view of the Chauri Chaura volunteers. Nationalism in the guise of the alms-seeking volunteer appeared literally outside Naujadi's door—"*Aa hamare duāre-pe aa-ke khara hoilān bhikmanga! Hamre jo-kuch jutal: chāur-dāl jutal, pisān jutal, diyāi.*" Whatever could be managed—rice, lentils, flour—was given. Since the peasant household parted with a portion of its food, it fell to the housewife to make arrangements for the upkeep of the (full-time) peripatetic volunteers.[128] They were not given the leftovers, as sannyasis were, according to their "stated rule";[129] "otiyars" claimed a fraction of the food grains at the point at which it was to be cooked by the housewife.

Chutki-giving for nonascetic or political purposes was not novel in the region: the militant kine protection leagues that had emerged in the 1890s to safeguard the Hindu community's holy cows from being slaughtered by butchers at Muslim religious festivals had laid down elaborate chutki-gathering rules:[130] "Each household was directed to set apart at each meal one chutki (equal in weight or value to one paisa) of foodstuff for each member of the family." And in keeping with the cow-centered discipline of the *sabhās*, "the eating of food without setting apart the chutki" was tantamount to eating beef! Agents were deputed to garner the "contributions." They were to convert chutki-grain into hard cash and remit the money to provincial chiefs.[131]

An analogous network of converting chutki to cash and its onward transmission to headquarters was proposed by the Gorakhpur

Congress Committee in 1921. In a front-page notice, *Swadesh*, the nationalist weekly, exhorted "each and every village . . . claiming *shraddha* in Mahatma Gandhi" to "take out chutki . . . and *khalihāni*."[132] Raghupati Sahai—the famous poet Firaq Gorakhpuri of later years—was initially in charge of these collections; Maulvi Subhanullah, the District Congress Committee president, replaced him in May 1921. In a public notice, Firaq enjoined "one or two persons in every village to take responsibility for the collection of *muthia* and khalihāni." The responsible individuals were to sell the chutki grain "in the village or a nearby bazaar" and forward the cash by "money order" to the District Congress Committee in Gorakhpur. The preferred mode was for the collectors to come over to the headquarters and deposit the cash personally.[133] "Chutki registers" were in existence in villages like Burha Dih, near Pipraich and in Padrauna *tahsil* (subdivision).[134] Small wonder that the 1921–22 budget of the District Congress Committee had estimated an income of Rs. 5 lakhs from the chutki-muthia collection. A realization rate of one-half *chatāk* chutki daily per house of ten persons, with a 33 percent "discount for unrealized houses," when sold at an average rate of twelve seers to the rupee, yielded an annual value of Rs. 509,352 for the entire district.[135] The rate of conversion was arrived at keeping in mind the different foodstuff—*pisān, chāur, dāl,* in Naujadi's composite phrase—that were offered as chutki. As the secretary of the Gorakhpur Town Congress Committee informed the court, "various corns [*sic!*] were collected in the handfuls [*muthia*?], so it was considered that they will sell for 12 standard seers to the rupee."[136]

For the Congress Committee, chutki was a subscription; it was another name for chanda. It had to be collected, forwarded, and accounted for. Lists of authorized chutki and chanda collectors were often published in nationalist newspapers.[137] District account ledgers have such entries as "direct muthia from a Salempur village, Rs.7–12."[138] Chutki or muthia collections were certainly not meant for the upkeep of local volunteers—there was no provision for it in the budget of 1921–22.[139] When Hakeem Arif came to Dumri on 13 January, "he told Lal Mohammad and Nazar Ali and [Shikari] to make over to Bhagwati Bania the subscriptions . . . (chanda and chutki) collected by us."[140] This order, Shikari testified in court, was not obeyed. "Collections . . . made by Lal Mohammad and Nazar Ali" were "apparently embezzled," opined the judge, on the basis of the approver's testimony.[141]

The Feast of 4 February

All this is a far cry from Naujadi's idea of chutki. Chutki for Naujadi was what sustained full-time volunteers; it was not a chanda meant for ultimate deposit in the District Congress treasury.[142] Naujadi's otiyars in fact straddled the distance that separated chutki, a public levy, from chanda, a nationalist subscription. The surplus chutki was laid aside (*dharāt rahal*) in the village for a suitable public use.[143] According to Naujadi, the big Dumri gathering of 4 February feasted on the chutki collected by the volunteers of Chauri Chaura. Shikari in his statement did not mention the storage and the feast; he alluded, however, to the *gur* that had been collected for refreshment at the meeting.[144] Naujadi maintained that it was a regular feast (and not "modest provisions," as the judge noted) that took place on the day of the clash with the police: "Arē mītha āil rahal, mane mītha, tarkāri āil rahal, dāl-chāur āil rahal, dūsar-tīsar āil rahal . . . banal, khailān-piyalān, tab uthlān" (I mean there were sweets, there were vegetables, there were rice and dal, this and that. All this was cooked, they ate, they drank, and only then did they move). It is difficult to miss the hyperbole in that statement. But it is precisely the excess of description that enables Naujadi to under-score the public and festive nature of the *"bator"* (literally, gathering) of that day, when issues were debated, food was consumed, oaths were administered, and the march to the thāna commenced amid fanfare:

> *Suni! te Magh-ke mahinna mein inhān bator bhail.* Are you listen-ing! In the month of Magh, there was a gathering here. It is the same month [now]. There was a gathering; everybody came. All the chutki that had been kept—all that chutki—was sent to the *kāli-mai-ke-than*. It was at that place that the feast took place [*Ohi-ja banal bhandāra*]. They ate and drank; thick, real thick garlands were pre-pared; and drums and *dholaks* started "singing."

It was from such a meeting that the otiyars marched, singing and shouting (*gāwat-bajāwat*), to the thana.[145] Note the effervescent nature of the Dumri sabha, but note especially the feast that Naujadi repeat-edly emphasizes. Brought up on a diet of Indian anthropology, I wished to know whether the grain was cooked or offered uncooked, *sattu*-like.[146] Naujadi had lost her patience:

> Now, whether they cooked it or consumed it *kaccha*, this I did not see with my own eyes. I didn't see who ate and who didn't, did I? It was in his house—in Mir Shikari's house . . . and in Salamat's house

[Shikari's daughter's in-laws] that all the stuff was kept. . . . Everybody, young and old [*larka, parāni, manahi*], everybody carted the stuff away. Whether people cooked it and ate it, or they didn't eat it—the stuff left [Shikari's] house.

"I am telling you, all the grain was sent for the feast—*Ajji! sajji jinisiya gail khāe-piye ke; Bhandāra mein chal gail.*" The construction of this passage is significant. It is not that the grain (*jinis*) was kept in a storehouse (*bhandār*). In fact, on the morning of the fourth, it was sent out to the *bhandāra* (a sister word, *bhandāri*, is still used in Mundera for Sant Baksh Singh's provisioning of the police-*fauj*).[147] Now, *bhandāra* means both "storehouse" and a "feast"—of *jogīs*, sannyasis, and the like. "Bāba-ka bhandāra bhar-pūr rahe" was a benediction of plentitude that the alms-seeking mendicant showered on the householder. The beggar's second cry, "Mhāre bhandāre mein sājha kar-ke māi, mhāre bhandāre mein," was an invitation to the alms-giving housewife to "share" in the mendicant's feast/storehouse in the next world.[148] In Naujadi's recall, chutki and bhandāra unite the individual volunteer to other volunteers and to the *paulic* (public) at large. The *bhīk* given to the otiyars remained in the village, but it went a long way.

Do not the terms *bhīk*, *chutki*, and *bhandāra* suggest that Naujadi's "otiyars" be meaningfully considered as sadhus and sannyasis? I do not think so. There are several reasons for this. First, Naujadi during her exposition on chutki (and she talked about it at considerable length) nowhere employs these familiar terms. She repeatedly uses the descriptive *bhikmanga* (beggar), not *Bāba*, the generic term for religious mendicant. *Bābas* asking for *dāl* and pisān (pulse and lentils) is how a Bhojpuri poet was to describe the usual chutki-seeking "renouncers" of eastern UP.[149] Naujadi, however, refrains from characterizing Nazar Ali, Shikari, or Nageshar, her brother-in-law, as Bābas in nationalist garb. Even when someone glossed over her comment on *gerua* clothes with the stock phrase, "vairāgya mein aa gaye" (they appeared as renouncers), Naujadi refuses to give her assent. For Naujadi, the chutki-seekers of 1922 were political activists from the village: householders all, whom she knew, and whose physical strength and organizational skill she admired. They begged *bhikmanga*-like for chutki,[150] but that did not make them into sannyasis.

A new term, an idea—"volunteer"—comes into the village. This word is not translated into the standard Hindi, *swayamsēvak*, or absorbed into the more common *Bāba* or *sannyasi*. The word is peasantized. I don't think we gain anything by translating Naujadi's *otiyars* into yet another "native" term.

Gerua-rang

The chutki-seekers of Naujadi wore *gulābi* or *gerua* clothes. In our second meeting in February 1989, Naujadi elaborated on the colored clothes of the volunteers as follows:

> When Gandhi-Bāba came—what did he give [us]? He took out [*karhlān*] otiyars. Otiyars he took out. He first sent word that people should become otiyars. Red, black—no, not black—red—*geru* . . . everything *geru*. Then the cap was dyed, this, whatisitsname—dhoti was dyed. And this big flag and lāthi. . . . And the flag was used for gathering chutki.

Now the dyeing of dhotīs was not the norm in eastern UP and Bihar. *Mārkīn* (machine-made cloth, with the distinguishing "mark" of a Lancashire or Bombay mill) was the cloth most used for dhotīs, and it was usually white.[151] Shikari's uncle recalled seeing "a large number of men" going toward the thana, "some with yellow and *some with ordinary cloth*."[152] Where white was the norm, the dyeing of cloth had a special significance attached to it. Dhotīs are still dyed primarily for marriages and other ceremonials, and they are dyed by the *rangrez*, the professional dyer commonly pronounced *angrez*! Buchanan-Hamilton, that trusted companion of medieval and modern historians, comes in handy here. "The dyers in most parts of the district," he wrote in his notice on Bhagalpur,

> are chiefly employed to dye the clothes of those who attend marriage parties, . . . and during the three months that the ceremonies last, the dyers make very high wages; but at other times they have little employment.
>
> [Those in the town of Munger] dye chiefly with safflower, with which they give two colours, kusami [*kusumbi*, "cloth dyed with safflower"], a bright pomegranate red, and golabi, a fine red like rose; and each colour is of two different shades. . . . The safflower, *Carthamus tinctorious* or kusum is most in demand.[153]

Gulābi, *lāl*, and *geru* were used interchangeably by Naujadi; in the court records, *gerua bastar*, red or simply "coloured" clothes described the *pahirāwa* (dress) of the Chauri Chaura volunteers.[154] In fact, the various volunteer corps, as they sprang up in the early 1920s, revealed a marked preference for colored uniforms.[155] A Criminal Investigations Department (CID) report noted that "the yellow [*gerua*] shirt" was especially popular among the volunteers in UP; in North Bihar, nationalist "battalions" were dressed in khaddar of "yellow *ramraj* colour." Rahul Sankrityayan, who raised one such "colorful army" (*sēna* of *rangīn vardi-dhari swayam-sēvaks*), also tried his hand at dyeing by looking up the nationalist-chemist P. C. Ray's book on color.[156] The Bihar Sēwak Dal (formed in late 1921 to "do *baghāwat*") had a wide range of color uniforms: white for Hajipur, red for Muzaffarpur, and green dhotīs for those enlisting in Sitamarhi district.[157] The UP Provincial Volunteer Board for its part reserved these "swaraj colours" for shoulder straps; it recommended kusumbi and *zafrāni* (safflower and saffron) as the preferred colors for khaddar uniforms.[158] All this was in total disregard of Gandhi's express instructions on proper nationalist attire.

The Requirements of Khaddar

For Gandhi, the satyagrahi had to wear white khaddar; colored clothes were out, at least until swaraj was attained. The Mahatma was willing to compromise on certain things: one's bedding, for instance, could still be of "foreign or mill-made cloth," as there were "difficulties in the way of immediate self-purification to this extent."[159] No such difficulty was countenanced for khaddar as apparel. Those who could not afford to buy khaddar worth Rs. 5 or Rs. 10 for their clothes "could certainly borrow this amount . . . and become volunteer(s)."[160] It was not "at all difficult," wrote Gandhi in late 1921, to "use khadi for one's clothes." A "very poor man" could "limit himself to a loin-cloth, but this should be of khadi."[161]

The semiotics of khaddar consisted in three qualities: sparseness, coarseness, and whiteness. Handloomed silk and woolen clothes were to be abjured, unless "when . . . required by climatic or other urgent considerations. . . . The fashion certainly should be . . . to wear coarse khaddar."[162]

The clothes of the Gandhian volunteer had to be coarse khaddar and white. "India will lose nothing by wearing only white clothes for some time to come. Let them fill in colours after they have, clad in white, achieved their goal," Gandhi quoted approvingly from an unlikely source. He added, "We wear white khaddar because we have no time to get it dyed. Moreover, many of us do not like colours, as they are of foreign make."[163]

In early 1922, at the height of the volunteer movement (ninety-six thousand had signed up in UP alone), Gandhi's instructions on proper khaddar wear were being ignored. "Hardly fifty could be found dressed in hand-spun khaddar from top to toe" in Allahabad and Banaras. Others "wore khaddar for outer covering, all the rest being foreign cloth."[164] In Calcutta, Gandhi ruefully cataloged, "hundreds who have gone to jail know nothing about the pledge, are not dressed in khaddar, are not dressed even in Indian mill-made cloth but have gone to jail wearing foreign cloth, and . . . they have had no training in nonviolence."[165]

What the Otiyars Wore

The picture in Chauri Chaura was no different. For Naujadi, it was Gandhi who had "created" volunteers, but she is clearer that the "otiyars" wore gerua rather than khaddar.[166] In inquiries and testimonies, khaddar and gerua often appear as exclusive categories. A report on the occurrence published in the *Pioneer* spoke of a three-thousand-strong "procession . . . headed by *four or five volunteers in khaddar uniform.*"[167] The unofficial Congress inquiry talked in turn of five or six hundred volunteers, all "clad in gerua-coloured clothes . . . accompanied by a large crowd."[168] In the first version, it was texture; in the second, it was color that marked a Chauri Chaura volunteer.

At innumerable places in the court records, we get the equation of gerua clothes with volunteers.[169] Bhagwan Ahir, himself a leading actor, stated, "Some [were] dressed in white and *some dressed as volunteers.*"[170] It was not as if none wore khaddar. Dwarka Pandey of Barhampur mandal was in his khaddar *dhoti-kurta* when he was put up for identification in the district jail. The magistrate had to make special arrangements—two persons were asked to don khaddar clothes and stand beside Dwarka—to make the identification proceedings "fair" to the accused.[171] But even Dwarka, reminiscing fifty years later, talked about "a four-hundred–strong contingent of gerua-clad volunteers supervising the conduct of the five-thousand-strong crowd."[172]

The distinction between color and texture breaks down in several recollections in the courtroom. Meghu Tiwari, the chief villain in the dishonoring of the darogāin, was denounced as a volunteer who "used to wear gerua khaddar . . . before . . . [and] on Chaura riot day."[173] Identifying eight men from his village, Mahatam of Kusmhi testified, "They were all dressed in gerua khaddar. They told me they were going to Dumri sabha. Volunteers wear gerua cloth."[174] We are back once again to gerua as the distinguishing marker.

Sarju Kahar, a domestic servant at the thāna, was certain that "the volunteers had gerua cloth on and were crying Mahatmaji's *jai*. The four men I identified had gerua cloth on."[175] One of these four, Bhagwan Ahir, the subaltern pensioner from the Mesopotamia campaign, was not wearing gerua. On 4 February, Bhagwan was sporting, as usual, his "khaki sarkari coat," an appropriate attire for the "drill-master" of Chaura volunteers. Bhagwan, it seems, never took his coat off, even while in hiding. Constable Jai Ram arrested him on 10 March in the northern jungle by the River Gandak, "because of his [khaki] uniform."[176] Such was the metonymic connection gerua-otiyar that Sarju Kahar persisted in identifying Bhagwan-volunteer by his non-existent gerua uniform.

The association between otiyars and a particular color was so strong that in the courtroom reconstruction of the riot, those proved to be wearing *white clothes* were presumed to be "spectators" and not "volunteers." The counsels for the accused spent considerable time getting the approvers to admit of *this distinction* between *geru* and *white*. "I meant by 'spectators' the people who were wearing white, not coloured clothes," Shikari stated at the beginning of his cross-examination. The defense pushed him further: "I considered the persons wearing coloured clothes to be volunteers. And I thought the persons who were not wearing coloured clothes were not volunteers. In those 4,000 [outside the thāna] were volunteers, non-volunteers, and spectators."[177] Thakur, the second approver, also stated under cross-examination, "The volunteers had on ochre-colored clothing [*gerua bastar*]."[178] These were not abstract characterizations. What the approvers made of a man's attire was a matter of life and death for the person in the dock. Shikari had "named" Shahadat as "taking part in the riot," but was unclear about his volunteer status. Under cross-examination, Shikari replied that Shahadat of Dumri was "not a volunteer *because* he wore white clothes." The judge seemed to agree. Shahadat's clothes, inter alia, was why Holmes of Gorakhpur "did not think it . . . safe to convict him."[179] Clothes like Shahadat's testified to the presence of "nonvolunteers and spectators" in the crowd. White, coarse khaddar was not a markedly nationalist sign in Chauri Chaura.

"What significance do we ascribe to gerua, then?" I can hear the reader ask as I turn to the final theme of this essay. How much reflexivity should be assigned to the wearing of these garments? Were the volunteers conscious of their clothes being different from the ones prescribed by Gandhi? Did not the District Congress know about the dress of the Dumri volunteers? One can only debate such questions.

For Naujadi and many others, chutki and gerua *defined* the volunteers.[180] True, these terms have histories of their own.[181] But the old woman has no urge to hurl her "otiyars" back into the enveloping fold of a meaningful past. Naujadi remembers them in relation to a specific present, namely, the time of "Gandhi-raj" and of the "*utpāt* [tumult] we all created" on 4 February 1922. Naujadi's usage of *hamman*, the first-person plural, embraces the otiyars and their families in a collective act of great national significance for which they still await an adequate recompense.

Witness to a History

> SITA: Chauri Chaura is really the first "case" in connection with *surāj*.
> NAUJADI: No doubt about it, it is Chauri Chaura for sure—and Dumri is the place from where everything started. . . . Everybody has got their raj, our raj never came. It's us who created the *utpāt*, and look what we got—nothing!

The old widow is, of course, complaining about Rameshar's political pension, which is intercepted by local politicos who parade the "relatives of the rioters" in Lucknow and Delhi for their own ends. Naujadi no longer has "her paper with '172' written on it." It has been taken away by Rajbansi Sainthwar, a politician from Bansgaon *tahsīl*. Her poverty, the bully Rajbansi, the pension that never comes, the arrival of Gandhi, the sabha at Dumri—all are jumbled together in a poignant statement. Naujadi breaks down, and the historian hears himself mumble foolishly: "What else do I ask you?"

> Listen! In the month of Māgh, chutki-gathering started, and this event also happened in the month of Māgh. This *kānd* took place after a year. After one year this, whatisitsname—sabha—took place. Are you listening? One hundred seventy-two persons there are on

my paper, and Rajbansi has taken it away. [Breaks down.] My son had died [and I had to go to Delhi with Rajbansi]. I said to Rajbansi, Oh *nēta*, I said, I can't make it. He replied, I'll beat your arse blue if you carry on like this. *Eh Bābu*! Hearing this my daughter started crying. Rajbansi also took away hundred rupees from me. *Babua-lōg*, give me something to keep me going.

Historical Fieldwork

Naujadi's story is not just about the event of 1922. It is equally about the iniquitous recognition of the "freedom fighters." Our long conversations somehow missed out on how it felt to be the wife or the son of a convicted "rioter." Rather, the memory of privation, when the householder was locked up for eight to fifteen years (or indeed hanged), was enveloped by the quest for the political pension that was now due to the family. Recollections of the "riot" in Dumri are invariably interspersed with graphic accounts of a recent trip to New Delhi—to "Rajiv's house," to Jantar Mantar, or to the Rashtrapati Bhavan. The successful insertion of that infamous event into the life of the nation has both freed and framed familial memories.

If the inaccessibility of the actors' speech in court and in nationalist records pushes the possibility of narrating the event to the limit, historical fieldwork—the grasping after "experience" through its recall, "memory"—cannot by itself unify all extant and emerging accounts. Testimony to the incompleteness of record, familial memories are themselves witness to another history, that of the recent nationalization of the event.

The enormous conceptual and narratological complications here are obvious by being on display. So, clearly, I am not suggesting that what we now have on record is the voice and consciousness of the actors as it played itself out in early 1922. I simply note that the problems of capturing 1922 through interviews in 1990 are considerable, as are the pitfalls of a pragmatic reliance on contemporary evidence. This essay is an attempt to trace the event in the memory that incites it today. Processes and encounters external to "Chauri Chaura," but not to its retellings, play their part. While according primacy to local speech, I have refrained from an ethnoreportage. I have sought to reproduce specific, personalized, often eccentric accounts, but I have also invoked the authorized texts of historiography: court records, contemporary tracts, ethnological notices, even the dictionary. This is historiography's way of shaping events (and their recall) into context; it is especially required of any writing based on historical fieldwork. The historian who seeks to garner memories of an event officially labeled "crime" would do well to march outward from the archives. Refusal to recognize the prior presence of law, "the state's emissary,"[182] is unlikely to lead to a better dialogue at the present site of past actions.

As the last of the *puraniyās* (old folk) die, familial recall will no doubt lose out in intensity and facticity, but the investment made in "Chauri Chaura" by the local politicians will help keep the stories alive—the stories of Gandhi's men, the beating of volunteers, the firing on the crowd, the attack on the thāna, the arrival of the avenging "force," the circumstances that saved the locality, the punishment, and the betrayal of the families by New Delhi and the nation.

Subject to the Nation

The nation, of course, has its own ways of remembering the event. Now that the "riot" has been incorporated within the Freedom Struggle,[183] a space has been created for a monument, so tall that lights flicker over it at night, warning the planes making their way to the Gorakhpur airport. Across the railway track and adjacent to the station stands the old Chauri Chaura memorial, inaugurated in February 1924 by the then lieutenant governor. The monument unveiled seventy years ago to honor the policemen dead has been nationalized. The legend that the colonial masters engraved on it was gouged out by Baba Raghav Das, the prominent Gandhian of eastern UP, on 15 August 1947.[184] The postcolonial government did more than just smooth the rough-cut edges of nationalist chisels. It chose to inscribe "Jai Hind" on the police memorial, a slogan with which prime ministers of India end their Independence Day perorations from the Red Fort in Delhi. Both policemen and volunteers, it now appears, laid down their lives for the nation.

A few years ago, the otiyars received another gift from the nation. A super-fast train, named Shaheed Express in honor of the Chauri Chaura martyrs, was started between Delhi and Gorakhpur. Inaugurated on 2 October, Gandhi's birthday, it terminates at the district headquarters, fifteen miles short of Chauri Chaura.

Notes

This chapter began as a contribution to a special issue of *Subaltern Studies VIII* (1996) and emerged as a book, *Event, Metaphor, Memory: Chauri Chaura, 1922–1992* (Delhi: Oxford University Press; Berkeley: University of California Press, 1995). The present version is being published for the first time, very much as the long essay it originally was in 1992, with minor changes and additions.

1. Mohandas K. Gandhi, "The Crime of Chauri Chaura," 16 February 1922; "Divine Warning," 19 February 1922; and "Gorakhpur's Crime," 12 February 1922; in *Collected Works of Mahatma Gandhi*, vol. 22 (Ahmedabad, 1966), pp. 386–87, 415–21 (hereafter *CWMG*). For a contemporary official version, see *United Provinces Gazette*, March 25, 1922 (pt. 8), pp. 220–22.

2. P. C. Verma, *Gandhi-ki Larāi, urf Satyagraha Itihās* (Bulandshahr, 1931), Proscribed Pamphlet, Hindi, B 247, India Office Library, London.

3. Rajendra Prasad, "A Brief Sketch of the Non-Co-operation Movement," dated 31 August 1922, in *Young India, 1921–22,* by Mahatma Gandhi, ed. Rajendra Prasad (Madras, 1922), p. lxi.

4. Sampurnanand, *Memories and Reflections* (Bombay, 1961), p. 35. Sampurnanand was arrested on 24 December 1921 and released in July 1922.

5. The records of the Chauri Chaura Trials nos. 44–45 of 1922 are available in the District Record Room, Gorakhpur. Those generated in the High Court are preserved picklelike in the Museum of the Court in Allahabad; for nearly a decade, I was allowed only a "taste," till the perseverance of Rajeev Bhushan, Saad Saidullah, and above all Justice Khanna enabled me to sample the full fare.

6. Partha Chatterjee, "Gandhi and the Critique of Civil Society," in Ranajit Guha, ed., *Subaltern Studies III* (Delhi, 1984), p. 182. See also Ravinder Kumar, ed., *Essays on Gandhian Politics: The Rowlatt Satyagraha of 1919* (Oxford, 1971), and Ranajit Guha, "The Mahatma and the Mob," a review article, in *South Asia*, no. 3 (August 1973): 107–11.

7. Gandhi, "Democracy versus Mobocracy," 8 September 1920, *CWMG*, vol. 18, p. 240.

8. For a conceptualization of the problem, see Ranajit Guha, "Discipline and Mobilize," in Partha Chatterjee and Gyanendra Pandey, eds., *Subaltern Studies VII* (Delhi, 1992).

9. Ibid., p. 244. *Darshan*: paying homage to a holy object or a revered person by presenting oneself in the vicinity of the object or person.

10. Gandhi, "Some Illustrations," *CWMG*, vol. 18, p. 275. See also Chatterjee's comments on this passage, "Gandhi and the Critique of Civil Society," pp. 185–86.

11. Guha, "Discipline and Mobilize," p. 107.

12. Gandhi, *CWMG*, vol. 18, p. 240, cited in Guha, "Discipline and Mobilize."

13. The standard English version of the pledge form, as drafted by Gandhi, is printed in *CWMG*, vol. 22, pp. 100–101.

14. The sketch of the event that follows is based on court records and fieldwork done in Chauri Chaura. It remains very much my own account. I have not tried to silence my voice from this brief history; it is meant to help the reader along. For the ways in which the event was constructed in the courtroom and in the judges' prose, see Shahid Amin, "Approver's Testimony, Judicial Discourse: The Case of Chauri Chaura," in Ranajit Guha, ed., *Subaltern Studies V* (Delhi, 1987).

15. I have not found it worthwhile to detail the precise relationship between the Khilafat and noncooperation in Chauri Chaura and the surrounding villages. That part

of the story must await another occasion. Hakeem Niaz Ahmad Arif of Basantpur *mohalla*, Gorakhpur, was also the vice president of the Gorakhpur District Khilafat Committee. Maulvi Subhanullah, a leading Khilafatist, was in turn the president of the Gorakhpur District Congress Committee.

16. Drawing on the root "to possess," the term *malik* has a wide range of connotations in popular Hindustani. *A New Hindustani Dictionary, with Illustrations from Hindustani Literature and Folklore*, by S. W. Fallon (Banaras, 1879), gives the following: "1. owner; proprietor; 2. master; lord; 3. God; 4. husband; 5. *one empowered; an employer*" (emphasis added). The "māliks" of the crowd were those who had been clearly "empowered" by the Dumri meeting. A *thānedār* is an officer in charge of a police station, or *thāna*; also referred to as a subinspector or, in indigenous parlance, a *daroga*.

17. Cf. Haidar chaukidār: "The volunteers said the thanadar had no spirit left, *his rectum had split*"; evidence in the Sessions Court, Chauri Chaura Trials, II, p. 217. The proceedings of the committing magistrate reproduce the abuse with its Bhojpuri inflection. Rameshar, chaukidār of Satrohanpur, is quoted: "Some volunteers clapped their hands saying, . . . *'Thāna ki gānd phat gayil'*"; Chauri Chaura Trials, I, p. 318.

18. In all, about 1,000 "suspects" were listed and 225 put on trial. Not all, of course, had pledge forms pinned to their name. Many were arrested and tried on the basis of information supplied by local landlords or by the "coaccused."

19. Chauri Chaura Trials, I, p. 535.

20. Chauri Chaura Records (Gorakhpur), I, pp. 555, 556, 557, 759, 639 (hereafter CCR).

21. Shahid Amin, "Approver's Testimony, Judicial Discourse."

22. I am here borrowing Veena Das's characterization of Shikari's testimony. See her "Subaltern as Perspective," in Ranajit Guha, ed., *Subaltern Studies VI* (Delhi, 1989), pp. 315–16. See also Renato Rosaldo, "From the Door of His Tent: The Field-worker and the Inquisitor," in J. Clifford and G. E. Marcus, eds., *Writing Cultures: The Poetics and Politics of Ethnography* (Berkeley: University of California Press, 1986).

23. Upendra Baxi, "The State's Emissary: The Place of Law in Subaltern Studies," in Chatterjee and Pandey, eds., *Subaltern Studies VII*.

24. One such document in possession of Ramdihal Kewat's son reads as follows: "Pramān patra—Thāna Chauri Chaura: Pramānit kiya jāta hai ki Rudli putra Ramdihal Kewat, mauza Lakshmanpur, thāna Chauri Chaura, Gorakhpur, san 1922 ke Asahyog Āndolan (Chauri Chaura kānd) mein bhāg liye the. Inke viruddh dhāra 147/148/149/302 I.P.C. ka mukadma chala hai aur High Court adālat se phānsi ki saja pāe the. P.S. Chaura 10.2.1973 [Thumb impression]."

25. See the section "Chauri Chaura kānd," in *Swatantrata Sangrām ke Sainik (sankshipt parichay)*, vol. 35, *Gorakhpur* (Lucknow: Suchna Vibhag, 1972), pp. 10–12.

26. While *chitthiāon* (literally, lettering) was undertaken by Nazar Ali for the *bator* of 4 February, the news of the forthcoming "gathering" was spread in neighboring villages and bazaars by word of mouth. See the testimonies of Ugra, Nazir, Raghubir, and Bahadur, Committal Proceedings of 1.3.22, 20.3.22, 7.2.22, 8.2.22, CCR. For the importance of oral and unauthored speech and the metaphoric uses of writing by peasants, see Ranajit Guha, *Elementary Aspects of Peasant Insurgency in Colonial India* (Delhi, 1983), chap. 6.

27. These letters now figure as Exhibits nos. 93, 94, and 95 of the CCR.

28. Eighty of these pledge forms were produced in the court as incriminating evidence.

29. Testimony of Shikari, CCR, II, p. 2.

30. For a complete list, see "Fehrist barāmadagi māl baqabza Ahmad Husain wald

Hafiz Abdul Rahim wa Nur Baksh chaprāsi, Khilafat Committee, Gorakhpur" and "Fehrist ashiyāy Congress Committee, Gorakhpur," 5 February 1922, Exhibits nos. 121 and 122, CCR.

31. See "Fard talāshi mandal fehrist kāgzāt jo barāmad hue, mauza Burha Dih, be tarīkh, 19 farwari 1922, rūbru Ali Hasan wa Gobind ki bamaujūdgi sahib sub-inspector," Exhibit no. 114, CCR.

32. Exhibits nos. 115, 117, CCR.

33. The "search list" from Burha Dih mentions two bundles of "raddi kāghzāt" and "kāghaz sāda."

34. For the police officer, the twin peasant nationalists of Dumri had become one composite figure.

35. Ranajit Guha, *Elementary Aspects*, pp. 146 ff.

36. "Imposition of Collective Fines," Subdivisional Magistrate (SDM), Padrauna, 26.1.1943, xx-35-1942, Gorakhpur Records. The Committing Magistrate made this angry outburst on the destruction of the police turbans at the thāna: "The red turban was particularly offensive to the non-co-operation lamb. Minute strips of these turbans, two or three inches long and a quarter inch broad, were lying all over the place, as if the police force had been dispersed to the four quarters by that token. It appeared as if some men had been detailed for that attractive job"; Order by M. B. Dixit, 18 June 1922, p. 13, CCR.

37. "Pledge [Form] of Bhagirathi Pasi of Dumri," Exhibit no. 150, CCR.

38. On Gandhi's notion of the sacrificing volunteer, see Chatterjee, "Gandhi and the Critique of Civil Society."

39. General Note on Police Administration, Report of Gorakhpur Division for the year 1923, 4–5 March 1924, xx-5-1923-24, Gorakhpur Records.

40. Commissioner, Gorakhpur to Inspector General Police, 10 March 1925, xx-20-1924-25, Gorakhpur Records.

41. In all probability, what Komal shared with the Dumri volunteers was the district jail. Sita refers to how Komal wanted Neur (Sita's cousin) to escape along with him. Neur's courage failed him on the appointed day.

42. Interview with Mewa Lal Jaiswal and Ram Awadh "Bookseller," Mundera Bazaar, 22 February 1989.

43. Awadhu, when asked to comment on the oppressive nature of his master, proffered a diplomatic reply: "I cannot say about B[abu] Sant Baksh Singh being *zabardast*, he is considered to be a zamindar"; Chauri Chaura Trials, II, p. 500.

44. Evidence of Audhu, CCR, II, p. 498.

45. The High Court judge's comment is instructive: "Before the next morning's sun arose . . . each man felt himself marked out for the vengeance of the irresistible power which, in a moment of madness, he had challenged"; Theodore Piggott, *Outlaws I Have Known and Other Reminiscences of an Indian Judge* (Edinburgh, 1930), p. 281.

46. Evidence of Audhu Tiwari, CCR, II, pp. 500, 498; I, p. 507.

47. "From 4th to 11th I was mostly out at night, in the day I stayed at Chaura. . . . During the day time the villages in the neighbourhood [of Chaura] were mostly deserted. . . . I did not sleep on a bed any of these nights. Up to the 11th I had no opportunity of taking off my clothes. I became ill. I was ill after going back to Gorakhpur"; Evidence of Stanley Ray Mayers, Supt. of Police, Gorakhpur, CCR, II, pp. 657–58.

48. "Babu-saheb koi police station apne gāon ke pās nahīn banne dēte the— 'administration par asar parēga.' Gāon Gaunar rakkha—dēkhiye thāna [wahān] nahīn banne diya! Inki monopoly thi, jo man mein āta tha karte the"; interview with Shiv Shankar Tiwari, village Gaunar, 24 February 1989.

49. Evidence of Hasnu chaukidār of Mundera, Chauri Chaura Trials, II, p. 313.

50. Pirthi Rai, a peon of Mundera Bazaar, testified in court: "In the Chaura case, by order of the estate (of Babu Sant Baksh Singh), I arrested Baran Kalwar, Naipal Mallah and Ganga Kalwar, all of Mundera and Ramlagan Lohar of Pokharbhinda. I arrested . . . [them] in Mundera bazaar. After arresting them, I took them to the police Dy. Sahib in Chaura with their faces covered, because the Manager [of the estate] had ordered that after arrest they were to be taken to the thana with their faces covered [a technical requirement for the subsequent identification to be legal]"; CCR, II, p. 719.

51. Interview with Raghvendra Sharma Vaid, Mundera Bazaar, 22 February 1989.

52. The terms "sufferers" and "back-mein" are Mewa Lal Jaiswal's.

53. M. B. Dixit, Committing Magistrate, "Order," p. 10, CCR. On the social composition of the Chauri Chaura accused, see Lal Bahadur Varma, "Kshetrīya itihās ka pariprēkshya: Seemāin aur sambhāvanāin," in Uttar-Pradesh ka itihās (paper presented at the Gorakhpur University Conference, March 2–3, 1984), pp. 238–39.

54. Narrative of Janab Mohram Sheikh of Madanpur, 28 February 1989.

55. The Pathan traders of Madanpur make a parenthetic appearance in the confession of Ramrup Barai of Mundera: "There was much smoke and so they [the policemen] all came out of the thana. Nazar Ali and Shikari and *four or five Pathans of Madanpur* who were there said, "You all should keep watch so that no one may run away [*Tum kya māroge ham mārēnge*]." Exhibit no. 225, Chauri Chaura Records. Circle inspector Piare Lal and party raided Madanpur on the night of 23 February and arrested Ali Husain, Nawab, and Shubrati. All three were acquitted for want of evidence. "Thāna jalāne mein Madanpur ke Pathānon ka bahut hāth tha—wahi sab trader the," said Mewa Lal, who had heard it from his father.

56. The full Hindi version goes as follows: "Pahchānon mat! Āzadi ka sawāl hai! Yeh sab ke liye kiya gaya hai. [Pahchān] karōge to phānsi pa jāenge yeh log. Dēsh ke sāth ghaddāri hogi. Dēsh ko āzad karana hai, kam-se-kam itna to karo!"

57. CCR, II, pp. 785 ff.

58. This fact earned the veteran nationalist the following entry in an official directory: "In 1922 [he] specially resumed practice to plead on behalf of the famous Chouri Choura conspiracy case"; *Fighters for Freedom: 2: Varanasi Division* (Lucknow: Information Department, 1964), p. 512.

59. The memory of the Great Betrayal, which made the Sardars of Majitha village (Amritsar district in Punjab) into the leading landholders of Gorakhpur, still rankles with the people of Chauri Chaura. Naujadi referred deprecatingly to the Majithias who owned Dumri, and much else besides in Keotali *tappa*, as "Sardarwa"; even the Majithias' estate functionaries were accorded the title "Maharaj" in the 1920s. Mewa Lal Jaiswal even more severe: "The Majithias," he said, "will always remain *ghaddārs* in this area, *chāhe jitna uth jāen.*"

60. Both Shikari and Thakur Ahir went to Harcharan Singh's *kothi* in Chaura Bazaar before offering themselves (and their stories) to the police; see Judgment of H. E. Holmes, Sessions Judge, Gorakhpur, pp. 23, 25, CCR.

61. Shikari is described in the court records as "son of Mir Qurban, saiyid, 24 . . . cultivator and hideseller."

62. This was just one of the stratagems in the face of high rates of infant mortality. The other custom, "when a family happen[ed] to lose several children in succession," was to get the nose of the nextborn bored on the right nostril. The surviving child then bore the name Nakcched. Chotki Dumri had its own Nakcched Kahar, the schoolboy who functioned as "writer" to Nazar Ali and Shikari. On nose-piercing as a survival strategy, see *North Indian Notes and Queries*, no. 247 (September 1894).

63. In Mundera, the same phrase, in chaste Hindi, was used to describe the power of Bansu Singh, the manager of the bazaar.

64. Interview with Sita Ahir. *Pace* Gandhi: "I would advise those who feel guilty and repentent to hand themselves voluntarily to the Government for punishment and make a clear confession." Gandhi also exhorted the Gorakhpur Congress "workers . . . to find out the evil-doers and urge them to deliver themselves into custody"; Gandhi, *CWMG*, vol. 22, p. 420.

65. *Tāp-ki-kham-kham* is the standard phonetic rendering of the sound of horses' hoofs in Hindustani; see Vidyanivas Misr, *Hindi ki shabd sampada* (New Delhi: Rajkamal, 1982), p. 22.

66. Memorandum of Examination, Abdulla alias Sukhi, son of Gobar of Rajdhani, *Churihar*, 23 May 1922, CCR.

67. See p. 238 in this chapter.

68. The quotations in this paragraph are taken from Piggott, *Outlaws I Have Known*, pp. 287–89. Piggott was one of the two judges of the High Court who passed the final sentence in the Chauri Chaura case.

69. Ibid., p. 288.

70. Douglas Hay, "Property, Authority, and Criminal Law" in Hay et al., eds., *Albion's Fatal Tree: Crime and Society in Eighteenth-Century England* (New York, 1975), esp. pp. 40–49.

71. Piggott, *Outlaws I Have Known*, p. 288.

72. In answer to the question about the location of the trial, Sita also mentioned 172, but in a garbled way. Here it was 372—*bahattar* seems to be important—who were sentenced to death at Gorakhpur, and this number was reduced to 172 at Allahabad due to the efforts of Madan Mohan Malaviya. To quote Sita: "Mokadma jehel mein chale. Inhān [Gorakhpur] ke judge jehaliya mein jaa aur case kare Chauri Chaura ke. Te okre baad ee phaisla kar dihlān—aa 372 admi ke saja-e-phānsi de dehlān. Madan Maalvi ji—itthi—'appeal' kar dihlān—High Court. High Court se 172 admi ke saja-i-phānsi bhail. Aur admi choot gailān. Har itvār jehaliya mein bhent kihal jaa."

73. "Hān rahlān!" Sita replied to a question. "Pahila phānsi Abdullah ke hai." The Criminal Appeal no. 51, decided on 30 April 1923 from the Order of Special Sessions Judge, Gorakhpur, was titled *Abdullah and Others versus King Emperor*. "A whole lot were punished; we [their family members] have got [copies of] the judgment"; Sita Ahir then dwells on the three orders of punishment: jail, *dāmul* (transportation for life, in effect fourteen years' rigorous imprisonment in the Andaman islands), and *phānsi* (death by hanging). "Dāmul," the popular term for transportation for life used by Sita, is a peasantized abridgment of the Persian legal term *Dāyam-ul-habs*, literally, enclosed/imprisoned forever.

74. See the account of the hanging of Sita's uncle, Bikram Ahir, on p. 213 in this chapter.

75. See Shahid Amin, "Approver's Testimony, Judicial Discourse," in Guha, ed., *Subaltern Studies V*, pp. 191–92.

76. "The above offences are alleged to have been committed in the course of an occurrence, the *main features* of which . . . [as] proved by unimpeachable evidence are not disputed"; Sessions Trial nos. 44–45 of 1922, Judgment of Sessions Judge, Gorakhpur, p. 8 (emphasis added), CCR.

77. Ibid., p. 8.

78. Cited in Piggott, *Outlaws I Have Known*, p. 295.

79. Appeal no. 51 of 1923, *Abdullah and Others vs. King Emperor*, Judgment of the Allahabad High Court, 30 April 1923, pp. 16–17.

80. Extract from the District Khilafat Committee's [confiscated] Papers: "Āmad-ke kāgzāt ka Ragister," Exhibit no. 95, CCR. I have modified the translation from the one given in the High Court Judgment, p. 16.

81. *Abdullah and Others vs. King Emperor*, Judgment, High Court, p. 16.

82. See pp. 183 and 205 in this chapter.

83. Judgment, Sessions Judge, p. 9, CCR.

84. For Gandhi's reception at Chauri Chaura, see Shahid Amin, "Gandhi as Mahatma," in Guha, ed., *Subaltern Studies III* pp. 19–20.

85. To quote Sita's recollection: "Gānhi-bāba ke dekhle rahlīn. Gora, patra-ke rahlān. Lamba. Bhāsan karlān. Bahūt bheer! . . . maare log—kaccha paisa chale, sab dekh pāven. Hamre laikhan dhoti karke aur sab ke, chāru oor ghoom ke hathva joren. Ail rahlān terain se, ruklān . . . taniye hamse karēr rahlān Gandhi-ji, aur tar-uupar karke—hai-tare—hāth joren, panchan-ke hāth joren." The throwing of coins (Sita's *kaccha-paisa*, the regionally minted copper-coins used extensively in Mundera Bazaar) is also emphasized in the account of Gandhi's stopover published in *Swadesh*, 13 February 1922: "At Chauri Chaura one Marwari gentleman managed to hand something over to . . . [Gandhiji]. Then there was no stopping. A sheet was spread and currency notes and coins started raining. It was a sight."

86. *Barhani/Barhni*: "The broom used by women in sweeping out the house . . . , so called because the family is supposed to prosper [*barhna*]." *Hēnga* is "the flat plank dragged along the ground to break the clods after ploughing, while a man stands on it to give it weight"; see William Crooke, *A Glossary of North Indian Peasant Life*, ed. Shahid Amin (Delhi, 1989), paras. 34, 21.

87. For a brief discussion of these two themes, see Shahid Amin, "Gandhi as Mahatma," in Guha, ed., *Subaltern Studies III*, pp. 52–53.

88. For a description of Gandhi's reception at Chauri Chaura, see *Swadesh*, 13 February 1922. See also Amin, "Gandhi as Mahatma," p. 19.

89. I am grateful to David Arnold, Partha Chatterjee, and Nicholas Dirks for helpful suggestions on this section.

90. In this paragraph, I have combined the two accounts that Sita provided in August 1988 and February 1989.

91. Subsequent discussion on why meat, fish, and liquor were picketed failed to elicit a clear answer from Sita. His responses to my questions were as follows: "Don't eat, don't drink: *paulic* is unnecessarily throwing away money on these commodities; if these things are not sold, there would be nobody to consume them"; "No, volunteers were doing this on their own, Gandhiji hadn't said so"; "Volunteers were against the taking of life." For a brief discussion of some of these issues, see Amin, "Approver's Testimony, Judicial Discourse," p. 197, and Amin, "Gandhi as Mahatma."

92. Judgment, Sessions Judge, p. 36, CCR.

93. On police firing on crowds, see the debate contained in Police File no. 548B of 1894, North-Western Provinces (NWP) & Oudh, United Provinces (UP) Archives, Lucknow. In 1894, a new paragraph was added to the Police Orders and Regulations (Rule 97, sec. X, para. 66), requiring "a Magistrate or an officer in charge of a police station . . . to give beforehand to *the mob* the fullest warning of his intention, warning *the rioters that the fire will be effective* and *that blank cartridges will not be used*" (emphasis added). Subsequent to "Chauri Chaura," the attention of all district officers in UP was drawn to the standing orders forbidding firing in the air. What the police officers called "effective firing" was to be aimed at the front ranks of the crowds, where "leaders" were most likely to be found; firing in the air might injure or kill "spectators" or "stragglers." It was in this context that the "whole import" of the above instructions was considered to be

"humane"; see Government of India (GOI), Home to Govt. UP, telegram, dated 8 February 1922, KW 10 Police File 57 of 1921, and Note by Secretary, NWP & Oudh, to Governor, dated 28 August 1894, Police File 548B, KW 19, UP State Archives, Lucknow.

94. Evidence of Audhu, CCR, II, p. 501.

95. *Gārad* was the common translation of "armed guards" in Bhojpuri and regional Urdu alike. See "Yāddāsht" (Chauri Chaura), by Ajodhya Das, barrister-at-law, in *Mashriq*, 16 February 1922, p. 3.

96. Report on the Goraits of Gorakhpur, by E. J. Mardon, NWP & Oudh Police Progs., June 1894, no. 103, para. 9.

97. Of the 7,543 goraits in 1894, 83 percent belonged to the Chamar-Dusadh-Bhar lower-caste cluster, with the Chamars accounting for a high 60 percent. Among the chaukidārs, Ahirs (the caste to which Sita's family belonged), with 26 percent, and Muslims, with 22 percent, were the largest groups. Chamars and Dusadhs, by contrast, accounted for no more that 7 percent of the 2,302 chaukidārs; statistics from Report on the Goraits of Gorakhpur.

98. After a protracted debate, the "office" of gorait was merged with that of the chaukidār. Under this scheme, many goraits lost their posts. Provisions were made to prevent the dispossession of rent-free allotments of these former goraits; see Gorakhpur Goraits Act, 1919 (UP Act 1 of 1919), in Rev. A Progs., March 1919, nos. 6–41.

99. The duties expected of the chaukidārs were truly fantastic; they are described in the NWP Village and Road Police Act, 1873.

100. I am here following the remarks of Guha in his *Elementary Aspects of Peasant Insurgency*, p. 66.

101. "Order" by M. B. Dixit, 18 June 1922, p. 13, CCR.

102. CCR, II, p. 274.

103. The evidence of the chaukidars from CCR, II, pp. 274; I, pp. 281, 39; II, p. 257; and II, p. 448.

104. See the evidence of Harpal, chaukidār of Dumri, CCR, II, pp. 244–48.

105. Nos. 227 to 240 in this list, dated 27 January 1922, were from Dumri village. The list for the village was topped by Nazar Ali, followed by Shikari, with Nageshar Pasi, Naujadi's brother-in-law, in the fourth position. The marginal comment in the daroga's hand reads: "In this portion of the police station there are fine estates. Owner of each should be asked to suppress the movement. . . . Shikari Sekh is the leader. Evidence can be had under sec. 107, CPC."

106. The proverb is reproduced in *Indian Notes and Queries* 4, no. 116 (1886). For a stylized attack on darogas, see the poem "Naghmāt Pulis Nāseh," in *Report of the Committee to Enquire into Police Administration of the NWP & Oudh* (Allahabad, 1891), para. 53. Constable Ram Saran Singh of Chaura thāna had been set upon by volunteers in January and beaten with lathis; see CCR, II, pp. 729–31.

107. For a brief account of Bikram in the narrative of his grandson, see pp. 191–92 in this chapter.

108. Memo of Bikram Ahir, 25 May 1922, CCR.

109. On Neur Ahir, Sita's cousin and Bikram's son, see CCR, I, p. 506; Judgment, Sessions Judge, p. 187, CCR.

110. Entry no. 782, Register of Volunteers of Gorakhpur, Unnumbered Exhibit, CCR.

111. CCR, II, p. 245.

112. Judgment, Sessions Judge, p. 120, CCR.

113. Interview with Raghvendra Sharma Vaid, Mundera Bazaar, 22 February 1989.

114. Committal Order by M. B. Dixit, p. 12; Judgment, Sessions Judge, pp. 176–77, CCR.

236 / *Shahid Amin*

115. Musammat Rajmani Kaur, "Answers to Interrogatories," CCR, II, p. 379b. Under the Evidence Act, there was a special procedure for taking the evidence of women in purdah.

116. Committal Order, p. 12.

117. CCR, II, p. 379a.

118. The ambiguity arises in part from Naujadi's attempt to speak like the darogāin.

119. For the full text of the darogāin's testimony, see CCR, II, pp. 379a-379c.

120. The *buzurg*, glowingly described as "qaddāwar jawān, first-class-ki-dārhi, amama pahine-hue," prayed successfully for the Madanpur undertrials. In addition, it was because of his "powers" that the police raiding party had difficulty locating the village on the night of 18 March; interview with Moharam Sheikh, Deoria Sadar, 28 February 1989.

121. *Dāda* (grandfather in Hindustani) stands for "father" in the kinship terminology of rural east UP. The Bhojpuri exclamation *Āhi-ho-Dāda!* is the exact equivalent of the Hindustani *Bāp-re-Bāp!* Both correspond to the English "Oh, my God!"

122. Naujadi offered this clarification in answer to my question. *Khariyāni*, derived from *khalihān*, harvest floor, refers to dues collected at the threshing floor. District Congress records mention khaliyāni dues that were to be collected in the villages.

123. CCR, II, p. 2.

124. CCR, I, pp. 161ff; II, pp. 245, 705, 707.

125. Fallon, *A New Hindustani Dictionary*, s.v. "Chutki."

126. "They did not ask for it every day, did they? . . . It was given every third day or so."

127. The full statement on "chutki" runs as follows:
    AMIN: Te otiyar-log ka karat rahlān?
    NAUJADI: Otiyar! Aise bata de-een! Ohi chutikiya mānge.
    AMIN: Ka kah-ke mānge?
    NAUJADI: Mānge! Bhikiya jaise māngal jaa-la—sab-ke jāhil na rahe! Chāhe dāl-e banāve, chāhe bhāt banāve, chāhe pisān banāve, jo-kuch banāve unke khātir kārh-ke dhara-ja.
    AMIN: Te kāhe log unkar batiya mānat rahlān bhāi?
    NAUJADI: Batiya ee mānat rahlān—sarkār ke hukum deehal rahal, sarkār ke hukum rahal, sarkār ke oor se māngat rahlān.
    AMIN: Sarkār-ke, ki Gānhi Bāba ke?
    NAUJADI: Uhe! Gānhi-e-Bāba ke—te diya-jaa.
    AMIN: Te kā kah-ke māngat rahlān? Gānhi Bāba ke hukum ba? Gāna-ona gāt rahlān?
    NAUJADI: Roj nāhīn ne kaheen! . . . Nāhīn dusre-tisre din chutki diyāt rahal. . . . Unke niyuti-se teen din rasoi banāwal-ja—chāhe barhe chāhe ghate, unki chutki dhail rahe—te jehiya āwēn bhīk mānge, te unke diya jāe.

128. To quote Sita Ahir, "Olantiyar bhīk māngat rahlān. Olantiyar—koi kharcha de nāhīn—din-bhar ghoomen, aur khae-khātir mānge—khāeke." In court, the chaukidār of Bishembharpur named Buddhu and Iddan as volunteers. He "found out [that] they were volunteers when Budhu *went hither and thither asking for chutki*" (emphasis added); CCR, II, p. 423.

129. "According to the stated rule, they must not approach a house to beg until the regular meal-time is passed; what remains over is the portion of the mendicant"; A. S.

Gedden, "Asceticism (Hindu)," in J. Hastings, ed., *Encyclopedia of Religion and Ethics* (New York, 1910), vol. 2, p. 92.

130. Such chutki or *muthia* (from *mutthi*, fist) collections could, for instance, support full-time Sanskrit students at an informal *pathshāla*. For an example from north Bihar, see Rahul Sankrityayan, *Meri jeevan yatra* (Calcutta, 1951), p. 21.

131. Gen. [Admn.] Dept. Resolution of NWP Govt., 29 August 1893, para. 3(a), xvi-37/1898–1900, Commissioner's Records, Gorakhpur.

132. *Swadesh*, 10 April 1921.

133. "Notice by Raghupati Sahai," *Swadesh*, 1 May 1921, p. 8.

134. Exhibits nos. 121, 114, CCR; Trials of Volunteers in Padrauna tahsil, 1922, DIR Bastas, Gorakhpur Records.

135. *Chutki*, a pinch, had become *muthia*, a fistful; see "Budget 1921–22 of the District Congress Committee, Part B," Exhibit no. 82, CCR.

136. Evidence of Sadho Saran, CCR, II, p. 593.

137. See, for instance, the Report on Non-co-operation in Hata tahsil, *Swadesh*, 16 October 1921, p. 11.

138. Account of Income, 4.5.1921, Budget 1921–22 of the District Congress Committee, Gorakhpur, Exhibit no. 81, CCR.

139. See Exhibit no. 82, CCR.

140. Testimony of Shikari, CCR, II, p. 2.

141. Judgment, Sessions Judge, p. 18, CCR.

142. There was the further problem of the distribution of this collection between the Tilak Swaraj and the Khilafat Fund. A meeting of the Gorakhpur Committee had agreed in early January to divide the muthia collection in a "fixed proportion." In some other UP districts, the ratio was 25 percent for the Khilafat fund, with 75 percent reserved for the Tilak Fund; see Evidence of Maulvi Subhanullah and Hakim Arif, CCR, II, pp. 562, 687; Jawaharlal Nehru to Sec. AICC, 19 October 1921, *Selected Works of Jawaharlal Nehru*, vol. 1 (Delhi, 1972), p. 200.

143. On public levy, see Guha, *Elementary Aspects of Peasant Insurgency*, pp. 113–15.

144. Testimony of Shikari, CCR, II, p. 8; see also pp. 125, 514, 515.

145. "*Dholak baja rahe the aur jhande uthāe hue the*"; evidence of Sarju Kahar, CCR, *Tajwiz Awwal*, p. 358.

146. *Sattu*, or *satua*, flour of parched barley and gram, is a common *kachcha* food in eastern UP and Bihar. Sattu is mixed with water and kneaded into a dough and garnished with chilies and onions. A few pounds of sattu is enough for a peasant to subsist on for a couple of days.

147. See the recollection of Mewa Lal Jaiswal, cited p. 194 in this chapter.

148. S.v. "Bhandāra," in Fallon, *New Hindustani Dictionary*.

149. The "luckless peasant," in Ram Kumar Upadhyay "Vaid's" lament, goes hungry because of all manner of imposts, including "chutki" demanded by "Babas." See Ram Kumar Upadhyay "Vaid," *Vaid ki Lachari,* Jaunpur 1942, poem no. 47 in *Proscribed Literature in the U.P. State Archives* (Lucknow, 1987).

150. Gandhi regarded alms-seeking as a part of "the beggar problem," a "social nuisance," especially in the cities. In August 1921, he wrote strongly against "hundreds and thousands of people [who] do not work and live on alms, thereby putting their ochre robes to shame. . . . Today we simply have no work of a kind which we could offer to a beggar." The answer lay in the handloom and the spinning wheel. With village industry revived, "only Brahmins and fakirs who disseminated knowledge among the people will continue to live on alms. . . . Rogues will no longer be able to roam around in the

garb of sadhus and beg for alms." In his speech in January 1925, however, Gandhi employed the metaphor of "alms" and "begging" to help enlist volunteers at the Petlad Cultivator's Conference in Gujarat. The sources for the quotations are *CWMG*, vol. 72, pp. 136–37; vol. 22, p. 471; and vol. 25, p. 599.

151. That *mārkīn*, the mill cloth, was primarily white is attested by Sita Ahir's remark, "Mārkīn jyāda chale; rangīn kam chale." See also Ram Gharib Chaube, "Appx. B: On Cloth and the Clothes of the Natives of Eastern United Provinces," in William Crooke, *A Glossary of North Indian Peasant Life*, ed. Shahid Amin (Delhi, 1989), para. 726.

152. Evidence of Abdul Karim, CCR, I, p. 109.

153. Montgomery Martin, ed., *The History, Antiquities, Topography, and Statistics of Eastern India* (abridged ed. of Buchanan-Hamilton's manuscript account of Gorakhpur), vol. 2 (London, 1838), pp. 267–68; Fallon, *New Hindustani Dictionary*, s.v. "kusumbi."

154. CCR, II, pp. 38, 39, 49, 76, 115, 460. The organic dyes used in Gorakhpur to color the white *nān-gilāt* (long cloth) dhotīs were *kusum* (safflower), *haldi* (turmeric), the bark of the *tun* tree (*Cedrela toona*), and the flowers of *tesu* and *harsingār* (*Nyctanthes arbortristis*); written communication, Habib Ahmad, Gorakhpur. See also "List of Trees and Shrubs in the Gorakhpur Forest Division," in *Working Plan for the Forests of the Gorakhpur Division*, by R. G. Marriott (Allahabad, 1915), Appx. 4.

155. "The pathetic anxiety of all volunteer bodies to model themselves on the pattern of the military and police uniforms," as noticed by the Intelligence Bureau in 1939, belonged to a later period. In August 1940, with the war in full swing, "the wearing of unofficial uniforms bearing a colourful resemblance to military or official uniforms" was prohibited in India. See Note on Volunteer Movement in India, Pt. 3 by IB, June 1939, and copy of dispatch by Reuters, Simla, 5 August 1940, in L/PJ/8/678, India Office Library, London.

156. Note, dated 27 May 1922, by UP CID on Volunteer Movement, General Administration Department (GAD) File 658/1920, UP State Archives, Lucknow; Sankrityayan, *Meri Jeevan Yatra*, pp. 358–59, 355.

157. Bihar & Orissa Secret Abstracts, 17.2.1921, para. 2071, cited in Police Abstracts of Intelligence, UP, 7.1.1922, p. 41.

158. Instructions issued after the 3 December 1921, meeting of the (UP) Prantiya Swayam Sevak Dal, Exhibit no. 118, CCR.

159. Gandhi, *CWMG*, vol. 22, p. 152.

160. Ibid., p. 273.

161. Ibid., p. 152.

162. Ibid., p. 323.

163. Ibid., vol. 20, p. 451. The source of Gandhi's quotation was Pickthall, editor of the *Bombay Chronicle*.

164. Ibid., pp. 462–64. Cf. Hakeem Arif, "founder" of Dumri mandal: "I wear khaddar still as I did before. My upper garment is not khaddar nor are my trousers"; Evidence, 12.9.1922, CCR, II, p. 685.

165. Gandhi, *CWMG*, vol. 22, pp. 463–64.

166. When the Pandit of Malaon stated that he "remember[ed] the condition that *gārha* was not to be worn and khaddar was," he was implying that the rough hand-loomed cloth (*gārha*) of the locality was woven from mill-made yarn; CCR, II, p. 469.

167. *Pioneer*, 9 February 1922, cited in Sir C. Sankaran Nair, *Gandhi and Anarchy* (Madras, 1922), Appx. 12, "Gorakhpur Tragedy," p. 164.

168. Report by H. N. Kunzru, Maulvi Subhanullah, and C. K. Malaviya, *Leader*, 23 February 1922.

169. See CCR, I, pp. 49, 76, 115, 161; II, 38, 49, 76, 115, 245, 705, 707.

170. Statement by Bhagwan Ahir, 25 April 1922, CCR, I, p. 267.

171. Evidence of Pandit Mahesh Bal Dixit, Deputy Magistrate, CCR, II, p. 807. See also "Instructions re: Identification of Undertrial Prisoners in Jails," UP Police A Progs., September 1910, no. 4(a).

172. Interview with Dwarka Pandey, cited in Ram Murat Upadhyay, "Gorakhpur janpad mein Swatantrata Sangharsh, 1857–1947" (Ph.D. diss., Gorakhpur University, 1975), pp. 152–53.

173. Evidence of Thag Chamar, chaukidār, Gaunar, CCR, I, p. 303.

174. Evidence of Mahatam Sukul, CCR, I, p. 287.

175. CCR, I, pp. 273–74.

176. On Bhagwan Ahir's uniform, see testimonies of Bhagwan Ahir, Harcharan Singh, the Pandit of Malaon, and Constable Jai Ram, CCR, I, pp. 264ff., 366, 491, 82; II, p. 473.

177. Testimony of Shikari, Chauri Chaura Trials, II, pp. 38–39.

178. Testimony of Thakur Ahir, CCR, II, p. 49.

179. The quotations are taken from the judgment of Sessions Judge H. E. Holmes, pp. 234–35 (emphasis added), CCR.

180. There seems to have been general agreement about this in Dumri. "I understand what volunteers are," stated Subhag of Chotki Dumri in court. "Shikari, Nazar Ali, Nageshar, and Awadhi Pasi. These 4 are volunteers," he told the sessions judge. "I considered them to be volunteers because they *wore ochre-coloured clothes and demanded chutki*"; CCR, II, p. 481.

181. *Gerua*, from the Sanskrit *gairika*, that is, the color of *giri* or hills, is used by many Hindu sects as a prescriptive color for garments worn by those of their members who have renounced the world. As such, it came to symbolize the spirit of world-renunciation in Hindu religious thought and practice. Adopted by Hindu nationalist discourse of both literary and political genres since the middle of the last century, *gerua* has been operating in north Indian culture as an index of Hindu-nationalist sentiment with various idealist connotations, such as religiosity, patriotism, self-sacrifice, and so on. A well-known Bengali (Hindu) patriotic play, based on a fictionalized version of Shivaji's conflict with the Mughals, was called *Gairik patāka* (The saffron flag). As with so many other things, Bankimchandra Chattopadhyay's writings did much to promote the Hindu-nationalist symbolism of this particular color. The armed band of sannyasis whose exploits are celebrated in his novel, *Ānandamath*, were all clad in saffron robes. They called themselves *santān*, children of the Mother (i.e., Motherland), and stepped out of fiction into real life during the Swadeshi Movement, when many of its nationalist volunteers adopted the appellation and the dress. The arrival of such a band at the house of the liberal-landlord hero of Rabindranath Tagore's novel *Ghare baire* acts as a cue in the development of its plot; written communication from Ranajit Guha.

182. The phrase is Ranajit Guha's; see his "Chandra's Death," chapter 2 in this volume.

183. The official directory of accredited nationalists published by the Information Department of the UP Government in 1972 not only gives pride of place to the twenty "martyrs" hanged for their part in the "Chauri Chaura *kand*," it also affords an honorable mention to the five undertrials who expired (*divangat*) in jail; see *Swatantrata-sangrām ke sainik (sankshipt parichay)*, vol. 35, *Gorakhpur* (Lucknow, 1972), pp. 1–2.

184. Amodnath Tripathi, "Poorvi Uttar Pradesh ke jan-jeevan mein Baba Raghav Das ka Yogdān" (Ph.D. diss., Allahabad University, 1981), p. 135.

7 / The Nation and Its Women

Partha Chatterjee

The Paradox of the Women's Question

The "women's question" was a central issue in the most controversial debates over social reform in early and mid-nineteenth-century Bengal—the period of its so-called renaissance. Rammohan Roy's historical fame is largely built around his campaign against the practice of the immolation of widows, Vidyasagar's around his efforts to legalize widow remarriage and abolish Kulin polygamy; and the Brahmo Samaj was split twice in the 1870s over questions of marriage laws and the "age of consent." What has perplexed historians is the rather sudden disappearance of such issues from the agenda of public debate toward the close of the century. From then onward, questions regarding the position of women in society did not arouse the same degree of public passion and acrimony as they had only a few decades before. The overwhelming issues became directly political ones—concerning the politics of nationalism.

How are we to interpret this change? Ghulam Murshid states the problem in its most obvious, straightforward form.[1] If one takes seriously, that is to say, in their liberal, rationalist, and egalitarian content, the mid-nineteenth-century attempts in Bengal to "modernize" the condition of women, then what follows in the period of nationalism must be regarded as a clear retrogression. "Modernization" began in the first half of the nineteenth century because of the "penetration" of Western ideas. After some limited success, there was a perceptible decline in the reform movements as "popular attitudes" toward them "hardened." The new politics of nationalism "glorified India's past and

240

tended to defend everything traditional"; all attempts to change customs and lifestyles began to be seen as the aping of Western manners and thereby regarded with suspicion. Consequently, nationalism fostered a distinctly conservative attitude toward social beliefs and practices. The movement toward modernization was stalled by nationalist politics.

This critique of the social implications of nationalism follows from rather simple and linear historicist assumptions. Murshid not only accepts that the early attempts at social reform were impelled by the new nationalist and progressive ideas imported from Europe, he also presumes that the necessary historical culmination of such reforms in India ought to have been, as in the West, the full articulation of liberal values in social institutions and practices. From these assumptions, a critique of nationalist ideology and practices is inevitable. It would be the same sort of critique as that of the colonialist historians who argue that Indian nationalism was nothing but a scramble for sharing political power with the colonial rulers, its mass following only the successful activation of traditional patron-client relationships, its internal debates the squabbles of parochial factions, and its ideology a garb for xenophobia and racial exclusiveness.

Clearly, the problem of the diminished importance of the women's question in the period of nationalism deserves a different answer from the one given by Murshid. Sumit Sarkar has argued that the limitations of nationalist ideology in pushing forward a campaign for liberal and egalitarian social change cannot be seen as a retrogression from an earlier radical reformist phase.[2] Those limitations were in fact present in the earlier phase, as well. The "renaissance" reformers, he shows, were highly selective in their acceptance of liberal ideas from Europe. Fundamental elements of social conservatism, such as the maintenance of caste distinctions and patriarchal forms of authority in the family, acceptance of the sanctity of the shastras, and preference for symbolic rather than substantive changes in social practices, were conspicuous in the reform movements of the early and mid–nineteenth century.

Following from this, we could ask, How did the reformers select what they wanted? What, in other words, was the ideological sieve through which they put the newly imported ideas from Europe? If we can reconstruct this framework of the nationalist ideology, we will be in a far better position to locate where exactly the women's question fitted in with the claims of nationalism. We will find, if I may anticipate my argument in this essay, that nationalism did in fact provide an answer to the new social and cultural problems concerning the position of women in "modern" society and that this answer was posited not on an identity but on a difference with the perceived forms of cultural modernity in the West. I will argue, therefore, that the relative unimportance of the women's question in the last decades of the nineteenth century is to be explained not by the fact that it had been censored out of the reform agenda or overtaken by the more pressing and emotive issues of political struggle. The reason lies in nationalism's success in situating the "women's question" in an "inner" domain of sovereignty, far removed from the arena of political contest with the colonial state. This "inner" domain of national culture was constituted in the light of the discovery of "tradition."

The Women's Question in "Tradition"

Apart from the characterization of the political condition of India preceding the British conquest as a state of anarchy, lawlessness, and arbitrary despotism, a central element in the ideological justification of British colonial rule was the criticism of the "degenerate and barbaric" social customs of the Indian people, sanctioned, or so it was believed, by the religious tradition. Alongside the project of instituting orderly, lawful, and rational procedures of governance, therefore, colonialism also saw itself as performing a "civilizing mission." In identifying the tradition as "degenerate and barbaric," colonialist critics invariably repeated a long list of atrocities perpetrated on Indian women, not so much by men or certain classes of men, but by an entire body of scriptural canons and ritual practices that, they said, by rationalizing such atrocities within a complete framework of religious doctrine, made them appear to perpetrators and sufferers alike as the necessary marks of right conduct. By assuming a position of sympathy with the unfree and oppressed womanhood of India, the colonial mind was able to transform this figure of the Indian woman into a sign of the inherently oppressive and unfree nature of the entire cultural tradition of a country.

Take, for example, the following account of an early-nineteenth-century British traveler in India:

> At no period of life, in no condition of society, should a woman do any thing at her mere pleasure. Their fathers, their husbands, their sons, are verily called her protectors; but it is such protection! Day

and night must women be held by their protectors in a state of absolute dependence. A woman, it is affirmed, is never fit for independence, or to be trusted with liberty. Their deity has allotted to
women a love of their bed, of their seat, and of ornaments, impure
appetites, wrath, flexibility, desire of mischief and bad conduct.
Though her husband be devoid of all good qualities, yet, such is the
estimate they form of her moral discrimination and sensibilities, that
they bind the wife to revere him as a god, and to submit to his cor-
poreal chastisements, whenever he chooses to inflict them, by a cane
or a rope, on the back parts. . . . A state of dependence more strict,
contemptuous, and humiliating, than that which is ordained for the
weaker sex among the Hindoos, cannot easily be conceived; and to
consummate the stigma, to fill up the cup of bitter waters assigned to
woman, as if she deserved to be excluded from immortality as well
as from justice, from hope as well as from enjoyment, it is ruled that
a female has no business with the texts of the Veda—that having no
knowledge of expiatory texts, and no evidence of law, sinful woman
must be foul as falsehood itself, and incompetent to bear witness. To
them the fountain of wisdom is sealed, the streams of knowledge are
dried up; the springs of individual consolation, as promised in their
religion, are guarded and barred against women in their hour of des-
olate sorrow and parching anguish; and cast out, as she is, upon the
wilderness of bereavement and affliction, with her impoverished resources, her water may well be spent in the bottle; and, left as she is,
will it be a matter of wonder that, in the moment of despair, she will
embrace the burning pile and its scorching flames, instead of length-
ening solitude and degradation, of dark and humiliating suffering
and sorrow?[3]

An effervescent sympathy for the oppressed is combined in this breath-
less prose with a total moral condemnation of a tradition that was seen
to produce and sanctify these barbarous customs. And, of course, it
was "suttee" that came to provide the most clinching example in this
rhetoric of condemnation—"the first and most criminal of their customs," as William Bentinck, the governor-general who legislated its
abolition, described it. Indeed, the practical implication of the criticism
of Indian tradition was necessarily a project of "civilizing" the Indian
people: the entire edifice of colonialist discourse was fundamentally
constituted around this project.

Of course, within the discourse thus constituted, there was much
debate and controversy about the specific ways in which to carry out
this project. The options ranged from proselytization by Christian missionaries to legislative and administrative action by the colonial state

to a gradual spread of enlightened Western knowledge. Underlying each option was the liberal colonial idea that in the end Indians themselves must come to believe in the unworthiness of their traditional customs and embrace the new forms of civilized and rational social order.

Elsewhere, I have spoken of some of the political strategies of this civilizing mission.[4] What we must note here is that the so-called women's question in the agenda of Indian social reform in the early nineteenth century was not so much about the specific condition of women within a specific set of social relations as it was about the political encounter between a colonial state and the supposed "tradition" of a conquered people—a tradition that, as Lata Mani has shown in her study of the abolition of suttee,[5] was itself produced by colonialist discourse. It was colonialist discourse that, by assuming the hegemony of Brahmanical religious texts and the complete submission of all Hindus to the dictates of those texts, defined the tradition that was to be criticized and reformed. We will now see how Indian nationalism, in demarcating a political position opposed to colonial rule, took up the women's question as a problem already constituted for it: namely, a problem of Indian tradition.

The Women's Question in Nationalism

I have described elsewhere the way nationalism separated the domain of culture into two spheres—the material and the spiritual.[6] It was in the material sphere that the claims of Western civilization were the most powerful. Science, technology, rational forms of economic organization, modern methods of statecraft—these had given the European countries the strength to subjugate the non-European people and to impose their dominance over the whole world. To overcome this domination, the colonized people had to learn those superior techniques of organizing material life and incorporate them within their own cultures. This was one aspect of the nationalist project of rationalizing and reforming the traditional culture of their people. But this could not mean the imitation of the West in every aspect of life, for then the very distinction between the West and the East would vanish; the self-identity of national culture would itself be threatened. In fact, as Indian nationalists in the late nineteenth century argued, not only was it undesirable to imitate the West in anything other than the material aspects of life, it was even unnecessary to do so, because in the spiritual domain the East was superior to the West. What was necessary was to cultivate the material techniques of modern Western civilization while retaining and strengthening the distinctive spiritual essence of the national culture. This completed the formulation of the nationalist project, and as an ideological justification for the selective appropriation of Western modernity it continues to hold sway to this day.

The discourse of nationalism shows that the material/spiritual distinction was condensed into an analogous, but ideologically far more powerful, dichotomy: that between the outer and the inner. The material domain, argued nationalist writers, lies outside us—a mere external, which influences us, conditions us, and to which we are forced to adjust. But ultimately it is unimportant. It is the spiritual, which lies within, that is our true self; it is that which is genuinely essential. It followed that as long as India took care to retain the spiritual distinctiveness of its culture, it could make all the compromises and adjustments necessary to adapt itself to the requirements of a modern material world without losing its true identity. This was the key that nationalism supplied for resolving the ticklish problems posed by issues of social reform in the nineteenth century.

Applying the inner/outer distinction to the matter of concrete day-to-day living separates the social space into *ghar* and *bāhir*, the home and the world. The world is the external, the domain of the material; the home represents one's inner spiritual self, one's true identity. The world is a treacherous terrain of the pursuit of material interests, where practical considerations reign supreme. It is also typically the domain of the male. The home in its essence must remain unaffected by the profane activities of the material world—and woman is its representation. And so one gets an identification of social roles by gender to correspond with the separation of the social space into *ghar* and *bāhir*.

Thus far we have not obtained anything that is different from the typical conception of gender roles in traditional patriarchy. If we now find continuities in these social attitudes in the phase of social reform in the nineteenth century, we are tempted to label this, as indeed the liberal historiography of India has done, as "conservatism," a mere defense of traditional norms. But this would be a mistake. The colonial situation, and the ideological response of nationalism to the critique of Indian tradition, introduced an entirely new substance to these terms and effected their transformation. The material/spiritual dichotomy, to which the terms *world* and *home* corresponded, had acquired, as we have noted before, a very special significance in the nationalist mind. The world was where the European power had challenged the non-European peoples and, by virtue of its superior material culture, had subjugated them. But, the nationalists asserted, it had failed to colonize the inner, essential, identity of the East, which lay in its distinctive, and superior, spiritual culture. That is where the East was undominated, sovereign, master of its own fate. For a colonized people, the world was a distressing constraint, forced upon it by the fact of its material weakness. It was a place of oppression and daily humiliation, a place where the norms of the colonizer had perforce to be accepted. It was also the place, as nationalists were soon to argue, where the battle would be waged for national independence. This required that the subjugated learn from the West the modern sciences and arts of the material world. Then their strengths would be matched and ultimately the colonizer overthrown. But in the entire phase of the national struggle, the crucial need was to protect, preserve, and strengthen the inner core of the national culture, its spiritual essence. No encroachments by the colonizer must be allowed in that inner sanctum. In the world, imitation of and adaptation to Western norms was a necessity; at home, they were tantamount to annihilation of one's very identity.

Once we match this new meaning of the home/world dichotomy with the identification of social roles by gender, we get the ideological framework within which nationalism answered the women's question. It would be a grave error to see in this, as liberals are apt to in their despair at the many marks of social conservatism in nationalist practice, a total rejection of the West. Quite the contrary: the nationalist paradigm in fact supplied an ideological principle of *selection*. It was not a dismissal of modernity; the attempt was rather to make modernity consistent with the nationalist project.

Difference as a Principle of Selection

It is striking how much of the literature on women in the nineteenth century concerns the threatened Westernization of Bengali women. This theme was taken up in virtually every form of written, oral, and visual communication—from the ponderous essays of nineteenth-century moralists, to novels, farces, skits, and jingles, to the paintings of the *paṭuā* (folk painters). Social parody was the most popular and effective medium of this ideological propagation. From Iswarchandra Gupta

(1812–59) and the *kabiyāl* (popular singers) of the early nineteenth century to the celebrated pioneers of modern Bengali theater—Michael Madhusudan Dutt (1824–73), Dinabandhu Mitra, Jyotirindranath Tagore (1849–1925), Upendranath Das (1848–95), Amritalal Bose (1853–1929)—everyone picked up the theme. To ridicule the idea of a Bengali woman trying to imitate the ways of a memsahib (and it was very much an idea, for it is hard to find historical evidence that even in the most Westernized families of Calcutta in the mid-nineteenth century there were actually any women who even remotely resembled these gross caricatures) was a recipe sure to evoke raucous laughter and moral condemnation in both male and female audiences. It was, of course, a criticism of manners, of new items of clothing such as the blouse, the petticoat, and shoes (all, curiously, considered vulgar, although they clothed the body far better than the single length of sari that was customary for Bengali women, irrespective of wealth and social status, until the middle of the nineteenth century), of the use of Western cosmetics and jewelry, of the reading of novels, of needle-work (considered a useless and expensive pastime), of riding in open carriages. What made the ridicule stronger was the constant suggestion that the Westernized woman was fond of useless luxury and cared little for the well-being of the home. One can hardly miss in all this a criticism—reproach mixed with envy—of the wealth and luxury of the new social elite emerging around the institutions of colonial administration and trade.

Take, for example, a character called "Mister Dhurandhar Pakrashi," whose educated wife calls him a "fool" and a "rascal" (in English) and wants to become a "lady novelist" like Mary Correlli. This is how their daughter, Phulkumari, makes her entrance:

> PHULKUMARI: Papa! Papa! I want to go to the races, please take me with you.
> DHURANDHAR: Finished with your tennis?
> PHULKUMARI: Yes, now I want to go to the races. And you have to get me a new bicycle. I won't ride the one you got me last year. And my football is torn: you have to get me another one. And Papa, please buy me a self-driving car. And also a nice pony. And please fix an electric lamp in my drawing-room; I can't see very well in the gaslight.
> DHURANDHAR: Nothing else? How about asking the Banerjee Company to rebuild this house upside down, ceiling at the bottom and floor on top?
> PHULKUMARI: How can that be, Papa? You can't give me an education and then expect me to have low tastes.[7]

Or take the following scene, which combines a parody of the pretensions to Westernized manners of the reformists with a comment on their utter impotence against the violence and contempt of the British. A group of enlightened men, accompanied by their educated wives, are meeting to discuss plans for "female emancipation," when they are interrupted by three English soldiers called—yes!—James, Frederick, and Peter. (Most of the scene is in English in the original.)

JAMES: What is the matter? my dear—something cheering seems to take place here?

UNNATA BABU: Cheering indeed, as ninety against twenty—a meeting for the Hindu female liberty.

JAMES: A meeting for the Hindu female liberty? A nice thing indeed amidst poverty.

FREDERICK: Who sit there, both males and females together?

PETER: These seem to be the Hindu Heroes, met to unveil their wives' veiled nose.

FREDERICK: Nose alone won't do—if eyes and head be set to full liberty, Hindu ladies are sure to be the objects of curiosity.

PETER: Curiosity, nicety, and charity too.

UNNATA BABU: This is offensive—this is offensive.

JAMES: Nothing offensive—nothing offensive.

UNNATA BABU: Go hence, ye foreigners. Why come here, ye vain intruders?

JAMES: To dance, to sing and to feast—
With our rising cousins of the East.

He takes Unnata Babu's wife by her hand, sings and dances with her and then kisses her.

UNNATA BABU: [Catches James by the hand] Leave her, leave her. She is my wife, my married wife.

JAMES: [Throws Unnata to the ground]
O! thou nigger of butter and wax made,
Dared come, my hand to shake!
If Jupiter himself with his thunder-bolt in hand,
Comes to fight us, we will here him withstand.
[Takes out his sword]
Look, look, here is my sword.
Come, please, stain it with your blood.
[Frederick and Peter also take out their swords]
Strike him, strike the devil right and left,
We both better strike the rest.

The English soldiers make their exit with the following words to Unnata's wife:

> JAMES: . . . O! pretty poor lady! We good-bye,
> Pray you—go, go forward—
> Wait upon, and guard your husband,
> A treacherous, bloody coward.[8]

The literature of parody and satire in the first half of the nineteenth century clearly contained much that was prompted by a straightforward defense of existing practices and outright rejection of the new. The nationalist paradigm had still not emerged in clear outline. In hindsight, this appears as a period of great social turmoil and ideological confusion among the literati—the period from Rammohan to Vidyasagar. And then a new discourse, drawing from various sources, began to form in the second half of the century—the discourse of nationalism.

In 1851, for instance, a prize essay on "Hindu female education" was trying to marshal evidence that women's education was encouraged in ancient India and that it was not only not harmful but positively beneficial for women to be educated.[9] It went into numerous practical considerations on how women from respectable families could learn to read and write without any harm to their caste or their honor. In 1870, however, a tract on the duties of wives was declaring that the old prejudices about women's education had virtually disappeared. "Now the times are such that most people believe that . . . by educating women the condition of the country will improve and that there will be happiness, welfare, and civilized manners in social life."[10]

The point of the new discussions was to define the social and moral principles for locating the position of women in the "modern" world of the nation. Let us take as an example one of the most clearly formulated tracts on the subject: Bhudeb Mukhopadhyay's *Pāribārik prabandha* (Essays on the family), published in 1882. Bhudeb states the problem in his characteristic matter-of-fact style:

> Because of the hankering for the external glitter and ostentation
> of the English way of life . . . an upheaval is under way within our
> homes. The men learn English and become sahibs. The women do
> not learn English but nevertheless try to become *bibis*. In households

that manage an income of a hundred rupees, the women no longer cook, sweep, or make the bed . . . everything is done by servants and maids; [the women] only read books, sew carpets, and play cards. What is the result? The house and furniture get untidy, the meals poor, the health of every member of the family is ruined; children are born weak and rickety, constantly plagued by illness—they die early.

Many reform movements are being conducted today; the education of women, in particular, is constantly talked about. But we rarely hear of those great arts in which women were once trained—a training that, if it had still been in vogue, would have enabled us to tide over this crisis caused by injudicious imitation. I suppose we will never hear of this training again.[11]

The problem is put here in the empirical terms of a positive sociology, a genre much favored by serious Bengali writers of Bhudeb's time. But the sense of crisis that he expresses was very much a reality. Bhudeb is voicing the feelings of large sections of the newly emergent middle class of Bengal when he says that the very institutions of home and family were threatened under the peculiar conditions of colonial rule. A quite unprecedented external condition had been thrust upon us; we were being forced to adjust to those conditions, for which a certain degree of imitation of alien ways was unavoidable. But could this wave of imitation be allowed to enter our homes? Would that not destroy our inner identity? Yet it was clear that a mere restatement of the old norms of family life would not suffice; they were breaking down because of the inexorable force of circumstance. New norms were needed, which would be more appropriate to the external conditions of the modern world and yet not a mere imitation of the West. What were the principles by which these new norms could be constructed?

Bhudeb supplies the characteristic nationalist answer. In an essay entitled "Modesty,"[12] he talks of the natural and social principles that provide the basis for the feminine virtues. Modesty, or decorum in manner and conduct, he says, is a specifically human trait; it does not exist in animal nature. It is human aversion to the purely animal traits that gives rise to virtues such as modesty. In this aspect, human beings seek to cultivate in themselves, and in their civilization, spiritual or godlike qualities wholly opposed to the forms of behavior that prevail in animal nature. Further, within the human species, women cultivate and cherish these godlike qualities far more than do men. Protected to a certain extent from the purely material pursuits of securing a livelihood in the external world, women express in their appearance and behavior the spiritual qualities that are characteristic of civilized and refined human society.

The relevant dichotomies and analogies are all here. The material/spiritual dichotomy corresponds to that between animal/godlike qualities, which in turn corresponds to masculine/feminine virtues. Bhudeb then invests this ideological form with its specifically nationalist content:

> In a society where men and women meet together, converse together at all times, eat and drink together, travel together, the manners of women are likely to be somewhat coarse, devoid of spiritual qualities and relatively prominent in animal traits. For this reason, I do not think the customs of such a society are free from all defect. Some argue that because of such close association with women, the characters of men acquire certain tender and spiritual qualities. Let me concede the point. But can the loss caused by coarseness and degeneration in the female character be compensated by the acquisition of a certain degree of tenderness in the male?

The point is then hammered home:

> Those who laid down our religious codes discovered the inner spiritual quality that resides within even the most animal pursuits that humans must perform, and thus removed the animal qualities from those actions. This has not happened in Europe. Religion there is completely divorced from [material] life. Europeans do not feel inclined to regulate all aspects of their life by the norms of religion; they condemn it as clericalism. . . . In the Arya system there is a preponderance of spiritualism, in the European system a preponderance of material pleasure. In the Arya system, the wife is a goddess. In the European system, she is a partner and companion.[13]

The new norm for organizing family life and determining the right conduct for women in the conditions of the modern world could now be deduced with ease. Adjustments would have to be made in the external world of material activity, and men would bear the brunt of this task. To the extent that the family was itself entangled in wider social relations, it, too, could not be insulated from the influence of changes in the outside world. Consequently, the organization and ways of life at home would also have to be changed. But the crucial requirement was to retain the inner spirituality of indigenous social life. The home was the principal site for expressing the spiritual quality of the national culture, and women must take the main responsibility for protecting and nurturing this quality. No matter what the changes in the external conditions of life for women, they must not lose their essentially spiritual (that is, feminine) virtues; they must not, in other words, become essentially Westernized. It followed, as a simple criterion for judging the desirability of reform, that the essential distinction between the social roles of men and women in terms of material and spiritual virtues must at all times be maintained. There would have to be a marked *difference* in the degree and manner of Westernization of women, as distinct from men, in the modern world of the nation.

A Genealogy of the Resolution

This was the central principle by which nationalism resolved the women's question in terms of its own historical project. The details were not, of course, worked out immediately. In fact, from the middle of the nineteenth century right up to the present day, there have been many controversies about the precise application of the home/world, spiritual/material, feminine/masculine dichotomies in various matters concerning the everyday life of the "modern" woman—her dress, food, manners, and education; her role in organizing life at home; her role outside the home. The concrete problems arose out of the rapidly changing situation, both external and internal, in which the new middle-class family found itself; the specific solutions were drawn from a variety of sources—a reconstructed "classical" tradition, modernized folk forms, the utilitarian logic of bureaucratic and industrial practices, the legal idea of equality in a liberal democratic state. The content of the resolution was neither predetermined nor unchanging, but its form had to be consistent with the system of dichotomies that shaped and contained the nationalist project.

The new woman defined in this way was subjected to a *new* patriarchy. In fact, the social order connecting the home and the world in which nationalists placed the new woman was not only contrasted with that of modern Western society; it was also explicitly distinguished from the patriarchy of indigenous tradition, the same tradition that had been put on the dock by colonial interrogators. Sure enough, nationalism adopted several elements from tradition as marks of its native cultural identity, but this was now a "classicized" tradition—reformed, reconstructed, fortified against charges of barbarism and irrationality.

The new patriarchy was also sharply distinguished from the immediate social and cultural condition in which the majority of the people lived, for the "new" woman was quite the reverse of the "common" woman, who was coarse, vulgar, loud, quarrelsome, devoid of superior moral sense, sexually promiscuous, and subjected to brutal physical oppression by males. Alongside the parody of the Westernized woman, this other construct is repeatedly emphasized in the literature of the nineteenth century through a host of lower-class female characters who make their appearance in the social milieu of the new middle class—maidservants, washer women, barbers, peddlers, procuresses, prostitutes. It was precisely this degenerate condition of women that nationalism claimed it would reform, and it was through these contrasts that the new woman of nationalist ideology was accorded a status of cultural superiority to the Westernized women of the wealthy parvenu families spawned by the colonial connection, as well as the common women of the lower classes. Attainment by her own efforts of a superior national culture was the mark of woman's newly acquired freedom. This was the central ideological strength of the nationalist resolution of the women's question.

We can follow the form of this resolution in several specific aspects in which the life and the condition of middle-class women have changed over the last one hundred years or so. Take the case of female education, that contentious subject that engaged so much of the attention of social reformers in the nineteenth century.[14] Some of the early opposition to the opening of schools for women was backed by an appeal to tradition, which supposedly prohibited women from being introduced to bookish learning, but this argument hardly gained much support. The real threat was seen to lie in the fact that the early schools, and arrangements for teaching women at home, were organized by Christian missionaries; there was thus the fear of both proselytization and the exposure of women to harmful Western influences.[15] The threat was removed when in the 1850s Indians themselves began to open schools for girls. The spread of formal education among middle-class women in Bengal in the second half of the nineteenth century was remarkable. From 95 girls' schools with an attendance of 2,500 in 1863, the figures went up to 2,238 schools in 1890 with a total of more than 80,000 students.[16] In the area of higher education, Chandramukhi Bose (1860–1944) and Kadambini Ganguli (1861–1923) were celebrated as examples of what Bengali women could achieve in formal learning: they took their B.A. degrees from the University of Calcutta in 1883, before most British universities agreed to accept women on their examination rolls. Kadambini then went on to medical college and became the first professionally schooled woman doctor.

The development of an educative literature and teaching materials in the Bengali language undoubtedly made possible the quite general acceptance of formal education among middle-class women. The long debates of the nineteenth century on a proper "feminine curriculum" now seem to us somewhat quaint, but it is not difficult to identify the real point of concern. Much of the content of the modern school education was seen as important for the "new" woman, but to administer it in the English language was difficult in practical terms, irrelevant because the central place of the educated woman was still at home, and threatening because it might devalue and displace that central site where the social position of women was located. The problem was resolved through the efforts of the intelligentsia, which made it a fundamental task of the national project to create a modern language and literature suitable for a widening readership that would include newly educated women. Through textbooks, periodicals, and creative works, an important force that shaped the new literature of Bengal was the urge to make it accessible to women who could read only one language—their mother tongue.

Formal education became not only acceptable, but, in fact, a requirement for the new *bhadramahilā* (respectable woman), when it was demonstrated that it was possible for a woman to acquire the cultural refinements afforded by modern education without jeopardizing her place at home, that is, without becoming a *memsahib*. Indeed, the nationalist construct of the new woman derived its ideological strength from its goal of cultural refinement through education as a personal challenge for every woman, thus opening up a domain where woman was an autonomous subject. This explains to a large extent the remarkable degree of enthusiasm among middle-class women themselves to acquire and use for themselves the benefits of formal learning. It was a goal that they set for themselves in their personal lives and as the objects of their will: to achieve it was to achieve freedom.[17] Indeed, the achievement was marked by claims of cultural superiority in several different aspects: superiority over the Western woman for whom, it was believed, education meant only the acquisition of material skills to compete with men in the outside world and hence a loss of feminine (spiritual) virtues; superiority over the preceding generation of women in their own homes who had been denied the opportunity of freedom by an oppressive and degenerate social tradition; and superiority over women of the lower classes who were culturally incapable of appreciating the virtues of freedom.

It is this particular nationalist construction of reform as a project of both emancipation and self-emancipation of women (and hence a project in which both men and women must participate) that also explains why the early generation of educated women themselves so keenly propagated the nationalist idea of the "new woman." Recent historians of a liberal persuasion have often been somewhat embarrassed by the profuse evidence of women writers of the nineteenth century, including those at the forefront of the reform movements in middle-class homes, justifying the importance of the so-called "feminine virtues." Radharani Lahiri, for instance, wrote in 1875: "Of all the subjects that women might learn, housework is the most important. . . . Whatever knowledge she may acquire, she cannot claim any reputation unless she is proficient in housework."[18] Others spoke of the need for an educated woman to develop such womanly virtues as chastity, self-sacrifice, submission, devotion, kindness, patience, and the labors of love. The ideological point of view from which such protestations of "femininity" (and hence the acceptance of a new patriarchal order) were made inevitable was given precisely by the nationalist resolution of the problem, and Kundamala Devi, writing in 1870, expressed this well when she advised other women:

> If you have acquired real knowledge, then give no place in your heart to *memsahib*-like behavior. That is not becoming in a Bengali housewife. See how an educated woman can do housework thoughtfully and systematically in a way unknown to an ignorant, uneducated woman. And see how if God had not appointed us to this place in the home, how unhappy a place the world would be.[19]

Education then was meant to inculcate in women the virtues—the typically bourgeois virtues characteristic of the new social forms of "disciplining"—of orderliness, thrift, cleanliness, and a personal sense of responsibility, as well as the practical skills of literacy, accounting, and hygiene and the ability to run the household according to the new physical and economic conditions set by the outside world. For this, she would also need to have some idea of the world outside the home into which she could venture as long as it did not threaten her femininity. It is this latter criterion, now invested with a characteristically nationalist content, that made possible the displacement of the boundaries of the home from the physical confines earlier defined by the rules of purdah to a more flexible, but nonetheless culturally determinate, domain set by the *differences* between socially approved male and female conduct. Once the essential femininity of women was fixed in terms of certain culturally visible spiritual qualities, they could go to schools, travel in public conveyances, watch public entertainment programs, and in time even take up employment outside the home. But the "spiritual" signs of her femininity were now clearly marked—in her dress, her eating habits, her social demeanor, and her religiosity.

The specific markers were obtained from diverse sources, and in terms of their origins each had its specific history. The dress of the *bhadramahilā*, for instance, went through a whole phase of experimentation before what was known as the *brāhmikā* sari (a form of wearing the sari in combination with blouse, petticoat, and shoes made fashionable in Brahmo households) became accepted as standard for middle-class women.[20] Here, too, the necessary differences were signified in terms of national identity, social emancipation, and cultural refinement—differences, that is to say, from the memsahib, from women of earlier generations, and from women of the lower classes. Further, in this, as in other aspects of her life, the spirituality of her character had also to be stressed in contrast with the innumerable surrenders that men were having to make to the pressures of the material world. The need to adjust to the new conditions outside the home had forced upon men a whole series of changes in their dress, food habits, religious observances, and social relations. Each of these capitulations now had to be compensated for by an assertion of spiritual purity on the part of women. They must not eat, drink, or smoke in the same way as men; they must continue the observance of religious rituals that men were finding difficult to carry out; they must maintain the cohesiveness of family life and solidarity with the kin to which men could not now devote much attention. The new patriarchy advocated by nationalism conferred upon women the honor of a new social responsibility and, by associating the task of female emancipation with the historical goal of sovereign nationhood, bound them to a new, and yet entirely legitimate, subordination.

As with all hegemonic forms of exercising dominance, this patriarchy combined coercive authority with the subtle force of persuasion. This was expressed most generally in the inverted ideological form of the relation of power between the sexes: the adulation of woman as goddess or as mother. Whatever its sources in the classical religions of India or in medieval religious practices, it is undeniable that the specific ideological form in which we know the "Indian woman" construct in the literature and arts of India today is wholly a product of the development of a dominant middle-class culture coeval with the era of nationalism. It served to emphasize with all the force of mythological inspiration what had in any case become a dominant characteristic of femininity in the new construct of "woman" standing as a sign for "nation," namely, the spiritual qualities of self-sacrifice, benevolence, devotion, religiosity, and so on. This spirituality did not, as we have seen, impede the chances of the woman moving out of the physical confines of the home; on the contrary, it facilitated it, making it possible for her to go into the world under conditions that would not threaten her femininity. In fact, the image of woman as goddess or mother served to erase her sexuality in the world outside the home.

There are many important implications of this construct. To take one example, consider an observation often made: the relative absence of gender discrimination in middle-class occupations in India, an area that has been at the center of demands for women's rights in the capitalist West. Without denying the possibility that there are many complexities that lie behind this rather superficial observation, it is certainly paradoxical that, whereas middle-class employment has been an area of bitter competition between cultural groups distinguished by caste, religion, language, and so on, in the entire period of nationalist and postcolonial politics in India, gender has never been an issue of public contention. Similarly, the new constitution of independent India gave women the vote without any major debate on the question and without there ever having been a movement for women's suffrage at any period of nationalist politics in India. The fact that everyone assumed that women would naturally have the vote indicates a complete transposition of the terms in which the old patriarchy of tradition was constituted. The fixing by nationalist ideology of masculine/feminine qualities in terms of the material/spiritual dichotomy does not make women who have entered professional occupations competitors to male job seekers, because in this construct there are no specific cultural signs that distinguish women from men in the material world.

In fact, the distinctions that often become significant are those that operate *between* women in the world outside the home. They can mark out women by their dress, eating habits (or drinking or smoking), adherence or otherwise to religious marks of feminine status, behavior toward men, and so on, and classify them as "Westernized," "traditional," or "low-class" (or subtler variations on those distinctions)—all signifying a deviation from the acceptable norm. A woman identified as "Westernized," for instance, would invite the ascription of all that the "normal" woman (mother/sister/wife/daughter) is not—brazen, avaricious, irreligious, sexually promiscuous—and this not only from males but also from women who see themselves as conforming to the legitimate norm, which is precisely an indicator of the hegemonic status of the ideological construct. An analogous set of distinctions would mark out the "low-class" or "common" woman from the "normal." (Perhaps the most extreme object of contempt for the nationalist is the stereotype of the Anglo-Indian *ṭnyāś* (half-breed)—Westernized and common at the same time.) Not surprisingly, deviation from the norm also carries with it the possibility of a variety of ambiguous meanings—signs of illegitimacy become the sanction for behavior not permitted with those who are "normal"—and these are the sorts of meaning exploited to the full by, for instance, the commercial media of film, advertising, and fashion. Here is one more instance of the displacement in nationalist ideology of the construct of woman as a sex object in Western patriarchy: the nationalist male thinks of his own wife/sister/daughter as "normal" precisely because she is not a "sex object," while those who could be "sex objects" are not "normal."

Elements of a Critique of the Resolution

I end this chapter by pointing out another significant feature of the way in which nationalism sought to resolve the women's question in accordance with its historical project. This has to do with the one aspect of the question that was directly political, concerning relations with the state. Nationalism, as we have noticed before, located its own subjectivity in the spiritual domain of culture, where it considered itself superior to the West and hence undominated and sovereign. It could not permit an encroachment by the colonial power in that domain. This determined the characteristically nationalist response to proposals for effecting social reform through the legislative enactments of the colonial state. Unlike the early reformers from Rammohan to Vidyasagar, nationalists of the late nineteenth century were in general opposed to such proposals, for such a method of reform seemed to deny the ability of the nation to act for itself even in a domain where it was sovereign. In the specific case of reforming the lives of women, consequently, the nationalist position was firmly based on the premise that this was an area where the nation was acting on its own, outside the purview of the guidance and intervention of the colonial state.

We now get the full answer to the historical problem I raised at the beginning of this chapter. The reason why the issue of "female emancipation" seems to disappear from the public agenda of nationalist agitation in the late nineteenth century is not because it was overtaken by the more emotive issues concerning political power. Rather, the reason lies in the refusal of nationalism to make the women's question an issue of political negotiation with the colonial state. The simple historical fact is that the lives of middle-class women, coming from that demographic section that effectively constituted the "nation" in late colonial India, changed most rapidly precisely during the period of the nationalist movement—indeed, so rapidly that women from each generation in the last hundred years could say quite truthfully that their lives were strikingly different from those led by the preceding generation. These changes took place in the colonial period mostly outside the arena of political agitation, in a domain where the nation thought of itself as already free. It was after independence, when the nation had acquired political sovereignty, that it became legitimate to embody the idea of reform in legislative enactments, about marriage rules, property rights, suffrage, equal pay, equality of opportunity, and so on. Now, of course, the women's question has once again become a political issue in the life of the nation-state.

Another problem on which we can now obtain a clearer perspective is that of the seeming absence of any autonomous struggle by women themselves for equality and freedom. We would be mistaken to look for evidence of such struggle in the public archives of political affairs, for unlike the women's movement in nineteenth- and twentieth-century Europe or America, the battle for the new idea of womanhood in the era of nationalism was waged in the home. We know from the evidence left behind in autobiographies, family histories, religious tracts, literature, theater, songs, paintings, and such other cultural artifacts that it was the home that became the principal site of the struggle through which the hegemonic construct of the new nationalist patriarchy had to be normalized. This is the real history of the women's question whose terrain our genealogical investigation into the nationalist idea of "woman" has identified. The nationalist discourse we have heard so far is a discourse about women; women do not speak here.

The location of the state in the nationalist resolution of the women's question in the colonial period has yet another implication. For sections of the middle class that felt themselves culturally excluded from the formation of the nation and that then organized themselves as politically distinct groups, the relative exclusion from the new nation-state would act as a further means of displacement of the legitimate agency of reform. In the case of Muslims in Bengal, for instance, the formation of a new middle class was delayed, for reasons that we need not go into here. Exactly the same sorts of ideological concerns typical of a nationalist response to issues of social reform in a colonial situation can be seen to operate among Muslims as well, with a difference in chronological time.[21] Nationalist reforms do not, however, reach political fruition in the case of the Muslims in independent India, because to the extent that the dominant cultural formation among them considers the community excluded from the state, a new colonial relation is brought into being. The system of dichotomies of inner/outer, home/world, feminine/masculine are once again activated. Reforms that touch upon what are considered the inner essence of the identity of the community can only be legitimately carried out by the community itself, not by the state. It is instructive to note how little institutional change has been allowed in the civil life of Indian Muslims since independence and to compare it with Muslim countries where nationalist cultural reform was part of the successful formation of an independent nation-state. The contrast is striking if one compares the position of middle-class Muslim women in West Bengal today with that of neighboring Bangladesh.

The continuance of a distinct cultural "problem" of the minorities is an index of the failure of the Indian nation to effectively include within its body the whole of the demographic mass that it claims to represent. The failure becomes evident when we note that the formation of a hegemonic "national culture" was *necessarily* built upon the privileging of an "essential tradition," which in turn was defined by a system of exclusions. Ideals of freedom, equality, and cultural refinement went hand in hand with a set of dichotomies that systematically excluded from the new life of the nation the vast masses of people whom the dominant elite would represent and lead, but who could never be culturally integrated with their leaders. Both colonial rulers and their nationalist opponents conspired to displace in the colonial world the original structure of meanings associated with Western liberal notions of right, freedom, equality, and so on. The inauguration of the national state in India could not mean a universalization of the bourgeois notion of "man."

Indeed, in setting up its new patriarchy as a hegemonic construct, nationalist discourse demarcated its cultural essence as distinct not only from that of the West, but also from the mass of the people. It has generalized itself among the new middle class, admittedly a widening class and large enough in absolute numbers to be self-reproducing, but is situated at a great distance from the large mass of subordinate classes. Our analysis of the nationalist construction of woman once again shows how, in the confrontation between colonialist and nationalist discourses, the dichotomies of spiritual/material, home/world, feminine/masculine, while enabling the production of a nationalist discourse that is different from that of colonialism, nonetheless remains trapped within its framework of false essentialisms.

Notes

1. Ghulam Murshid, *Reluctant Debutante: Response of Bengali Women to Modernization, 1849–1905* (Rajshahi: Rajshahi University Press, 1983).

2. Sumit Sarkar, *A Critique of Colonial India* (Calcutta: Papyrus, 1985), pp. 71–76.

3. J. W. Massie, *Continental India* (London: Thomas Ward, 1819), vol. 2, pp. 153–54.

4. Partha Chatterjee, *The Nation and Its Fragments* (Princeton: Princeton University Press, 1993), pp. 14–34.

5. Lata Mani, "The Production of an Official Discourse on *Sati* in Early Nineteenth-Century Bengal," *Economic and Political Weekly: Review of Women's Studies* 21 (April 1986): WS32–40; Mani, "Contentious Traditions: The Debate of *Sati* in Colonial India," in Kumkum Sangari and Sudesh Vaid, eds., *Recasting Women: Essays in Colonial History* (New Delhi: Kali for Women, 1989), pp. 88–126.

6. Partha Chatterjee, *Nationalist Thought and the Colonial World* (London: Zed Books, 1986).

7. Amarendranath Datta, *Majā* (Calcutta, 1900), pp. 7–8.

8. *Meye manṭār miṭiṃ* (Calcutta: Girish Vidyaratna, 1874), pp. 28–31.

9. Tarasankar Sharma, *Strīganer bidyā śikṣā* (Calcutta, 1851).

10. Sibchandra Jana, *Pātibratya-dharma-śikṣā* (Calcutta: Gupta Press, 1870).

11. Bhudeb Mukhopadhyay, "Gṛhakāryer byabasthā," in Pramathanath Bisi, ed., *Bhūdeb racanāsambhār* (Calcutta: Mitra and Ghosh, 1969), p. 480.

12. Bhudeb Mukhopadhyay, "Lajjāśīlatā," in Bisi, ed., *Bhūdeb racanāsambhār*, pp. 445–48.

13. Ibid., pp. 446, 447.

14. See the survey of these debates in Murshid, *Reluctant Debutante*, pp. 19–62;

Meredith Borthwick, *The Changing Role of Women in Bengal, 1849–1905* (Princeton: Princeton University Press, 1984), pp. 60–108; and Malavika Karlekar, "Kadambini and the Bhadralok: Early Debates over Women's Education in Bengal," *Economic and Political Weekly: Review of Women's Studies* 21 (April 1986): WS25–31.

15. M. A. Laird, *Missionaries and Education in Bengal, 1793–1837* (Oxford: Clarendon Press, 1972).

16. Murshid, *Reluctant Debutante*, p. 43.

17. The autobiographies of the early generation of educated middle-class women are infused with this spirit of achievement. For a recent study, see Malavika Karlekar, *Voices from Within: Early Personal Narratives of Bengali Women* (Delhi: Oxford University Press, 1991).

18. Cited in Murshid, *Reluctant Debutante*, p. 60.

19. Cited in Borthwick, *Changing Role of Women*, p. 105.

20. See ibid., pp. 245–56.

21. See Murshid, *Reluctant Debutante*.

8 / Postcoloniality and the Artifice of History: Who Speaks for "Indian" Pasts?

Dipesh Chakrabarty

Push thought to extremes.
—Louis Althusser

I

It has recently been said in praise of the postcolonial project of *Subaltern Studies* that it demonstrates, "perhaps for the first time since colonization," that "Indians are showing sustained signs of reappropriating the capacity to represent themselves [within the discipline of history]."[1] As a historian who is a member of the *Subaltern Studies* collective, I find the congratulation contained in this remark gratifying but premature. The purpose of this article is to problematize the idea of "Indians" "representing themselves in history." Let us put aside for the moment the messy problems of identity inherent in a transnational enterprise such as *Subaltern Studies*, where passports and commitments blur the distinctions of ethnicity in a manner that some would regard as characteristically postmodern. I have a more perverse proposition to argue. It is that insofar as the academic discourse of history—that is, "history" as a discourse produced at the institutional site of the university—is concerned, "Europe" remains the sovereign, theoretical subject of all histories, including the ones we call "Indian," "Chinese," "Kenyan," and so on. There is a peculiar way in which all these other histories tend to become variations on a master narrative that could be called "the history of Europe." In this sense, "Indian" history itself is in a position of subalternity: one can only articulate subaltern subject positions in the name of this history.

While the rest of this article will elaborate on this proposition, let me enter a few qualifications. "Europe" and "India" are treated here as hyperreal terms in that they refer to certain figures of imagination whose geographical referents remain somewhat indeterminate.[2] As figures of the imaginary they are, of course, subject to contestation, but for the moment I shall treat them as though they were given, reified categories, opposites paired in a structure of domination and subordination. I realize that in treating them thus I leave myself open to the charge of nativism, nationalism, or worse, the sin of sins, nostalgia. Liberal-minded scholars would immediately protest that any idea of a homogeneous, uncontested "Europe" dissolves under analysis. True, but just as the phenomenon of orientalism does not disappear simply because some of us have now attained a critical awareness of it, similarly a certain version of "Europe," reified and celebrated in the phenomenal world of everyday relationships of power as the scene of the birth of the modern, continues to dominate the discourse of history. Analysis does not make it go away.

That Europe works as a silent referent in historical knowledge itself becomes obvious in a highly ordinary way. There are at least two everyday symptoms of the subalternity of non-Western, third-world histories. Third-world historians feel a need to refer to works in European history; historians of Europe do not feel any need to reciprocate. Whether it is an Edward Thompson, a Le Roy Ladurie, a George Duby, a Carlo Ginzberg, a Lawrence Stone, a Robert Darnton, or a Natalie Davis—to take but a few names at random from our contemporary world—the "greats" and the models of the historian's enterprise are always at least culturally "European." "They" produce their work in relative ignorance of non-Western histories, and this does not seem to affect the quality of their work. This is a gesture, however, that "we" cannot return. We cannot even afford an equality or symmetry of ignorance at this level without taking the risk of appearing "old-fashioned" or "outdated."

The problem, I may add parenthetically, is not particular to historians. An unselfconscious but nevertheless blatant example of this "inequality of ignorance" in literary studies, for example, is the following sentence on Salman Rushdie from a recent text on postmodernism: "Though Saleem Sinai [of *Midnight's Children*] narrates in English . . .

his intertexts for both writing history and writing fiction are doubled: they are, on the one hand, from Indian legends, films, and literature and, on the other, from the West—*The Tin Drum, Tristram Shandy, One Hundred Years of Solitude*, and so on."[3] It is interesting to note how this sentence teases out only those references that are from "the West." The author is under no obligation here to be able to name with any authority and specificity the "Indian" allusions that make Rushdie's intertextuality "doubled." This ignorance shared and unstated is part of the assumed compact that makes it "easy" to include Rushdie in English department offerings on postcolonialism.

This problem of asymmetric ignorance is not simply a matter of "cultural cringe" (to let my Australian self speak) on our part or of cultural arrogance on the part of the European historian. These problems exist but can be relatively easily addressed. Nor do I mean to take anything away from the achievements of the historians I mentioned. Our footnotes bear rich testimony to the insights we have derived from their knowledge and creativity. The dominance of "Europe" as the subject of all histories is part of a much more profound theoretical condition under which historical knowledge is produced in the third world. This condition ordinarily expresses itself in a paradoxical manner. It is this paradox that I shall describe as the second everyday symptom of our subalternity, and it refers to the very nature of social science pronouncements themselves.

For generations now, philosophers and thinkers shaping the nature of social science have produced theories embracing the entirety of humanity. As we well know, these statements have been produced in relative, and sometimes absolute, ignorance of the majority of humankind—that is, those living in non-Western cultures. This in itself is not paradoxical, for the more self-conscious of European philosophers have always sought theoretically to justify this stance. The everyday paradox of third-world social science is that we find these theories, in spite of their inherent ignorance of "us," eminently useful in understanding our societies. What allowed the modern European sages to develop such clairvoyance with regard to societies of which they were empirically ignorant? Why cannot we, once again, return the gaze?

There is an answer to this question in the writings of philosophers who have read into European history an entelechy of universal reason, if we regard such philosophy as the self-consciousness of social science.

Only "Europe," the argument would appear to be, is *theoretically* (i.e., at the level of the fundamental categories that shape historical thinking) knowable; all other histories are matters of empirical research that fleshes out a theoretical skeleton that is substantially "Europe." There is one version of this argument in Edmund Husserl's Vienna lecture of 1935, in which he proposed that the fundamental difference between "oriental philosophies" (more specifically, Indian and Chinese) and "Greek-European science" (or as he added, "universally speaking: philosophy") was the capacity of the latter to produce "absolute theoretical insights," that is, "*theoria*" (universal science), while the former retained a "practical-universal," and hence "mythical-religious," character. This "practical-universal" philosophy was directed to the world in a "naive" and "straightforward" manner, while the world presented itself as a "thematic" to *theoria*, making possible a praxis "whose aim is to elevate mankind through universal scientific reason."[4]

A rather similar epistemological proposition underlies Marx's use of categories like "bourgeois" and "prebourgeois" or "capital" and "precapital." The prefix *pre-* here signifies a relationship that is both chronological and theoretical. The coming of the bourgeois or capitalist society, Marx argues in the *Grundrisse* and elsewhere, gives rise for the first time to a history that can be apprehended through a philosophical and universal category, "capital." History becomes, for the first time, *theoretically* knowable. All past histories are now to be known (theoretically, that is) from the vantage point of this category, that is in terms of their differences from it. Things reveal their categorical essence only when they reach their fullest development, or as Marx put it in that famous aphorism of the *Grundrisse*: "Human anatomy contains the key to the anatomy of the ape."[5] The category "capital," as I have discussed elsewhere, contains within itself the legal subject of Enlightenment thought.[6] Not surprisingly, Marx said in that very Hegelian first chapter of *Capital*, volume 1, that the secret of "capital," the category, "cannot be deciphered until the notion of human equality has acquired the fixity of a popular prejudice."[7] To continue with Marx's words:

> Even the most abstract categories, despite their validity—precisely because of their abstractness—for all epochs, are nevertheless . . . themselves . . . a product of historical relations. Bourgeois society is the most developed and the most complex historic organization of production. The categories which express its relations, the com-

prehension of its structure, thereby also allow insights into the structure and the relations of production of all the vanished social formations out of whose ruins and elements it built itself up, whose partly still unconquered remnants are carried along within it, whose mere nuances have developed explicit significance within it, etc. . . . The intimations of higher development among the subordinate animal species . . . can be understood only after the higher development is already known. The bourgeois economy thus supplies the key to the ancient.[8]

For "capital" or "bourgeois," I submit, read "Europe."

II

Neither Marx nor Husserl spoke—not at least in the words quoted above—in a historicist spirit. In parenthesis, we should also recall here that Marx's vision of emancipation entailed a journey beyond the rule of capital, in fact beyond the notion of juridical equality that liberalism holds so sacred. The maxim "From each according to his ability, to each according to his need" runs quite contrary to the principle of "Equal pay for equal work," and this is why Marx remains—the Berlin Wall notwithstanding (or not standing!)—a relevant and fundamental critic of both capitalism and liberalism and thus central to any postcolonial postmodern project of writing history. Yet Marx's methodological/epistemological statements have not always successfully resisted historicist readings. There has always remained enough ambiguity in these statements to make possible the emergence of "Marxist" historical narratives. These narratives turn around the theme of "historical transition." Most modern third-world histories are written within problematics posed by this transition narrative, of which the overriding (if often implicit) themes are those of development, modernization, and capitalism.

This tendency can be located in our own work in the *Subaltern Studies* project. My book on working-class history struggles with the problem.[9] Sumit Sarkar's (another colleague in the *Subaltern Studies* project) *Modern India*, justifiably regarded as one of the best textbooks on Indian history written primarily for Indian universities, opens with the following sentences:

The sixty years or so that lie between the foundation of the Indian National Congress in 1885 and the achievement of independence in

August 1947 witnessed perhaps the greatest transition in our country's long history. A transition, however, which in many ways remains grievously incomplete, and it is with this central ambiguity that it seems most convenient to begin our survey.[10]

What kind of a transition was it that remained "grievously incomplete"? Sarkar hints at the possibility of there having been several by naming three:

So many of the aspirations aroused in the course of the national struggle remained unfulfilled—the Gandhian dream of the peasant coming into his own in *Ram-rajya* [the rule of the legendary and the ideal god-king Ram], as much as the left ideals of social revolution. And as the history of independent India and Pakistan (and Bangladesh) was repeatedly to reveal, even the problems of a complete bourgeois transformation and successful capitalist development were not fully solved by the transfer of power of 1947.(P.4)

Neither the peasant's dream of a mythical and just kingdom, nor the Left's ideal of a social[ist] revolution, nor a "complete bourgeois transformation"—it is within these three absences, these "grievously incomplete" scenarios that Sarkar locates the story of modern India.

It is also with a similar reference to "absences"—the "failure" of a history to keep an appointment with its destiny (once again an instance of the "lazy native," shall we say?)—that we announced our project of *Subaltern Studies*:

It is the study of this *historic failure of the nation to come to its own* [emphasis added], a failure due to the inadequacy of the bourgeoisie as well as of the working class to lead it into a decisive victory over colonialism and a bourgeois-democratic revolution of the classic nineteenth-century type . . . or [of the] "new democracy" [type]—*it is the study of this failure which constitutes the central problematic of the historiography of colonial India.*[11]

The tendency to read Indian history in terms of a lack, an absence, or an incompleteness that translates into "inadequacy" is obvious in these excerpts. As a trope, however, it is an ancient one, going back to the hoary beginnings of colonial rule in India. The British conquered and represented the diversity of "Indian" pasts through a homogenizing narrative of transition from a "medieval" period to "modernity." The terms have changed with time. The "medieval" was once called "despotic" and the "modern," "the rule of law." "Feudal/capitalist" has been a later variant.

When it was first formulated in colonial histories of India, this transition narrative was an unashamed celebration of the imperialist's capacity for violence and conquest. To give only one example among the many available, Alexander Dow's *History of Hindostan*, first published in three volumes between 1770 and 1772, was dedicated to the king with a candor characteristic of the eighteenth century, when one did not need a Michel Foucault to uncover the connection between violence and knowledge: "The success of Your Majesty's arms," said Dow, "has laid open the East to the researches of the curious."[12] Underscoring this connection between violence and modernity, Dow added: "The British nation have become the conquerors of Bengal and they ought to extend some part of their fundamental jurisprudence to secure their conquest. . . . The sword is our tenure. It is an absolute conquest, and it is so considered by the world" (1:cxxxviii).

This "fundamental jurisprudence" was the "rule of law" that contrasted, in Dow's narrative, with a past rule that was "arbitrary" and "despotic." In a further gloss, Dow explained that "despotism" did not refer to a "government of mere caprice and whim," for he knew enough history to know that that was not true of India. Despotism was the opposite of English constitutional government; it was a system where "the legislative, the judicial and the executive power [were] vested in the prince." This was the past of unfreedom. With the establishment of British power, the Indian was to be made a legal subject, ruled by a government open to the pressures of private property ("the foundation of public prosperity," said Dow) and public opinion, and supervised by a judiciary where "the distributers of justice ought to be independent of everything but law [as] otherwise the officer [the judge] becomes a tool of oppression in the hands of despotism" (1:xcv, cl, cxl–cxli).

In the nineteenth and twentieth centuries, generations of elite Indian nationalists found their subject positions, as nationalists, within this transition narrative that, at various times and depending on one's ideology, hung the tapestry of "Indian history" between the two poles of the homologous sets of oppositions despotic/constitutional, medieval/modern, feudal/capitalist. Within this narrative shared between imperialist and nationalist imaginations, the "Indian" was always a figure of lack. There was always, in other words, room in this story for characters who embodied, on behalf of the native, the theme of "inadequacy" or "failure." Dow's recommendation of a "rule of law" for

Bengal/India came with the paradoxical assurance (to the British) that there was no danger of such a rule "infusing" in the natives "a spirit of freedom":

> To make the natives of the fertile soil of Bengal free, is beyond the power of political arrangement. . . . Their religion, their institutions, their manners, the very disposition of their minds, form them for passive obedience. To give them property would only bind them with stronger ties to our interests, and make them our subjects: or if the British nation prefers the name—more our slaves. (1:cxl-cxli)

We do not need to be reminded that this would remain the cornerstone of imperial ideology for many years to come—subjecthood but not citizenship, as the native was never adequate to the latter—and would eventually become a strand of liberal theory itself.[13] This was, of course, where nationalists differed. For Rammohun Roy as for Bankimchandra Chattopadhyay, two of India's most prominent nationalist intellectuals of the nineteenth century, British rule was a necessary period of tutelage that Indians had to undergo in order to prepare precisely for what the British denied but extolled as the end of all history: citizenship and the nation-state. Years later, in 1951, an "unknown" Indian who successfully sold his "obscurity" dedicated the story of his life thus:

> To the memory of the
> British Empire in India
> Which conferred subjecthood on us
> But withheld citizenship;
> To which yet
> Everyone of us threw out the challenge
> "Civis Britanicus Sum"
> Because
> All that was good and living
> Within us
> Was made, shaped, and quickened
> By the same British Rule.[14]

In nationalist versions of this narrative, as Partha Chatterjee has shown, it was the peasants and the workers, the subaltern classes, who were given to bear the cross of "inadequacy," for, according to this version, it was they who needed to be educated out of their ignorance, parochialism, or, depending on your preference, false consciousness.[15] Even today the Anglo-Indian word *communalism* refers to those who allegedly fail to measure up to the "secular" ideals of citizenship.

That British rule put in place the practices, institutions, and discourse of bourgeois individualism in the Indian soil is undeniable. Early expressions—that is, before the beginnings of nationalism—of this desire to be a "legal subject" make it clear that to Indians in the 1830s and 1840s, to be a "modern individual" was to become a "European." *The Literary Gleaner*, a magazine in colonial Calcutta, ran the following poem in 1842, written in English by a Bengali schoolboy eighteen years of age. The poem apparently was inspired by the sight of ships leaving the coast of Bengal "for the glorious shores of England":

> Oft like a sad bird I sigh
> To leave this land, though mine own land it be:
> Its green robed meads—gay flowers and cloudless sky
> Though passing fair, have but few charms for me.
> For I have dreamed of climes more bright and free
> Where virtue dwells and heaven born liberty
> Makes even the lowest happy;—where the eye
> Doth sicken not to see man bend the knee
> To sordid interest:—climes where science thrives,
> And genius doth receive her guerdon meet;
> Where man in his all his truest glory lives,
> And nature's face is exquisitely sweet:
> For those fair climes I heave the impatient sigh,
> There let me live and there let me die.[16]

In its echoes of Milton and seventeenth-century English radicalism, this is obviously a piece of colonial pastiche.[17] Michael Madhusudan Dutt, the young Bengali author of this poem, eventually realized the impossibility of being "European" and returned to Bengali literature to become one of our finest poets. Later Indian nationalists, however, abandoned such abject desire to be "Europeans" themselves. Nationalist thought was premised precisely on the assumed universality of the project of becoming individuals, on the assumption that "individual rights" and abstract "equality" were universals that could find home anywhere in the world, that one could be both an "Indian" and a "citizen" at the same time. We shall soon explore some of the contradictions of this project.

Many of the public and private rituals of modern individualism became visible in India in the nineteenth century. One sees this, for instance, in the sudden flourishing in this period of the four basic genres that help express the modern self: the novel, the biography, the autobiography, and history.[18] Along with these came modern industry, technology, medicine, and a quasi-bourgeois (although colonial) legal system supported by a state that nationalism was to take over and make its own. The transition narrative that I have been discussing underwrote, and was in turn underpinned by, these institutions. To think this narrative was to think these institutions at the apex of which sat the modern state,[19] and to think the modern state or the nation-state was to think a history whose theoretical subject was Europe. Gandhi realized this as early as 1909. Referring to the Indian nationalists' demands for more railways, modern medicine, and bourgeois law, he cannily remarked in his book *Hind Swaraj* that this was to "make India English" or, as he put it, to have "English rule without the Englishman."[20] This "Europe," as Michael Madhusudan Dutt's youthful and naive poetry shows, was of course nothing but a piece of fiction told to the colonized by the colonizer in the very process of fabricating colonial domination.[21] Gandhi's critique of this "Europe" is compromised on many points by his nationalism, and I do not intend to fetishize his text. But I find his gesture useful in developing the problematic of nonmetropolitan histories.

III

I shall now return to the themes of "failure," "lack," and "inadequacy" that so ubiquitously characterize the speaking subject of "Indian" history. As in the practice of the insurgent peasants of colonial India, the first step in a critical effort must arise from a gesture of inversion.[22] Let us begin from where the transition narrative ends and read "plenitude" and "creativity" where this narrative has made us read "lack" and "inadequacy."

According to the fable of their constitution, Indians today are all "citizens." The constitution embraces almost a classically liberal definition of citizenship. If the modern state and the modern individual, the citizen, are but the two inseparable sides of the same phenomenon, as William Connolly argues in *Political Theory and Modernity*, it would appear that the end of history is in sight for us in India.[23] This modern individual, however, whose political/public life is lived in citizenship, is also supposed to have an interiorized "private" self that pours out incessantly in diaries, letters, autobiographies, novels, and, of course, in what we say to our analysts. The bourgeois individual is not born until one discovers the pleasures of privacy. But this is a very special kind of "private"—it is, in fact, a deferred "public," for this bourgeois private, as Jürgen Habermas has reminded us, is "always already oriented to an audience [*Publikum*]."24

Indian public life may mimic on paper the bourgeois legal fiction of citizenship—the fiction is usually performed as a farce in India—but what about the bourgeois private and its history? Anyone who has tried to write "French" social history with Indian material would know how impossibly difficult the task is.25 It is not that the form of the bourgeois private did not come with European rule. There have been, since the middle of the nineteenth century, Indian novels, diaries, letters, and autobiographies, but they seldom yield pictures of an endlessly interiorized subject. Our autobiographies are remarkably "public" (with constructions of public life that are not necessarily modern) when written by men, and they tell the story of the extended family when written by women.26 In any case, autobiographies in the confessional mode are notable for their absence. The single paragraph (out of 963 pages) that Nirad Chaudhuri spends on describing the experience of his wedding night in the second volume of his celebrated and prize-winning autobiography is as good an example as any other and is worth quoting at some length. I should explain that this was an arranged marriage (Bengal, 1932), and Chaudhuri was anxious lest his wife should not appreciate his newly acquired but unaffordably expensive hobby of buying records of Western classical music. Our reading of Chaudhuri is handicapped in part by our lack of knowledge of the intertextuality of his prose—there may have been at work, for instance, an imbibed puritanical revulsion against revealing "too much." Yet the passage remains a telling exercise in the construction of memory, for it is about what Chaudhuri "remembers" and "forgets" of his "first night's experience." He screens off intimacy with expressions like "I do not remember" or "I do not know how" (not to mention the very Freudian "making a clean breast of"), and this self-constructed veil is no doubt a part of the self that speaks:

> I was terribly uneasy at the prospect of meeting as wife a girl who was a complete stranger to me and when she was brought in . . . and left standing before me I had nothing to say. I saw only a very shy smile on her face, and timidly she came and sat by my side on the edge of the bed. I do not know how after that both of us drifted to the pillows, to lie down side by side. [Chaudhuri adds in a footnote: "Of course, fully dressed. We Hindus . . . consider both extremes—

fully clad and fully nude—to be modest, and everything in-between as grossly immodest. No decent man wants his wife to be an *allumeuse.*"] Then the first words were exchanged. She took up one of my arms, felt it and said: "You are so thin. I shall take good care of you." I did not thank her, and I do not remember that beyond noting the words I even felt touched. The horrible suspense about European music had reawakened in my mind, and I decided to make a clean breast of it at once and look the sacrifice if it was called for straight in the face and begin romance on such terms as were offered to me. I asked her timidly after a while: "Have you listened to any European music?" She shook her head to say "No." Nonetheless, I took another chance and this time asked: "Have you heard the name of a man called Beethoven?" She nodded and signified "Yes." I was reassured, but not wholly satisfied. So I asked yet again: "Can you spell the name?" She said slowly: "B,E,E,T,H,O,V,E,N." I felt very encouraged . . . and [we] dozed off.[27]

The desire to be "modern" screams out of every sentence in the two volumes of Chaudhuri's autobiography. His legendary name now stands for the cultural history of Indo-British encounter. Yet in the fifteen-hundred-odd pages that he has written in English about his life, this is the only passage where the narrative of Chaudhuri's participation in public life and literary circles is interrupted to make room for something approaching the intimate. How do we read this text, this self-making of an Indian male who was second to no one in his ardor for the public life of the citizen, yet who seldom, if ever, reproduced in writing the other side of the modern citizen, the interiorized private self unceasingly reaching out for an audience? Public without private? Yet another instance of the "incompleteness" of bourgeois transformation in India?

These questions are themselves prompted by the transition narrative that in turn situates the modern individual at the very end of history. I do not wish to confer on Chaudhuri's autobiography a representativeness it may not have. Women's writings, as I have already said, are different, and scholars have just begun to explore the world of autobiographies in Indian history. But if one result of European imperialism in India was to introduce the modern state and the idea of the nation, with their attendant discourse of "citizenship," which by the very idea of "the citizen's rights" (i.e., "the rule of law") splits the figure of the modern individual into "public" and "private" parts of the self (as the young Marx once pointed out in his *On the Jewish Question*), these themes have existed in contestation, alliance, and miscegenation with other narratives of the self and community that do not look to the state/citizen bind as the ultimate construction of sociality.[28] This as such will not be disputed, but my point goes further. It is that these other constructions of self and community, while documentable in themselves, will never enjoy the privilege of providing the metanarratives or teleologies (assuming that there cannot be a narrative without at least an implicit teleology) of our histories. This is so partly because these narratives often themselves bespeak an antihistorical consciousness: that is, they entail subject positions and configurations of memory that challenge and undermine the subject that speaks in the name of history. "History" is precisely the site where the struggle goes on to appropriate, on behalf of the modern (my hyperreal Europe), these other collocations of memory.

To illustrate these propositions, I will now discuss a fragment of this contested history in which the modern private and the modern individual were embroiled in colonial India.[29]

IV

What I present here are the outlines, so to speak, of a chapter in the history of bourgeois domesticity in colonial Bengal. The material—in the main, texts produced in Bengali between 1850 and 1920 for teaching women that very Victorian subject, "domestic science"—relates to the Bengali Hindu middle class, the *bhadralok,* or "respectable people." British rule instituted into Indian life the trichotomous ideational division on which modern political structures rest, namely, the state, civil society, and the (bourgeois) family. It was therefore not surprising that ideas relating to bourgeois domesticity, privacy, and individuality should come to India via British rule. What I want to highlight here, however, through the example of the *bhadralok* are certain cultural operations by which the "Indians" challenged and modified these received ideas in such a way as to put in question two fundamental tenets underlying the idea of "modernity"—the nuclear family based on companionate marriage and the secular historical construction of time.

As Meredith Borthwick, Ghulam Murshid, and other scholars have shown, the eighteenth-century European idea of "civilization" culminated in early-nineteenth-century India in a full-blown imperialist critique of Indian/Hindu domestic life, which was now held to be inferior to what became mid-Victorian ideals of bourgeois domesticity.[30] The "condition of women" question in nineteenth-century India was part of that critique, as were the ideas of the "modern" individual, "freedom," "equality," and "rights." In passages remarkable for their combination of egalitarianism and orientalism, James Mill's *The History of British India* (1817) joined together the thematic of the family/nation and a teleology of "freedom":

> The condition of women is one of the most remarkable circumstances in the manners of nations. . . . The history of uncultivated nations uniformly represents the women as in a state of abject slavery, from which they slowly emerge as civilisation advances. . . . As society refines upon its enjoyments . . . the condition of the weaker sex is gradually improved till they associate on equal terms with the men and occupy the place of voluntary and useful coadjutors. A state of dependence more strict and humiliating than that which is ordained for the weaker sex among the Hindus cannot be easily conceived.[31]

As is well known, the Indian middle classes generally felt answerable to this charge. From the early nineteenth century onward a movement developed in Bengal (and other regions) to reform "women's conditions" and to give them formal education. Much of this discourse on women's education was emancipationist in that it spoke the language of "freedom," "equality," and "awakening," and was strongly influenced by Ruskinian ideals and idealization of bourgeois domesticity.[32] If one looks on this history as part of the history of the modern individual in India, an interesting feature emerges. It is that in this literature on women's education certain terms, after all, were much more vigorously debated than others. There was, for example, a degree of consensus over the desirability of domestic "discipline" and "hygiene" as practices reflective of a state of modernity, but the word *freedom*, yet another important term in the rhetoric of the modern, hardly ever acted as the register of such a social consensus. It was a passionately disputed word, and we would be wrong to assume that the passions reflected a simple and straightforward battle of the sexes. The word was assimilated to the nationalist need to construct cultural boundaries that supposedly separated the "European" from the "Indian." The dispute over this word was thus central to the discursive strategies through which a subject position was created, enabling the "Indian" to speak. It is this subject position that I want to discuss here in some detail.

What the Bengali literature on women's education played out was a battle between a nationalist construction of a cultural norm of the patriarchal, patrilocal, patrilineal extended family and the ideal of the patriarchal, bourgeois nuclear family that was implicit in the European/imperialist/universalist discourse on the "freedoms" of individualism, citizenship, and civil society.[33] The themes of "discipline" and "order" were critical in shaping nationalist imaginings of aesthetics and power. "Discipline" was seen as the key to the power of the colonial (i.e., modern) state, but it required certain procedures for redefining the self. The British were powerful, it was argued, because they were disciplined, orderly, and punctual in every detail of their lives, and this was made possible by the education of "their" women, who brought the virtues of discipline into the home. The "Indian" home, a colonial construct, now fared badly in nationalist writings on modern domesticity. To quote a Bengali text on women's education from 1877:

> The house of any civilised European is like the abode of gods. Every household object is clean, set in its proper place and decorated: nothing seems unclean or smells foul. . . . It is as if [the goddess of] order [*srinkhala*, "order, discipline"; *srinkhal*, "chains"] had become manifest to please the [human] eye. In the middle of the room would be a covered table with a bouquet of flowers on it, while around it would be [a few] chairs nicely arranged [with] everything sparkling clean. But enter a house in our country and you would feel as if you had been transported there by your destiny to make you atone for all the sins of your life. [A mass of] cow dung torturing the senses . . . dust in the air, a growing heap of ashes, flies buzzing around . . . a little boy urinating into the ground and putting the mess back into his mouth. . . . The whole place is dominated by a stench that seems to be running free. . . . There is no order anywhere, the household objects are so unclean that they only evoke disgust.[34]

This self-division of the colonial subject, the double movement of recognition by which it both knows its "present" as the site of disorder and yet moves away from this space in desiring a discipline that can only exist in an imagined but "historical" future, is a rehearsal, in the context of the discussion of the bourgeois domestic in colonial India, of the transition narrative we have encountered before. A historical construction of temporality (medieval/modern, separated by historical time), in other words, is precisely the axis along which the colonial subject splits itself. Or to put it differently, this split is what is history; writing history is performing this split over and over again.

The desire for order and discipline in the domestic sphere thus may be seen as having been a correlate of the nationalist, modernizing desire for a similar discipline in the public sphere, that is, for a rule of law enforced by the state. It is beyond the scope of this chapter to pursue this point further, but the connection between personal discipline and discipline in public life was to reveal itself in what the nationalists wrote about domestic hygiene and public health. The connection is recognizably modernist, and it is what the Indian modern shared with the European modern.[35] What I want to attend to, however, are the differences between the two. And this is where I turn to the other important aspect of the European modern, the rhetoric of "freedom" and "equality."

The argument about "freedom"—in the texts under discussion—was waged around the question of the Victorian ideals of the companionate marriage, that is, over the question as to whether or not the wife should also be a friend to the husband. Nothing threatened the ideal of the Bengali/Indian extended family (or the exalted position of the mother-in-law within that structure) more than this idea wrapped up in notions of bourgeois privacy, that the wife was also to be a friend or, to put it differently, that the woman was now to be a modern individual. I must mention here that the modern individual who asserts his or her individuality over the claims of the joint or extended family almost always appears in nineteenth- and early-twentieth-century Bengali literature as an embattled figure, often the subject of ridicule and scorn in the same Bengali fiction and essays that otherwise extolled the virtues of discipline and scientific rationality in personal and public lives. This irony had many expressions. The most well known Bengali fictional character who represents this moral censure of modern individuality is Nimchand Datta in Dinabandhu Mitra's play *Sadhabar ekadashi* (A married woman's widowhood) (1866). Nimchand, who is English-educated, quotes Shakespeare, Milton, or Locke at the slightest opportunity, uses this education arrogantly to ignore his duties toward his extended family, and finds his nemeses in alcohol and debauchery. This metonymic relationship between the love of "modern"/English education (which stood for the romantic individual in nineteenth-century Bengal) and the slippery path of alcohol is suggested in the play by a conversation between Nimchand and a Bengali official of the colonial bureaucracy, a deputy magistrate. Nimchand's supercilious braggadocio about his command of the English language quickly and inevitably runs to the subject of drinks (synonymous, in middle-class Bengali culture of the period, with absolute decadence): "I read English, write English, speechify in English, think in English, dream in English—mind you, it's no child's play—now tell me, my good fellow, what would you like to drink?—Claret for ladies, sherry for men, and brandy for heroes."[36]

A similar connection between the modern, "free" individual and selfishness was made in the literature on women's education. The construction was undisguisedly nationalist (and patriarchal). *Freedom* was used to mark a difference between what was "Indian" and what was "European/English." The ultrafree woman acted like a memsahib (European woman), selfish and shameless. As Kundamala Devi, a woman writing for a women's magazine *Bamabodhini patrika*, said in 1870: "Oh dear ones! If you have acquired real knowledge, then give no place in your heart to *memsahib*-like behavior. That is not becoming in a Bengali housewife."[37] The idea of "true modesty" was mobilized to build up this picture of the "really" Bengali woman.[38] Writing in 1920, Indira Devi dedicated her *Narir ukti* [A woman speaks]—interestingly enough, a defense of modern Bengali womanhood against criticisms by (predominantly) male writers—to generations of ideal Bengali women whom she thus described: "Unaffected by nature, of pleasant speech, untiring in their service [to others], oblivious of their own pleasures, [while] moved easily by the suffering of others, and capable of being content with very little."[39]

This model of the "modern" Bengali/Indian woman—educated enough to appreciate the modern regulations of the body and the state but yet "modest" enough to be unassertive and unselfish—was tied to the debates on "freedom." "Freedom" in the West, several authors argued, meant *jathechhachar*, to do as one pleased, the right to self-indulgence. In India, it was said, *freedom* meant freedom from the ego, the capacity to serve and obey voluntarily. Notice how the terms *freedom* and *slavery* have changed positions in the following quote:

> To be able to subordinate oneself to others and to *dharma* [duty/moral order/proper action] . . . [and] to free the soul from the slavery of the senses are the first tasks of human freedom. . . . That is why in Indian families boys and girls are subordinate to the parents, wife to the husband and to the parents-in-law, the disciple to the

guru, the student to the teacher, . . . the king to *dharma*, . . . the people to the king, [and one's] dignity and prestige to [that of] the community [*samaj*].⁴⁰

There was an ironical twist to this theorizing that needs to be noted. Quite clearly, this theory of "freedom-in-obedience" did not apply to the domestic servants who were sometimes mentioned in this literature as examples of the "truly" unfree, the nationalist point being that (European) observers commenting on the unfree status of Indian women often missed (so some nationalists argued) this crucial distinction between the housewife and the domestic. Obviously, the servants were not yet included in the India of the nationalist imagination.

Thus went the Bengali discourse on modern domesticity in a colonial period when the rise of a civil society and a quasi-modern state had already inserted the modern questions of "public" and "private" into middle-class Bengali lives. The received bourgeois ideas about domesticity and connections between the domestic and the national were modified here in two significant ways. One strategy, as I have sought to demonstrate, was to contrapose the cultural norm of the patriarchal extended family to the bourgeois patriarchal ideals of the companionate marriage, to oppose the new patriarchy with a redefined version of the old one(s). Thus was fought the idea of the modern private. The other strategy, equally significant, was to mobilize, on behalf of the extended family, forms and figurations of collective memory that challenged, albeit ambiguously, the seemingly absolute separation of "sacred" and "secular" time on which the very modern ("European") idea of history was/is based.⁴¹ The figure of the "truly educated," "truly modest," and "truly Indian" woman is invested, in this discussion of women's education, with a sacred authority by subordinating the question of domestic life to religious ideas of female auspiciousness that joined the heavenly with the mundane in a conceptualization of time that could be only antihistorical. The truly modern housewife, it was said, would be so auspicious as to mark the eternal return of the cosmic principle embodied in the goddess Lakshmi, the goddess of domestic well-being by whose grace the extended family and clan, and hence, by extending the sentiment, the nation (*Bharatlakshmi*), lived and prospered. Thus we read in a contemporary pamphlet: "Women are the Lakshmis of the community. If they undertake to improve themselves in the sphere of *dharma* and knowledge . . . there will be an automatic improvement in [the quality of] social life."[42] Lakshmi, regarded as the Hindu god Vishnu's wife by about A.D. 400, has for long been held up in popular Hinduism, and in the everyday pantheism of Hindu families, as the model of the Hindu wife, united in complete harmony with her husband (and his family) through willing submission, loyalty, devotion, and chastity.[43] When women did not follow her ideals, it was said, the (extended) family and the family line were destroyed by the spirit of Alakshmi (not-Lakshmi), the dark and malevolent reverse of the Lakshmi principle. While women's education and the idea of discipline as such were seldom opposed in this discourse regarding the modern individual in colonial Bengal, the line was drawn at the point where modernity and the demand for bourgeois privacy threatened the power and the pleasures of the extended family.

There is no question that the speaking subject here is nationalist and patriarchal, employing the clichéd orientalist categories "the East" and "the West."[44] However, of importance to us are the two denials on which this particular moment of subjectivity rests: the denial, or at least contestation, of the bourgeois private and, equally important, the denial of historical time by making the family a site where the sacred and the secular blended in a perpetual reenactment of a principle that was heavenly and divine.

The cultural space the antihistorical invoked was by no means harmonious or nonconflictual, although nationalist thought of necessity tried to portray it to be so. The antihistorical norms of the patriarchal extended family, for example, could only have had a contested existence, contested both by women's struggles and by those of the subaltern classes. But these struggles did not necessarily follow any lines that would allow us to construct emancipatory narratives by putting the "patriarchals" clearly on one side and the "liberals" on the other. The history of modern "Indian" individuality is caught up in too many contradictions to lend itself to such a treatment.

I do not have the space here to develop the point, so I will make do with one example. It comes from the autobiography of Ramabai Ranade, the wife of the famous nineteenth-century social reformer from the Bombay presidency, M. G. Ranade. Ramabai Ranade's struggle for self-respect was in part against the "old" patriarchal order of the extended family and for the "new" patriarchy of companionate marriage, which her reform-minded husband saw as the most civilized form of the conjugal bond. In pursuit of this ideal, Ramabai began to share her husband's commitment to public life and would often take part (in the 1880s) in public gatherings and deliberations of male and female social reformers. As she herself says, "It was at these meetings that I learnt what a meeting was and how one should conduct oneself at one."[45] Interestingly, however, one of the chief sources of opposition to Ramabai's efforts were (apart from men) the other women in the family. There is, of course, no doubt that they, her mother-in-law and her husband's sisters, spoke for the old patriarchal extended family. But it is quite instructive to listen to their voices (as they come across through Ramabai's text), for they also spoke for their own sense of self-respect and their own forms of struggle against men:

> You should not really go to these meetings [they said to Ramabai]. . . .
> Even if the men want you to do these things, you should ignore them.
> You need not say no: but after all, you need not do it. They will then
> give up out of sheer boredom. . . . You are outdoing even the Euro-
> pean women.

Or this:

> It is she [Ramabai] herself who loves this frivolousness of going
> to meetings. Dada [Mr. Ranade] is not at all so keen about it. But
> should she not have some sense of proportion of how much the
> women should actually do? If men tell you to do a hundred things,
> women should take up ten at the most. After all men do not under-
> stand these practical things! . . . The good woman [in the past] never
> turned frivolous like this. . . . That is why this large family . . . could
> live together in a respectable way. . . . But now it is all so different!
> If Dada suggests one thing, this woman is prepared to do three.
> How can we live with any sense of self-respect then and how can
> we endure all this? (Pp. 84–85)

These voices, combining the contradictory themes of nationalism, of patriarchal clan-based ideology, and of women's struggles against men, and opposed at the same time to friendship between husbands and wives, remind us of the deep ambivalences that marked the trajectory of the modern private and bourgeois individuality in colonial India. Yet historians manage, by maneuvers reminiscent of the old "dialectical" card trick called "negation of negation," to deny a subject position to this voice of ambivalence. The evidence of what I have called "the denial of the bourgeois private and of the historical subject" is acknowledged but subordinated in their accounts to the supposedly higher purpose of making Indian history look like yet another episode in the universal and (in their view, the ultimately victorious) march of citizenship, of the nation-state, of themes of human emancipation spelled out in the course of the European Enlightenment and after. It is the figure of the citizen that speaks through these histories. And so long as that happens, my hyperreal Europe will continually return to dominate the stories we tell. "The modern" will then continue to be understood, as Meaghan Morris has so aptly put it in discussing her own Australian context, "as a *known history*, something which has *already happened elsewhere*, and which is to be reproduced, mechanically or otherwise, with a local content." This can only leave us with a task of reproducing what Morris calls "the project of positive unoriginality."[46]

V

Yet the "originality"—I concede that this is a bad term—of the idioms through which struggles have been conducted in the Indian subcontinent has often been in the sphere of the nonmodern. One does not have to subscribe to the ideology of clannish patriarchy, for instance, to acknowledge that the metaphor of the sanctified and patriarchal extended family was one of the most important elements in the cultural politics of Indian nationalism. In the struggle against British rule, it was frequently the use of this idiom—in songs, poetry, and other forms of nationalist mobilization—that allowed "Indians" to fabricate a sense of community and to retrieve for themselves a subject position from which to address the British. I will illustrate this with an example from the life of Gandhi, "the father of the nation," to highlight the political importance of this cultural move on the part of the "Indian."

My example refers to the year 1946. There had been ghastly riots between the Hindus and the Muslims in Calcutta over the impending partition of the country into India and Pakistan. Gandhi was in the city, fasting in protest over the behavior of his own people. And here is how an Indian intellectual recalls the experience:

> Men would come back from their offices in the evening and find food prepared by the family [meaning the womenfolk] ready for them; but soon it would be revealed that the women of the home had not eaten the whole day. They [apparently] had not felt hungry. Pressed further, the wife or the mother would admit that they could not understand how they could go on [eating] when Gandhiji was

dying for their own crimes. Restaurants and amusement centres did little business; some of them were voluntarily closed by the proprietors. . . . The nerve of feeling had been restored; the pain began to be felt. . . . Gandhiji knew when to start the redemptive process.[47]

We do not have to take this description literally, but the nature of the community imagined in these lines is clear. It blends, in Gayatri Chakravorty Spivak's words, "the feeling of community that belongs to national links and political organizations" with "that other feeling of community whose structural model is the [clan or the extended] family."[48] Colonial Indian history is replete with instances where Indians arrogated subjecthood to themselves precisely by mobilizing, within the context of "modern" institutions and sometimes on behalf of the modernizing project of nationalism, devices of collective memory that were both antihistorical and antimodern.[49] This is not to deny the capacity of "Indians" to act as subjects endowed with what we in the universities would recognize as "a sense of history" (what Peter Burke calls "the renaissance of the past") but to insist at the same time that there were also contrary trends, that in the multifarious struggles that took place in colonial India, antihistorical constructions of the past often provided very powerful forms of collective memory.[50]

There is then this double bind through which the subject of "Indian" history articulates itself. On the one hand, it is both the subject and the object of modernity because it stands for an assumed unity called the "Indian people" that is always split into two—a modernizing elite and a yet-to-be-modernized peasantry. As such a split subject, however, it speaks from within a metanarrative that celebrates the nation-state; and of this metanarrative the theoretical subject can only be a hyperreal "Europe," a "Europe" constructed by the tales that both imperialism and nationalism have told the colonized. The mode of self-representation that the "Indian" can adopt here is what Homi Bhabha has justly called "mimetic."[51] Indian history, even in the most dedicated socialist or nationalist hands, remains a mimicry of a certain "modern" subject of "European" history and is bound to represent a sad figure of lack and failure. The transition narrative will always remain "grievously incomplete."

On the other hand, maneuvers are made within the space of the mimetic—and therefore within the project called "Indian" history—to represent the "difference" and the "originality" of the "Indian," and it is in this cause that the antihistorical devices of memory and the anti-historical "histories" of the subaltern classes are appropriated. Thus peasant-worker constructions of "mythical" kingdoms and "mythical" pasts and futures find a place in texts designated "Indian" history precisely through a procedure that subordinates these narratives to the rules of evidence and to the secular, linear calendar that the writing of "history" must follow. The antihistorical, antimodern subject, therefore, cannot speak itself as "theory" within the knowledge procedures of the university even when these knowledge procedures acknowledge and "document" its existence. Much like Spivak's "subaltern" (or the anthropologist's peasant who can only have a quoted existence in a larger statement that belongs to the anthropologist alone), this subject can only be spoken for and spoken of by the transition narrative that will always ultimately privilege the modern (i.e., "Europe").[52]

As long as one operates within the discourse of "history" produced at the institutional site of the university, it is not possible simply to walk out of the deep collusion between "history" and the modernizing narrative(s) of citizenship, bourgeois public and private, and the nation-state. "History" as a knowledge system is firmly embedded in institutional practices that invoke the nation-state at every step—witness the organization and politics of teaching, recruitment, promotions, and publication in history departments, politics that survive the occasional brave and heroic attempts by individual historians to liberate "history" from the metanarrative of the nation-state. One only has to ask, for instance, Why is history a compulsory part of education of the modern person in all countries today, including those that did quite comfortably without it until as late as the eighteenth century? Why should children all over the world today have to come to terms with a subject called "history" when we know that this compulsion is neither natural nor ancient?[53] It does not take much imagination to see that the reason for this lies in what European imperialism and third-world nationalisms have achieved together: the universalization of the nation-state as the most desirable form of political community. Nation-states have the capacity to enforce their truth games, and universities, their critical distance notwithstanding, are part of the battery of institutions complicit in this process. "Economics" and "history" are the knowledge forms that correspond to the two major institutions that the rise (and later universalization) of the bourgeois order has given to the world—the capitalist mode of production and the nation-state ("history" speaking to the figure of the citizen).[54] A critical historian has no choice but to negotiate this knowledge. She or he therefore needs to understand the state on its own terms, that is, in terms of its self-justificatory narratives of citizenship and modernity. Since these themes will always take us back to the universalist propositions of "modern" (European) political philosophy—even the "practical" science of economics that now seems "natural" to our constructions of world systems is (theoretically) rooted in the ideas of ethics in eighteenth-century Europe[55]—a third-world historian is condemned to knowing "Europe" as the original home of the "modern," whereas the "European" historian does not share a comparable predicament with regard to the pasts of the majority of humankind. Thus follows the everyday subalternity of non-Western histories with which I began this paper.

Yet the understanding that "we" all do "European" history with our different and often non-European archives opens up the possibility of a politics and project of alliance between the dominant metropolitan histories and the subaltern peripheral pasts. Let us call this the project of provincializing "Europe," the "Europe" that modern imperialism and (third-world) nationalism have, by their collaborative venture and violence, made universal. Philosophically, this project must ground itself in a radical critique and transcendence of liberalism (i.e., of the bureaucratic constructions of citizenship, modern state, and bourgeois privacy that classical political philosophy has produced), a ground that late Marx shares with certain moments in both poststructuralist thought and feminist philosophy. In particular, I am emboldened by Carole Pateman's courageous declaration—in her remarkable book *The Sexual Contract*—that the very conception of the modern individual belongs to patriarchal categories of thought.[56]

VI

The project of provincializing "Europe" refers to a history that does not yet exist: I can therefore only speak of it in a programmatic manner. To forestall misunderstanding, however, I must spell out what it is *not* while outlining what it could be.

To begin with, it does not call for a simplistic, out-of-hand rejection of modernity, liberal values, universals, science, reason, grand narratives, totalizing explanations, and so on. Fredric Jameson has recently reminded us that the easy equation often made between "a philosophical conception of totality" and "a political practice of totalitarianism" is "baleful."[57] What intervenes between the two is history—contradictory, plural, and heterogeneous struggles whose outcomes are never predictable even retrospectively, in accordance with schemas that seek to naturalize and domesticate this heterogeneity. These struggles include coercion (both on behalf of and against modernity)—physical, institutional, and symbolic violence, often dispensed with dreamy-eyed idealism—and it is this violence that plays a decisive role in the establishment of meaning, in the creation of truth regimes, in deciding, as it were, whose and which "universal" wins. As intellectuals operating in academia, we are not neutral to these struggles and cannot pretend to situate ourselves outside of the knowledge procedures of our institutions.

The project of provincializing "Europe" therefore cannot be a project of "cultural relativism." It cannot originate from the stance that the reason/science/universals that help define Europe as the modern are simply "culture-specific" and therefore only belong to the European cultures. For the point is not that Enlightenment rationalism is always unreasonable in itself, but it is rather a matter of documenting how—through what historical process—its "reason," which was not always self-evident to everyone, has been made to look "obvious" far beyond the ground where it originated. If a language, as has been said, is but a dialect backed up by an army, the same could be said of the narratives of "modernity" that, almost universally today, point to a certain "Europe" as the primary habitus of the modern.

This Europe, like "the West," is demonstrably an imaginary entity, but the demonstration as such does not lessen its appeal or power. The project of provincializing "Europe" has to include certain other additional moves: (1) the recognition that Europe's acquisition of the adjective *modern* for itself is a piece of global history of which an integral part is the story of European imperialism; and (2) the understanding that this equating of a certain version of Europe with "modernity" is not the work of Europeans alone; third-world nationalisms, as modernizing ideologies par excellence, have been equal partners in the process. I do not mean to overlook the anti-imperial moments in the careers of these nationalisms; I only underscore the point that the project of provincializing "Europe" cannot be a nationalist, nativist, or atavistic project. In unraveling the necessary entanglement of history—a disciplined and institutionally regulated form of collective memory—

with the grand narratives of "rights," "citizenship," the nation-state, and "public" and "private" spheres, one cannot but problematize "India" at the same time as one dismantles "Europe."

The idea is to write into the history of modernity the ambivalences, the contradictions, the use of force, and the tragedies and the ironies that attend it. That the rhetoric and the claims of (bourgeois) equality, of citizens' rights, of self-determination through a sovereign nation-state have in many circumstances empowered marginal social groups in their struggles is undeniable—this recognition is indispensable to the project of *Subaltern Studies*. What effectively is played down, however, in histories that either implicitly or explicitly celebrate the advent of the modern state and the idea of citizenship is the repression and violence that are as instrumental in the victory of the modern as is the persuasive power of its rhetorical strategies. Nowhere is this irony—the undemocratic foundations of "democracy"—more visible than in the history of modern medicine, public health, and personal hygiene, the discourses of which have been central in locating the body of the modern at the intersection of the public and the private (as defined by, and subject to negotiations with, the state). The triumph of this discourse, however, has always been dependent on the mobilization, on its behalf, of effective means of physical coercion. I say "always" because this coercion is originary/foundational (i.e., historic) as well as pandemic and quotidian. Of foundational violence, David Arnold gives a good example in his essay on the history of the prison in India. The coercion of the colonial prison, Arnold shows, was integral to some of the earliest, pioneering research on the medical, dietary, and demographic statistics of India, for the prison was where Indian bodies were accessible to modernizing investigators.[58] Of the coercion that continues in the names of the nation and modernity, a recent example comes from the Indian campaign to eradicate smallpox in the 1970s. Two American doctors (one of them presumably of "Indian" origin) who participated in the process thus describe their operations in a village of the Ho tribe in the Indian state of Bihar:

> In the middle of gentle Indian night, an intruder burst through the bamboo door of the simple adobe hut. He was a government vaccinator, under orders to break resistance against smallpox vaccination. Lakshmi Singh awoke screaming and scrambled to hide herself. Her husband leaped out of bed, grabbed an axe, and chased the intruder into the courtyard. Outside a squad of doctors and policemen quickly

overpowered Mohan Singh. The instant he was pinned to the ground, a second vaccinator jabbed smallpox vaccine into his arm. Mohan Singh, a wiry 40-year-old leader of the Ho tribe, squirmed away from the needle, causing the vaccination site to bleed. The government team held him until they had injected enough vaccine. . . . While the two policemen rebuffed him, the rest of the team overpowered the entire family and vaccinated each in turn. Lakshmi Singh bit deep into one doctor's hand, but to no avail.[59]

There is no escaping the idealism that accompanies this violence. The subtitle of the article in question unselfconsciously reproduces both the military and the do-gooding instincts of the enterprise. It reads: "How an Army of Samaritans Drove Smallpox from the Earth."

Histories that aim to displace a hyperreal Europe from the center toward which all historical imagination currently gravitates will have to seek out relentlessly this connection between violence and idealism that lies at the heart of the process by which the narratives of citizenship and modernity come to find a natural home in "history." I register a fundamental disagreement here with a position taken by Richard Rorty in an exchange with Jürgen Habermas. Rorty criticizes Habermas for the latter's conviction "that the story of modern philosophy is an important part of the story of the democratic societies' attempts at self-reassurance."[60] Rorty's statement follows the practice of many Europeanists who speak of the histories of these "democratic societies" as if they were self-contained histories complete in themselves, as if the self-fashioning of the West were something that occurred only within its self-assigned geographical boundaries. At the very least Rorty ignores the role that the "colonial theater" (both external and internal)— where the theme of "freedom" as defined by modern political philosophy was constantly invoked in aid of the ideas of "civilization," "progress," and, later, "development"—played in the process of engendering this "reassurance." The task, as I see it, will be to wrestle with ideas that legitimize the modern state and its attendant institutions, in order to return to political philosophy—in the same way as suspect coins returned to their owners in an Indian bazaar—its categories whose global currency can no longer be taken for granted.[61]

And finally—since "Europe" cannot after all be provincialized within the institutional site of the university, whose knowledge protocols will always take us back to the terrain where all contours follow that of my hyperreal Europe—the project of provincializing Europe must realize within itself its own impossibility. It therefore looks to a history that embodies this politics of despair. It will have been clear by now that this is not a call for cultural relativism or for atavistic, nativist histories. Nor is this a program for a simple rejection of modernity, which would be, in many situations, politically suicidal. I ask for a history that deliberately makes visible, within the very structure of its narrative forms, its own repressive strategies and practices, the part it plays in collusion with the narratives of citizenships in assimilating to the projects of the modern state all other possibilities of human solidarity. The politics of despair will require of such history that it lay bare to its readers the reasons why such a predicament is necessarily inescapable. This is a history that will attempt the impossible: to look toward its own death by tracing that which resists and escapes the best human effort at translation across cultural and other semiotic systems, so that the world may once again be imagined as radically heterogeneous. This, as I have said, is impossible within the knowledge protocols of academic history, for the globality of academia is not independent of the globality that the European modern has created. To attempt to provincialize this "Europe" is to see the modern as inevitably contested, to write over the given and privileged narratives of citizenship other narratives of human connections that draw sustenance from dreamed-up pasts and futures where collectivities are defined neither by the rituals of citizenship nor by the nightmare of "tradition" that "modernity" creates. There are, of course, no (infra)structural sites where such dreams could lodge themselves. Yet they will recur so long as the themes of citizenship and the nation-state dominate our narratives of historical transition, for these dreams are what the modern represses in order to be.

Notes

1. Ranajit Guha and Gayatri Chakravorty Spivak, eds., *Selected Subaltern Studies* (New York, 1988); Ronald Inden, "Orientalist Constructions of India," *Modern Asian Studies* 20, no. 3 (1986): 445.

2. I am indebted to Jean Baudrillard for the term *hyperreal* (see his *Simulations* [New York, 1983]), but my use differs from his.

3. Linda Hutcheon, *The Politics of Postmodernism* (London, 1989), p. 65.

4. Edmund Husserl, *The Crisis of European Sciences and Transcendental Philosophy*, trans. David Carr (Evanston, Ill., 1970), pp. 281–85. See also Wilhelm Halbfass, *India and Europe: An Essay in Understanding* (New York, 1988), pp. 167–68.

5. See the discussion in Karl Marx, *Grundrisse: Foundations of the Critique of Po-*

litical Economy, trans. Martin Nicholas (Harmondsworth, 1973), pp. 469–512; and in Marx, *Capital: A Critique of Political Economy*, vol. 3 (Moscow, 1971), pp. 593–613.

6. See Dipesh Chakrabarty, *Rethinking Working-Class History: Bengal, 1890–1940* (Princeton, N.J., 1989), chap. 7.

7. Marx, *Capital*, vol. 1, p. 60.

8. Marx, *Grundrisse*, p. 105.

9. See Chakrabarty, *Rethinking Working-Class History*, chap. 7, in particular.

10. Sumit Sarkar, *Modern India, 1885–1947* (Delhi, 1985), p. 1.

11. Guha and Spivak, *Selected Subaltern Studies*, p. 43. The words quoted here are Guha's. But I think they represent a sense of historiographical responsibility that is shared by all the members of the Subaltern Studies collective.

12. Alexander Dow, *History of Hindostan*, 3 vols. (London, 1812–16), dedication, vol. 1.

13. See L. T. Hobhouse, *Liberalism* (New York, 1964), pp. 26–27.

14. Nirad C. Chaudhuri, *The Autobiography of an Unknown Indian* (New York, 1989), dedication page.

15. Partha Chatterjee, *Nationalist Thought and the Colonial World: A Derivative Discourse?* (London, 1986).

16. *Madhusudan racanabali* (in Bengali) (Calcutta, 1965), p. 449. See also Jogindranath Basu, *Michael Madhusudan Datter jibancarit* (in Bengali) (Calcutta, 1978), p. 86.

17. My understanding of this poem has been enriched by discussions with Marjorie Levinson and David Bennett.

18. I am not making the claim that all of these genres necessarily emerge with bourgeois individualism. See Natalie Zemon Davis, "Fame and Secrecy: Leon Modena's *Life* as an Early Modern Autobiography," *History and Theory* 27 (1988): 103–18, and Davis, "Boundaries and Sense of Self in Sixteenth-Century France," in Thomas C. Heller et al., eds., *Reconstructing Individualism: Autonomy, Individuality, and the Self in Western Thought* (Stanford, Calif., 1986), pp. 53–63. See also Philippe Lejeune, *On Autobiography*, trans. Katherine Leary (Minneapolis, 1989), pp. 163–84.

19. See the chapter on Nehru in Chatterjee, *Nationalist Thought*.

20. M. K. Gandhi, *Hind swaraj* (1909), in *Collected Works of Mahatma Gandhi*, vol. 10 (Ahmedabad, 1963), p. 15.

21. See the discussion in Gauri Viswanathan, *Masks of Conquest: Literary Studies and British Rule in India* (London, 1989), pp. 128–41 passim.

22. Ranajit Guha, *Elementary Aspects of Peasant Insurgency in Colonial India* (New Delhi, 1983), chap. 2.

23. William E. Connolly, *Political Theory and Modernity* (Oxford, 1989). See also David Bennett, "Postmodernism and Vision: Ways of Seeing (at) the End of History" (forthcoming).

24. Jürgen Habermas, *The Structural Transformation of the Public Sphere: An Inquiry into a Category of Bourgeois Society* (Cambridge, Mass., 1989), p. 49.

25. See Sumit Sarkar, "Social History: Predicament and Possibilities," in Iqbal Khan, ed., *Fresh Perspective on India and Pakistan: Essays on Economics, Politics, and Culture* (Oxford, 1985), pp. 256–74.

26. For reasons of space, I shall leave this claim here unsubstantiated, although I hope to have an opportunity to discuss it in detail elsewhere. I should qualify the statement by mentioning that in the main it refers to autobiographies published between 1850 and 1910. Once women join the public sphere in the twentieth century, their self-fashioning takes on different dimensions.

27. Nirad C. Chaudhuri, *Thy Hand, Great Anarch! India, 1921–1952* (London, 1987), pp. 350–51.

28. See Karl Marx, *On the Jewish Question*, in *Early Writings* (Harmondsworth, 1975), pp. 215–22.

29. For a more detailed treatment of what follows, see Dipesh Chakrabarty, "The Difference-Deferral of a Colonial Modernity: Public Debates on Domesticity in British India," in David Arnold and David Hardiman, eds., *Subaltern Studies VIII* (Delhi, 1994), pp. 50–88.

30. Meredith Borthwick, *The Changing Role of Women in Bengal, 1849–1905* (Princeton, N.J., 1984); Ghulam Murshid, *Reluctant Debutante: Response of Bengali Women to Modernisation, 1849–1905* (Rajshahi, 1983). On the history of the word *civilization*, see Lucien Febvre, "Civilisation: Evolution of a Word and a Group of Ideas," in Peter Burke, ed., *A New Kind of History: From the Writings of Febvre*, trans K. Folca (London, 1973), pp. 219–57. I owe this reference to Peter Sahlins.

31. James Mill, *The History of British India*, vol. 1, ed. H. H. Wilson (London, 1840), pp. 309–10.

32. Borthwick, *Changing Role*.

33. The classic text where this assumption has been worked up into philosophy is, of course, *Hegel's Philosophy of Right*, trans. T. M. Knox (Oxford, 1967), pp. 110–22. See also Joanna Hodge, "Women and the Hegelian State," in Ellen Kennedy and Susan Mendus, eds., *Women in Western Philosophy* (Brighton, 1987), pp. 127–58; Simon During, "Rousseau's Heirs: Primitivism, Romance, and Other Relations between the Modern and the Nonmodern" (forthcoming); Joan B. Landes, *Women and the Public Sphere in the Age of the French Revolution* (Ithaca, N.Y., 1988); and Mary Ryan, *Women in Public: Between Banners and Ballots, 1825–1880* (Baltimore, 1990).

34. *Streesiksha*, vol. 1 (Calcutta, 1877), pp. 28–29.

35. I develop this argument further in Dipesh Chakrabarty, "Open Space/Public Place: Garbage, Modernity, and India," *South Asia* 14, no. 1 (1991): 15–31.

36. *Dinabandhu racanabali*, ed. Kshetra Gupta (Calcutta, 1981), p. 138.

37. Borthwick, *Changing Role*, p. 105.

38. I discuss this in more detail in Chakrabarty, "The Difference-Deferral of Colonial Modernity."

39. Indira Devi, *Narir ukti* (Calcutta, 1920), dedication page.

40. Deenanath Bandyopadhyaya, *Nanabisayak prabandha* (Calcutta, 1887), pp. 30–31. For a genealogy of the terms *slavery* and *freedom* as used in the colonial discourse of British India, see Gyan Prakash, *Bonded Histories: Genealogies of Labor Servitude in Colonial India* (Cambridge, 1990).

41. Peter Burke, *The Renaissance Sense of the Past* (London, 1970).

42. Bhikshuk [Chandrasekhar Sen], *Ki holo!* (Calcutta, 1876), p. 77.

43. David Kinsley, *Hindu Goddesses: Visions of the Divine Feminine in the Hindu Religious Tradition* (Berkeley, Calif., 1988), pp. 19–31; Manomohan Basu, *Hindu acar byabahar* (Calcutta, 1873), p. 60; H. D. Bhattacharya, "Minor Religious Sects," in R. C. Majumdar, ed., *The History and Culture of the Indian People: The Age of Imperial Unity*, vol. 2 (Bombay, 1951), pp. 469–71; Upendranath Dhal, *Goddess Lakshmi: Origin and Development* (Delhi, 1978). The expression "everyday pantheism" was suggested to me by Gayatri Chakravorty Spivak (personal communication).

44. See the chapter on Bankim in Chatterjee, *Nationalist Thought*.

45. *Ranade: His Wife's Reminiscences*, trans. Kusumavati Deshpande (Delhi, 1963), p. 77.

46. Meaghan Morris, "Metamorphoses at Sydney Tower," *New Formations* 11 (summer 1990): 10.

47. Amiya Chakravarty, quoted in Bhikhu Parekh, *Gandhi's Political Discourse* (London, 1989), p. 163.

48. Gayatri Chakravorty Spivak, "Can the Subaltern Speak?" in Cary Nelson and Lawrence Grossberg, eds., *Marxism and the Interpretation of Culture* (Urbana, Ill., 1988), p. 277.

49. See *Subaltern Studies* I–VII (Delhi, 1982–91), and Ashis Nandy, *The Intimate Enemy: Loss and Recovery of Self under Colonialism* (Delhi, 1983).

50. *Subaltern Studies* I–VII; Guha, *Elementary Aspects*.

51. Homi Bhabha, "Of Mimicry and Man: The Ambivalence of Colonial Discourse," in Annette Michelson et. al., eds., *October: The First Decade, 1976–1986* (Cambridge, Mass., 1987), pp. 317–26; also Bhabha, ed., *Nation and Narration* (London, 1990).

52. Spivak, "Can the Subaltern Speak?" Also see Spivak's interview published in *Socialist Review* 20, no. 3 (July–September 1990): 81–98.

53. On the close connection between imperialist ideologies and the teaching of history in colonial India, see Ranajit Guha, *An Indian Historiography of India: A Nineteenth-Century Agenda and Its Implications* (Calcutta, 1988).

54. Without in any way implicating them in the entirety of this argument, I may mention that there are parallels here between my statement and what Gyan Prakash and Nicholas Dirks have argued elsewhere; see Gyan Prakash, "Writing Post-Orientalist Histories of the Third World: Perspectives from Indian Historiography," *Comparative Studies in Society and History* 32, no. 2 (April 1990): 383–408; Nicholas B. Dirks, "History as a Sign of the Modern," *Public Culture* 2, no. 2 (spring 1990): 25–33.

55. See Amartya Kumar Sen, *Of Ethics and Economics* (Oxford, 1987). Tessa Morris-Suzuki's *A History of Japanese Economic Thought* (London, 1989) makes interesting reading in this regard. I am grateful to Gavan McCormack for bringing this book to my attention.

56. Carole Pateman, *The Sexual Contract* (Stanford, Calif., 1988), p. 184.

57. Fredric Jameson, "Cognitive Mapping," in Nelson and Grossberg, eds., *Marxism and the Interpretation of Culture*, p. 354.

58. David Arnold, "The Colonial Prison: Power, Knowledge, and Penology in Nineteenth-Century India," chapter 5 in this volume. I have discussed some of these issues in a Bengali article: Dipesh Chakrabarty, "Sarir, samaj o rashtra: Oupanibeshik bharate mahamari o janasangskriti," *Anustup*, 1988.

59. Lawrence Brilliant with Girija Brilliant, "Death for a Killer Disease," *Quest*, May/June 1978, p. 3. I owe this reference to Paul Greenough.

60. Richard Rorty, "Habermas and Lyotard on Postmodernity," in Richard J. Bernstein, ed., *Habermas and Modernity* (Cambridge, Mass., 1986), p. 169.

61. For an interesting and revisionist reading of Hegel in this regard, see the exchange between Charles Taylor and Partha Chatterjee in *Public Culture* 3, no. 1 (1990). My book *Rethinking Working Class History* attempts a small beginning in this direction.

Contributors

Shahid Amin is professor of history at Delhi University. He is the author of *Sugarcane and Sugar in Gorakhpur* (1984) and *Event, Metaphor, Memory: Chauri Chaura, 1922–1992* (1995).

David Arnold is professor of South Asian history, School of Oriental and African Studies, London. His published work includes studies of the police in colonial South India and colonial medicine (*Colonizing the Body: State Medicine and Epidemic Disease in Nineteenth-Century India*, 1993). Professor Arnold is currently working on environmental history and has recently published *The Problem of Nature: Environment, Culture, and the Expansion of Europe* (1996).

Gautam Bhadra has taught history at the University of Calcutta and is now professor at the Centre for Studies in Social Sciences, Calcutta. He is the author of two books in Bengali on peasants in Mughal India and on religiosity in peasant consciousness in Bengal.

Dipesh Chakrabarty is professor in the Department of South Asian Languages and Civilizations at the University of Chicago. He is the author of *Rethinking Working-Class History: Bengal 1890–1940* (1989) and is coeditor (with Shahid Amin) of *Subaltern Studies IX* (1996).

Partha Chatterjee is professor of political science at the Centre for Studies in Social Sciences, Calcutta, and the author of *Bengal, 1920–1947: The Land Question* (1985), *Nationalist Thought and the Colonial World* (1986), and *The Nation and Its Fragments* (1993).

Ranajit Guha has edited *Subaltern Studies I-VI* (1982–89). His publications include *A Rule of Property for Bengal: An Essay on the Idea of Permanent Settlement* (1963, 1982, 1996), *Elementary Aspects of Peasant Insurgency in Colonial India* (1983), and *Dominance without Hegemony: History and Power in Colonial India* (forthcoming). He has served in teaching and research positions at a number of universities in India, England, the United States, and Australia. Now retired, he lives in Canberra, Australia.

David Hardiman was based during the 1980s at the Centre for Social Studies, Surat, where he carried out the research and writing for *The Coming of the Devi: Adivasi Assertion in Western India* (1987). Now based at the University of Warwick, his most recent book is *Feeding the Baniya: Usurers and Peasants in Western India* (1996).

Gyanendra Pandey is professor of history at the University of Delhi. He has taught at universities in India, Great Britain, Australia, and the United States. He is the author of *The Ascendancy of the Congress in Uttar Pradesh* (1978) and *The Construction of Communalism in Colonial North India* (1990), and editor of *Hindus and Others: The Question of Identity in India Today* (1993), among other publications.

Index